Images and Cultures of Law in Early Modern England

This book offers a unique interpretation of the hidden culture of the early modern legal profession and its influence on the development of the English constitution. It locates an alternative site of political sovereignty in the legal communities at the Inns of Court in London, examining the signs of legitimacy by which they sought to validate the claim that common law represented sovereign constitutional authority.

The role of symbols in the culture of English law is central to the book's analysis. Within the framework of a cultural history of the legal profession from 1558 to 1660, the book considers the social presence of the law, revealed in its various signs. It analyses how institutional existence at the Inns of Court presented the legal community as an emblematic template for the English nation-state, defending the sovereignty of the Ancient Constitution by reference to the immemorial provenance of common law.

PAUL RAFFIELD was tutor in Constitutional Law and a guest lecturer in legal history, law and literature, Birkbeck College, University of London.

Cambridge Studies in Early Modern British History

Series editors

ANTHONY FLETCHER
Victoria County History, Institute of Historical Research, University of London

JOHN GUY
Fellow, Clare College, Cambridge

JOHN MORRILL
*Professor of British and Irish History, University of Cambridge, and
Vice-Master of Selwyn College*

This is a series of monographs and studies covering many aspects of the history of the British Isles between the late fifteenth century and the early eighteenth century. It includes the work of established scholars and pioneers work by a new generation of scholars. It includes both reviews and revisions of major topics and books, which open up new historical terrain or which reveal startling new perspectives on familiar subjects. All the volumes set detailed research into our broader perspectives and the books are intended for the use of students as well as of their teachers.

For a list of titles in the series, see end of book.

IMAGES AND CULTURES OF LAW IN EARLY MODERN ENGLAND

Justice and Political Power, 1558–1660

PAUL RAFFIELD

CAMBRIDGE UNIVERSITY PRESS
Cambridge, New York, Melbourne, Madrid, Cape Town, Singapore, São Paulo

Cambridge University Press
The Edinburgh Building, Cambridge CB2 8RU, UK

Published in the United States of America by Cambridge University Press, New York

www.cambridge.org
Information on this title: www.cambridge.org/9780521827393

© Paul Raffield 2004

This publication is in copyright. Subject to statutory exception
and to the provisions of relevant collective licensing agreements,
no reproduction of any part may take place without the written
permission of Cambridge University Press.

First published 2004
This digitally printed version 2007

A catalogue record for this publication is available from the British Library

ISBN 978-0-521-82739-3 hardback
ISBN 978-0-521-04453-0 paperback

In memory of my father
Bill Raffield

CONTENTS

List of illustrations *page* viii
Acknowledgements ix

    Introduction 1
1 Eating, learning and revering the law: oral traditions and the religious inheritance 9
2 Architecture and heraldry: bodies of law, myth and honour 43
3 Revels, feasting and role-playing: dreamland, drunkenness and the Utopian state 84
4 The theatre of law: dramatic symbols of crown, common law and the Ancient Constitution 124
5 Reformation, regulation and the image: the English state and the subject of law 157
6 Common lawyers, fundamental law and the idolatrous mask of Charles I 190
7 Interregnum: *lex*, *ius* and de facto government 227
    Conclusion 263

Bibliography 270
Index 285

ILLUSTRATIONS

1 Dissection scene from *Master John Banister, Anatomical Tables* (*c.* 1580) (ms. Hunter 364, V.1.1, frontispiece). By permission of Glasgow University Library, Department of Special Collections.   *page* 56
2 'Embleme 29' (Lord Stanhope), *The Mirrour of Maiestie* (1618) (shelfmark c.71.d.17). By permission of the British Library.   68
3 'Embleme 28' (Lord Wotton), *The Mirrour of Maiestie* (1618) (shelfmark c.71.d.17). By permission of the British Library.   70
4 The St Simon Light. Detail from the 'Van Linge' window in the south front of Lincoln's Inn Chapel. By permission of the treasurer and masters of the bench of Lincoln's Inn.   186
5 *Equestrian Portrait of Charles I* (*c.* 1638). Anthony Van Dyck. By permission of the National Gallery, London.   212

ACKNOWLEDGEMENTS

I wish to thank the staff and students of the School of Law, Birkbeck College, for their support and inspiration during research for this book. My especial thanks go to Peter Goodrich for his unceasing encouragement and enthusiasm. His comments and criticisms were consistently illuminating and incisive. Costas Douzinas, Adam Gearey and Piyel Haldar all contributed ideas that helped to formulate the themes I have developed. Lindsay Farmer and Ian Ward made invaluable criticisms of the content and style of the text, while Valerie Hoare has provided indispensable assistance throughout the project.

William Davies at Cambridge University Press has given me excellent practical advice. Staff at the libraries and Treasuries of Gray's Inn, the Inner Temple, the Middle Temple and Lincoln's Inn willingly gave their time and expertise, furnishing me with all the information I requested in relation to the Inns of Court. Guy Holborn, the librarian of Lincoln's Inn, has been extremely helpful. My thanks go also to Margaret Daly at the National Gallery and all the staff at the British Library, who have been unfailingly co-operative since I started research for this book.

The article on which parts of chapter 2 are based was published in the *International Journal for the Semiotics of Law* 13 (2000); parts of chapters 3 and 5 are based on articles published in *Law and Critique* (8 (1997) and 13 (2002)); parts of chapter 4 are based on an article published in *The Journal of Legal History* 20 (1999).

Finally, my greatest debt of thanks is to my wife, Emily Jackson. Her example is inspirational, her tolerance, patience and encouragement never less than astonishing. Thank you.

P. R.

Introduction

A mile downstream from Westminster, in the enclosed environs of the Inns of Court, the English legal profession of the sixteenth and early seventeenth centuries created a commonwealth of lawyers. The content of its constitution was founded on a code of manners, integrating the moral and ethical precepts of Judaeo-Christian theology and Neoplatonic humanism. The self-governing legal community gave physical expression to a Utopian ideal: an autonomous state governed by the equitable principles of common law ideology. The physical structure of the Inns and the institutional existence of their members provided a microcosm of the ideal English state, in which the ethical subject of law was acknowledged as a constitutional entity and the embryonic social contract between subject and ruler was nourished and enhanced. The legal community represented and articulated this unprecedented relationship, and through the regulation of its quotidian existence delineated the rights, obligations and restrictions that attached to it.

In jurisprudential terms, the principal achievement of the Henrician Reformation was to establish the primacy and sovereignty of a secular legal system, albeit one strongly informed by its religious inheritance. Common lawyers demarcated the boundaries of jurisdiction between ecclesiastical and common law, but it is evident that the English legal system derived most of its traditions from the laws and customs of the Roman Church. As the authority of crown and church became coextensive during the reign of Henry VIII, following the Act of Supremacy, so common law acquired much of the jurisdiction previously associated with ecclesiastical law. A principal argument of this book is that through the various signs of its legitimacy and sovereignty the English constitution was consciously developed to represent the indivisibility of divine law and common law within a classically ordered cosmos.[1] Although common lawyers and jurists of the early modern period argued that

---

[1] Goodrich refers to the religious basis of the constitution as a type of legal theology, in which the eternal presence is represented. P. Goodrich, *Languages of Law: From Logics of Memory to Nomadic Masks* (London: Weidenfeld & Nicolson, 1990), p. 6.

the English legal system represented the coalescence of divine law, human reason and natural law,[2] the constitution was characterised principally by its unwritten nature, unfettered by formal constraints. In such a system, willing subjection by the individual to the authority of law is determined by the perceived legitimacy of the legal institution. Unblemished institutional provenance is therefore a crucial indication of lawful authority. The absence of textual codification necessitates that the legitimacy of the legal institution, and of the constitution that it embodies, is established with reference to a system of representations and visual signs. This system can be described broadly as the aesthetics of law: the idea that governmentality expresses the 'art' of law.[3] It is an art in which the perception of the image or sign is manipulated so that the subject of law attaches itself willingly to the authority of the legal institution.

The sign system of the early modern legal profession was predicated on the theory that the origins of common law lie beyond the memory of man. Jurists argued that substantive law derived from the distillation of ancient custom and was therefore largely unwritten, the principles enshrined in common law having their textual origins in Judaeo-Christian scripture. These practices attain the authority of law by means of the form through which they manifest themselves, or are 'presenced' in social life. The legal community at the Inns of Court was the principal architect in shaping and constructing all such representations. Following its expansion and standardisation during the sixteenth century, the political influence of the legal profession was such that it became the pre-eminent institutional body to affect directly the shape of an emergent constitution, in which common law was sovereign. The Inns of Court, which developed on an unprecedented scale throughout this period, were symbols and embodiments not only of the self-proclaimed status of the legal profession as legitimate guardians of the constitution, but also of the values inherent in the constitution itself. Their world within a world endeavoured to constitute an exemplary community of impeccable genealogy, whose self-governing status was essential to the regulation of that community.[4] Through the active intervention of their governing bodies, the

---

[2] See, for example, J. Fortescue, *De Laudibus Legum Angliae*, ed. J. Selden (Savoy: R. Gosling, 1737); C. St German, *Two Dialogues in English, Between a Doctor of Divinity, and a Student in the Laws of England, of the Grounds of the said Laws, And of Conscience* (London: the Assigns of R. & E. Atkins, 1709); W. Dugdale, *Origines Juridiciales or Historical Memorials of the English Laws* (London: F. & T. Warren, 1666).

[3] On the constitutional and ethical importance of governmentality, see M. Foucault, *Ethics, Subjectivity and Truth: Essential Works of Foucault, 1954–1984*, ed. P. Rabinow (London: Penguin, 2000), Introduction, p. xvii.

[4] On the self-governing status of the Inns as a symbol of a specific community's identity, see P. Goodrich, 'Signs Taken for Wonders: Community, Identity, and *A History of Sumptuary Law*', *Law and Social Inquiry*, 23 (1998), 720.

Inns of Court legislated for a living constitution within their own sovereign realm. The regulation of every aspect of diurnal life was intended to be instrumental in the realisation of an ideal commonwealth, whose citizens were guided and united by their shared belief that the common law embodied ethical principles, adherence to which would ultimately ensure the effectuation of a Utopian state. Central to the creation of this state is the Platonic notion of order as a symbol of perfection; its achievement, in the state or in the individual, depends upon the correct ordering of parts and the performance by each part of its allotted function.[5]

My analysis is founded on the historical and philological observation that the sources of the Ancient Constitution are classical and continental, rather than indigenous. That the insular tradition is a foreign importation supports the normative argument that it is the symbolic presence and value of legality, the semiotic or appearance of a native law that is the reality of the tradition, rather than its quotidian judgments and other elaborations of rules. The integration of Christianity and Neoplatonic humanism, represented at a cultural level by the artistic and literary achievements of the European Renaissance, manifested itself in a unique and unprecedented manner in the struggle for political sovereignty in post-Reformation England. Successive Tudor monarchs consolidated and enhanced the independent status of the nation-state, providing stability and security through increased use of the royal prerogative. Common lawyers responded to the threat of absolutism by citing the Ancient Constitution as the amorphous symbol of fundamental rights and freedoms.

The order of signs created by the Elizabethan Inns of Court articulated a particular constitutional relationship between governor and governed, the basis of which was the classical concept of *justitia*, or right relations between men. The idea that the common law predated the memory of man and that the legitimacy of the Ancient Constitution was guaranteed by the usage of ancient, English custom was fictive. The theory of constitutional provenance expounded by jurists of the Elizabethan and Jacobean periods accredits mythical (and notably foreign) archetypes such as Brutus and Solon with the foundation of English law. Apart from demonstrating the importance of iconic archetypes of national unity to the foundation of the body politic, this accreditation betrays the tacit acceptance by common lawyers of the classical and continental origins of English law. The relevance of these origins to constitutional theory is their foundations in the city-states of the ancient world, and the nature of the civic freedoms and obligations that

---

[5] See Book IV of Plato, *The Republic*, trans. D. Lee (London: Penguin, 1987), 427D–434C, 441C–445B. On the cosmos, temperance and justice, see also Plato's *Gorgias*, in *Lysis, Symposium, Gorgias*, trans. W. R. M. Lamb (London: W. Heinemann, 1946), 507E–508A.

such provenance implies, in particular the relationship between citizens and between subject and ruler. The constitutional model proposed by Hooker in *Of the Laws of Ecclesiastical Polity* broadly suggests that the English legal system embodied a code of tradition, manners or honour. This model finds its classical equivalent and original in *The Republic* of Plato, in which *justitia* referred to the ideal goodness of society and not exclusively to the application of formal law. Of seminal influence also was *The Politics* of Aristotle, in particular its suggestion that the bonds of friendship between citizens provided the essential basis for the ideal *polis*.[6]

In the course of the sixteenth century the English nation-state gradually supplanted the medieval, feudal model of government. Implicit in the former model was an unprecedented, reciprocal system of governance in which individuals were guaranteed the benefits of subject status in return for the relinquishment of their natural rights and their willing submission to the legitimate authority of a sovereign power. In other words, this period in English history witnessed the transition from a society that was determined and delineated by status to one in which contract was the defining factor of societal relations.[7] The resurgence and reinterpretation of classical texts, and their sudden availability due to the innovative printing processes, provided the intellectual impetus for the creation of the model *polis*, reinvented by Hooker as a religious commonwealth. As self-regulating, independent communities of the law, the Inns of Court were the ideal (and probably the only) institution through which the representation of this commonwealth could be manifested. Through the exercise of their executive and legislative powers, the governing bodies of the four Inns regulated the symbols of their communities in order that the images of the legal institution could give form and substance to the invisible principles of governance and legitimate rule. The visibility of the symbolic order of law and the real presence of power suggested by the image were crucial developments in the perception of the early modern legal profession as an embodiment of political, ethical and moral sovereignty. The details of quotidian existence at the Inns were regulated to present an emblem of community that could usefully serve as a template for the larger community of the nation.[8]

Although I refer extensively to two seminal texts by Sir John Fortescue, *De Laudibus Legum Angliae* and *The Governance of England*, and occasionally to relevant aspects of Henrician, Marian and Edwardian rule, my substantive analysis of the English legal profession concentrates on the

---

[6] On Aristotle, ethics and the ancient *polis*, see A. Macintyre, *After Virtue: a Study in Moral Theory* (London: Duckworth, 1981), pp. 124–7.

[7] H. Maine, *Ancient Law* (London: Dent, 1917), p. 100.

[8] On the regulation of the visual image at the Inns of Court, see Goodrich, 'Signs Taken for Wonders', 721.

period between the accession of Elizabeth I and the Restoration of the monarchy in 1660. Fortescue was significant both for articulating the constitutional theory of mixed monarchy and for placing the English legal profession in its ethical context as the guardian of common law rights and the arbiter of disputes between magistrate and subject. But the idea that the Inns of Court represented an ideal commonwealth of responsible citizens, in which the governance of the state could be enacted in microcosm, only attained its physical manifestation during the period of architectural, cultural and institutional expansion in the reign of Elizabeth I.[9]

The political relevance of the intellectual arguments for a constitutional monarchy (made variously by Fortescue, St German and Hooker) became apparent during the last decade of Elizabethan rule and throughout the reign of James I. Increased emphasis by the monarch on the constitutional primacy of the divine right of kings threatened to destroy the social contract between magistrate and subject. The political necessity to restrict the personal power of the monarch in the interests of individual liberty became a matter of urgent practical significance during the reign of Charles I, in relation to his excessive and unlawful use of the royal prerogative. In the latter part of the book I consider the veracity of claims by common lawyer MPs that they sought a constitutional settlement, the effect of which would entrench the political sovereignty of common law and abolish absolute monarchy and the conditions under which absolutism could flourish. Pursuant to this analysis, I examine the body politic of the English republic, and consider its resemblance to the ideal constitutions for which the Inns of Court had legislated. As Plato remarked in *The Republic*, every political system derives, however slightly, from a Utopian ideal.

My approach is thematic rather than strictly chronological, although within this stylistic framework I outline the development of the legal profession and the English constitution from 1558 to 1660. Chapter 1 traces the emergence of a secular legal profession from its ecclesiastical origins in the monastic orders. In particular I examine the oral traditions of common law. The centrality of oratory and narrative to the English legal system was crucial in determining the form of legal practice. The spirituality of common law and common lawyers was expressed unequivocally through the act of communal dining at the Inns of Court. This practice was inherited from the monasteries, in whose refectories the Word of God was symbolically eaten at dinner and spoken during the readings. The effect of the printing revolution and the increased textualisation of English law and law reporting was not so

---

[9] On Coke and the influence of *De Laudibus Legum Angliae*, see J. P. Sommerville, *Royalists and Patriots: Politics and Ideology in England, 1603–1640* (Harlow: Pearson Education, 1999), p. 83.

much to create an empirical, rational legal system as to initiate the evolution of legal hermeneutics: the emergence of the lawyer as author, critic and poet.

In chapter 2 I consider those public manifestations of the legal institution that collectively comprise the corpus of law. In this analysis of the semiotics of legal architecture, the buildings of the Inns are perceived as eclectic symbols of an ethical rather than a legalistic code. This unwritten law, or *lex terrae*, derives from classical principles but corresponds to the imperatives of a Christian nation-state of the Renaissance period.[10] The religious commonwealth described by Hooker in *Of the Laws of Ecclesiastical Polity* is given permanence and visibility in the physical structure of the Inns.[11] Throughout this chapter, the theme of the genealogy of law predominates: only these images of 'perfect blood'[12] guarantee the legitimacy of the constitution. I attempt to construe from these architectural icons the content of the unwritten constitution, just as rights and obligations can be construed from a written document.

Chapter 3 examines the depictions of a Utopian state, envisaged during the annual, seasonal festivities known as the revels. During the course of these elaborate and extravagant entertainments, the patriarchs of the Inns of Court ceded their governing authority to junior members. The theatricality of the ensuing enactment of governance and the decision of the revellers to present a parody of the hierarchic structure of English society does not detract from the didactic function of the revels. Their social relevance was to imply that in the interests of the community or commonwealth, law acts as a repressive force upon the primitive desires of the individual. The artifice of political order and the foundation of utility can be identified clearly as central themes of the revels.[13] Through an examination of two of the revels of the Inns of Court, in 1561 and 1594, I analyse the response of the legal profession to constitutional developments at the start and during the last decade of Elizabethan rule. I characterise the revels as the search for a new Utopia: a landscape that is simultaneously real and imaginary, in which the common law aspires to create the necessary political, social and spiritual conditions for the realisation of the ideal state.[14]

---

[10] On the evolution of the nation-state and the development of the European legal systems, see J. M. Kelly, *A Short History of Western Legal Theory* (Oxford: Clarendon, 1992), pp. 159–68.

[11] On the religious commonwealth and Elizabethan political theory, see C. MacEachern, *The Poetics of English Nationhood* (Cambridge University Press, 1996).

[12] J. Ferne, *The Blazon of Gentrie* (London: Winder, 1586), ff. 86–7.

[13] Hume's theory of the artificial basis of political order is discussed in I. Ward, *Shakespeare and the Legal Imagination* (London: Butterworth, 1999), pp. 144–5. See D. Hume, *A Treatise of Human Nature* (Oxford University Press, 1978), pp. 494–5.

[14] On the influence of the fictional land of Cockaygne over the evolution of modern socialism, see A. L. Morton, *The English Utopia* (London: Lawrence & Wishart, 1952), p. 33. On the presentation of Utopia in Shakespeare's England, see Ward, *Legal Imagination*, p. 142.

In chapter 4 I examine the representation of law in theatre and the utility of the visual and dramatic image in facilitating the comprehension of invisible concepts such as governmentality, rationality and divine law. I analyse various dramatic entertainments presented at the Inns of Court during the Elizabethan and Jacobean periods, and their status as legal texts that embody the content of the Ancient Constitution. The didactic function of the masques was to facilitate the visible expression of the poetics of law, in which human reason interacts with nature to create an ordered and perceptible realm, governed by the equitable judgments of common law. The chapter concludes with an analysis of the image of law, both as icon and idol. The doctrinal distinction indicates the importance of the particular form of the sign, both to the legitimacy of the legal institution and to the acceptance of common law as the human manifestation of divine law.

Chapter 5 assesses the constitutional status of the individual in the early modern state, within the context of sumptuary legislation enacted by the crown and the governing bodies of the Inns of Court. The crown demonstrated its respect for the independence and autonomous status of the Inns of Court by exempting them from any of the strictures of sixteenth-century sumptuary legislation. The governing bodies of the Inns responded to this freedom by manipulating the image of the lawyer to represent the inherent divinity of common law. The synthesis of classical and Christian values and their impact on the development of an ethical relationship between subject and governor demonstrates the importance of the Renaissance as a force for political change. The regulation of the image at the Inns of Court was effective in ensuring that the legal profession was perceived as a secular priesthood, whose appearance exactly reflected its spiritual role.

In chapter 6 I consider the gradual erosion of the autonomous power of the Inns, as the personal rule of Charles I encroached upon their traditional independence. Through the vociferous character of the common lawyer William Prynne, I explore the reaction of the legal profession to the increased isolation and idolatry of the royal court. For Prynne (and many other lawyers) the decadence of the Caroline court reflected the intrinsic corruption and decay of absolute government. The venality of the Inns of Court was symbolised by the extravagant masque jointly performed by their members in honour of the king and queen, *The Triumph of Peace*. This was a vacuous entertainment, intended primarily to ingratiate the Inns with their sovereign master. As the legal institution continued to compromise its independence by compliance with the edicts of the king, the voice of libertarian dissent shifted perceptibly from the Inns of Court to Parliament. From this public forum, the unprecedented number of lawyer MPs provided the only effective opposition to the arbitrary acts of the king. With the dissolution of Parliament in 1629 and the debilitating effect on the legal institution of the civil war, the printed pamphlet attained unprecedented significance as the means through which articulate opposition was expressed. The latter part of this chapter considers the ascendancy of the pamphlet, with particular reference to the use of literary tropes as a means of expressing common law principles of freedom and justice.

Finally, in chapter 7 I address the extent to which the English republic adopted the Aristotelian model of government provided by the humanist commonwealths of the legal community. Despite increasing numbers of admissions during the years of the Protectorate, the political influence of the Inns declined throughout the Interregnum as their cultural activities were proscribed and their oral learning exercises fell into disuse. In the history of constitutional jurisprudence, this period signals the ascendancy of legal positivism and the irrelevance of natural law to the strong government of the state by a de facto ruler. The claims to liberty, equity and conscience made by the Levellers resembled those made previously by Coke. Their pleas were ignored and the movement crushed by a régime intent on the suppression of dissent and anarchy. The pervasive influence of constitutional libertarianism was demonstrated by attempts to balance the power of the sovereign with the liberty of the individual: the Instrument of Government and the Humble Petition and Advice both reflected common law principles of restricted sovereignty. But the pragmatic government of arms, proposed by Machiavelli in *The Prince* and supported by Harrington in *Oceana*, was incompatible with the ethereal constructs of the Ancient Constitution. The appeal of this fictive charter to immemorial custom was fatally at odds with a political climate in which equity and justice were not recognised as formal law, but (as Hobbes suggested) were mere qualities disposing subjects towards peace and obedience.[15]

[15] T. Hobbes, *Leviathan*, ed. J. C. A. Gaskin (Oxford University Press, 1996), p. 177.

1

Eating, learning and revering the law: oral traditions and the religious inheritance

COMMONS AND THE DISCIPLES OF COMMON LAW

... we, who are the Ministerial Officers, who sit and preside in the Courts of Justice, are therefore not improperly called; Sacerdotes (Priests): The import of the Latin Word (Sacerdos) being one who gives or teaches Holy Things.[1]

The suggestion that the primary purpose of the judiciary was to fulfil a sacerdotal role represents a pervasive opinion in the early modern English legal profession that jurisprudence was a form of theology, the meaning of which could be expounded only by common lawyers. It is not coincidental that, as the jurisdiction of common law encroached upon areas previously administered by the ecclesiastical courts, common lawyers should seek to establish the unimpeachable probity of their profession. After the Henrician ban on the teaching of canon law in England and the statutory recognition in 1532 of the professional status of barristers, it became incumbent upon the Inns of Court to shape the development of the legal profession along the religious lines originally suggested by Fortescue. Although the Inns were founded for pragmatic reasons, allowing lawyers to gather as a corporate body and providing easy access to the courts of justice, during the sixteenth century the regulation of members in accordance with strict religious principles became their primary symbolic role. Commons developed from its simple dietary function to become a potent symbol not only of the oral basis to the common law tradition, but also of the religious commonwealth of lawyers. From the diurnal rites of the legal community emerged the prototype of an ideal society, governed by the perfect reason of common law, inspired by divine law and articulated by common lawyers. Communion rites were enacted during commons, at which senior and junior members shared a mandatory, frugal meal. In iconic fashion (as at the supper at Emmaus), the bonds of a religious community were enforced and strengthened through the communal act of dining. The Word was made flesh and eaten, reflecting the oral

---

[1] J. Fortescue, *De Laudibus Legum Angliae*, ed. J. Selden (Savoy: R. Gosling, 1737), pp. 4–5.

tradition of the English legal system.² Dining embodied the immemorial custom of common law; food (and the strict regulations governing its consumption) became its physical expression. In hall the past was honoured and evoked by the food offered, representing that which otherwise would not be present.³

The derivation of commons from the refectories and oratories of the monasteries, and the strict rules governing the ascetic nature of the quotidian dining regime, represented the coalescence of common law principles and sacrament-based Anglicanism. Implicit in the rules of the Benedictine Order is the correlation between the will of God, the spoken word and the law. Of particular importance to the institutional communities of monks and common lawyers was the Christian injunction against pride, a recurring theme in the sumptuary laws of the Inns of Court, with regard both to sartorial and alimentary regulation. The Benedictine monk is enjoined to 'ask all to pray for him, that God may keep him from the spirit of pride'.⁴ Stripped of the decadent and idolatrous excesses popularly associated with Rome and the pre-Reformation monasteries, the arcane rituals of the early modern legal profession were suggestive of a unique English Catholicism and strongly imply the centrality of this ethnocentric faith to the governance of the religious commonwealth of England. Significant also to an analysis of the oral traditions of English law and their religious affiliations is the fact that the educational exercises of the Inns took place in the sacred precinct of hall, usually as an adjunct to the rituals of dining. That common law was considered by the legal profession to be the Word of God can be construed from the fact that educational exercises were originally practised in the place of worship. A Council of Lincoln's Inn, held on 13 May 1623, records that moots were held in the old chapel prior to the consecration of the new chapel in 1623. Council 'ordered that the said exercise shall not hereafter be used in that Chappell, nor in the new Chappell; and that from henceforth the Barristers that shall sitt att the said exercises shall sitt at the Barr table on the Bench side in the Hall'.⁵ The resemblance to the Rule of the Order of Saint Benedict is notable: '[r]eading must not be wanting while the brethren eat

---

² For an analysis of the Last Supper, the Eucharist and the law, see P. Goodrich, *Languages of Law: From Logics of Memory to Nomadic Masks* (London: Weidenfeld & Nicolson, 1990), p. 54.

³ The theory of representation and the value of substitution are discussed in L. Marin, *Portrait of the King*, trans. M. M. Houle (Basingstoke: Macmillan, 1988), p. 5. On the aesthetics of dining, see M. Visser, *The Rituals of Dinner: the Origins, Evolution, Eccentricities, and Meaning of Table Manners* (Toronto: HarperCollins, 1991). See also R. C. Wood, *The Sociology of the Meal* (Edinburgh University Press, 1995).

⁴ D. O. H. Blair (ed.), *The Rule of our Most Holy Father Saint Benedict* (London: Burns & Oates, 1886), p. 117.

⁵ *Black Books of Lincoln's Inn*, ed. J. D. Walker, 5 vols. (London: Lincoln's Inn, 1897), II, p. 242.

at table . . . let this verse be said thrice in the Oratory, he himself beginning it: "*Domine, labia mea aperies, et os meum annuntiabit laudem tuam*". [O Lord, Thou shalt open my lips, and my mouth shall declare Thy praise].'[6] The nourishment of body and soul was perceived as coextensive, and it is noteworthy that reference is made to the opening of the lips, in order that the law may be spoken and eaten.

Pollock and Maitland were the first legal historians to observe that the laws of the Inns resembled those governing Christian religious societies, noting that they shared a system of constitutional law that endowed the overseer (*episcopus*) of every congregation with extensive powers.[7] The Inns inherited from the monasteries a system of punitive law, whereby the offender might be excluded from all participation in the symbolic rituals of the legal community, and therefore from communion with his peers. In the Benedictine Order, those who absented themselves from the readings that accompanied dinner were liable to the severe punishment of exclusion from the community: 'let him not be admitted to share in the common table, but be separated from the companionship of all, and eat alone'.[8] The effect of exclusion was experienced at two levels, the social and the religious. At the social or civic level, offenders were unable to participate as active citizens in the commonwealth. In Aristotelian terms they had breached the bonds of friendship that formed the basis of the *polis* and therefore could exert no influence over the governance of their institution. At a religious level, offenders were excluded from the communion of the faithful, and their incapacity to receive the Word made flesh was the effective equivalent of excommunication. Consequently, orders concerning exclusion from commons were couched in appropriate biblical terms, such as the following injunction from Gray's Inn: '. . . if any Fellow of the Society being out of Commons, send for beer or bread into the Buttery, he is to be cast into half Commons'.[9]

The origins of the English Bar are traceable to the monastic orders, whose members regularly acted as advocates in local disputes and whose legal advice was routinely heeded by potential litigants. Dugdale notes that 'divers Monks of Abingdon, amongst which Sacolus and Godric are specially remembered, were persons so expert in the Laws, that others in divers parts did easily submit to their judgment'.[10] The word *advocatus* was originally

---

[6] Blair, *Saint Benedict*, p. 117.
[7] F. Pollock and F. Maitland, *History of English Law*, 2 vols. (Cambridge University Press, 1898), I, p. 2. The origin of the common law (and particularly early pleaders or narrators) in the monasteries is considered in J. H. Baker, *The Order of Serjeants at Law* (London: Selden Society, 1984).
[8] Blair, *Saint Benedict*, p. 131.
[9] W. Dugdale, *Origines Juridiciales or Historical Memorials of the English Laws* (London: F. & T. Warren, 1666), fo. 287.
[10] *Ibid.*, fo. 21.

used to describe a person in the ecclesiastical courts who fulfilled the equivalent function of the 'narrator' in the king's court during the first half of the thirteenth century.[11] Prelates were called upon to administer secular law in medieval England, and their knowledge of ecclesiastical law was an important influence on the development of both common law and the infant legal profession. A unique feature of the Anglo-Saxon judicial system is that there was no rigid distinction between spiritual and temporal courts, and their jurisdictions frequently overlapped.[12] As Dugdale notes, the itinerant justices of the king's courts were 'antiently persons in holy Orders', a definition that included bishops, abbots, deans, canons of cathedral churches and archdeacons.[13] Henry II made the prelates of the Church his justices, ensuring that common law was rationalised under the influence of canon law. English law was administered by the judges ordinary of the Church's courts, men learned in ecclesiastical law. For example, a court sitting in July 1195 consisted of Hubert Walter (Archbishop of Canterbury), Godfrey Lucy (bishop of Winchester), Richard Fitzneal (bishop of London), Gilbert Glanville (bishop of Rochester), Richard Barre (archdeacon of Ely), Ralph Foliot (archdeacon of Hereford), William of Chimelli (archdeacon of Richmond), William of Ste Mère l'Église (afterwards bishop of London), and only four lay members.[14]

Megarry suggests that an Ordinance of Edward I in 1292 was indirectly responsible for the formation of the Inns of Court as the physical centre of a secular legal profession.[15] The Ordinance, prohibiting members of the clergy from acting as advocates in secular actions, had the obvious effect of facilitating the emergence of an unprecedented body of non-clerical lawyers. Edward I (who was given the apt sobriquet of 'the English Justinian') was responsible for providing the conditions necessary for the emergence of a professional organisation of secular lawyers. In the twentieth year of his reign, he appointed the Lord Chief Justice, John de Metingham, to 'provide and ordain, from every County, certain Attorneys and Lawyers, of the best and most apt for their learning and skill, who might do services to his Court'.[16] That the lawyers should choose to congregate as unincorporated associations, close to the royal court and the courts of justice, was a corollary of institutional expansion. The foundations for a centralised legal system were laid at Westminster in the courts of Common Pleas, King's Bench and Exchequer. Physical proximity to the king was expedient as, for many students,

---

[11] P. Brand, *The Origins of the English Legal Profession* (Oxford University Press, 1992), p. 48.
[12] Pollock and Maitland, *English Law*, I, p. 40.
[13] Dugdale, *Origines Juridiciales*, fo. 141.
[14] Pollock and Maitland, *English Law*, I, p. 4.
[15] R. Megarry, *Inns Ancient and Modern* (London: Selden Society, 1972), p. 10.
[16] Dugdale, *Origines Juridiciales*, fo. 141.

the study of law was secondary to the principal purpose of elevation to the royal court. Dugdale notes that 'the Students in them, did there, not only study the Laws, but use such other exercises as might make them serviceable to the King's Court'.[17] Beyond the close proximity of the Inns of Court to the royal court, of fundamental institutional importance was the fact that their evolution provided the unified corporate structure necessary for the standardization of the legal profession and for the influence it subsequently wielded over the development of the constitution.

The ecclesiastical courts were administered by civil lawyers, but many eminent prelates, whose influence in the wider political sphere was considerable, were members of the Inns of Court. These included archbishops Whitgift, Bancroft, Laud and Ussher, all of Gray's Inn. Impeached in 1640 for endeavouring to introduce popery and arbitrary government, Laud suggested during his trial that his prosecutor 'fears both Ceremonies and Doctrine. But in both he fears where no fear is'.[18] Laud's emphasis on the beauty of holiness and the primacy of ceremony in liturgical proceedings provided his opponents with highly visible grounds for initiating his downfall. Throughout the sixteenth and seventeenth centuries, the Inns of Court remained immune to censure from iconoclasts, despite their extensive use of symbols and ceremony to represent the legitimacy of common law and its divine origins. For example, at Gray's Inn and the Middle Temple, a symbolic meal of calves' heads was eaten to celebrate the resurrection of Christ: '[h]e [the chief cook] was wont yearly every Easter Term to bestow upon the whole Society a Break-fast of Calves heads, for which every Gentleman gave xiid. Or more, according to his discretion'.[19] The consecration of calves' heads and their ritualistic consumption was a tradition traceable to medieval England: '[f]yrste on that daye [Easter Sunday] he shall serve a calfe sodden and blessyd and then sodden egges with grene sauce, and set them before the most pryncypall estate'.[20] Of course, the calf was a symbol of classical as well as Christian sacrifice, a symbol of kingship, procreation and fertility.[21]

The significance of pre-Christian sacrificial rites to the particular form of English religious worship was noted by Coke in the preface to Part Three of

---

[17] *Ibid.*
[18] Anon., *The History of the Troubles and Tryal of William Laud, Arch-Bishop of Canterbury* (London: R. Chiswell, 1695), fo. 310. See H. Trevor-Roper, *Archbishop Laud* (London: Phoenix, 2000); for an analysis of the trial of Laud, see D. Alan Orr, *Treason and the State: Law, Politics and Ideology in the English Civil War* (Cambridge University Press, 2002), pp. 101–40.
[19] Dugdale, *Origines Juridiciales*, fo. 199.
[20] Anon., 'The Boke of Kervynge' (1413), in F. J. Furnivall (ed.), *Early English Meals and Manners* (London: Bungay, 1868), pp. 160–1.
[21] M. Bakhtin, *Rabelais and His World*, trans. H. Iswolsky (Bloomington: Indiana University Press, 1984), p. 202.

The Reports: '[n]ow for matters of religion, Strabo in his 4th book observeth, that the Britains worshipped Ceres and Proserpina, and sacrificed unto them according to the Greek form of superstition'.[22] The dining rituals of the Inns forged a seminal link between the common law and the ancient world, reinforcing the idea that the origins of English law preceded the memory of man. To the early modern jurist, the antiquity of English law was the basis of its legitimacy and ultimately of its constitutional supremacy: 'the Common Laws of England are grounded upon the Law of God, and extend themselves to the original Law of Nature, and the universal Law of Nations; and that they are not originally *Leges scriptae*'.[23] The Inns commemorated the ancient status of English law and its embodiment in custom rather than text through their elaborate order of dining. Hence at the Inner Temple and the Middle Temple a gilded horn is blown by the panyer-man to summon members to dinner,[24] recalling the rites of ancient Greek sacrifice, at which the horns of the victim (calf, goat or sheep) were gilded.[25] As with the Eucharist, ritual transforms quotidian details into symbolic acts of sacred importance, and the association between communal dining and communion with God is reinforced nightly at commons.

Respect for the rituals of communal dining was recognised in the Benedictine Order as central to their diurnal life. The Rule of St. Benedict issued the following instruction to the 'Cellarer', responsible for catering arrangements: '[l]et him look upon all the vessels and goods of the Monastery as though they were the consecrated vessels of the altar'.[26] At the Inns of Court, particular types of food and unique utensils associated with their preparation or consumption reflected the religious significance of commons as well as the ancient provenance of their dining rites. Indeed, a Council at Lincoln's Inn in 1551 alluded to the correlation between bread eaten in commons and the Host received at Holy Communion. It records an allowance of '8s. 6d. to Thomas Townerowe, the Butler, for bread and wine for the Chapel'.[27] In hall and chapel, the butler was responsible for providing mundane objects, transmuted through the symbolic act of communion into phantasms of an absent presence. At the Inner Temple, until the second year of Elizabeth's reign, wine was drunk from cups made from ash-wood, 'but then those were laid aside, and green Earthern Pots introduced'.[28] The tradition of drinking

---

[22] E. Coke, *The Reports*, 7 vols. (London: Rivington, 1777), Part III, preface, p. ix.
[23] Dugdale, *Origines Juridiciales*, fo. 3. [24] *Ibid.*, fo. 200.
[25] G. Hersey, *The Lost Meaning of Classical Architecture* (Cambridge, Mass.: MIT, 1988), pp. 15–16; see F. Lissarague, *The Aesthetics of the Greek Banquet: Images of Wine and Ritual*, trans. A. Szegedy-Maszak (New Jersey: Princeton University Press, 1990).
[26] Blair, *Saint Benedict*, p. 103. [27] *Black Books*, I, p. 299.
[28] Dugdale, *Origines Juridiciales*, fo. 148.

from wooden cups was inherited from the Knights Templar,[29] suggesting not only the religious and nationalist affiliations of common law, but also its antiquity.

The above examples demonstrate that the quotidian régime of commons was iconic rather than idolatrous. The licit use of signs directs the viewer from the visible to the invisible, from the human to the divine, thus consummating the union between man and God through the sacraments. In relation to the ecclesiastical polity of the Inns of Court and the early modern English state, Richard Hooker played a crucial role in defining the particular form of religious commonwealth in which common law determined the rights and obligations of magistrate and subject. It is plausible that the three main elements in Hooker's concept of worship (prayer, sacraments and ceremonial forms) were suggested to him by his presence at commons while master of Temple church. The daily repetition by the legal community of sacrament-centred (but not popish) ceremony symbolised an English Protestant polity. It represented an existing tradition that was an acceptable alternative to the idolatrous excesses of Roman Catholicism and the threat to existing constitutional norms implicit in Presbyterianism.[30]

The presence of the body of law, or *corpus iuris*, is witnessed in institutional structures, just as the presence of God is symbolised by His church and witnessed in the Host by means of an institutional ritual, the Eucharist. The overriding theme of the Eucharist is recognition: it signifies the continuing presence of deity while referring to and remembering the past. The analogy of Eucharistic recognition applies also to a legal system founded on the distillation of ancient custom and perfect reason, sanctioned by holy writ but not enshrined in any single document. Concerning the rival claims of text and image, the history of English law mirrors the history of the church in England. This comparison is particularly apt in connection with the central theological debate over the institutional authority of the established church and the textual authority of the printed word.[31] The reformers saw the sacrament as *verba visibilia*: correspondingly the semiotics of legal presence concern the spirit of law being made visible in architecture, dress and other *insignia armorum* of law.

---

[29] *Calendar of Inner Temple Records*, ed. F. A. Inderwick, 5 vols. (London: H. Sotheran, 1896), I, preface.

[30] On Hooker and the Protestant alternative to English Calvinism, see P. Lake, *Anglicans and Puritans? Presbyterianism and English Conformist Thought from Whitgift to Hooker* (London: Unwin Hyman, 1988), pp. 228–30.

[31] On the social, cultural and political effects of the innovative printing process, see E. Eisenstein, *The Printing Press as an Agent of Change* (Cambridge University Press, 1980); L. Febvre and H.-J. Martin, *The Coming of the Book* (London: New Left Books, 1976); H. J. Graff, *The Legacies of Literacy* (Bloomington: Indiana University Press, 1987).

16   *Images and Cultures of Law in Early Modern England*

As authority moved from church to state, from theology to jurisprudence, so presence was predicated not on the recognition of deity but on recognition of the body politic.³² The constitutional sacrifice implicit in the social contract between subject and ruler replaced the continuing sacrifice of Christ in the Eucharist. As the church sought to assert its authority as sole guardian of the Word, in which resided the exclusive right to interpret God's will, so the legal profession sought to establish its exclusive right to interpret the Ancient Constitution. Sir Thomas More remarked on the significant similarity between the threat to the church posed by the reliance on textual as opposed to institutional authority, and the threat to the authority of the law posed by textualisation.³³ In the context of the Elizabethan legal institution, More's fears were reflected in Coke's advice that it is 'a desperate and dangerous matter for civilians and canonists (I speak what I know, and not without just cause) to write either of the common laws of England which they profess not, or against them which they know not'.³⁴ The power of the printed word was fully appreciated by Elizabeth I, in whose reign the Stationers' Company policed the presses and received their instructions from the Privy Council.³⁵ At a symbolic level the debate concerned the relative status of text and sign; the evidence of the written word challenged institutional authority and the iconic signs of that authority.

TEMPERANCE, ORDER AND THE SACRIFICIAL RITE OF DINING

The quotidian fare offered in hall typically consisted of cheap cuts of meat, an allowance of cheese and a limited quantity of wine or beer: mutton was the 'usual Supper-meat of this Society [the Middle Temple], there being seldome any other joynt served in the Hall'.³⁶ The sheep was of great symbolic importance to the Middle Temple, as their emblem was the paschal lamb and flag. The sacrificial rites of ancient societies derived from the belief that the qualities of the victim were absorbed by the person who ate it (or him).³⁷ At a religious and sacrificial level, the consumption of mutton at the Middle

---

[32] On the relationship between law and theology, see Marin, *Portrait of the King*, pp. 3–15; also E. Kantorowicz, *The King's Two Bodies: A Study in Medieval Political Theology* (New Jersey: Princeton University Press, 1957).

[33] T. More, 'The Confutacyon of Tyndale's Answere by Sir Thomas More Knyght Lorde Chancellor of England', *The Yale Edition of the Complete Works of St. Thomas More*, ed. L. A. Schuster, R. C. Marius, J. P. Lusardi and R. J. Schoeck, 15 vols. (New Haven: Yale University Press, 1973), VIII, p. 291.

[34] Coke, *Reports*, Part X, preface, p. xvii.

[35] J. Guy, *Tudor England* (Oxford University Press, 1990), p. 416.

[36] Dugdale, *Origines Juridiciales*, fo. 199.

[37] On the cannibalistic rites of ancient societies, see Visser, *Rituals of Dinner*, pp. 3–12; see also Bakhtin, *Rabelais*, p. 281.

Temple re-enacts the conclusive sacrifice of Christ on the cross and represents His presence in the body of law. The eating rite witnessed here is analogous to the sacraments, in building a community of the faithful and an order of privileged knowledge. Christ is the Word made flesh, and that impossible unity of divinity and humanity, of spirit and corporeality, is closely linked to the foundation of community in communal eating. Commons celebrates the presence of God in hall and in the common law. The Word has been passed down to His priests in the form of law, and they reaffirm their faith through the sacramental rite of dining. There is a notable similarity between the Eucharistic rites of the church and the ritual enacted at the Middle Temple on the feast of All Saints:

there is delivered unto every Barister, a Towell, with Wafers in it; and unto every Gentleman under the Bar, a wooden Bowl, filled with Ipocras, with which they march in order into the Hall, the Reader with his white Rod, going formost... and then, after a low solemn Congee made, the Gentlemen of the Bar first carry the Wafers; the rest, with the new Reader, standing in their places. At their return, they all make another solemn low Congee, and then the Gentlemen under the Bar, carry their Bowles of Ipocras to the Judges: and returning, when the Judges have drank, they make the like solemn Congee, and so all depart.[38]

Wafers were eaten and wine was drunk in a replication of the Eucharistic act.

The public veneration of God was, of course, a crucial aspect of the diurnal life of the Inns. At the Middle Temple, for example, 'they have every day three Masses said; one after the other: And the first Masse doth begin in the morning at seaven of the Clock, or thereabouts. The Festivall days they have Mattens and Masse solemnly sung; and during the Matyns singing, they have three Masses said'.[39] Attendance at religious services was compulsory, as was attendance at commons for at least eight weeks every year, during term; absence from either could result in expulsion from the Inn. A Council at Lincoln's Inn in 1575 records that 'Mr Peterson, Mr Gilbert, Mr Barney, Mr Basset, Mr Abbot, Mr Johnson, Mr Skydmore, and Mr Wye are to be talked with all at the Benche for not receiving the Communyon.'[40] The correlation between professional advancement and religious observance (specifically, active participation by common lawyers in the Eucharistic rite) is instanced by the decision of Council (16 May 1602) that Mr Henry Denne, having satisfied all other criteria, should be called to the Bar of Lincoln's Inn only 'yf he satisfie Mr Tindall touchinge his nott receyvinge of the Communion in the Chappell of this Howse'.[41] The rituals of religious services held in chapel mirrored those of commons in hall; in both, the authority of the

---

[38] Dugdale, *Origines Juridiciales*, fo. 205.
[39] *Ibid.*, fo. 196.   [40] *Black Books*, I, p. 398.   [41] *Ibid.*, II, p. 73.

Father was replicated through an act of communion. The presence of God was invoked every night before and after dinner: at the Inner Temple, the words 'Benedictus benedicat' were spoken before dinner, and after dinner, 'Benedicto benedicatur'.[42] Members were considered to have attended dinner only if they were present when the invocation of blessing upon the food was offered.

In connection with food and the law, there is an extensive literature from the sixteenth century offering advice on diet to intending lawyers. Fulbecke insisted that '[a] Student [of common law] must in his diet be temperat, and abstinent . . . Continency in dyet is the step to wisedom. A fat and full belly yeeldeth nothing to a man but grosse spirits, by which the sharp edge of the minde is dulled and refracted, and too much meate cast into the stomack doth ingender nothing but cruditie and diseases.'[43] Coke explicitly referred to the act of eating the law: '[i]n reading these and others of my Reports, I desire the Reader, that he would not read (and as it were swallow) too much at once; for greedy appetites are not of the best digestion; the whole is to be attained by parts.'[44] In the advice Fulbecke offered to students of common law, his instructions for the careful maintenance of the 'body' of law were explicit: '[t]he next thing I require in a Student is temperance . . . a restreint of the minde from all voluptuousness and lust, as namely from covetousness, excesse of diet, wantonness, and all other unlawfull delights.' The body of law was healthily maintained by temperance, 'the mother of order'.[45]

Dugdale referred to the '[d]egrees of Tables in the Hall', providing evidence that commons was the primary medium through which order was expressed. Seating was arranged according to seniority, and the overriding concern with antiquity and oral skills manifested itself in the delineation of individual rank. The most junior members were inner-barristers, the least experienced of whom were termed 'clerks commons'. Inner-barristers of approximately two years' membership were known as 'masters commons'. Utter-barristers had been members for between five and eight years, and had to 'plead, argue, and dispute some doubtful matter in the Law' during term or the grand vacations of Lent and summer: 'the same manner of argument or disputations is called Motyng'. Benchers had been utter-barristers for at least twelve years, and were chosen to 'reade, expound, and declare some Estatute openly unto

---

[42] J. H. Baker, *The Inner Temple: A Brief Historical Description* (London: Inner Temple, 1991), p. 14.

[43] W. Fulbecke, *A Direction or Preparative to the study of the Lawe*, (London: T. Wight, 1600), fo. 12a. See also W. Phillips, *Studii Legalis Ratio or Directions for the Study of Law* (London: Kirkman, 1667); M. Montaigne, 'Of Sumptuary Laws', in *The Complete Works of Montaigne*, trans. D. M. Frame (London: Hamish Hamilton, 1958), p. 196; T. Wilson, *The Art of Rhetorique* (London: G. Robinson, 1585).

[44] Coke, *Reports*, Part VI, preface, p. x.

[45] Fulbecke, *A Direction or Preparative*, ff. 12a, 15b.

all the Company of the House' in the grand vacation.[46] A bencher who had completed two readings was called a 'Double Reader', and from their ranks 'the King makes choice of his Attorney, and Sollicitor general'[47] and elected the serjeants-at-law. There were separate tables for benchers, utter-barristers, inner-barristers (with two tables for masters commons and one for clerks commons) and one 'without the Skreen, for the Benchers Clerks, called the Yeomans Table'.[48]

The religious and sacrificial significance of the tables should not be overlooked. The association with the *tabulata* of the ancient world, on which offerings were laid outside the temple, is obvious. Fortescue would certainly have been aware, when he compared the judiciary to *sacerdotes*, that *sacra* was the Latin word commonly used to describe sacrifices and religious festivals.[49] Desecration of the venerable ritual of commons and of hall, the sacred place in which the Eucharistic act was performed, was regarded by the governing bodies of the Inns as sacrilegious, recalling another meaning of *sacer* as accursed, criminal or infamous. Such acts were punishable 'either by payment of money, or by putting him forth of commens; which is, that he shall take no meate nor drynke among the fellowship'.[50] Consequently, at Lincoln's Inn in 1581, receipts included '3s. 4d. from Maisters junior for snatching a dish of meat from the Steward'.[51] Exclusion from the legal community was a severe sanction, which, according to Fortescue, members 'dread more than Criminals do Imprisonment and Irons'.[52] Respect for the artificial order of social community was a central theme of commons. It was enforced not only by the governing bodies of the Inns, but on at least one occasion by the most senior member of the judiciary, the Lord Chief Justice, on the explicit order of the king. On the eve of the feast of Saint Thomas in 1639, several members of the Middle Temple broke open the doors of hall, the buttery and the kitchen: '[t]hese gentlemen, with others, continued to keep Christmas with commons and play until they were convented before the Lord Chief Justice, and were commanded by him, by his Majesty's special direction, to break up their commons and conform to the order.'[53]

The *minutiae* of the order of dining is notable for its obsessive regard for hierarchy and its implicit insistence on humility. Clerks commons served masters commons their food; if two members of masters commons sat at a mess, then an equal amount of meat was divided between three members of clerks commons; 'and when three of the Masters commens doth syt at

---

[46] Dugdale, *Origines Juridiciales*, fo. 193. [47] *Ibid.*, fo. 144. [48] *Ibid.*, fo. 158.
[49] Hersey, *Classical Architecture*, pp. 30, 43. [50] Dugdale, *Origines Juridiciales*, fo. 196.
[51] *Black Books*, I, p. 422. [52] Fortescue, *De Laudibus*, p. 112.
[53] *A Calendar of the Middle Temple Records*, ed. C. H. Hopwood, 4 vols. (London: Butterworth, 1903), II, p. 888.

a Messe, then doth foure of the Clerks commens sit at so much meat'.[54] The menu throughout the year (with the exception of the seasonal feasts) was repetitive and frugal, reflecting temperance and respect for immutable custom. For dinner at the Middle Temple, '[b]etwene two of the Masters commens, is served meat to the value of iiid. And the third part of iid. Betwene three of the Masters commens, at Supper, is served meat to the value of iiid.'[55] Wine was the usual accompaniment to the food offered: 'one pottle of Claret Wine at every meal'.[56] It was customary for commons to be attended only by members of the Inn, and it is notable that records emphasise the exclusion of non-members from the sacred rite of dining. For example, at the Inner Temple there was a requirement '[t]hat no stranger be suffered to stand in the Skreen in Meal-times'.[57] The discipleship of the legal community and the bonds of apostolic fraternity that united members were emphasised and enforced by the exclusivity of its rituals.

MOOTS AND READINGS: THE ACQUISITION OF ORAL SKILLS

The correlation between eating and learning the law was emphasised by the coexistence of commons and the educational exercises that invariably followed the communal rites of dining. At the Middle Temple, the office of chief butler exemplified the indissoluble and symbolic link between common law and the consumption of food. His mandatory unmarried status was indicative of his elevated role within the male hegemony of hall. The Parliament of the Inner Temple decided in 1579 that cooks and other members of staff were prohibited from allowing women into the kitchen, 'upon pain that the officer to whom such person shall resort to lose his office or place.'[58] The chief butler was responsible for keeping the 'Buttry-book', in which were recorded orders for food and drink. But it was his responsibility also to record 'all such as perform any Moot or Exercise, either within the House or abroad, to the end he may give a true accompt thereof when he is thereunto called'.[59] Oral exercises took place after dinner; at the Inner Temple before the start of the clerks commons exercise, the most senior of the inner-barristers, known as the 'abbot', approached the bar-table at the end of dinner and informed the utter-barristers that they 'have a Case to put their Masterships'. Exercises took place on three nights of the week, throughout the vacations. But only after the tables were laid and the panyer-man had summoned the members to dinner, 'he that is to put the Case, layeth a Case fair written in paper, upon the Salt, giving thereby notice, of the Case to be

---

[54] Dugdale, *Origines Juridiciales*, ff. 193, 195.
[55] Ibid., ff. 195–6.   [56] Ibid., fo. 278.   [57] Ibid., fo. 287.
[58] *Inner Temple Records*, I, p. 299.   [59] Dugdale, *Origines Juridiciales*, fo. 198.

argued after Dinner'.[60] Although the case to be argued was transcribed onto paper, the particular techniques practised by students were exclusively oral. Every night after dinner, students would sit at their tables in groups of three, to dispute 'some doubtfull question in the Law'.[61]

Before he could be called to the Bar, a student had to participate in twelve grand moots and twenty-four petty moots at the Inns of Chancery. Following his call to the Bar, he would take part in a moot at his Inn of Court during each of the Lent and summer vacations for the following three years.[62] The moot was by far the most important single exercise in the education of law students, and senior members of the Inn were obliged to attend them. Dugdale records that in 1560 at the Inner Temple, 'every single Reader should be at three Mootes in every Term, and in Michaelmas Term at four Mootes. And every Bencher not a Reader, to be at five Mootes in every Term, and in Michaelmas Term at six, upon payn of five shillings every Moote'.[63] Readings offered similar opportunities for the development of adversarial skills. After the reader had offered up a case, it would then be argued by utter-barristers. Following their disputation, 'the Judges and Benchers argue according to their antiquity, the puisne Bencher beginning first; and so everyone after another, till the antientest Judge or Bencher have argued the Case'.[64] Throughout the sixteenth century, students at the Inns undertook educational exercises in law-French, as the following description of a moot held at the Middle Temple during the grand vacation records:

before three of the Elders or Benchers at the leste, is pleadyd and declared in homely Law-french, by such as are young Lerners, some doubtfull matter, or question in the Law; which afterwards an Utter-Barister doth reherse, and doth argue and reason to it in the Law-frenche: and after him another Utter-Barrister doth reason in the contrary part, in Law-frenche also; and then do the three Benchers declare their myndes in English; and this is that they call motyng.[65]

It is notable that although the pleadings and arguments were in law-French, the judgment was given in English, the language associated by common lawyers with wisdom and justice. This practice represents a symbolic rejection of subjugation to the Norman yoke and reflected the popular opinion that the English were God's chosen people. Such a belief was expressed by Bishop Aylmer, who said of the English, concerning their enemies abroad: 'you have right and truth, and seek not to do them wrong, but to defend your right. Think not that God will suffer you to be soiled at their hands, for your fall is his dishonour.'[66]

---

[60] *Ibid.*, fo. 158.   [61] *Ibid.*, fo. 194.   [62] *Ibid.*, fo. 159.
[63] *Ibid.*, fo. 148.   [64] *Ibid.*, fo. 160.   [65] *Ibid.*, fo. 194.
[66] Bishop Aylmer, *An Harborowe for Faithfull and Trewe Subjectes* (Strasborowe, 1559), sig. iiia–ivb.

A statute enacted in 1363 (36 Edw. 3. C. 15) ordered that all pleadings, arguments and disputations of law should henceforth be performed in English, rather than law-French, although the oral exercises of the Inns were explicitly excluded from its provisions. As Prest has observed, by the early modern period the use of law-French outside the Inns was confined to the brief annotation of case notes. Apart from the relative ease with which the jargon could be acquired (taking between two and ten days),[67] the principal virtue of law-French, as far as the English legal profession was concerned, was that it differentiated common law at a linguistic level from civil and canon law. Law-French represented an attempt by the legal institution to popularise itself and to communicate with a wider (and often uneducated) audience, who could respond to aural, but not literary, stimuli.[68] The following extract demonstrates the attraction of this unique idiom to unlettered listeners:

Home ad un Molyn, & l'eaw courge per le terr d'une auter al dit Molyn, le Tenant del terre mis stakes deins le dit eaw sur y il edify un meason, per reason de quell l'eaw ne poit vener cy bien al dit Molin come devant: Le Tenant del Molyn enter en la dit terre, & enrasa les stakes, per y la dit Meison eschew: Et in Trespas pur entry en la dit terr & enraser la meason; tout cest matter pur avoider le dit Nusance fuit plede per le defendant & tenus bon Iustification.[69]

The widespread availability of books, facilitated by the innovative printing process, was a crucial factor in altering the form and content of legal education at the Inns. The rediscovery of ancient texts and their distribution at the Inns of Court ensured that the common law was taught, developed and disseminated under the influence of classical philosophers such as Plato and Aristotle, and that the rhetorical techniques of Quintilian, Cicero and Tacitus were imitated by the legal community. Rhetorical handbooks such as *The Arte or Crafte of Rhethoryke* (1529) by Leonard Cox and *The Art of Rhetorique* (1553) by Thomas Wilson drew extensively from the ancient rhetorical tradition and provided a classical foundation for the skills of forensic oratory acquired at the Inns of Court. The acquisition of rhetorical techniques from the Graeco-Roman world became a crucial aspect of legal education. The Inns of Court realigned the republican values of the Utopian states imagined by Plato and Aristotle, within the Anglican confines of the religious commonwealth envisaged by Hooker. This fact was of fundamental

---

[67] W. R. Prest, *The Rise of the Barristers: A Social History of the English Bar, 1590–1640* (Oxford: Clarendon, 1991), pp. 108–9; see also J. H. Baker, *Manual of law-French* (Amersham: Avebury, 1979), pp. 9–14.

[68] D. Manderson, '*Statuta* v. Acts: Interpretation, Music, and Early English Legislation', *Yale Journal of Law & the Humanities*, 7 (1995), 341.

[69] J. Doderidge, *The English Lawyer. Describing A Method for the managing of the Lawes of this Land* (London: I. More, 1631), p. 220.

importance to the development of a unique body of English law and its representation within the constitution. The integration of classical and Christian philosophy determined the particular form of religious commonwealth that the Inns sought to represent.

As their alternative title of 'the Third University' implies, the educational function of the Inns was not confined to the indoctrination of substantive law and rhetorical techniques. Fortescue had ascribed to them a broader, social and cultural role, and their contribution to the sphere of juristic thought was considerable. For example, readings and moots were not mere educational devices, intended only to develop the oratorical skills of advocacy necessary for the common lawyer. They provide evidence that the Inns of Court contributed to the creation of a distinct body of law. Baker has suggested that the evolution of criminal law can be attributed to the educational practice of readings at the Inns.[70] The earliest readings on criminal law concerned offences such as homicide and the related defences of duress, insanity and automatism. Relevant to the claim that the Inns functioned partly as legal innovators is the fact that these and other areas of law (such as negligence and abortion) were debated at the Inns long before their appearance in the law reports. As Baker observes, the Inns were not only responsible for systematising and rationalising English law; they also prompted and directed the manner in which jurisprudence was effected by the courts.[71]

THE LAWYER AS ACTOR

What maketh the Lawyer to have such utteraunce: Practise.[72]

In his *Brutus*, Cicero defined the successful advocate in terms of his acting prowess. His courtroom, or judge's tribunal, was a theatre in which all the benches were filled and an expectant audience congregated. As he stood to speak, the crowd became silent, breaking into spontaneous applause at appropriate moments in appreciation of the speaker's histrionic skills. The level of noise was such that distant passers-by were aurally alerted to the effect the orator was having on his audience.[73] It is unsurprising that, in Cicero's vivid description of the advocate's craft, he should emphasise the theatrical skills of the forensic orator rather than his legal knowledge, as at the time of writing there was no law of evidence. In general, orators were not trained in law and neither were most of the judges who presided over cases.

---

[70] J. H. Baker, 'Why the History of English Law Has Not Been Finished', *Cambridge Law Journal*, 59 (2000), 81–2.
[71] *Ibid.*, 82. On Readings at the Inns, see J. H. Baker, *The Third University of England: the Inns of Court and the Common Law Tradition* (London: Selden Society, 1990), p. 20.
[72] Wilson, *Art of Rhetorique*, fo. 4.
[73] Cicero, *Brutus*, trans. G. L. Hendrickson (London: William Heinemann, 1962), p. 290.

Legal practice had not been appropriated by an independent profession; it was inhabited almost entirely by rhetors and orators, and the success of an individual pleader depended as much on his effectiveness at moving an audience as it did on his knowledge of law.

Adulation of the rhetorician's craft was commonplace in ancient Greece and Rome, where the earliest laws took the form of myths and stories; the great law-givers – Solon, Lycurgus and Plato – were all successful narrators. The ancient trial advocate was both actor and poet, applying his stylistic judgment to interpret events. He rearranged certain aspects of the narrative to give a selective and highly stylised version of events.[74] Historically, there is extensive and eloquent opposition to the idea that law and aesthetics are indivisible. In *The Laws*, Plato argued that the language of the legal text must be unambiguous and clear in order to ensure the consistency and certainty of law. He suggested that such clarity was inconsistent with poetry, a craft in which the ambiguities of human nature were exposed and expressed.[75] Protected from the hazards of misinterpretation, laws were more likely to be incontestable. But the poetic craft, which Plato found incompatible with law, was central to the practice of English law. The adversarial nature of English law necessitated that, in every action, two conflicting interpretations of the same events were offered by the plaintiff and the defendant, each of whom employed a narrator to convince the court that his interpretation of events was the most convincing. It is noteworthy in this context that the traditional Latin word to describe members of the Order of Serjeants at Law was 'narratores'.[76] The dependence on storytelling, and the preservation of these narratives in texts or law reports, characterised to a considerable extent the practice of common law in the early modern period.[77]

The exploration by the European Renaissance of classical art, literature and philosophy facilitated the resurgence of rhetorical skills in legal education. The relevance of Ciceronian techniques to sixteenth-century English rhetoricians was reflected in the respect afforded Cicero by the numerous writers of rhetorical manuals, who depicted him as an archetype of classical rhetoric. Sir Thomas Wilson, for example, suggested that 'rhetorique is an Arte to set foorth by utterance of words, matter at large, or (as Cicero doth say) it is learned, or rather an artificiall declaration of the mynd, in the

---

[74] On the correlation between rhetoric, law and theatre in the ancient world, see B. W. Vickers, *In Defence of Rhetoric* (Oxford University Press, 1988). The link between performance of law and power is emphasised in R. Warrington and C. Douzinas, 'The Trials of Law and Literature', *Law and Critique*, 6 (1995), 135–65; see also J. White, *Heracles' Bow: Essays on the Rhetoric and Poetics of Law* (Madison: University of Wisconsin Press, 1985).
[75] Plato, *The Laws*, trans. T. J. Saunders (Harmondsworth: Penguin, 1970), p. 180.
[76] Dugdale, *Origines Juridiciales*, fo. 110.
[77] On law as a narrative representation of human behaviour, see B. Jackson, *Law, Fact and Narrative Coherence* (Roby: Deborah Charles, 1988), p. 91.

handling of any cause, called in contention, that may through reason largely be discussed'.[78] Wilson emphasised the utility of rhetoric as a persuasive political device: 'if the worthinesse of Eloquence maie moove us, what worthier thing can there bee, then with a word to winne Cities and whole Countries?'[79] A large proportion of the barrister's training was dedicated to the acquisition of these skills, whose association with the ancient world contributed to the fiction that common law was of immemorial origin. Although the sources of common law and the foreign influences on the origins of the English legal system were investigated during the early modern period by jurists and legal historians such as Selden, this had no noticeable effect on the polemical treatise that common law was of antique, English provenance.[80] The extreme antiquity of the common law is a recurring theme of *The Reports* of Sir Edward Coke. Pocock has remarked upon the peculiar insularity of Coke's mind, but concedes that there was no reason why a common lawyer should compare English law with its continental counterparts, other than to satisfy intellectual curiosity outside the everyday needs of the profession.[81] Sir Henry Spelman contributed greatly to the understanding of the origins of common law, which he related to the history of other peoples (largely Germanic), rather than indulging in the manufacture of insular legend.[82] But accurate analysis was of no practical use to Coke, who asserted the ancient sovereignty of common law, emphasising its antique origins and unique ethnocentricity. As the claim to ancient provenance was a fundamental tenet of the common law tradition, so the acquisition of classical skills was considered appropriate to the training of barristers. Consequently, the performance of poetic drama (whose themes were predominantly drawn from the myths of the ancient world) became an important medium through which these skills were acquired and demonstrated at the Inns of Court.

In chapter 4, I consider the function of the masques presented at the Elizabethan and Jacobean Inns of Court as a continuing narrative of polemical tracts, containing oblique references to the monarch, the constitution and the royal prerogative. But the staging of drama was also an effective educational device, employed by the Inns to instil the skills of oratory and

---

[78] Wilson, *Art of Rhetorique*, fo. 1.
[79] *Ibid.*, 'The Epistle', fo. 2. See also L. Cox, *The Arte or Crafte of Rhetoryke* (London: R. Redman, 1529); P. Sidney, *The Defense of Poesy* (Glasgow: R. Urie, 1752); H. Peacham, *The Garden of Eloquence* (London: H. Jackson, 1593). Observations on the study of rhetoric by sixteenth-century law students include D. S. Bland, 'Rhetoric and the Law Student in Sixteenth Century England', *Studies in Philology*, 54 (1957), 498–508; and R. J. Schoeck, 'Rhetoric and Law in Sixteenth Century England', *Studies in Philology*, 50 (1953), 110–27.
[80] See D. R. Kelley, 'History, English Law and the Renaissance', *Past & Present*, 65 (1974), 30.
[81] J. G. A. Pocock, *The Ancient Constitution and the Feudal Law: A Study of English Historical Thought in the Seventeenth Century* (Cambridge University Press, 1987), p. 56.
[82] H. Spelman, *Of the Four Law Terms: A Discourse* (London: Gillyflower, 1684).

performance that were central to the work of the successful common lawyer. There is an obvious parallel between the *agon* of the trial and the intrinsic conflict of drama, a correlation that was identified and examined by Cicero, in *Brutus*.[83] The poetic medium of drama was also the means through which the Inns expressed the principle that the development of the early modern English state should be grounded in the existence of an ethically informed jurisprudence. The relationship between the oral origins of law, the narratives of the ancient world and the classical arts of oratory and forensic rhetoric was explored in the dramas performed by junior barristers and students of the Inns of Court. The classical themes of rational governance and political order as a microcosm of cosmic order were also intended to propagate in the junior ranks of the legal profession the common law ethos of spirituality, community and political sovereignty.

At the Middle Temple during the Christmas period of 1598, it is probable that members of the Inn acted all the parts in an early version of Shakespeare's *Troilus and Cressida*, prior to its first public performance.[84] Records suggest that the governing body of the Middle Temple intended that the entertainment provided at this time should not be of the usual type. A Parliament of the Middle Temple, held on 24 November 1598, decreed that '[t]he feast of Christmas shall be kept solemnly, not grandly. Commons shall be continued till next term. A cartload of coal and 40s. for the minstrels shall be allowed to those who remain.'[85] The dramatist John Marston (a member of the Middle Temple and, like many other Middle Templars, a neighbour of Shakespeare in Warwickshire) wrote a comic play entitled *Histrio-Mastix Or, the Player whipt!*, which was performed at the Middle Temple in 1599. Reference to the performance of *Troilus and Cressida* and its author, Shakespeare, is included in the text of Marston's play:

Come *Cressida* my Cresset light,
Thy face doth shine both day and night,
Behold, behold, thy garter blue,
Thy knight his valiant elboe weares,
That when he shakes his furious Speare,
The foe in shivering fearefull sort,
May lay him downe in death to snort.[86]

There are several other comic references to the work of Shakespeare in *Histrio-Mastix*, the most obvious of which is the staging of a play by a

---

[83] On the trial in literature, see Warrington and Douzinas, 'Trials of Law and Literature', 138.
[84] The convincing argument that the play received its first performance on this occasion was presented in J. L. Hotson, 'Love's Labours Won', in *Shakespeare's Sonnets Dated* (London: R. Hart-Davis, 1949), pp. 37–56.
[85] *Middle Temple Records*, I, p. 390.
[86] J. Marston, *Histrio-Mastix Or, The Player whipt!* (London: T. Thorp, 1610), fo. C4a; see P. J. Finkelpearl, *John Marston of the Middle Temple: An Elizabethan Dramatist in his Social Setting* (Cambridge, Mass.: Harvard University Press, 1969).

troupe of incompetent amateurs, going under the name of 'Sir Oliver Owlet's Men'.[87] Three of these characters, Belch the Beard-maker, Gutt the Fiddle-string-maker and Incle the Pedler, have their counterparts in Bottom the weaver, Flute the bellows-mender and Snout the tinker, three of the artisans in Shakespeare's *A Midsummer Night's Dream* (written three years before *Histrio-Mastix*), who perform their version of *Pyramus and Thisbe* for Duke Theseus and the royal court in the final act of the play. A reference to Shakespeare himself (both to his acting skills and his prolific output of plays) may be construed from the character of 'Post-hast the Poet', the fourth of Marston's artisan-actors. He describes Sir Oliver Owlet's men as 'Politician Players',[88] alluding possibly to the predominant political themes of *Troilus and Cressida*. That reference to *A Midsummer Night's Dream* was intended can be inferred from Marston's stage direction for the entrance of these characters: 'Enter a sort of Russetings and Mechanicalls'; in Shakespeare's play, Puck describes the amateur actors as 'A crew of patches, rude mechanicals'.[89] The choice of 'beard-maker' as the craft of Belch was possibly influenced by Bottom's quandary concerning the style of beard he should wear for the part of Pyramus: 'I will discharge it in either your straw-colour beard, your orange-tawny beard, your purple-in-grain beard, or your French-crown-colour beard, your perfect yellow'.[90]

The cross-references to Shakespeare, and the repeated themes of theatre and the performance of plays by amateur actors, allude to the staging of *Troilus and Cressida* the previous year by members of the Middle Temple. They also demonstrate the crucial role played by drama in the education and social life of common lawyers. The protagonists of Marston's comic interlude are two common lawyers, Fourcher and Vourcher. They are familiar with the disputatious nature of legal education at the Inns of Court. To the question, 'How shall we best imploy this idle time?' Fourcher answers, 'Lets argue on some case for exercise'.[91] But when asked how they should spend the afternoon, Fourcher replies: 'Fayth lets goe see a Play'; when he is told that plays are 'a deale of prating to so little purpose', he replies that 'going to a play is now all in the fashion'.[92] Fourcher and Vourcher are cynical manipulators of the forensic craft, the latter complaining on their joint behalf:

And sweet contention (Lawyers best content)
Is sent by drowsie Peace to banishment.[93]

Encouraged by the allegorical character of 'Pride' to use their wisdom in order to enrich themselves 'In buildings, ryot, garments, gallantry', Vourcher

---

[87] Marston, *Histrio-Mastix*, fo. B1a.   [88] *Ibid.*
[89] *Ibid.*, fo. F3b; *A Midsummer Night's Dream*, III. ii. 9. Unless otherwise indicated, line references are to the New Penguin Shakespeare edition.
[90] *Ibid.*, I. ii. 86–9.   [91] Marston, *Histrio-Mastix*, fo. D1b.
[92] *Ibid.*, fo. B1b.   [93] *Ibid.*, fo. D1b.

replies that 'wee have Lawes to limitte our attire',[94] a reference to the sumptuary legislation enacted and enforced by the Elizabethan Inns of Court. Typical of the seasonal entertainments presented at the Inns of Court during this period, *Histrio-Mastix* ends with a felicitous affirmation of monarchic governance and the familiar iconic representation of Queen Elizabeth as *Astraea*:

Whose glory, which thy solid vertues wonne,
Shall honour *Europe* whil'st there shines a Sunne.[95]

Marston's presence at the Middle Temple during this period is recorded by a Parliament held on 8 February 1600: 'Mr. John Marston was readmitted to the chamber to which his father was lately admitted with Mr. Haule.' In *Histrio-Mastix*, he gently parodied the theatrical efforts of his fellow Middle Templars in their rendition of Shakespeare's play. The association between Shakespeare and the Middle Temple is well documented. His cousin, Thomas Greene, became Treasurer in 1629, and his friends and neighbours in Stratford, William and Thomas Combe, took over the chambers of their great-uncle, William Combe (also of Stratford), a bencher of the Middle Temple. Other members of the Stratford gentry who joined the Middle Temple during this period include William Catesby, Fulke Greville, Henry Rainsford, William Barnes, Edward Fisher, Leonard Kempson and Henry Goodere.[96] In 1609, when *Troilus and Cressida* was released for publication, the preface stated that the play was 'never stal'd with the Stage, never clapper-clawd with the palmes of the vulgar, and yet passing full of the palme comicall'.[97] This would suggest that the play had never been performed in front of a paying audience, at least not with the knowledge of its 'grand possessors', mentioned in the same preface: a probable allusion to the Honourable Society of the Middle Temple. The play was ideally suited to performance by a large, amateur company of young men, containing twenty-four male and four female roles. Its intellectual, cynical, and satirical style suggests too that the play was intended originally for a different audience from that which usually attended Shakespeare's plays. A possible indication of the importance with which this exercise was regarded is that the punishment for those members who did not attend was especially severe. Parliament of 9 February 1599 fined twenty-seven members of the Middle Temple '20s. each for absence and being out of commons at Christmas 1598'.[98]

The natural order, articulated and embodied in *Troilus and Cressida* by the character of Ulysses, is congruent with the Platonic notion of justice, upon

---

[94] *Ibid.*, fo. D1b–D2a.   [95] *Ibid.*, fo. H2b.   [96] Hotson, 'Love's Labours Won', p. 44.
[97] The preface is discussed in the Arden edition of *Troilus and Cressida*, ed. D. Bevington (Walton-on-Thames: T. Nelson, 1998), introduction.
[98] *Middle Temple Records*, I, p. 391.

which the ethos of the Inns of Court was founded. The speeches of Ulysses, delivered in the consistent rhythm of iambic pentameter, provide an aural affirmation of the coextensive nature of reason, polity and natural order (and a rejection of their antithesis, chaos). It is a noteworthy paradox, in connection with the use of poetry as a means of comprehending natural and political order, that Plato opposed the presence of poets in *The Republic*, fearing the threat inherent in language to the maintenance of reason and order. It can be argued that Plato's fears were realised in the Elizabethan and Jacobean Inns, where poetic drama was the chosen medium through which the mores of existing governmental norms were challenged and alternatives posited.[99] The form and content of Elizabethan and Jacobean poetic drama illustrate the Aristotelian relationship between ethics and rhetoric, and the importance of their indivisibility to the legitimacy of common law and the legal profession. This connection applies both to the oral skills of the forensic orator and to the linguistic and hermeneutic skills of the poet, which were to attain great significance as judgments and law reporting were standardised in textual form.

The poetics of law were explored in a unique fashion in *Troilus and Cressida*, which expresses the congruency of communality, social order and cosmic order within the structured boundaries of an undeviating verse form. The fact that all the parts in the play were acted by members of the Middle Temple demonstrates both the prominence of rhetoric in legal education and the lawyer's role as actor. It is self-evident that such skills (unchanged in substance since the rhetorical manuals of Aristotle, Cicero, and Tacitus were written) were of fundamental importance to the prospective barrister. But the performance of *Troilus and Cressida* was important too in demonstrating the relevance of ethics to the forensic rhetorician. Education was considered important not merely as a desirable end in itself but (as Sir Thomas Elyot argued in *The Book Named the Governor* and as David Hume was to suggest in *A Treatise of Human Nature*) as the necessary means whereby the political order of the community could be facilitated and realised. The Inns of Court played a central educational role in creating an ordered community which reflected and embodied ethical principles of justice, never more clearly demonstrated than in the peculiar juristic themes of Shakespeare's *Troilus and Cressida*.[100] At one level, the play functioned as a teaching device for the

---

[99] On Plato, poetry and the state, see I. Ward, *Shakespeare and the Legal Imagination* (London: Butterworth, 1999), p. 143; on the quarrel between philosophy and poetry in relation to law and literature, see Warrington and Douzinas, 'Trials of Law and Literature', 139; see also T. Gould, *The Ancient Quarrel between Poetry and Philosophy* (New Jersey: Princeton University Press, 1990).

[100] D. Hume, *A Treatise of Human Nature* (Oxford University Press, 1978), pp. 494–5. On the role of education in Plato's *Republic*, see Ward, *Legal Imagination*, p. 142;

lawyer-actors, through which certain classical, oratorical techniques were acquired. These rhetorical skills are evidence of the common law's stylistic conformity to the exposition of narrative through oral disputation. The acquisition of rhetorical skills was not merely a technical necessity for the successful barrister, although such expertise was essential. Of great significance is the fact that rhetoric and morality were perceived at the Inns as indivisible. In accordance with the first of Aristotle's four uses of rhetoric, it is the means by which truth and justice maintain and assert their natural superiority to falsehood and injustice.[101]

Troilus and Cressida, was atypical of the rumbustious entertainment normally associated with Christmas revels at the Inns. Hotson suggests that Shakespeare's friend, Richard Martin, an organiser of the revels at the Middle Temple, persuaded him to write for them. Martin had been enthroned as 'Prince d'Amour' for the Middle Temple performance of *The Masque of the Passions* at the royal court on Twelfth Night, 1598, and was therefore aware of the type of play best suited to performance by his fellow members.[102] *Troilus and Cressida* lacks either the farcical excess of *The Comedy of Errors* (performed at Gray's Inn in 1594) or the preponderance of comic characters in *Twelfth Night* (performed at the Middle Temple in 1602). Whereas professional actors performed these two plays, only members of the Middle Temple acted in *Troilus and Cressida*, a play memorable for its debate of social topics, the function of law in society being foremost among them. For example, Hector warns Troilus and Paris: 'There is a law in each well-ordered nation/ To curb those raging appetites that are/ Most disobedient and refractory.'[103] Given the auditorium in which the play was performed (Middle Temple hall), the theory of law propounded by Hector suggests that the Middle Temple is a microcosm of the 'well-ordered nation' of Britain. There was a strong appreciation among early modern English jurists of the affinity between London and ancient Troy. Brutus was reputed to have arrived in Britain from Troy, and was credited by Fortescue with the foundation of the 'dominium politicum et regale'.[104] This is of particular relevance to the political morality of the community, and the congruency of the natural and political order within the commonwealth, as described by Ulysses in *Troilus and Cressida*.[105] Ulysses, more than any other character in

[101] *The Rhetoric of Aristotle*, trans. J. E. C. Welldon (London: Macmillan, 1886), pp. 6–8.
[102] Hotson, 'Love's Labours Won', p. 48.
[103] *Troilus and Cressida*, II. ii. 181–3. On the relevance of Shakespeare's constitution to contemporary legal and literary theory, see I. Ward, 'A Kingdom for a Stage, Princes to Act: Shakespeare and the Art of Government', *Law and Critique*, 8 (1997), 189–213.
[104] J. Fortescue, *The Governance of England*, ed. C. Plummer (Oxford: Clarendon Press, 1885), p. 112. On London and 'Troynovant', see D. Bruster, ' "The Alteration of Men": *Troilus and Cressida*, Troynovant and Trade', in *idem, Drama and the Market in the Age of Shakespeare* (Cambridge University Press, 1992), pp. 97–117.
[105] On Ulysses as the personification of reason and order in the play, see E. Tillyard, *Shakespeare's Problem Plays* (London: Athlone, 1993), p. 77.

the play, embodies the artificial reason of man-made law and its relationship with the natural order of the cosmos. His respect for '[o]ffice and custom, in all line of order' is congruent with the opinion of Elizabethan common lawyers that alteration to the received wisdom of English law was not merely foolish and unnecessary, but that the immutable rectitude of common law was threatened by challenges to its ancient authority. Fulbecke, for example, asked the rhetorical question of the law: 'for what authority or force should it have, if it did always change like the Moon'?[106] Arguing from a more pragmatic perspective, against incursions by the royal prerogative into common law traditions, Coke invoked the threat of chaos that was the likely consequence of change to ancient customs: 'the alteration of any of them is most dangerous; for that which hath been refined and perfected by all the wisest men in former succession of ages . . . cannot without great hazard and danger be altered and changed'.[107] Implicit in the didactic content of *Troilus and Cressida* was the injunction that it would be the responsibility of the actors, in their capacity as lawyers, to maintain and strengthen the existing social order by preserving the customs of common law and the legal profession.

The fundamental question of order and the concomitant need to curb disobedient, 'raging appetites' had a particular relevance in the last few years of Elizabethan rule, which were notable for their descent into factionalism. The struggle for patronage and power was personified by the rival camps of the Cecils (led by Burghley and his younger son, Robert) and Robert Devereux, second earl of Essex. The latter's love of military posturing, his predilection for warfare as opposed to the peaceful resolution of conflict, and his dedication to a chivalric code of conduct embodied by Sir Philip Sidney (he married Sidney's widow, Frances) is accurately represented in *Troilus and Cressida* by the character of Achilles. George Chapman made a more flattering comparison between Essex and Achilles in his translation of the seven books of the *Iliad*, published in 1598. The rebellion and execution of Essex in February 1601 were the tragic consequences of his own 'raging' appetite for power and his wilful disregard for the intrinsic dangers posed by the formation of 'hollow factions', as Ulysses describes them in Shakespeare's play. Ulysses suggests that Achilles, '[h]aving his ear full of his airy fame,/ Grows dainty of his worth'.[108] The identical, apt and resonant charge could reasonably be made of Essex.

From Hector's lines, concerning the laws of well-ordered nations, can be inferred the ethical context in which the rhetorical exercises were undertaken by law students. In the same speech, Hector refers to 'moral laws/ Of nature

[106] Fulbecke, *A Direction or Preparative*, fo. 6a.   [107] Coke, IV *Reports*, preface, p. vi.
[108] *Troilus and Cressida*, I. iii. 80, 144–5. On Essex and the Tudor *fin de siècle*, see Guy, *Tudor England*, pp. 437–52; see also R. Lacey, *Robert, Earl of Essex: An Elizabethan Icarus* (London: Phoenix, 2001).

and of nations' which 'speak aloud', providing a definition of common law similar to that provided by early modern jurists such as Dugdale, who represents English law as the felicitous integration of the laws of God, nature and nations.[109] These moral laws can only 'speak aloud' if they are articulated by those schooled in the art of speaking law. Hence in addition to the play's emphasis on the correlation between law and morality in an ordered society, there are numerous references within it to specific rhetorical exercises undertaken by students at the Inns of Court, such as bolts and moots. The action of *Troilus and Cressida* starts with a playful exchange between Pandarus and Troilus on the purpose of 'bolting'. Shakespeare thereby implies a strong institutional link between Trojan legal forms and the ancient practices of the English legal profession. 'Bolt' derives from a 13th-century, Old French word, 'bulter', meaning to examine and separate. This is an example of the 'few hunting terms and peddlars French in the lousye law' to which Bishop Aylmer referred, excusing their presence on the grounds that 'the language and the customs bee Englyshe and Saxonyshe'.[110] The Anglo-Saxon provenance of 'moot' is genuine: the moot was an assembly that dealt with local legal and administrative affairs (from the Old English, 'gemot').[111] The Prologue to *Troilus and Cressida* promises some 'correspondent and fulfilling bolts' and later a moot is presented, in which Troilus, Paris and Hector each present an argument before the revered Priam, who poses them the moral and legal dilemma: should the Trojans deliver up Helen to the Greeks? Characters offer advice on the practical skills of public speaking and the importance of these in facilitating the maintenance of order in society. A complex rhetorical device, the poetic drama, was employed to persuade the participants and audience of the practical importance and social significance of the rhetorician's craft.

The five qualities which classical orators shared with their Elizabethan descendants were enumerated by Thomas Wilson, as follows: '(i) Invention of matters (ii) Disposition of the same (iii) Elocution (iv) Memorie (v) Utteraunce'.[112] In addition to acquiring these skills through the performance of classical drama, law students learned other performance skills, common to actor and orator: '[t]o teach. To delight. And to persuade . . . to tell his tale, that the hearers may well knowe what he meaneth'.[113] *Troilus and Cressida* makes reverential allusion to the founder of the art of rhetoric, Aristotle. Hector criticises Paris and Troilus for debating an issue 'but superficially – not much/ Unlike young men whom Aristotle thought/ Unfit to hear moral philosophy'.[114] Artful reference is made to the ancient and

---

[109] Dugdale, *Origines Juridiciales*, fo. 3.   [110] Bishop Aylmer, *An Harborowe*, sig. q2v.
[111] On the administration of early English law courts, see Brand, *English Legal Profession*.
[112] Wilson, *Art of Rhetorique*, fo. 6.
[113] Ibid., fo. 2.   [114] *Troilus and Cressida*, II. ii. 166–8.

mysterious link between art, order and law. Speaking of the necessity for order and respect for hierarchy, Ulysses insists that: 'Take but degree away, untune that string,/ And hark what discord follows!'[115] It was, of course, the lyre of Orpheus that charmed beasts, recording the moment when law was first introduced into ancient Greece. In Elizabethan England, Hooker adopted the harp as a symbol of social harmony within an Anglican commonwealth whose principles were informed by Aristotelian, civic values. Concerning the constitutional relationship between ruler and subject of law, he used a musical metaphor to represent the harmony that should characterise interaction between king and law.[116] In the context of the performance at the Middle Temple in 1598, the above lines of Ulysses provide evidence that the Inns of Court shared Hooker's belief that the authority of the civil magistrate was grounded rather in an original social contract than in the preexistence of patriarchal right. They are a possible indication also of the level of influence exerted by the Inns over Hooker's political thought and in particular of the exalted constitutional status of common law within his imagined commonwealth.[117] Only if the king was subject to the law, as interpreted for the benefit of his subjects by common lawyers, could the social harmony to which Ulysses and Hooker refer be attained. The analogy between music, social harmony and law is Platonic in origin: men must reproduce in themselves and in society the harmony that unites the universe.[118] The earliest laws were poems (for example, the *Iliad* and the *Odyssey*), through which the Greeks learned of their ancestors' deeds and of divine edicts. Law and morality were inextricably linked with the commands and pronouncements of previous generations and expressed through the medium of poetry.[119]

The extensive dissemination of classical literature during the Renaissance ensured that the military imagery of *Troilus and Cressida* was familiar to Elizabethan audiences. The plot, derived from the *Iliad*, devotes considerable attention to speeches made by army leaders in council and at soldiers' assemblies. The stylised, Greek military costumes were a powerful visual trope, suggestive of the cultural links between the ancient world and the Western legal tradition. The particular representation of ancient Greece would create expectations in the audience at the start of the play that a

---

[115] *Ibid.*, I. iii. 109–10.
[116] R. Hooker, *Of the Laws of Ecclesiastical Polity*, ed. A. S. McGrade (Cambridge University Press, 1989), pp. 146–7.
[117] On Hooker, common law and constitutional theory, see Lake, *Anglicans and Puritans?*, pp. 197–207; also A. Cromartie, 'Theology and Politics in Richard Hooker's Thought', *History of Political Thought*, 21 (2000), 42–3.
[118] Plato, *The Republic*, trans. D. Lee (London: Penguin, 1987), pp. 137–46, 158–64.
[119] Hersey, *Classical Architecture*, p. 5. On the association between Orpheus's lyre and public powers, see G. Vico, *La Scienza nuova seconda*, trans. T. G. Bergin and M. H. Fisch (Ithaca: Cornell University Press, 1948).

demonstration of rhetorical skills in the form of a dialogue of orators was imminent. The military costumes were images of the cardinal virtues, representing the congruency of rhetoric and ethics, and their applicability to the practice of common law. The association between the legal orator and the soldier, and the centrality of conflict to both professions, was emphasised by Elizabethan commentators to imply the existence of courage and reason in the common lawyer. Fulbecke, for example, insisted that '[t]he first and chiefe thing that I doe require in him [the student of common law], is, to have the true knowledge, and feare of God, without which his other knowledge is but as a sword in the hand of a frantike person.'[120]

Waterhouse suggested that every aspect of the barrister's craft actively incorporated the actor's skills: '[a]n Advocate then is a Patron who undertakes the cause of men in Judgment . . . and he acts divers parts, that of an Oratour in proper wording it; that of an Attorney in diligently watching and observing, that no advantage be taken against the Cause, that of a Lawyer, in producing Arguments from the Text, to maintain and support it.'[121] That rhetoric should provide the basis of education from early childhood was emphasised by Sir Thomas Elyot in *The Book Named the Governor*. Outlining the ideal order of learning for young noblemen under the age of seven years, he suggested that in addition to being introduced to the alphabet, 'there is no better allective to noble wits than to induce them into a contention with their inferior companions'.[122] Elyot would prefer to have even the servants of the household conversing in fluent Latin, but if they speak only English, then it should be 'clean, polite, perfectly and articulately pronounced, omitting no letter or syllable'.[123] Elyot's overriding concern was with verbal dexterity and the necessity of cultivating this skill from childhood. This corresponds with a legal system based on oral traditions, on customs handed down by storytellers (*narratores*), recalling the oral origins of law itself in ancient Greek poems.

Abraham Fraunce, the Elizabethan rhetorician and member of Lincoln's Inn, attacked those legal orators who 'omit orderly distribution; obscure things purposely; amplify; change; and turn all things upside down'. It is not the art or craft of rhetoric that is impugned, but the unethical practice of it, particularly at the Inns of Court, where (according to Fraunce) 'the greedy desire of a superficial show in unnecessary trifles makes us want the true substance'.[124] This concern is articulated to virtuosic effect in *Troilus and*

---

[120] Fulbecke, *A Direction or Preparative*, fo. 10a.
[121] E. Waterhouse, *A Commentary On That Nervous Treatise De Laudibus Legum Angliae* (London, 1663), fo. 136.
[122] T. Elyot, *The Book Named the Governor* (London: Dent, 1962), p. 17.
[123] *Ibid.*, p. 18.
[124] A. Fraunce, *The Lawiers Logike, exemplifying the praecepts of logike by the practice of the common law* (London: How, 1588), ff. 89b, 61b–2a.

Cressida by the character of Thersites, a 'deformed and scurrilous Grecian': Shakespeare's succinct character note appears in the *dramatis personae* of the play. Given Thersites' rhetorical skills, his cynical opinion of humanity, and his amoral conduct, he most resembles those common lawyers with whom Fraunce expressed his unmitigated disgust. Thersites is invited by his master, Achilles, to demonstrate his discursive skills. It is an offer he accepts with alacrity:

THERSITES: Agamemnon is a fool, Achilles is a fool, Thersites is a fool, and, as aforesaid, Patroclus is a fool.
ACHILLES: Derive this; come.
THERSITES: Agamemnon is a fool to offer to command Achilles, Achilles is a fool to be commanded of Agamemnon, Thersites is a fool to serve such a fool, and Patroclus is a fool positive.[125]

Thersites is granted a licence to question, ridicule and insult, a privilege analogous to the immunity of barristers from prosecution for defamation, concerning remarks made in judicial proceedings.[126] His dexterous manipulation of language is such that the epigrammatic style overrides the content of his argument. The accusations made by Thersites in the above quotation are defamatory. But the rhetorical skill with which he deploys his argument is consummate, and compels the audience to consider his remarks seriously. Crucially, his oratorical technique is the essence of the argument. The elegance of Thersites' language, at odds with his 'deformed and scurrilous' appearance, becomes the argument itself. He offers only insults, but in such a skilful manner that the audience is convinced of his erudition, if not his integrity.

The ethical dilemma posed by Thersites' undeniable eloquence is whether rhetoric should exist in a moral vacuum. For Aristotle, there was no doubt that rhetoric was inextricably linked to moral concepts such as truth and justice. Thersites is not a gentleman of noble blood: somebody of equivalent social status in Elizabethan England would have been ineligible for membership of the Inns of Court on the basis of their flawed genealogy. The audience at the Middle Temple in 1598 would not have expected Thersites' mastery of rhetorical skills to be allied to nobility, honour and virtue. Such an alliance would have been considered impossible, as these qualities were the exclusive preserve of a distinct social group, to which Thersites could never belong. In *The Blazon of Gentrie*, Sir John Ferne described the Inns of Court as consisting of 'many gentlemen of bloud and coate-armour, so perfect and

---

[125] *Troilus and Cressida*, II. iii. 57–74.
[126] See *Munster v. Lamb* [1883] 11 QB 588, 603–604, per Brett, M.R.; also *Rondel v. Worsley* [1969] 1 AC 191.

auncient, that their number exceedeth anye assembly of men, which I can remember'.[127] Ferne enumerates the signs of a legitimate order – tradition, memory and genealogy – and asserts the importance of these to the English legal profession. He insists that 'no man can be properly called a Gentleman, except he be a Gentleman of bloud, possessing vertue'. A gentleman can be 'perfect in his bloud' only if there have been five previous generations of 'gentlemen of bloud'.[128] Thersites, whom Ajax describes as a 'bitch-wolf's son',[129] is amoral due to an accident of birth. He has neither honour nor virtue because he is not a gentleman: his deformed appearance is the physical representation of his moral and social destitution. Consequently, Thersites is a mere rhetorical technician, albeit one with an innate wit. To the Elizabethan audience at the Middle Temple, his diminished social status would automatically deprive him of any awareness that there existed an ethical dimension to the art of rhetoric.

The eulogistic style of Ferne's writing is typical of many commentators and jurists from the early modern period, who represented English law in historical terms, not as a code of positive law but as a body of tradition. Gerard Legh adopted a style of epideictic rhetoric similar to that employed by Ferne to describe the membership of the Inner Temple: '[f]or that the best of their people from tender yeres trained up in precepts of Justice, it could not chose, but yelde forth a profitable people to a wise common weale.'[130] The original of this genre is *De Laudibus Legum Angliae*, written nearly a hundred years before Legh's account of his visit to the Inner Temple. In it, Fortescue describes the study of law at the Inns as 'pleasant, excellently well adapted for Proficiency, and every way worthy of Your Esteem and Encouragement'.[131] The genealogy of common law (which, despite its uncertain provenance, was depicted by its apologists as unimpeachable because of its implied descent from an absolute, divine original) is the fundamental basis of its legitimacy. The following extract from *A Commentary On That Nervous Treatise De Laudibus Legum Angliae*, by Edward Waterhouse, exemplifies the belief that the excellence of English law was predicated upon its unblemished antiquity: 'there is no humane Law within the Circuit of the whole World by infinite degrees, so apt and profitable, for the honourable, peaceable, and prosperous Government of this Kingdom, as these antient and excellent Laws of England be'.[132] The memories of its habitual past were presented as justification for a system of precedent that bound not only the

---

[127] J. Ferne, *The Blazon of Gentrie* (London: Winder, 1586), fo. 92. On the contribution of the Inns of Court to the socio-political development of early modern England, see K. Wrightson, *English Society, 1580–1680* (London: Routledge, 1982), pp. 189–93.
[128] Ferne, *Blazon of Gentrie*, ff. 86–7.   [129] *Troilus and Cressida*, II. i. 10.
[130] G. Legh, *The Accedens of Armory* (London: R. Tottel, 1576), fo. 120a.
[131] Fortescue, *De Laudibus*, p. 112.   [132] Waterhouse, *Nervous Treatise*, fo. 236.

decisions of its judges, but also the prejudices and predilections of successive generations of common lawyers.

FROM ORALITY TO TEXTUALISATION: THE COMMON LAWYER AS POET

Rhetoric and law were rationalised in the sixteenth century under the influence of the innovative printing process, which incidentally introduced Neoplatonic humanism to a wide audience. The pre-modern, medieval judge has been characterised by Kantorowicz as a poet and sovereign artist who incorporated the fictions of natural law into the practices and decisions of the legal institution.[133] This definition implies that the post-medieval judge applied a scientific system of reasoning, incorporating unambiguous language and style in order to apply the law consistently and with certainty. While it is undeniable that a primary effect of the printing revolution was the standardisation and systematisation of the common law, it is fanciful to imagine that the decisions of the common law judiciary were subsequently based on an empirical and flawless reductionism. The transition from orality to textualisation can be characterised partly as the emergence of the judge as author and critic. It was in the Renaissance period that the poetics of English law emerged most clearly: common lawyers created those literary images of virtue by which Sir Philip Sidney identified the true poet. The poetic imagination of judges, which manifests itself in the *Reports* of Coke, proves the efficacy of legal aesthetics in capturing the imagination of the subject and effecting his willing subordination to the ancient authority of common law: '[t]o the reader my advice is, that in reading of these or any new reports, he neglect not in any case the reading of the old books of years reported in former ages, for assuredly out of the old fields must spring and grow the new corn.'[134] For Coke, the poetic imagination of common lawyers was indissolubly linked to unassailable faith in the fiction of the Ancient Constitution. He represents the idea that truth and justice are embedded in the antique and mysterious traditions of a sacrosanct legal institution, rather than in the prosaic and ambiguous texts of legislators and reformers.

Oratorical skills would always be important to the common lawyer, but as the written word became more widely available in the sixteenth century hermeneutics attained vital significance in the practice of common law. As written judgments began to be recorded in a systematised manner, so law reports (which hitherto had been fragmented and idiosyncratic) developed a

---

[133] E. Kantorowicz, 'The Sovereignty of the Legal Artist: A Note on Legal Maxims and Renaissance Theories in Art', in *idem, Selected Studies* (New York: J. J. Augustin, 1965), p. 118.
[134] Coke, I *Reports*, preface.

recognisable stylistic conformity.¹³⁵ In addition to the influence of new printing processes, this awareness of literary style can be attributed largely to the fact that in the sixteenth century law reports ceased to be anonymous, as they had been in the Year Books. They were accredited to particular writers, who tended to be distinguished members of the legal profession. Publication, and the knowledge that reports would be published and attributed, encouraged a greater consciousness of literary style. The reports of Davis, Bulstrode, Style, Calthorpe, March, Clayton and Jenkins were all written with publication in mind.¹³⁶

The Year Books preceded the era of printing and mass publication and consequently belonged to an oral, rather than a literary, legal tradition.¹³⁷ Their intrinsic fault was, as Holdsworth complained, a predilection for giving discursive accounts of the events that occurred in court. Activities incidental to the courtroom were given equal if not greater weight than the *ratio decidendi*: often there was no record of any decision.¹³⁸ For example, in the case of *Sharrington* v. *Sharrington* (reported in 1566), although the arguments were lengthy, the judgment was so brief that Plowden felt compelled to ask the judges for their reasons, which are contained in a few sentences.¹³⁹ In the case of *Wrotesley* v. *Adams*, Plowden informs us that Brown, J. did not argue because he was senile and inaudible.¹⁴⁰ In the absence of reasons for a particular decision, the reporter was content to record irrelevant aspects of courtroom behaviour, such as the illicit eating habits of the jury.¹⁴¹ In addition to their general refusal to acknowledge the vital importance of recording the decision and the reasons for that decision, the Year Books display a complete lack of narrative logic. The modern judge, as Dworkin suggests, is an author as well as a critic. He or she adds to the narrative of existing law, acting as the current author of a chain novel. New customs may emerge and evolve, but judges use their skills as storytellers to contribute to the seamless web of common law, from which the meaning is to be teased by subsequent authors in the chain.¹⁴² It is improbable that judgment should follow the model of the syllogism: the application of the major premise, law, to the

---

¹³⁵ On the genres, production, presentation and distribution of legal texts during this period, see I. Maclean, *Interpretation and Meaning in the Renaissance* (Cambridge University Press, 1992), pp. 30–50. On aesthetics and the post-medieval rationalisation of law, see P. Halder, 'The Function of the Ornament', in C. Douzinas and L. Nead (eds.), *Law and the Image: The Authority of Art and the Aesthetics of Law* (University of Chicago Press, 1999), p. 118.
¹³⁶ W. S. Holdsworth, *A History of English Law*, 17 vols. (London: Methuen, 1924), V, pp. 355, 364, 365.
¹³⁷ Baker, *The Third University*, p. 19.
¹³⁸ Holdsworth, *History of English Law*, V, p. 369. On the Year Books and reporting prior to the mid-sixteenth century, see L. W. Abbott, *Law Reporting in England, 1485–1585* (London: Athlone, 1973).
¹³⁹ Holdsworth, *History of English Law*, V, p. 370, n. 1.   ¹⁴⁰ *Ibid.*, p. 370.   ¹⁴¹ *Ibid.*
¹⁴² R. Dworkin, *Law's Empire* (London: Fontana, 1986), pp. 229–39.

minor premise, facts. Judgment is more likely to be based upon the choice of the most coherent, plausible narrative available.[143]

The standardisation of law reporting, and the concentration on the reasons for the decision, were crucial factors in the evolution of the chain of law. Crucial also to the stylistic development of the reported judgment and *ratio decidendi* was the intellectual impact of the Renaissance, which greatly affected the study of law and history. Scholars such as Bacon, Camden, Clarendon, Selden and Spelman were reinterpreting historical and legal norms in the context of this intellectual enlightenment.[144] The evolution of common law from 'common learning' into strict case law had an obvious and attendant destructive effect on the oral traditions of legal education at the Inns of Court.[145] Literary and hermeneutic skills usually associated with the craft of the poet became of unprecedented importance to common lawyers, whose judgments and arguments were reported and subsequently interpreted.[146] For Sir Philip Sidney, as for Aristotle, the true poet was not someone adept merely at versification. A clear ethical content had to manifest itself through his craft:

it is not rhyming and versing that maketh a poet (no more than a long gown maketh an advocate, who, though he pleaded in armour, should be an advocate and no soldier;) but it is that feigning notable images of virtues, vices, or what else, with that delightful teaching, which must be the right describing note to know a poet by.[147]

Sidney was a member of Gray's Inn, a poet and a soldier. He died in 1586 of wounds received fighting the Spanish at Zutphen, on an expedition organised by his uncle, the earl of Leicester. It is interesting, particularly in the context of the performance of *Troilus and Cressida* at the Middle Temple, that Sidney should have implied a correlation between poetry and law. In the play, noble characters of 'gentle blood' meet the requirement of Sidney's that the true poet should create images of virtue and provide a strong ethical context for the verse. Hence, on the desirability and indivisibility of order, hierarchy and

---

[143] See H. White, 'The Value of Narrativity in the Representation of Reality', in W. J. T. Mitchell (ed.), *On Narrative* (University of Chicago Press, 1980), p. 1; M. Minnow, 'Stories in Law', in P. Brooks and P. Gewirtz (eds.), *Law's Stories* (New Haven: Yale University Press, 1996), p. 24.
[144] Holdsworth, *History of English Law*, V, p. 402.
[145] Baker, *The Third University*, p. 21.
[146] The poetic and narrative skills of the modern common law judge in general, and of Lord Denning in particular, are considered in D. R. Klinck, ' "This Other Eden": Lord Denning's Pastoral Vision', *Oxford Journal of Legal Studies*, 14 (1994), 25–55.
[147] Sidney, *Defense of Poesy*, p. 22; on Sidney, see J. Buxton, *Sir Philip Sidney and the English Renaissance* (London: Macmillan, 1987); also A. Stewart, *Philip Sidney: A Double Life* (London: Pimlico, 2001). On the poetics of law, see Peacham, *Garden of Eloquence*; G. Puttenham, *The Arte of English Poesie* (London: Field, 1589).

community, Ulysses exhorts his audience to '[o]bserve degree, priority, and place,/ Insisture, course, proportion, season, form'.[148]

The correlation between poet and lawyer was not coincidental. Common law had never been a code or table of laws. Its legitimate continuance depended on the inheritance of oral traditions, represented by the rituals of the Inns of Court. The rhetorical techniques of the actor had always been relevant to the practice of common law, and were developed to a considerable extent by the active participation of law students in educational exercises. Maitland noted that law books were uncommon until the middle of the sixteenth century, which accounted for the institutional importance attached to oral and disputatious skills before this period.[149] During the mid-sixteenth century, however, law underwent its own renaissance. The sudden availability, in vast numbers, of hitherto unprinted medieval books was partly responsible for the belief that common law had existed unchanged for hundreds of years. Much of what was put into print was of medieval origin and had been current in manuscript. Maitland cites, for example, Littleton's *Tenures*, *The Old Tenures*, Statham's *Abridgement* and St German's *Doctor and Student*.[150] During the second half of the sixteenth century and the early seventeenth century there was an attempt to standardise English law, and to subject the developing legal profession and its arcane practices to some of the rigours of Renaissance learning. In *The Exposicions of the Terms of the Laws of England*, published in 1566, Rastell made the explicit association between law and science: '*ignorantis terminis ignoratur et ars* – he that is ignorant of the terms of any science, must needs be ignorant of the science'. In the early seventeeth century John Cowell (professor of civil law at Cambridge) produced *The Interpreter*, an English law dictionary that set out to systematise common law, cataloguing writs and offices, and endeavouring to subject English law to codified procedural rules.[151]

The progression towards textualisation was not uniformly welcomed by common lawyers, correctly perceiving in its genesis a threat not only to their unassailable institutional authority, but also to the immutability of common law. Writing in 1572, on the subject of sumptuary laws, Montaigne articulated the popular concern that change to existing social norms was a prelude

---

[148] *Troilus and Cressida*, I. iii. 86–7.
[149] F. W. Maitland, *English Law and the Renaissance* (Cambridge University Press, 1901), pp. 27–9.
[150] *Ibid.*, p. 29.
[151] J. Rastell, *The Exposicions of the Terms of the Laws of England* (London: Totell, 1566), ff. Aiiia-b; J. Cowell, *The Interpreter; or Booke Containing the Signification of Words* (Cambridge: J. Legate, 1607); see also J. Cowell, *The Institutes of the Laws of England, Digested into the Method of the Civill or Imperiall Institutions* (London: Roycroft, 1651). On Cowell and the systematisation of common law, see Goodrich, *Languages of Law*, pp. 111–12.

to cosmic disorder: apart from cases in which something was intrinsically bad, change of any sort was abhorrent. Montaigne applied this rule to seasonal, climatic and alimentary changes, but especially to changes in the law, arguing that laws were not truly honoured unless they were of ancient and divine provenance.[152] In Part Four of the *Reports*, Coke expressed concern about the encroachment of statute into areas of common law jurisdiction, with particular reference to the destruction of ancient rights to title in property. He compared 'certain late inventions and devises' with a statute enacted in the reign of Edward I, *De Donis Conditionalibus*, 'which intended to give every man power to create a new found estate in tail ... against a fundamental rule of the common law, that all estates of inheritance were fee-simple'. The disastrous consequences of this textual assault on the sovereignty of common law were experienced in a practical sense by English landowners: 'purchasers defeated, leases evicted, other estates and grants made upon just and good consideration were avoided, creditors defrauded af their just and due debts, offenders imboldened to commit capital offences, and many other inconveniencies followed'. Coke equates the best interests of the individual subject of law with the benevolent certainties of common law, and represents the gradual erosion of institutional authority by statute as the cause of 'infinite troubles, questions, suits, and difficulties'.[153]

At an institutional level, the development of a textual system of law enabled the hermeneutic skills of the poet to be practised and improved in the working environment of the courtroom. Judgment became a task of literary interpretation: the meaning of previously recorded, written narratives was inferred and construed, to a greater or lesser extent, according to the subjective understanding of individual judges. The Year Books had been available to previous generations of barristers and judges, but the innovative printing processes enabled an unprecedented distribution of law reports, and therefore greater standardisation, both of judgment and reporting. The narrator or storyteller of the ancient world was still relevant to English common law of this period; the adversarial nature of courtroom proceedings ensured the survival of the virtuosic orator. But print pushed rhetoric more firmly towards *interpretatio scripti*, or what is now termed hermeneutics. In *Poetic Justice*, Nussbaum refers to Walt Whitman's 'Phantom gigantic superb', and his contention that only poets were capable of embodying norms of judgment because of their archetypal equability.[154] As Nussbaum reminds us, Aristotle developed an identical conception of equitable judgment in relation to judicial reasoning.

[152] Montaigne, 'Of sumptuary laws', p. 197.
[153] Coke, IV *Reports*, preface, pp. vi–vii.
[154] M. Nussbaum, *Poetic Justice: the Literary Imagination and Public Life* (Boston, Mass.: Beacon Press, 1995), pp. 80–2.

The relevance of the correlation between poet and judge is that the true poet presents equitable judgments that adapt to the human complexities of each case. Of course, there are certain institutional constraints that prevent the lawyer from being simply a poet, or even simply an equable man; but these qualities supplement and complement other aspects of legal reasoning. The narrative character of common law, whose judgments contained those 'notable images of virtues, vices, or what else' (to which Sidney referred, concerning the poet's craft), made it uniquely susceptible to a form of artificial reasoning. Its legitimacy was founded on the authority of tradition over the written word. The advent of standardised case law in the sixteenth century heralded the arrival of judicial positivism and a diminution in the practical relevance of oral skills acquired at the Inns of Court, but the symbolic importance of their rituals was undiminished. The relevance of ceremony to the public perception of English law was enhanced by the guardians of the English legal tradition, whose practices reflected a preference for the immediacy of communication inherent in the signs of their institutional authority, to the semantic uncertainty of the written word. Opposition to the insidious threat of the civilian code, implicit in the systematisation of common law, continued to be articulated by common lawyers in subsequent centuries. The following rebuttal of textual primacy by Lord Mansfield, C. J. represents the immutable custom of common law and its embodiment in the ancient and arcane rites of the English legal profession: '[m]atters of practice are not to be known from books. What passes at a judge's chambers is matter of tradition: it rests in memory'.[155]

---

[155] *R. v. Wilkes* [1770] 4 *Burr.* 2527, *per* Lord Mansfield CJ, 2566.

2

Architecture and heraldry: bodies of law, myth and honour

INSTITUTIONAL MEMORIALS OF UNWRITTEN LAW

But the fairest structure belonging to this House, is the Hall, it being very large and stately; the first preparation whereunto, was in the year 1562. (5 Eliz.) though not finished till the year 1572. 14 Eliz.[1]

The enormous expense of building Middle Temple hall was met entirely by the Honourable Society of the Middle Temple, reflecting the institutional expansion of the Elizabethan legal profession. The double hammer-beam roof was the largest of its kind, imitated though not exceeded in size by that of Trinity College, Cambridge. Overall cost of the new hall 'put the House much in debt; and that it was not discharged of divers years after'.[2] Given the symbolic centrality of hall to the institutional existence of common lawyers, the erection of this imposing and confident structure was unsurprising. Hall was the setting for the continuous and undeviating repetition of legal ritual. Participation in these ceremonial rites affirmed the faith of students and practitioners in the legitimacy of common law. Such rites were exclusive: only members of the Inn could practise them on a regular basis. Guests may occasionally have attended these rites, but their status was always that of outsiders. Their spiritual exclusion from the Eucharist enacted at commons was compounded by their physical exclusion from the site when the ritual was practised. Common law was manifested and revealed to its disciples through the oral traditions of its exclusive communities, but for those subjects of law who did not have access to these rites, legitimacy and authority were communicated through an alternative system of signs.

It is axiomatic of the English legal system that no single document embodies the constitution. The authority of the invisible, unwritten constitution

---

[1] W. Dugdale, *Origines Juridiciales or Historical Memorials of the English Laws* (London: F. & T. Warren, 1666), fo. 188.
[2] *Ibid*. On institutional architecture of this period, see J. Summerson, *Architecture in Britain, 1530–1830* (Harmondsworth: Penguin, 1953).

rests in visual representations of its legitimacy. The sign rather than the text is the predominant means through which law is understood by its subjects. In this chapter I relate legal architecture to the *lex terrae*, the unwritten, and so embodied, geographical knowledge of law. The buildings of the legal community were repositories for the memory of law: bodies of tradition and ancient, institutional memorials.³ Similarities between the monumental representations of the law and the church are evident; in relation to monasteries, those outside the church were addressed by architectural images, persuading pilgrims to renounce the world for a short period and head for the *stabilitas* of the sacred centre.⁴ The early modern legal profession demonstrated its independence from executive interference by the extent and nature of architectural development at the Inns of Court. Between the reigns of Henry VIII and James I, building work proceeded at an unprecedented pace. In the words of Sir George Buc, 'since that time it hath beene much enlarged, and beautified with goodly buildings . . . the Benchers have Builded many very faire Lodgings, and Chambers, and will continue in building, and enlarging, and beautifying of it'.⁵

The Inns developed in the form of miniature city-states, drawing their inspiration from the Utopian states of classical and Christian philosophers, in particular those of Plato and St Augustine. The reassessment of classical texts by writers such as More and Elyot, and the development of the Inns of Court as Neoplatonic academies of humanist thinking, were crucial in defining the ideal republic to which the buildings of the legal community gave form and substance. The graphic images of the legal institution represented the synthesis of classical and Judaeo-Christian philosophies. Rhetorical devices redolent of natural law, divine law and ancient custom were interwoven into the architecture of the Inns of Court. These distinct jurisprudences were bound together inextricably (and have been since before the memory of man, according to legal orthodoxy) in the institutional body of common law. The immemorial fiction of English law was presented as fact by Fortescue in *De Laudibus Legum Angliae*, as for example: '[n]or in short, are the Laws of any other Kingdom in the world so venerable for their Antiquity'.⁶ English legal architecture confirmed the presence of common law in the body politic and re-presented the Ancient Constitution to the subjects of law. It elucidated the content of the constitution, while exposing the fundamental duality of the common law. One half of this duality was characterised by

---

³ On the memory of law, see P. Goodrich, *Languages of Law: From Logics of Memory to Nomadic Masks* (London: Weidenfeld & Nicolson, 1990), pp. 32–52.
⁴ See M. Camille, *Image on the Edge: The Margins of Medieval Art* (London: Reaktion, 1992), p. 56.
⁵ G. Buc, *The Third Universitie of England* (London: Society of Stationers, 1615), fo. 973.
⁶ J. Fortescue, *De Laudibus Legum Angliae*, ed. J. Selden (London: R. Gosling, 1737), pp. 33–4.

nationalist, xenophobic immutability that actively excluded strangers from any discourse; the other was exemplified by Neoplatonic humanism and represented the ideal of community, inclusion and scholarship.

The semiotics of law considers and analyses the various means by which law is understood and through which a specific way of life is instituted. It is through symbols and the form of its public representation that law is recognised as the legitimate action of a sovereign power. The reach of legal semiotics extends far beyond linguistics and the spoken word to embrace physical objects.[7] Consequently it can reasonably be argued that the buildings of the Inns of Court presented a graphic image of the law. The heraldic devices that adorned legal architecture can be interpreted as symbols both of judicial independence and of the law of honour that the Inns actively enforce. This honourable code was a fundamental and implied characteristic of the unwritten constitution. It emphasised the importance of the cardinal virtues to the legitimacy of common law. The law of honour lent unambiguous support to the hierarchic organisational structure of the Inns and to their role as ancient guardians of the common law.

THE BODY POLITIC: *JUSTITIA* AND THE CITY OF GOD

The ecclesiastical origins of the legal profession and the perceived correlation between theology and jurisprudence were reflected in the architectural configuration of the Inns of Court. They were a physical representation of the city of God envisaged by St Augustine. Their philosophical origins are Platonic rather than Augustinian, and can be traced to the discussion concerning justice, the state and the individual in *The Republic*. Relevant to the thesis that the sixteenth-century Inns of Court were miniature representations of Plato's ideal state is the emphasis in *The Republic* on the importance of the microcosm as a means of understanding invisible concepts such as justice.[8] St Augustine's divine city was the Christian descendant of Plato's *Republic*, the ethos of whose ideal city was based on right and instinct. In Plato's city a state of righteousness exists: a system of right relations between men. For St Augustine, righteousness concerned right relations between man and God (and also, consequently, between men). For Plato and St Augustine, righteousness referred to the ideal goodness of society: an ethical rather than a legal concept. Law and justice were not necessarily synonymous, but human law was a phantasm of natural or divine law, and the maintenance of cosmic order (in the classical and the Judaeo-Christian worlds) was necessarily dependent upon the visible embodiment of justice in the legal institution.

---

[7] On the contextual function of signs, see R. Kevelson, *The Law as a System of Signs* (New York: Plenum, 1988), p. 10.
[8] Plato, *The Republic*, trans. D. Lee (London: Penguin, 1987), p. 149.

In their use of the word *justitia*, the Romans adopted a strictly juridical interpretation of the Greek word for righteousness, which in the original had wider connotations than the exclusively legal. In classical terms, *justitia* was a goddess, but familiar monumental depictions suggest femininity rather than divinity, and allude to her humanity and implicit fairness. Selden referred to 'the Lady Common Law',[9] and the *Digest* itself stated that law was the queen of all things divine and human.

The Inns of Court lent material form or presence to the four grades of human society distinguished by St Augustine. These were *domus*, or the household; *civitas*, which originally referred to the city but was extended (as Rome grew from a city to a state) to mean the state; *orbis terrae*, or the earth and human society; and *mundus*, which included the universe, heaven and earth, God, the angels, departed souls, and human society on earth. St Augustine argued that the city of God transcended the grade of *civitas*. It was coextensive with *mundus*, the great society of the universe.[10] The significance of these distinctions to the Inns is that they embodied elements of all four grades. Indeed, the importance of the household, with its implication of familial governance, is such that during dinner at the Inns a toast is proposed to *domus*. The invisible concepts of truth, love, and eternity that St Augustine invoked as essential components of the ideal city (and by extension, the ideal state) could be represented only in images. It is significant that St Augustine founded a religious and legal community that combined elements of the divine and the secular, and was possessed of the same fraternal ethos as the Inns of Court. At a fundamental level, he organised a clerical community living a common life under a rule. He had judicial and clerical duties, both of which influenced his community and its laws.

As Fortescue observed, the ethos of the Inns and the knowledge of law acquired therein were not narrowly confined to the legalistic interpretation of *justitia* provided by Roman Christendom. Righteousness at the Third University referred to the ideal good of society in a whole range of its communal activities. According to Fortescue it was an educational establishment of which the ancient philosophers would have approved: 'a Sort of an Academy, or Gymnasium, fit for Persons of their Station . . . there is a constant Harmony amongst them, the greatest Friendship and a general Freedom of Conversation'.[11] He suggests that the Inns combined these classical values with the moral precepts of Judaeo-Christian theology: 'Laws which are made by Men, (who for the very End and Purpose receive their

---

[9] J. Selden, *Titles of Honour* (London: Stansby, 1614), fo. a3b. On the historical importance of the effigy or statue in legal iconology, see P. Goodrich, *Oedipus Lex: Psychoanalysis, History, Law* (Los Angeles: University of California Press, 1995), pp. 108–15.

[10] St Augustine, *The City of God*, trans. J. Healey (London: Dent, 1931), intro., p. xvi.

[11] Fortescue, *De Laudibus*, pp. 111–12.

Power from God) may also be affirmed to be made by God'.[12] Implicit in the title of Fortescue's *De Laudibus Legum Angliae* was a nationalist interpretation of common law, but the humanising, Neoplatonic influence of the Renaissance was also apparent. When Fulbecke published *A Direction or Preparative to the study of the Lawe*, in 1599, the influence of the ancient world had permeated all areas of education, not least the study of common law, as the following classical allusion indicates: '. . . it were as hard a matter for a young gentleman to gaine the knowledge of the lawe, as it was for Phaeton to ascend unto the Chariot of the Sunne, who ere he could accomplish that, was to passe through uncouth wayes, and by the ghastly formes of deformed creatures, by the terrible Signes of the Bull, the Lion, and the Scorpion'.[13] Fulbecke and other commentators developed an entire compendium of epigrammatic dicta, in which the ancients were eulogised for their insightful pronouncements on law and its relationship with order, society and the state. The insertion of a Latin sentence into the predominantly vernacular text was a rhetorical device, intended to lend additional authority to the writer's thesis. For example, Fulbecke asserts that '. . . true is that saying of Cicero, *Omnia incerta sunt cum a iure discessum est*. If you depart from Law there is no certain state of anything.'[14]

The legal system depicted by Fortescue and his juridical descendants represented the coalescence of divine law and human reason that St Augustine envisaged in the city of God. Such depictions presumed that the Ancient Constitution, upon whose legitimacy the authority of the body politic depended, represented the synthesis of *civitas dei* and *terrena civitas*. As institutional structures of the common law, the buildings of the Inns of Court acted as physical hosts through which these ancient traditions or memories could materialise,[15] hence the importance of the genealogical argument that *The Republic* and *The City of God* provided models for the emblematic legal community. The lawyers made the Word into stone and into image, into signs and into manners (the tacit and illiterate consensus of men). By this means the unwritten constitution, the theology of law and the Inns of Court were rendered coextensive and indivisible.

The original occupants of the Temple, the Knights Templar, laid the physical foundations for the Inner and Middle Temple and initiated the establishment of a self-contained, self-governing community. As Buc observed

---

[12] *Ibid.*, p. 5.
[13] W. Fulbecke, *A Direction or Preparative to the study of the Lawe* (London: T. Wight, 1600), fo. 9a.
[14] *Ibid.*, fo. 4b. See also J. Doderidge, *The English Lawyer. Describing A Method for the managing of the Lawes of this Land* (London: More, 1631), p. 7.
[15] On the Inns of Court as a home for the body of law, see D. Evans, 'Theatre of Deferral: The Image of the Law and the Architecture of the Inns of Court', *Law and Critique*, 10 (1999), 17.

of the Templars, '. . . [they] purchased certayne Landes and Messuages in Fleete Streete . . . and thereupon built a goodly large and magnificent house, together with that fayre round synagogue-like Church or Temple yet standing, and flourishing, and which was dedicated to the service of God by Heraclius patriarch of Jerusalem, Anno Domini, one Thousand one hundred eighty and five'.[16] A robust, nationalist version of Christianity was an identifiable feature of much of the early iconography that sought to link divine and common law. At the Temple the themes of Christianity, law, morality, nationalism and xenophobia were unified and represented in the image of the Knights Templar. They were both archetype and icon, as Buc's enthusiastic description demonstrates:

> Their vow and profession was to defend the Temple of Jerusalem, and to beare Armes, and make Warre against all Infidells, and to preserve the holy Sepulcre of our Lord and blessed saviour Jesus Christ from spoyle and prophanation attempted and practised by Turkes, Sarrazens, Agarens, and other Barbarous and cruell miscreants, who blasphemed the most sacred name of Christ, and pursued with all Malice, Rage, and Hostilitie, all professors of Christianity.[17]

In Temple church the effigies of eight knights lie recumbent on the floor, as they have since the thirteenth century. The Knights Templar erected a bar of posts, rails and a chain (eventually replaced by a gate) around the perimeter of their land, marking the boundary with the city beyond.[18] The body of common law was being defined and delineated by members of a religious organisation before the Inns of Court were established. Their immediate descendants, the Knights Hospitallers of the Order of Saint John, were experienced in the practice of law and legal administration in local courts.[19] When ownership of the Temple passed from an order of Christian knights to a secular legal community, many of the prejudices and predilections of their religious forebears were inherited. Adherence to Christianity and nationalism and an instinctive mistrust of foreigners and foreign jurisdictions were principal among these. Fortescue, for example, suggested that 'the Will of God' was discoverable through knowledge of English law in particular, articulating a popular belief in the incontrovertible link between God and common law.[20]

A nationalist interpretation of Christianity permeated the judgment and institutions of common law throughout the sixteenth and early seventeenth centuries. The language of common lawyers was characterised not only by

---

[16] Buc, *Third Universitie*, fo. 970. On the Order of Knights Templar, see P. P. Read, *The Templars* (London: Phoenix, 2001).
[17] Buc, *Third Universitie*, fo. 970.
[18] R. F. Roxburgh, 'Lawyers in the New Temple', *Law Quarterly Review*, 88 (1972), 415–16.
[19] *Ibid.*, 417.   [20] Fortescue, *De Laudibus*, p. 3.

the extreme nationalism of its content, but also by its biblical form. In some advice offered to young lawyers, Coke advised them to 'cast thine eye upon the sages of the law, that have been before thee, and never shalt thou find any that hath excelled in the knowledge of these laws, but hath sucked from the breast of that divine knowledge',[21] thus preserving the ancient credentials of common law in perpetuity. The image of the father was always present; Coke instilled in a new generation of lawyers the belief that God Almighty, the father of mankind, was the ultimate object of their allegiance. For Coke and his contemporaries the significance of divinity and theology was practical rather than theoretical, affecting the development of substantive law. Coke explicitly invoked the Holy Ghost in an attack against monopolies: 'the Monopolist that taketh away a mans trade, taketh away his life, and, therefore is so much more odious because he is *vir sanguinis*. Against these Inventors and Propounders of evill things, the holy ghost hath spoken'.[22] Theology was thus elevated to jurisprudence, a necessary development in the opinion of Pollock and Maitland, if theology was to influence the body politic of a nation.[23]

As the Inns of Court expanded during the sixteenth century a complex body of law evolved. The Christian tenets that underscored the fundamental ethos of common law were not eschewed, but the classical theories of the ideal state that the European Renaissance had rediscovered and reinvented were assimilated into the body. The particular form of architectural expansion at the Inns during this period reflected such influence. The erection of high walls, emulating the city-states of Renaissance Europe, defined the physical boundaries of the Inns, implying the autonomy and exclusivity of the legal community: '[t]he Wall betwixt the Thames and the Garden, was begun in 16 H. 8. Mr John Pakington (afterwards Serjeant at Law) and Mr. Rice being appointed Overseers of the work ... In 31 Eliz. Two sides of the Garden were inclosed with a brick wall'.[24] By 1598, when John Stow's *The Survey of London* was published, civic existence was the prototypical symbol of order. Its unimpeachable status was guaranteed both by divine and secular lawgivers: 'this civill life approacheth neerest to the shape of that mysticall body whereof Christ is the head, and men be the members: whereupon both at the first, that man of God Moses, in the commonwealth of the Israelites, and the Governours of all Countries in all ages sithence, have continually maintained the same'.[25] Stow articulated the aspiration of

---

[21] E. Coke, *The Reports*, 7 vols. (London: Rivington, 1777), Part II, preface, pp. x–xi.
[22] E. Coke, *The Third Part of the Institutes of the Laws of England* (London: Flesher, 1644), p. 181.
[23] F. Pollock and F. Maitland, *History of English Law*, 2 vols. (Cambridge University Press, 1898), I, p. 5.
[24] Dugdale, *Origines Juridiciales*, ff. 146, 147.
[25] J. Stow, *The Survey of London* (London: N. Bourne, 1633), fo. 693.

Elizabethan society to create the city of God on earth, linking the civic virtues of ancient Greece and Rome with the spiritual values espoused by Christ in the gospels. Stow incorporated Christ into the anatomical metaphor of an ideal body politic, whose governors acknowledged and approved the coextension of spiritual and temporal phenomena in the creation of a Utopian state. Moses (whom William Lambard cited as one of the original founders of English law)[26] was invoked to suggest archetypal, ancient credentials and divine approval. In the city of God the source of divine and common law was identical.

In ancient Israel the courts of justice were located in the gates of cities. Major trials and appeals were held there; in one such court the prophet Jeremiah, condemned to death by the Consistory of Priests, 'was by the Consistory of Princes secular, or Judges sitting in the Gate, absolved and dischardged. And the reason thereof was (as tis very probable) partly that the equity of their proceedings might be seen by all; and partly that none might go out of the Common way to seek for Justice'.[27] Visibility of justice and access to law attained unique significance in the unwritten constitution because its legitimacy depended on the acceptance of visual signs of ancient authority. In the iconography, historiography and literature of law, the gate is a recurrent and resonant symbol. It is an immutable determinant of access to law. In the history of any legal institution, the sites of entrance to the law attain peculiar symbolic importance. The monumental gates of a city are suggestive of inclusion and exclusion, of access and concealment. In *At the Door of the Law*,[28] Kafka fictionalised the characters of the gatekeeper and the subject of law, the latter being denied access to law for the duration of his life by the former. Derrida has interpreted this symbolic encounter between the legal institution and the subject of law as the discourse of law guarding the law, repeatedly deferring if not prohibiting access to law itself.[29] Common to these interpretations is the idea that although the legitimacy and authority of law are promised, exposition of the law is deferred indefinitely.

Dugdale notes that the 'Porter hath his lodging under the Middle Temple gate ... his Office being to shut and open that Gate at due hours, and to keep out Beggars, and such loose kind of people'.[30] The gate is the visible entrance to the law: it defines the exit from the secular world. For the student of common law it was the gate of humility through which lay 'the way to the

---

[26] W. Lambard, *Archeion or Discourse upon the High Courts of Justice in England* (London: Seile, 1591), p. 55.
[27] Dugdale, *Origines Juridiciales*, fo. 22.
[28] F. Kafka, 'At the Door of the Law', *Franz Kafka: Stories, 1904–1924*, trans. J. A. Underwood (London: Abacus, 1995), pp. 194–5.
[29] J. Derrida, 'Before the Law', in D. Attridge (ed.), *Acts of Literature* (New York: Routledge, 1992), p. 192.
[30] Dugdale, *Origines Juridiciales*, fo. 197.

hight of knowledge'.³¹ The great gate connecting the Middle Temple with Fleet Street fixed an impression of legitimacy on the subject of law, through the imposition of an order of signs: 'Sir Amias Paulet Knight about the 7th year of King Henry the 8th. who, being upon an old grudge, sent for up to the Cardinal, and commanded not to depart London without License, lodg'd in this Gatehouse, which he re-edified and sumptuously beautified on the outside, with the Cardinal's Armes, Hat, Cognisance, Badges, and other Devices, in a glorious manner'. In similar eulogistic terms, Buc describes the considerable sums expended on the expansion of Gray's Inn. Part of 'the great cost bestowed therein' was attributed to a 'fayre Gate, and a gatehouse for a more convenient, more honorable passage into the high streete of Holborne, whereof this house stood in much neede for the other former Gates were rather Posterns than Gates'.³² A memory is made, an impression fixed, of a law that attains legitimacy through the representation of an undeviating code of honour, the graphic symbols of which are the armorial devices described above, inscribed on the material body of law. Discussing the early history of man, when writing was first inscribed on the human body, Nietzsche recorded a sinister system of mnemonics whereby something was burnt on so as to remain in the memory.³³ It was through such acts as the building of this elaborate and beautiful gate that the memory of law was retained. The public representation of antique credentials was the means by which legitimacy could be conferred, a practice acquired from ancient Rome. Sir John Ferne wrote that

[a]mongst the Romaines, untill the time of their Caesars, it was a common use, to erect Images or Statuaes, in token of Generositie, so that, whosoever he were, which could not produce some publike Image of some of his Auncestors, he was called by them *Homo novus, terrae filius, a ses ortus*, a newe fellowe, a sonne of the dunghill, one without father, or parents.³⁴

On the foundation of England, Sir Thomas Wilson confidently asserted that 'this Kingdome is an absolute Imperiall Monarchy held nether of Pope, Emperor, nor any but of God alone, and so hath bene ever since the year of the World 2855, which was 1108 yeares before Christ'.³⁵ Specificity as to the date of foundation lent a spurious gloss of authority to the fiction of the Ancient Constitution.

---

[31] Fulbecke, *A Direction or Preparative*, fo. 11b. There is an architectural representation of Humility's Gate at Gonville and Caius College, Cambridge; see N. Ray, *Cambridge Architecture* (Cambridge University Press, 1994).
[32] Dugdale, *Origines Juridiciales*, fo. 188; Buc, *Third Universitie*, fo. 974.
[33] F. Nietzsche, *The Genealogy of Morals*, trans. W. Kaufmann and R. J. Hollingdale (New York: Random House, 1969).
[34] J. Ferne, *The Blazon of Gentrie* (London: Winder, 1586), fo. 150.
[35] T. Wilson, *The State of England, Anno Dom. 1600*, ed. F. J. Fisher, Camden Miscellany 16 (1936), 1.

A major cultural achievement of the Renaissance was to revitalise popular interest in the mythology of the classical world, whose metaphors and narratives were incorporated into architectural design and ornamentation. Consequently the erection of public representations of ancestry became a highly visible aspect of civic existence at the Inns of Court: symbols of their ancient (and therefore lawful) provenance. The devices in honour of Cardinal Wolsey, depicted on the magnificent gate erected by Sir Amias Paulet, prove a line of descent traceable to the founders of the Christian church, to whom Wolsey could trace the office of Cardinal. The arms bore witness to the thesis that common law was grounded in the law of God and was not originally, nor is essentially, *leges scriptae*. Of course, Wolsey fulfilled a secular role as Lord Chancellor as well as a spiritual one as a prince of the church. The congruency of the divine and the secular, embodied in common law, is explained by jurists in terms of a law that has evolved through the development of human customs but is informed primarily by biblical principles.

Although the common law was perceived as being derived ultimately from divine law, it was 'of Human Institution'.[36] As Dugdale explained, 'it being no other than pure and tried Reason ... or the absolute perfection of Reason, as Sir Edward Coke affirmeth, adding, that the ground thereof is beyond the memory or Register of any beginning'.[37] Divine provenance bestowed legitimacy on the common law, but, as Dugdale acknowledged in the above passage, human reason determined its shape, substance and practice. It can be understood therefore that the great gate of the Middle Temple represented the perfect congruency of human reason and divine law. The ornate gates separating the realm of law from the city of London performed a function identical to the public images of antiquity in ancient Rome, to which Ferne refers above. They were plastic and graphic forms of epideictic rhetoric; a category concerned with eulogising honour and nobility, and censuring disgrace and shamefulness. Aristotle suggested that epideictic rhetoric (as opposed to deliberative and forensic rhetoric, which were concerned respectively with the future and the past) was necessarily concerned with the present, 'as it is always existing facts which form the grounds of eulogy or censure'.[38] Plato and Aristotle related epideictic to ethics: praise being the correct response to virtue, and blame the correct response to vice. In *The Republic* of Plato, although poets were banished from the state, the poetry of praise to gods and good men was permitted.[39] Quintilian made the important observation that the function of epideictic was not limited exclusively to a celebration of the majesty, power and exploits of the gods; it was useful also for praising

---

[36] Fortescue, *De Laudibus*, p. 5.   [37] Dugdale, *Origines Juridiciales*, fo. 3.
[38] Aristotle, *The Rhetoric*, trans. J. E. C. Welldon (London: Macmillan, 1886), p. 23.
[39] Plato, *The Republic*, p. 375.

parents and ancestors, thereby bestowing institutional legitimacy on their paternal authority. It is noteworthy in connection with the civic qualities of the Inns of Court that Quintilian suggested that cities could be praised in a similar way to men, because their virtues and vices were identical to those of private individuals.[40] At a symbolic level, Sir Amias Paulet's gate praised the legitimacy of the immemorial *lex terrae*: the unwritten, embodied foundation of the English constitution.

Fortescue made similar claims for the legitimacy of a legal system whose authority was predicated upon the veneration of ancient custom. In *De Laudibus Legum Angliae*, he argued that civil law encouraged fornication because it recognised the hereditary rights of illegitimate offspring: '[i]ndeed I give Preference to the Law which does most effectually cast out Sin, and establish Virtue'.[41] In other words, common law was the essential catalyst through which the city of God could materialise on earth. It was not merely a collection of legal rules, but a force for the protection of English society in general, and the material happiness of its subjects in particular: '[t]hey are fed, in great Abundance, with all Sorts of Flesh and Fish, of which they have plenty everywhere; they are cloathed thro'out in good Woollens.'[42] Fortescue depicted an idyllic English realm, one with which the French equivalent did not favourably compare: 'the Peasants live in great Hardship and Misery. Their constant Drink is Water ... Their clothing consists of Frocks, or little short Jerkins made of Canvass no better than common Sackcloth.'[43] Fortescue suggested that their poverty was due entirely to the high rate of taxation imposed by the king, who was not answerable (as the kings of England were) to Parliament. He argued that common law had created the social and moral conditions necessary for the manifestation of this Utopian vision and that the Inns of Court offered a microcosmic vision of this ideal society. The students of common law did not concern themselves with the study of substantive law alone. Their education had a strong spiritual dimension: 'they employ themselves in the Study of Sacred and Prophane History: Here every Thing which is Good and Virtuous is to be learnt. All Vice is discouraged and Banisht.'[44] This corresponds with St Augustine's injunction that the divine city is the city only of the righteous: no unclean thing may enter into it.

It was through the institutional structures of common law, represented by the physical bodies of the Inns of Court, that Fortescue's rhetoric was

---

[40] M. F. Quintilianus, *The Institutio Oratoria*, trans. H. E. Butler (New York: Loeb, 1920), Book III. VII. XXVI.
[41] Fortescue, *De Laudibus*, p. 93.   [42] *Ibid.*, p. 83.
[43] *Ibid.*, pp. 80–1. Ward notes that Fortescue's contact with 'peasants' was fleeting; he passed them on his Gloucestershire estate as they went about their daily work. See I. Ward, *A State of Mind? The English Constitution and the Popular Imagination* (Stroud: Sutton, 2000).
[44] Fortescue, *De Laudibus*, p. 111.

translated into architectural images of the perfectly proportioned body, the well-ordered state, the city of God on earth. Although it must be emphasised that the architectural expansion of the Inns started during the century following the publication of *De Laudibus Legum Angliae*, it is reasonable to suggest that Fortescue's idealised depiction of an autonomous and sacerdotal legal profession was inspirational in the form of their development. The constitution of the Inns honoured the cardinal virtues of wisdom, courage, self-discipline and justice, which Plato considered to be crucial components of the ideal state.[45] Their physical expansion during and after the reign of Elizabeth was aligned strongly with the Aristotelian principle that the ultimate purpose of the state was to enable men to live well as virtuous citizens, in accordance with Hooker's insistence on the interdependence of spiritual and secular values.[46]

THE BODY AND THE LAW: ART, ARCHITECTURE AND ECLECTICISM

The analogy between buildings and body parts is a common one, particularly in the historiography of the Inns of Court. Megarry, for example, refers to the old hall of Lincoln's Inn as the heart of legal London and to Chancery Lane as the backbone.[47] A topographical examination of the four Inns of Court demonstrates the accuracy of Megarry's observation. If the anatomical metaphor of the body of law is accepted then Gray's Inn (the northernmost of the Inns) is the head, Lincoln's Inn is the heart, and the Middle and Inner Temples are the lungs. Chancery Lane (and at its southernmost point, Middle Temple Lane) provides the backbone, connecting the head (Gray's Inn) to the rest of the body. The four Inns were individual organs that collectively made up the body of law. They formed an independent city-state or *civitas*, enabling the body politic to be represented in architectural terms.

Evans argues that the labyrinthine passages, thoroughfares and thresholds of the Inns promise revelation of the law, while constantly deferring

---

[45] Plato, *The Republic*, p. 138.

[46] On Hooker and Aristotle, see P. Lake, *Anglicans and Puritans? Presbyterianism and English Conformist Thought from Whitgift to Hooker* (London: Unwin Hyman, 1988), 207; also A. Cromartie, 'Theology and Politics in Richard Hooker's Thought', *History of Political Thought*, 21 (2000), 55.

[47] R. Megarry, *Inns Ancient and Modern* (London: Selden Society, 1972), pp. 4, 6. See P. Goodrich (ed.), *Law and the Unconscious: A Legendre Reader* (London: Macmillan, 1997), intro., p. xvi; C. Douzinas, '*Whistler v. Ruskin*: Law's fear of images', *Art History*, 19 (1996), 355. In Shakespeare's *Coriolanus*, Menenius develops the anatomical analogy of the body politic, the 'good belly' of the Roman Senate nourishing the limbs of the populace: *Coriolanus*, I. i. 94–103, 126–38, 146–53.

Architecture and heraldry: bodies of law, myth and honour

any such exposition. He places the structure and constitution of the Inns in the medieval period,[48] citing their autonomous status as planning authorities and self-governing bodies in support of this claim. It is certain that the Inns were inhabited exclusively by lawyers during the reign of Edward III. Baker refers to 1339 as the year in which a servant of the apprentices of the King's Court killed a man in the Temple, and therefore a legal community may already have been formed there.[49] Although the exact date of foundation is unknown, the architectural development of the Inns in their existing form began not in the medieval period but during the reign of Henry VIII, gathering momentum under the subsequent Tudor and Stuart monarchs. The point of this distinction is that the buildings were representations not of medieval fiefdoms but of the Renaissance nation-state and its classical progenitor, the walled city-state of ancient Greece. As Aristotle observed in connection with Athens, and John Stow in relation to sixteenth-century London, the city provided the physical framework for the creation of the ideal *polis*. Insofar as the Inns embodied this *polis*, they represented the body politic of early modern rather than medieval England. In particular, they reflected the influence of Neoplatonic humanism on the immutable nationalism and ancient customs of the common law tradition. Medieval buildings remained, notably Temple church, but these buildings were part of an eclectic whole, mirroring the indeterminate nature of the Ancient Constitution.

The four Inns of Court were at the heart of the Elizabethan city-state. The arteries of High Holborn, Holborn, Strand, Fleet Street and the river Thames linked them to the other organs of the body politic. The image of the city or State as a human body evolved during the Renaissance. The body politic was literally anatomised: this was a metaphor that, apart from anything else, made the workings of the state comprehensible to a largely uneducated and illiterate populace. Illustrated anatomical textbooks in the sixteenth century provided graphic images of the dissected body and its constituent parts.[50] The body was represented in images by contemporary artists, including Michelangelo, Leonardo da Vinci and Nicholas Hilliard. In the dissection scene from the *Anatomical Tables of John Banister*[51] (attributed to Nicholas

---

[48] Evans, 'Theatre of Deferral', 4.
[49] J. H. Baker, *The Inner Temple, A Brief Historical Description* (London: The Honourable Society of the Inner Temple, 1991), p. 4. On the uncertain origins of the Inns of Court see R. F. Roxburgh, 'Lincoln's Inns of the Fourteenth Century', *Law Quarterly Review*, 94 (1978), 363–82.
[50] See for example, C. Estienne, *De Dissectione partium corporis humani* (Paris, 1545); T. Geminus, *Compendiosa totius anatomie delineatio* (London: J. Herfordie, 1545); and most famously, A. Vesalius, *De humani corporis fabrica librorum epitome* (Basle, 1543).
[51] Frontispiece, ms. Hunter 364 (V.1.1), Department of Special Collections, Glasgow University Library.

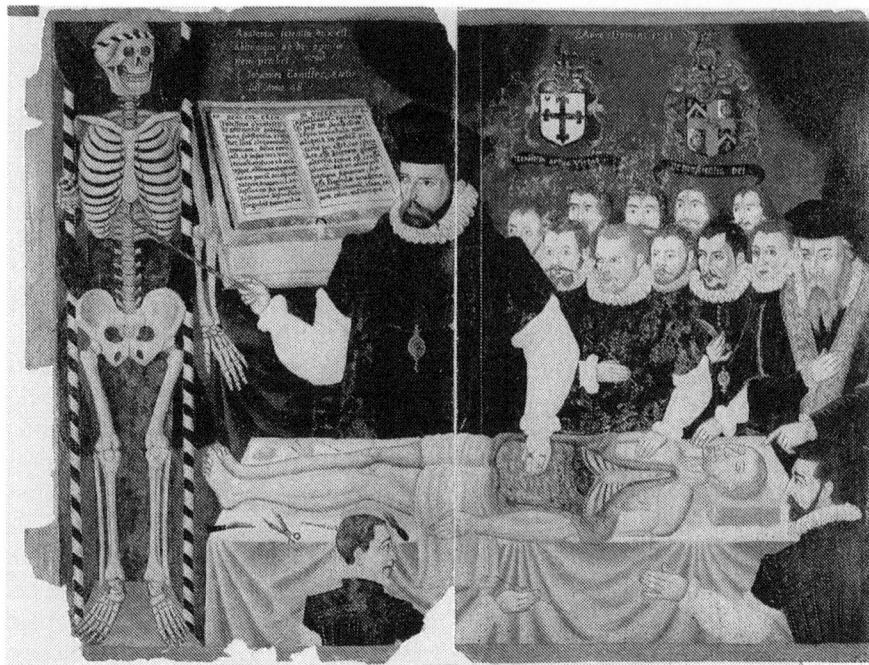

Fig. 1. Dissection scene from *Master John Banister, Anatomical Tables* (c. 1580).

Hilliard, c. 1580; see Fig. 1), a cadaver lies on an operating table whose resemblance to a sacrificial altar is enhanced by its ornate white drapes. The body is slit from throat to groin. John Banister, wearing a master's robe and surgeon's white sleeves, rests his left hand on the exposed intestines of the corpse. His right hand holds a silver-mounted cane, pointing to the abdominal cavity of a skeleton. In the foreground one of four assistants, also wearing surgeon's white sleeves, passes a surgical instrument to another. To the left of Banister a group of students attends. An old doctor, with long white beard and fur-lined robe, points to the head of the corpse. On a lectern between the skeleton and the lecturer rests an anatomical textbook. Above it, in red letters, are the words: '*Anatomia scientiae dux est / aditumque ad dei agnitio = / nem praebet. / Iohannes Banister Aetatis / sui Anno 48 Anno Domini 1581.*' Two heraldic blazons adorn the back wall of the lecture theatre, each bearing a motto, respectively '*Tendit in ardua Virtus*' and '*De praescientia Dei*'. It is plausible to draw an analogy between this scene and the order of dining at the Inns of Court. The symbolic components of both rites are identical: the sacrificial table on which the victim is laid and dissected; the Reader, offering an interpretation of a text; the attendance of students, masters and doctors, solemnly participating in the observance of an exclusive custom; and the lineage and legitimacy bestowed on the proceedings by the coats of arms, indicating ancient institutional genealogy.[52]

Da Vinci's *Vitruvian Man* (his arms and legs spread to form a Star of David within a circle, suggesting the crucified Christ) reflects the basic principles of divine proportion in the human form. Vitruvius set down the tenets of classical architecture using geometric principles that sought to connect the city of God with the city of man.[53] The depiction of the architectural equivalent of divine proportion can be seen in Massacio's *Trinità*, in which the crucified Christ is at the centre of an arch which is supported on either side by symmetrical columns and capitals.[54] These interpretations of the order of the body complement anatomical metaphors used by Renaissance jurists to describe the constitution of the ideal state. For example, Sir Thomas Elyot suggested that 'a public weal is a body living'.[55] The anatomical metaphor was famously incorporated into substantive law in *Calvin's Case*. The report referred to the two bodies of the king, and is notable for its images of physical frailty on the one hand, and those of ethereality on the other. The body natural of the king was 'subject to all Infirmities that come by Nature or Accident, to the Imbecility of Infancy or old Age, and to the like Defects that happen to the natural Bodies of other People. But his Body politic is a Body that cannot be seen or handled, consisting of Policy and Government, and constituted for the Direction of the People, and the Management of the public weal'.[56] In this definition of the king's two bodies, the symbol of the body as the representation of the ordered state has become reality. The dialectic is religious in tone, and specifically Christian in its interpretation: *hoc est*

---

[52] On the semiotic status of the coats of arms at the Inns of Court, see P. Goodrich, 'Eating Law: Commons, Common Land, Common Law', *The Journal of Legal History*, 12 (1991), 248. On the history of anatomical art, see D. Petherbridge, *The Quick and the Dead: Artists and Anatomy* (Manchester: Cornerhouse, 1997). On sacrifice, sacrificial ritual and the power of symbols, see R. Girard, *Violence and the Sacred* (Baltimore: Johns Hopkins University Press, 1977).

[53] See G. Hersey, *The Lost Meaning of Classical Architecture* (Cambridge, Mass.: MIT, 1988).

[54] For the theory that Christ was an architect, see G. Strachan, *Jesus The Master Builder* (Edinburgh: Floris, 1998).

[55] T. Elyot, *The Book Named the Governor* (London: Dent, 1962), p. 1. Elyot develops the organic analogy in Book III of the *Governor*.

[56] E. Plowden, *Commentaries or Reports* (London: Brooke, 1816), p. 212a. Coke refers to this case in VII *Reports*, p. 10. For a detailed analysis of the phenomenon, see E. Kantorowicz, *The King's Two Bodies: A Study in Medieval Political Theology* (New Jersey: Princeton University Press, 1957), pp. 7–23. The organic analogy is found in *Aristotle's Politics and Athenian Constitution*, trans. J. Warrington (London: Dent, 1959), Book V, 1302b–3b. For sixteenth-century comparisons between man's bodily structure and the state, see T. Spencer, *Shakespeare and the Nature of Man* (New York: Macmillan, 1949).

corpus meum. According to the judgment in *Calvin's Case* the body politic cannot be seen or handled, but the image of the lawful authority of the state can be represented.

The image of the human body recurs throughout the historiography of law and its institutions. Fulbecke employed the metaphor of the body and soul to represent respectively the state and the law: 'the law is as necessary for the government of a state, as the soule and mind is for the preservation of the bodie'. Fulbecke wrote of the law being 'trodde under foote' by the Godless,[57] as though it were either a living creature or a discernible area of sacred earth (literally *lex terrae*) that should be accorded appropriate respect. The connection between law and cultivated land is well documented. For example, Stow mentions the link between the city and arable land: the Latin word for 'city', *urbs*, was derived from *urbare* (to mark out by plough) 'because the first inclosure of them was described with the draught of a Plow'.[58] Ferne refers to the urban nature of common law and its ethical correlation with the Aristotelian concept of citizenship: 'for the law is said, the bond of the city, the foundation of liberty, a flowing spring of equity, the mind, the soul, and the definite sentence of the city'.[59] In *The Republic*, Plato attributes to justice a discernible physical characteristic, suggesting that it permanently lurks under our feet.[60] According to Plato, of the four prerequisite constituents of the ideal state (wisdom, courage, self-discipline and justice), justice determines the existence and preservation of the three remaining cardinal virtues, but is notoriously difficult to define. Consequently he acknowledges the importance of the visual image in providing an instantly recognisable representation of justice.[61]

At the Inner Temple in 1561, Gerard Legh encountered and described the prototypical body of law, the Prince, at whose feast by virtue of his love of honour, Legh was a guest. The Prince, personification of common law virtues, was 'a man of tall personage, of manlye countenaunce, somewhat browne of visage, stronglye featured, and thereto comely proporcioned in all lineaments of bodye'.[62] It is clear from the above description that there was an attempt to liken the invisible principles of common law to the complex workings of the human body. The interest in the perfect physiognomy is axiomatic of

---

[57] Fulbecke, *A Direction or Preparative*, at ff. 8a, 1a. On the correlation between corporeal and moral order in ancient Greece, see M. Foucault, *The Use of Pleasure*, trans. R. Hurley, 2 vols. (London: Penguin, 1987), II, p. 102.

[58] Stow, *Survey of London*, fo. 691. The linguistic origin of '*urbs*' is noted in *The Digest of Justinian*: see Goodrich, 'Eating Law', 260. On the plough and the law see Y. Hachamovitch, 'The Ideal Object of Transmission: An essay on the faith which attaches to instruments (*de fide Instrumentorum*)', *Law and Critique*, 2 (1991), 85–101.

[59] Ferne, *Blazon of Gentrie*, fo. 41.   [60] Plato, *The Republic*, p. 144.   [61] *Ibid*.

[62] G. Legh, *The Accedens of Armory* (London: R. Tottel, 1576), fo. 123b.

Renaissance appreciation of bodily proportion, extending through visual art to architecture, in which proportion becomes a symbol of order, hierarchy and the divine plan.

The eighteenth-century jurist, Giambattista Vico, suggested that words for law were derived from words for tendons: they were the sinews of the body politic.[63] These body parts were delineated in the architecture of the Inns of Court, but elucidation of the character of the body is problematic. Like the common law itself, the provenance of the Inns of Court is uncertain, and the eclecticism of their architecture reflected this fact. Eventually, 'the reverend, aunciente professors of the Lawes in the Raiyne of Kinge Edward the Third, obtayned a very large or as I might say, a perpetuall lease of this Temple',[64] but uncertainty surrounds the exact dates of occupation and origin. Rival claims have been made for the title of founder of Lincoln's Inn: Thomas de Lincoln (a serjeant-at-law) and the earl of Lincoln were two contenders. There is a religious background to the physical proximity of Lincoln's Inn, since its home was acquired from land belonging to the bishops of Chichester.[65] Of crucial significance to the legitimacy of common law, the Inns (like their honourable members) were represented as being 'of discent from gentile and noble parents, and aunceaters'.[66]

Viewed separately, the buildings of the Inns suggested a disparate mixture of styles, but collectively they represented the order of an enclosed Christian community, informed by the Neoplatonic ideals of Renaissance humanism. They were a microcosm of the 'public weal' to which Elyot referred. Sir Thomas More, a member of Lincoln's Inn, personified the synthesis of Christianity and classical, humanist philosophy. His friend Erasmus remarked on the extraordinary similarity between More's household and Plato's Academy.[67] The overriding significance of *The Republic* to More's *Utopia* is the suggestion in the former that the ideal state recognised the interdependence of political power and philosophy.[68] More repeated Plato's assertion that society would never achieve a state of absolute happiness until

---

[63] G. Vico, *La Scienza nuova seconda*, trans. T. G. Bergin and M. H. Fisch (Ithaca: Cornell University Press, 1948). On Vico and social harmony, see Hersey, *Classical Architecture*, p. 5. For a recent study of Vico, see D. P. Verene, *The New Art of Autobiography: An Essay on the Life of Giambattista Vico Written by Himself* (Oxford: Clarendon, 1991).

[64] Buc, *Third Universitie*, fo. 971.

[65] See Roxburgh, 'Lincoln's Inns', 363–82, for a detailed study of Lincoln's Inn's origins.

[66] Buc, *Third Universitie*, fo. 968.

[67] T. Stapleton, 'The Life and Illustrious Martyrdom of Sir Thomas More', in *Tres Thomae*, trans. P. E. Hallett (London: Burns, Oates & Washbourne, 1928), p. 94. On the influence of Platonism in early modern England, see E. Barker, 'The Education of the English Gentleman in the Sixteenth Century', in *Traditions of Civility: Eight Essays* (Cambridge University Press, 1948), p. 148. See also P. Ackroyd, *The Life of Thomas More* (London: Random House, 1998).

[68] Plato, *The Republic*, p. 203.

philosophers became kings, or kings studied philosophy.[69] The just society envisaged by More was modelled to a limited extent on the communality of the Inns of Court. The customs of hall were replicated in the fictional state of More's *Utopia*, and provided a template for the bonds of community through which the ethical precepts of the constitution were enacted and represented. The offices of steward and bencher, whose importance respectively to the quotidian existence and governance of the Inns was crucial, are clearly discernible in the imaginary 'Styward' and 'Bencheater' of *Utopia*. More was a reader at Lincoln's Inn; his father and grandfather had been butlers there, and his grandfather had also been a steward. The order of dining in the communities of *Utopia* is almost identical to the form of commons at the Inns. A horn is blown to summon the community to dinner; the place of honour is the high table, at which the most venerable members sit; diners are divided into messes of four people; and lunch and supper are accompanied by readings from educational literature.[70] More's description in *Utopia* of the hierarchic organisation of communal dining is mirrored by the delineation of rank applied by the Inns to the seating arrangements at commons. The major significance of *domus* to the commonwealth of the Inns of Court is apparent from the extensive erection of domestic buildings during the second half of the sixteenth century. At the Inner Temple, for example, '[i]n 1 Marie the Kitchin was new built, every Knight and double Reader being taxed at xs. towards the chardge thereof'.[71]

The development of the Inns as autonomous communities extended beyond their buildings to the creation of elaborate gardens. In More's *Utopia*, gardens were a source of communal enjoyment and a representation of cosmic order.[72] The gardens of the Inns of Court were powerful symbols not only of the harmonious coexistence of natural law, divine law and human reason, but also of the absorption of classical influences into the nationalist bastions of common law. They were simultaneously idylls of English rural life and imitations of ancient classical temples. The gardens were extensively developed throughout the sixteenth century after the erection of encircling walls had defined their status as autonomous entities. At the Inner Temple, the wall between the Thames and the garden was built in 1524. In 1589 two sides of the garden were enclosed with a brick wall and 'the Posts whereon the xii Celestial Signes are placed, then set up'.[73] It is significant that the twelve signs of the zodiacal constellations should be incorporated into the garden, as their presence symbolised the coalescence of the order of the heavens (divine law), nature (natural law), and man (common law).

[69] T. More, *Utopia*, trans. P. Turner (Harmondsworth: Penguin, 1965), p. 57.
[70] More, *Utopia*, pp. 74, 81, 82.   [71] Dugdale, *Origines Juridiciales*, fo. 146.
[72] More, *Utopia*, p. 73.   [73] Dugdale, *Origines Juridiciales*, fo. 147.

The gardens were an idyllic representation of St German's theory that the universal laws of God and Nature were both antecedent to and coexistent with English common law and equity. Maine suggested that natural law was not so much a theory guiding practice as an article of speculative faith. It was a doctrine that propounded the fundamental equality of human beings. He referred to Rousseau's theory that perfect social order could be evolved from the unassisted consideration of the natural state, a social order wholly irrespective of the actual condition of the world. In this respect, it was an order not dissimilar to the self-contained communities of the Inns of Court.[74]

There is a notable similarity between the architectural configurations of the Renaissance Inns of Court and the temples of ancient Greece. The latter were not single buildings but rather architectural representations of Arcadia. In Greek legend, the pastoral association of Arcadia derives from the fact that Arcas (son of Zeus and Callisto) taught the Arcadians to grow corn, bake and spin. A similar sense of autonomy and self-sufficiency was evident at the Inns.[75] The original temple of Aphrodite at Paphos, one of the oldest Greek holy places, was built in approximately 1200BC and consisted of colonnades, halls, pavements, gardens and sacred trees.[76] The garden is an idealised, pastoral landscape; it is nostalgic in the literal sense, that of longing for a lost home. It seeks to establish a *locus amoenus*, a delightful place, in which subjects share a harmonious existence. This sense of nostalgia for a pastoral idyll, of stylistic conformity to a fictional past,[77] is an integral part of the Ancient Constitution.

In symbolic terms, the gardens of the four Inns of Court represented the rationalisation of English law under the cultural influence of the Renaissance, of human reason acting upon and in conjunction with the natural order, to realise the will of God. In this respect the gardens act as a visual trope: a physical manifestation of a popular, Elizabethan literary conceit. Shakespeare incorporated this device into a scene in *Richard II*, in which the gardeners of the duke of York compare their husbandry of the land to the governance of England. One gardener ruefully observes that in the course of their work they

---

[74] H. Maine, *Ancient Law* (London: Dent, 1917). The relationship between natural law, divine law and common law is discussed in J. Guy, *Christopher St. German On Chancery And Statute* (London: Selden Society, 1985), p. 19.
[75] On the legend of Arcadia, see P. Grimal, *The Dictionary of Classical Mythology*, ed. S. Kershaw (London: Penguin, 1991), p. 52; see also A. Fraunce, *The Arcadian Rhetorike* (Oxford: Blackwell, 1950).
[76] Hersey, *Classical Architecture*, pp. 47, 71.
[77] See P. Goodrich, 'Poor Illiterate Reason: History, Nationalism and Common Law', *Social and Legal Studies*, 1 (1992), 11. The idea of the English as a 'rustic' race is discussed in T. Smith, *De Republica Anglorum* (Cambridge University Press, 1906), pp. 60–71.

> Keep law and form and due proportion,
> Showing as in a model our firm estate,
> When our sea-wallèd garden, the whole land,
> Is full of weeds, her fairest flowers choked up.[78]

This contrasts starkly with the nostalgic description of England by John of Gaunt as 'This other Eden – demi-paradise . . . This blessèd plot, this earth, this realm, this England'.[79] The pastoral vision of England, with its emphasis on the importance of the soil and the creation of a biblical paradise on earth, was incorporated into the construction of the literary constitution. The ordered garden of the legal community represented the inherent order of an ideal state, cultivated under the benevolent and rational husbandry of common law. Like the gardeners in *Richard II*, the legal institution ensured that 'All must be even in our government'.[80] The walls surrounding the gardens of the law exemplified the inviolability of English soil. They also represented the constitutional and linguistic correlation between the earth, the plough, the city and the defined limits of jurisdiction. But there is an inherent paradox in the symbolism of the gardens. Despite the insularity of the common law and its institutions, represented by the erection of walls intended to exclude strangers from the gardens of the legal community, the perceived enemy was already within. The architectural structure of the gardens was based on the classical model of ancient Greek temples, a development that could not have taken place without detailed knowledge of the classical world.

Despite the influence of Platonic philosophy on the exercise of political power in *Utopia*, the unassailable authority of the church was crucial to More's understanding and interpretation of law. Immediately after being called to the bar of Lincoln's Inn 'he redde for a good space a publike lecture of St. Augustine, *de civitate dei*, in the Churche of St Lawrens'.[81] He was opposed to the dissemination of legal knowledge, suggesting that 'be they of the church or the realm . . . to put out books in writing abroad among the people against them, that I would neither do myself, nor in the doing commend any man that does'.[82] This paradox at the heart of More's life, the Neoplatonist implacably opposed to the dissemination of knowledge, mirrors the duality of the Inns of Court. The heavenly city that had love for its law simultaneously exercised a policy of xenophobic exclusion. Although Fortescue suggested that the Inns were academies of harmony, friendship

---

[78] *Richard II*, III. Scene iv. 41–4.
[79] *Ibid.*, II. i. 42–50. On the depiction of Richard II as a monarch in the continental, absolutist style, see Ward, *Legal Imagination*, pp. 32–9. See also A. Tuck, *Richard II and the English Nobility* (London: Edward Arnold, 1973); Kantorowicz, *King's Two Bodies*, pp. 24–41.
[80] *Richard II*, III. iv. 36.
[81] W. Roper, *The Lyfe of Sir Thomas Moore, knighte* (Oxford University Press, 1935), p. 6.
[82] T. More, *The Debellacyon of Salem and Bizance* (London: W. Rastell, 1533), ff. q viii a–q ix a.

and freedom of speech, it was English law that was learned there because 'the Laws and Customs of England are not only Good, but the very Best'.[83] The xenophobic predisposition of English common law was reflected in the legislation of the Inns, which excluded strangers and foreigners from their environs as well as from their rituals. For example, at the Middle Temple in 1612 legislation was enacted 'forbidding any Gentleman to lodg any Stranger in his Chamber'.[84] In symbolic terms, the obvious effect of high walls and gates was to define the boundaries of common law and to determine access to it. The labyrinthine alleys within the walls had a similar effect: knowledge of the legal maze was essential in order to gain access to the heart of law.

No single architectural style defined or delineated the common law. Obviously there was an ecclesiastical style to Temple church and the chapels of Gray's Inn and Lincoln's Inn. But in other respects the architecture was a representation of Renaissance Neoplatonism: it suggested antiquity but lacked any specific, definable shape.[85] There is a correlation between the eclectic character of English legal architecture and the indistinct nature of the Ancient Constitution. Despite the increased textualisation and systematisation of law during the sixteenth century, *lex terrae* was located in ancient national custom, textual justification for which was to be found in the Bible. Coke made an identical assertion in relation to *The Mirror of Justices*: '[t]he law whereof this summary is made, is of ancient usages warranted by holy scripture; and because it is generally given to all, it is therefore called Common.'[86] The divine provenance of common law provided the spiritual foundation for the religious commonwealth that the architecture of the Elizabethan and Jacobean Inns embodied, and which the *corpus* of common law represented. The Inns did not depict the legalistic, Roman interpretation of *justitia*: codification and definition through exposition of the text were not represented. Instead they provided the context in which the legal community could be socially active. The cohesiveness of this society was a strong symbolic feature of its buildings, delineating the meaning of the legal institution and its relationship to the commonwealth.[87]

The relative importance of text and icon is crucial in any attempt to decipher the imagistic character of the Ancient Constitution. The text played

---

[83] Fortescue, *De Laudibus*, p. 33.   [84] Dugdale, *Origines Juridiciales*, fo. 192.
[85] J. M. Major, *Sir Thomas Elyot and Renaissance Humanism* (Lincoln, Nebr.: University of Nebraska, 1964), p. 173.
[86] Coke, *Reports*, Part IX, preface, p. I; A. Horne, *The Mirrour of Justices*, trans. W. Hughes (New York: Augustus M. Kelley, 1968).
[87] See K. Fischer Taylor, *In the Theater of Criminal Justice* (New Jersey: Princeton University Press, 1993), introduction, p. xx. On power and institutional architecture, see M. Foucault, *Discipline and Punish: the Birth of the Prison*, trans. A. Sheridan (London: Penguin, 1991), pp. 195–228.

its part in the elucidation of common law, but there was no single statute that defined either the legitimate limits to executive action or the concomitant rights of subjects. Although one function of statute law was to clarify or reject case law, thus giving the law irrefutable definition, Coke and his contemporary legal practitioners articulated the opinion that such clarity and certainty were self-evident in case law, which represented the epitome of human reason. Coke stated that the judgments of the common law courts represented sovereign constitutional authority: 'the common law will control acts of Parliament, and sometimes adjudge them to be utterly void: for when an act of Parliament is against common right and reason, or repugnant or impossible to be performed, the common law will controul it, and adjudge such act to be void'.[88] The absence of systematic codification necessitated that common law manifested its corporeality in images other than texts. The Inns were the public image of common law and in terms of the constitution of which they were the physical representation it is useful to recall the linguistic provenance of 'inn'. The word is translated from the Latin *hospitium*: a town house or mansion (particularly if used as a hostel for students).[89] The architectural iconography did not imply magnificence, nor did it represent the authority of the text or the sovereignty of kingship. Rather it addressed the issues of communality and *justitia*: the public weal 'made of sundry estates and degrees of men'.[90]

THE CITY-STATE: EXCLUSION, CITIZENSHIP AND THE CONSTITUTION

A unique feature of English common law is the principle of inviolability of private land in the area of constitutional law. The most celebrated example of a private action for trespass and its constitutional implications is *Entick* v. *Carrington*.[91] Hereafter inviolability of the Englishman's home was established in case law as constitutional principle. Magna Carta is the prototype of such rights and liberties, enumerating concessions extracted from the crown rather than delineating fundamental constitutional rights. The unwritten tradition of manners, chivalry or the intrinsically English phenomenon of fair play was regarded by common lawyers as immemorial custom and thus a guiding constitutional precept. Case law has confirmed the perception that private ownership and enjoyment of land are the sacred right of every Englishman.[92] Divine law and the rights it bestows on its subjects

---

[88] Coke, VIII *Reports* [*Dr. Bonham's Case*], p. 118a.
[89] Megarry, *Inns Ancient and Modern*, p. 11.
[90] Elyot, *the Governor*, p. 1.   [91] *Entick v. Carrington* (1765) 19 St. Tr. 1030.
[92] On the inviolability of English soil and the perceived fairness of English manners as a protection against tyrannical governance, see Goodrich, *Languages of Law*, p. 215.

take precedence over the crown, which has no right of entry into privately owned property, not even on the grounds of state necessity or reasonable suspicion.[93] The sacred right of the English subject to secure his property was asserted in textual and iconic form by the Inns and their governing bodies. The Temple has always been a separate local authority, outside the jurisdiction of the city and its agencies of law enforcement. It shared this self-policing status with other London institutions. Stow cites a Common Council held in 1542 concerning St Bartholomew's Hospital: 'none of the Officers or Ministers of the City, should doe or execute any Arrest within the Precinct of the said Hospitall'.[94] The surrounding walls of the Inns, built during the reigns of Elizabeth I and James I, were representations not only of immunity and independence, but also of a fear of the stranger or other, a fear that underpins the sacred right to security. The initial expansion of the Inns during the reign of Henry VIII reflected the emergence of an independent nation-state and the establishment of a separate, sovereign jurisdiction. The building of elaborate walls and gates in the Elizabethan period, and the enactment of legislation prohibiting the presence of strangers at the Inns, reflected fears concerning national security and in particular the threat of Spanish invasion.[95]

The obverse of this nationalist dialectic that fears, resents and legislates against the presence of foreigners is the spirit of *civitas* or citizenship, derived from the classical world and forming the opposite half of the dichotomous constitution. In *The Survey of London*, Stow examined the linguistic provenance of the city and in so doing accidentally highlighted a fundamental dilemma faced by the Inns of Court and the English legal institution. Stow observed that 'cities and well peopled places be called *Oppida* [Towns] in Latine, either *ab ope danda* [from power granted], or *ab opibus* [with power], or *ab opponendo se hostibus* [setting himself against enemies]. They bee named also *Civitates a coeundo* [Citizenship by assembly] . . . or else *ab orbe* [world, circle], for the round compasse that they at the first had.'[96] Aside from the plausible suggestion that the linguistic roots of *oppida* derived from a level of power devolved from the state, and those of *urbs* from a degree of self-containment and enclosure,[97] there is an inevitable conflict between his two remaining definitions. The contrasting principles of *opponendo se*

---

[93] *Entick v. Carrington*; see also *Bruce v. Rawlins* (1770) 95 *Eng. Rep.* 123.
[94] Stow, *Survey of London*, fo. 936. On the separate status of Inner Temple and the improper intrusion into its environs by the Lord Mayor and his swordbearer, see Baker, *The Inner Temple*, p. 17.
[95] See 'The War With Spain', in J. Guy, *Tudor England* (Oxford University Press, 1990), pp. 331–51.
[96] Stow, *Survey of London*, fo. 691.
[97] Stow also observes that the Saxon word for town, tun, 'derived of the word Tynan, to enclose or tyne, as some yet speake', *ibid.*

hostibus and *civitates a coeundo* represented the dilemma confronting the city-state. The walls that defined the exclusive rights of Englishmen also encouraged *civitas*. Gerard Legh's account of his visit to the Inner Temple in 1561 recalls this ancient quality and notes its perceived benefit to the commonwealth: 'gentlemen of al countries in there young yeres, norished together in one place, with suche comely order, and dailie conference are knit by continual acquaintaunce in such unitie of minds and manners, as lightly never after is severid, then which is nothinge more profitable to the comon weale'.[98] The spirit of *civitas* persuaded the members of the Inner Temple to welcome Legh into their home and admit him to their feast even though, as Legh admits, 'I was a straunger'.[99]

An attitude of defensive insularity was discernible in the administration of the City of London during the sixteenth century. Stow cites a statute 'for the Reformation of Divers Abuses Used In the Wardmote Inquest', concerned with various bylaws in the City of London: 'you suffer no stranger borne out of the Realme, to bee of the Common Councell, nor to exercise or use any other Office within this City'.[100] He quotes also from the 'Old Lawes and Customes of this City': 'No man which is a Forraine, shall not buy nor sell within the liberties of this City with another Forraine, under paine of forfeiture of the goods so forraine bought and sold.'[101] This civic legislation was identical in intent to the restrictive legislation of the Inns of Court. Foreigners, strangers and those unacquainted with the 'Old Lawes and Customes' were not merely unwelcome; they were prohibited. Stow depicted an idyllic civic life that contrasted starkly with the xenophobic legislation of the City of London and the Inns of Court. In Stow's ideal walled city, 'men by this neerenesse of conversation, are withdrawne from barbarous ferity and force, to a certaine mildnesse of manners and to humanity and justice: whereby they are contented to give and take right, to and from their equals and inferiors'.[102] The complex legal significance of manners and tradition to which Stow alludes is central to the exposition of content in the constitution. Sir John Davies, for example, asserted that 'the common law of England is a Tradition and learned by Tradition as well as by Books'.[103] If it is accepted that the fundamental law consists of a code of manners or tradition, then the architecture of the walled city which facilitated this code provided the context and occasion for its exposition. The dichotomy inherent in the constitution is demonstrated by the fact that such tolerance (which Stow terms *urbanitas* or 'good behavior' and insists is 'rather found in Cities, than elsewhere'[104]) was not to be found in the pronouncements of common lawyers,

[98] Legh, *The Accedens*, fo. 119a.   [99] *Ibid.*, fo. 120a.
[100] Stow, *Survey of London*, fo. 672.   [101] *Ibid.*, fo. 668.   [102] *Ibid.*, fo. 692.
[103] J. Davies, *A Discourse of Law and Lawyers* (private circulation, 1876), p. 254.
[104] Stow, *Survey of London*, fo. 692.

especially concerning foreign jurisdictions. For example, the stated purpose of *De Laudibus Legum Angliae* was to 'prove the Law of England eminently to excel'.[105]

Fortescue's preference for a legal system that established virtue and banished sin found its visual equivalent in the various books of emblems published during the Renaissance.[106] *The Mirrour of Maiestie* is a late-Jacobean example of the genre, depicting the emblems of English nobility and the offices of the crown, and praising their holders in verse. It provides graphic evidence of the assimilation and interpretation of the Anglican commonwealth envisaged by Hooker in *Of the Laws of Ecclesiastical Polity*, in particular the principle that political supremacy derives from the entire commonwealth and necessarily implies the interdependence of secular and spiritual values. Pictorial and poetic imagery evoked an idyllic English landscape defined and governed by God, king and common law. The constitution was delineated, its fundamental contents exposed, and the image of the walled city was invariably the chosen form through which such exposition took place. Two emblems in particular are worthy of consideration here for their contrasting symbolism. The first, Lord Stanhope's emblem, is an illustration of the defensive model of civic architecture, *ab opponendo se hostibus* (see Fig. 2). It represents the insular nationalism of common law and the concomitant fear of foreign invasion.

At the centre of the illustration a church stands above three tiers of castellated battlements. The citadel is perched on a stone pedestal high above a mountainous landscape. On the roof of the church presides the victorious figure of Christ; in one hand he holds a cross, in the other the flag of Saint George. At the entrance to the church stands Saint Peter, holding the key to the kingdom of heaven. At the other end of the church is Saint Paul, holding a sword. Beneath, guarding the ramparts, are the symbols of the four evangelists: the lawgivers, defending the city of God. Outside the citadel, beneath the imposing stone walls stand a peasant, a pope, a cardinal and a scholar. They are engulfed in flames. The accompanying verse celebrates their destruction:

> Imagine heere, *Christ* strongly fortifi'd,
> Against the *Popes* bold heresie and pride:
> And thinke, whilst his Accomplices combine
> The Castle of *Christs* truth, to undermine;
> A flame breakes forth, which doth consume them all.[107]

---

[105] Fortescue, *De Laudibus*, p. 29.
[106] The exemplary form of this genre is A. Alciatus, *Emblemata* (Lugudini: M. Bonhomme, 1550); see J. Manning, *The Emblem* (London: Reaktion, 2002).
[107] H. G., *The Mirrour of Maiestie: or, the Badges of Honour Conceitedly Emblazoned: with Emblems Annexed, Poetically Unfolded* (London: W. Jones, 1618), p. 57.

I Magine heere, *Christ* strongly fortifi'd,
Against the *Popes* bold heresie and pride:
And thinke, whilst his Accomplices combine
The Castle of *christs* truth, to vndermine;
A flame breakes forth, which doth consume them all:
So seeking his, they meete with their owne fall.
And thus whilst heretickes (like wretched elues)
Out-stare the *Truth*, they doe condemne themselues,
Subiected to the twofold victory
Of *Truth*, and of their owne impietie.
Take refuge then, in Heau'ns eternall rest,
And see Christs foes against themselues addrest.

Fig. 2. 'Embleme 29' (Lord Stanhope), *The Mirrour of Maiestie* (1618).

The symbolism suggests that the city of God is English, hence Christ is depicted holding the flag of Saint George in his right hand. The intention of the illustration and the verse is to suggest that the son of God is by disposition an Englishman. This supposition was not uncommon: Bishop Aylmer, for example, remarked of the English that 'first you have God, and all his army on your side'.[108] The pope, the cardinal and the scholar depicted here are graphic symbols of the rival claimants to legal primacy: the canonists and civilians. They also represent (in particular the scholar) the threat posed to the city of God by the dissemination of knowledge. This illustration provides, in an iconic form of fundamental importance, confirmation of the constitutional principle that it is the sacred right of every Englishman to secure his property against all trespassers, regardless of their power, knowledge or authority.

The second emblem, Lord Wotton's, offers a different perspective on the significance of the walled city (see Fig. 3). The city is depicted as a place of learning, inside whose walls wisdom is acquired. The classical influences of the Renaissance are evident: the winged figure of Time bears a defining characteristic of the satyr, cloven hoofs. In one hand he holds a laurel-wreath, an allusion to the imposition of Apollonian order on the primeval power of Dionysus; in the other he holds the sands of time. He stands before the gateway to a walled city. A traveller, in cloak and hat, approaches him, holding an open book. Time presents the wreath to him. Beneath the illustration the motto reads, '*Tempus coronat Industriam*'. The following verse accompanies the illustration:

> Th'ascending Path that up to wisedome leades
> Is rough, uneven, steepe ...
> Yet led by *Labour*, and a quicke *Desire*
> Of fairest *Ends* scrambles, and clambers higher
> Then *Common reach* ... till he come at last
> Up to *Her* gate, where *Learning* keepes the key,
> And lets him in, *Her* best things to survey.[109]

The city contains many ornate buildings; there is one arched entrance to the city, with steps leading up to it and circular towers on either side. The illustration bears a noticeable resemblance to 'Aircastle', the town in which Parliament meets in More's *Utopia*, surrounded by high walls, with imposing towers and gatehouses.[110] The steep, 'ascending Path' leads away from the gate to the hostile terrain beyond the city of wisdom. In Lord Stanhope's emblem the walls signify the defence of divine and common law against the

---

[108] Bishop Aylmer, *An Harborowe for Faithfull and Trewe Subjectes* (Strasborowe: n.p., 1559), sig. iiia–ivb.
[109] *Mirrour of Maiestie*, p. 55.   [110] More, *Utopia*, p. 72.

TH'afcending Path that vp to wifedome leades
Is rough, vneuen, fteepe : and he that treades
Therein, muft many a tedious *Danger* meet,
That, or trips vp , or clogs his wearied feet:
Yet led by *Labour*, and a quicke *Defire*
Of faireft *Ends* fcrambles, and clambers higher
Then *Common reach* : ftill catching to holde faft
On ftrong'ft *Occafion*, till he come at laft
Vp to *Her* gate, where *Learning* keepes the key,
And lets him in, *Her* beft Things to furuay :
There he vnkend (though to himfelfe beft knowne)
Takes reft, till Time prefents him with a Crowne :
In queft of this rich Prize, your toyle's thus graced :
Euer to be in Times beft Border placed.

Fig. 3. 'Embleme 28' (Lord Wotton), *The Mirrour of Maiestie* (1618).

Architecture and heraldry: bodies of law, myth and honour

threat of canonists and civilians. In Lord Wotton's, they signify *civitas* and *urbanitas*: the Utopian commonwealth of Stow's idealised city.[111]

These emblems mirror the duality of the English legal institution. Commentators such as Legh and Stow reflected the humanising influence of the Renaissance over indigenous practices and institutions. The other half of this duality was represented by opposition to the influence of alternative jurisdictions in particular and the dissemination of knowledge in general. *The Mirrour of Maiestie* represents a national code descended more closely from divine and natural law than from any legal system then extant. Honour, manners and inviolability were essential components of this immemorial law. An untitled emblem in *The Mirrour*, symbolising the indivisibility of crown and church, demonstrates both the sacred significance of such a code and the continued relevance of Hooker's religious commonwealth in Jacobean England. A crown and mitre are placed on an altar; the motto '*Rex et Sacredo Dei*' surrounds them, accompanied by the lines:

> Why be these marshal'd equall, as you see?
> Are they dis-rankt, or not? No: they should be
> Thus plac'd: for Common-weales doe tottering stand,
> Not under-propt thus by the mutuall hand
> Of *King* and *Priest*, by Gods and humane lawes:
> Divine assistance most effectuall drawes
> Kings to confesse, that t'heav'n they homage owe;
> Which consequently leads a King to knowe,
> That, that *Ambition's* by dead Embers fir'd,
> Which ha's no: beyond earth to heav'n aspir'd:
> Earth can but make a King of earth partaker,
> But Knowledge makes him neerest like his maker.
> For mans meere power not built on Wisdomes fort,
> Does rather pluck downe Kingdomes than support.
> Perfectly mixt, thus *Power* and *Knowledge* move
> About thy *just* designes, ensphear'd with *love*;
> Which (as a glasse) serve neighbour-Kings, to see
> How best to follow, though not equall thee.[112]

The icon of national unity, the crown, is of paramount importance: the monarchy is a *sine qua non* of the constitution.[113] But the visual and literary imagery is most striking for its redolence of Book VIII of *Of the Laws of Ecclesiastical Polity*, in particular, Hooker's suggestion that 'where the King

---

[111] For a discussion of form, content and aesthetics in legal history see W. P. MacNeil, 'Living On: Borderlines – Law/History', *Law and Critique*, 6 (1995), 167–91; see also H. White, *The Content of the Form: Narrative Discourse and Historical Representation* (Baltimore: Johns Hopkins University Press, 1987).
[112] *Mirrour of Maiestie*, p. 2.
[113] On the enduring popularity of the English monarchy, see T. Nairn, *The Enchanted Glass* (London: Radius, 1988).

doth guide the state and the law the King, that commonwealth is like an harp or melodious instrument', neatly summated in the Latin maxim, *rex nihil potest nisi quod iure potest*.[114] *The Mirrour of Maiestie* was published eight years after the pronouncement of King James in 1610 that '[t]he state of monarchy is the supremest thing upon earth; for Kings are not only God's lieutenants upon earth and sit upon God's throne, but even by God himself they are called gods.' Whilst this statement of constitutional supremacy was compatible with Thomist principles of Providentialism[115] (whereby a godly sovereign was not subject to the constraints of civil law and there was no theological facility for civil disobedience), it was irreconcilable with common law theories of limited monarchy. Indeed, in *The Reverse or Back-Face of the English Janus*, published in 1610, Sir John Selden implied that the judiciary not only enacted the sacerdotal role attributed to it by Fortescue, but that the judiciary (rather than the monarch) reflected an inherent divinity: 'the Eternal and Sacred Scriptures do more than once call judges by that most holy name Elohim, that is, Gods'.[116]

The authority of the sacred image was utilised by Coke to enhance the perception of the judiciary as oracles of divine law. Only two years prior to the publication of *The Mirrour of Maiestie*, he was dismissed from the office of Chief Justice of the King's Bench for his continued judicial opposition to acts of prerogative rule. James I increasingly usurped the legislative powers of Parliament by his use of proclamations. These created new offences, unknown to the law, and demanded that the accused be brought before tribunals not legally authorised to try offences, despite the fact that proclamations had no statutory authority, since the enabling legislation (31 Hen. 8 C. 8) had been repealed. Characteristically, Coke defined the legal limits of proclamations, arguing that 'the King hath no prerogative but that which the law of the land allows him'. Coke defined the legal limits of proclamations, thus: 'the King by his proclamation cannot create any offence which was not an offence before... the law of England is divided into three parts, common law, statute law, and custom, but the King's proclamation is none of them'.[117] The continued threat to judicial independence posed by the king was as unpalatable to Coke as the usurpation of the legislative process: '[o]n

---

[114] R. Hooker, *Of the Laws of Ecclesiastical Polity*, ed. A. S. McGrade (Cambridge University Press, 1989), Book VIII, ch. II, XII, p. 146. On Hooker's subjection of the monarch to the interests of society, see Lake, *Anglicans and Puritans*, pp. 109, 201.

[115] There is a discussion of Thomist Providentialism and its influence on early modern jurisprudence in I. Ward, *An Introduction to Critical Legal Theory* (London: Cavendish, 1998), pp. 12–22.

[116] J. Selden, *The Reverse or Back-Face of the English Janus*, trans. R. Westcot (London: T. Bassett & R. Chiswell, 1682), fo. 4.

[117] Coke, XII *Reports*, quoted in J. R. Tanner, *Constitutional Documents of the Reign of James I* (Cambridge University Press, 1930), p. 188.

Architecture and heraldry: bodies of law, myth and honour

Nov. 2, 1608, the King had said that he was the supreme judge, "inferior judges his shadows and ministers ... and the King may, if he please, sit and judge in Westminster Hall in any Court there, and call their Judgments in question. The King beinge the author of the Lawe is the interpreter of the Lawe".[118] Coke responded with a rebuttal of this presumption: 'true it was that God had endowed his Majesty with excellent science and great endowments of nature, but his Majesty was not learned in the laws of his realm of England ... *quod Rex non debet esse sub homine sed sub Deo et lege*'.[119]

The reference to a king constrained by God and law was expressed in visual and literary terms by the above representation of godly kingship, in *The Mirrour of Maiestie*. The emblems and accompanying verses of this text occupy an important area in the *corpora* of law.[120] They offer elucidation of a constitution predicated upon the recognition of an ethical code: the Aristotelian principle of a bond between citizens that establishes a *polis*, founded upon the virtue of friendship and a shared interest in the good of the commonwealth.[121] *Justitia* or righteousness, represented by the 'civill life' to which Stow refers, takes precedence over legal positivism: manners not rules are at the heart of the constitution. *The Mirrour of Maiestie* enabled the constitution to be sensed,[122] despite uncertainty as to the sources of that constitution's legitimacy or whether the claims of ancient, national identity were more convincing than those of Neoplatonic humanism. While *The Mirrour* provided textual and iconic exposition of the Ancient Constitution, the Inns of Court fulfilled a similar function through the medium of architecture. They provided a home for the body of law: their buildings were the embodiment of ancient, institutional memory. The eclectic architectural style of the individual organs in the body signified an uncertainty that extended not only to the origins of the common law, but also to the fundamental nature of the constitution. Insularity and exclusion define Britain, in a geographical and historical sense. But, as the emblem of godly kingship in *The Mirrour of Maiestie* suggests: wisdom, knowledge, love and goodness were the salient features of the English constitution. Collectively, these qualities formed a fundamental law of manners, one that was recognised in a line of descent from Fortescue to Hooker. As the same emblem indicates, the biblical

---

[118] Caesar's notes in Lansdowne MS. 160, ff. 426–28, quoted in W. Holdsworth, *A History of English Law*, 17 vols. (London: Methuen, 1924), V, p. 428, n. 5.

[119] Coke, XII *Reports*, quoted in Tanner, *Constitutional Documents*, p. 187.

[120] On the interdependence of the English constitution, the monarchy and literature in the sixteenth century, see I. Ward, *Law and Literature* (Cambridge University Press, 1995), pp. 60–6.

[121] See A. Macintyre, *After Virtue: a Study in Moral Theory* (London: Duckworth, 1981), p. 146.

[122] On the ethereal and amorphous nature of the British constitution, see A. T. Denning, *The Changing Law* (London: Stevens, 1953), p. 2.

injunction to love thy neighbour was entrenched in the constitution represented by *The Mirrour of Maiestie*. The institutional use of 'Power and Knowledge' was guaranteed to the subjects of law as equitable and just because it was 'ensphear'd with love'. Implicit in this constitution was a legal system based on an ethical code, guaranteeing to the subject of law benevolent governance by a divinely ordained monarch. Symbol and allegory were incorporated into a public declaration of intent to create the city of God on earth, 'that heavenly city which has Truth for its King, Love for its Law, and Eternity for its Measure'.[123]

EMBLEMS AND JUDICIAL INTERPRETATION

Post-Reformation England witnessed the rebuilding of the halls at Gray's Inn, Middle Temple and Staple Inn. The roof of Gray's Inn was entirely Gothic in style apart from some classical mouldings and pendants on the hammer-beams, suggesting Christian credentials and classical virtues. The capacity of the legal profession to adapt its customs to prevailing conditions and influences was clearly represented by these symbols of authority and legitimacy. The heraldic devices of the Inns of Court demonstrated the pragmatism of the Bar: absorbing and adapting the aesthetic influences of the Renaissance while maintaining a distinct, nationalist façade. These emblems present a pictorial narrative of common law, depicting the mythology both of its immediate past and its immemorial origins. The lamb and flag of the Middle Temple refer specifically to the deeds of the Knights Templar, and the mythical battles fought by Christians against the powers of darkness. This emblem bears the closest resemblance to the arms of the Knights Templar: 'a Shield argent, Charged with a Crosse Gules, and upon the Nombrill thereof, a holy Lambe'.[124] The choice of colours is significant: it constitutes a graphic illustration of the code of honour informing the ethos of the Knights Templar and their secular descendants at the Middle Temple. In *The Accedens of Armory*, Legh records that the inclusion of *Argent* with *Gules* in a coat of arms denoted one who was 'bolde in all honestie'.[125] The symbolic significance of colour is conclusive proof that the sign is never innocent;[126] it points always to the authority of the original, implying the flawless descent of the legal institution.

Concerning the Judaic provenance of the griffin, emblem of Gray's Inn, Legh observed that 'the Jewishe Rabbies upon the xiii of Deuteronomion do write that this is a fierse beast, & keepeth the Hyperborian Mountaynes,

---

[123] St Augustine, *City of God*, introduction, p. xii.
[124] Buc, *Third Universitie*, fo. 972.   [125] Legh, *The Accedens*, fo. 5a.
[126] As a general introduction to signs and semiotics, see M. Blonsky (ed.), *On Signs* (Baltimore: Johns Hopkins University Press, 1985).

where are precious stones'. The choice of the griffin indicates a degree of rivalry between Gray's Inn and the Inner Temple, whose members adapted the device of the Knights Templar, depicting two men astride a horse. According to legend, as related by Legh, griffins bore 'great enmitie to man and horse, and are them selves of such a merveilous strength, that though the man bee armed, and on horsebacke, yet they take the one with the other, quite from the ground, and carye them cleane away'.[127] The particular emblems of the Inns were peculiar for the preference shown to a fictional (and in the case of Gray's Inn and the Inner Temple, a fantastical) line of descent. Buc suggested that, in the case of Gray's Inn, it might 'beare the Armes of the Lord Gray, the auncient possessor, or inhabitant of this house, but differenced with a border Argent, and Azure counter charged . . . But the Gentlemen of Grayes Inne have not long since chosen for device or Ensigne of their House, A Grifon Or. In a field sables, and so they are furnished already very well.'[128] The choice of colour is significant, as a *Sable* background with *Or* denotes 'honor with long life'.[129]

The preference for mythological rather than genuine ancestry concerned Buc. He castigated Lincoln's Inn for its choice of emblem: 'a Lyon purple rampant in a Shield Or: finding the same in the windows of the Hall at their coming thither, and with which as a thing more propper, and authentical, I would have wished to be empaled, the Armes of the bishops of Chichester, the auncient Lordes of this house'. The lion was the emblem of the earl of Lincoln, although Buc was adamant that the lion was not as 'authentical' as the arms of the bishops of Chichester. Sir Henry Lacy, Earl of Lincoln, had after all only 'enjoyed that part of it which was made out of the oulde monastery of the blacke friers given to him by King Edward the first'.[130] Buc implies that the genuine ancestry of the Inn demanded it be called Chichester Inn. However, the benchers clearly believed that the lion of the earl of Lincoln was a more appropriate device than the gold cross on an azure background, the emblem of the bishops of Chichester. Apart from the heroic and majestic attributes of the lion, Legh records that the designated colour of the Lincoln's Inn lion, purple, is 'a princely colour'; that the planet associated with the colour is Mercury, '[t]he Poets call him, the God of Oratours'; and that the stone associated with the colour is amethyst, 'enemy to dronkennes, and gyddy braines, and causes a man to have good forecast, and a quick mind, removeth ydle thoughtes, and encreaseth good understanding'.[131] The authentic ancestry of Lincoln's Inn was anything but heroic, and explains the preference for a mythical genealogy. William de Haverhyll, treasurer to

---

[127] Legh, *The Accedens*, fo. 61a.
[128] Buc, *Third Universitie*, fo. 974.
[129] Legh, *The Accedens*, fo. 8a.
[130] Buc, *Third Universitie*, fo. 974.
[131] Legh, *The Accedens*, ff. 10a, 10b.

Henry III, owned the mansion house on the site of the present Inn. His land was given to Raphe, Chancellor of England and bishop of Chichester, after de Haverhyll was charged with treason.

Through the creation of such emblems the patriarchs of the common law can be seen to interpret their provenance not impartially but according to their predilections and prejudices, and with deference to an ancient code of honour. This law of honour was intended to guarantee to the subjects of law the integrity of common lawyers and their right to be recognised as legitimate, ordained lawgivers. They were 'registred by the stile and name of Gentlemen'. Recognition of this peculiar English title legitimised the actions of common lawyers: 'a matter of race, and of blood, and of discent, from gentile and noble parents, and auncesters'. The imaginative interpretation of history was demonstrated to exemplary effect in the choice of Pegasus as the emblem of the Inner Temple. Buc expressed a preference for the earliest emblem of the Knights Templar: 'before they took this device, they bare a horse . . . with two menne ryding uppon him'. This emblem 'had a very honorable beginning and was a symbole of piety'.[132] He was shocked that the device was interpreted by some to suggest that the order of Knights Templar was a poor one, and that its members could afford only to share one horse between two riders: 'they which loved to deprave, and make scandalous, and ridiculous, interpretations . . . would have it supposed that it was taken, and devised to shew and express the poore, and needy beginnings . . . of this order, as beeing driven for lacke of horses to ride two upon one Horse'. The truth offered a more charitable explanation, concerned with love for fellow Christians: 'these religious Knightes, who being martiall men, and men of noble minds, when they hapned to see any other Christian Souldier Wounded, or Hurte, or Sicke, lying upon the Way, they woulde take him uppe uppon their owne horse, and carry him out of daunger, and into some place of safety where hee might have cure, and releese'.[133] Despite this noble ancestry, the emblem of the horse bearing two riders was open to misinterpretation as a sign of poverty.

For Buc, the material wealth of lawyers was the reward of virtue and enabled such men to become 'honoured magistrates in this Kingdome, and founders of many worshipfull, and Noble Families in this Realme'.[134] Fulbecke insisted that the diligent lawyer 'is rewarded by the dignitie, credit, and ample fortune which belongeth unto it . . . they ought to be incited and allured to proceede in their studies by the excellent and honorable rewardes of the same'.[135] The correlation of wealth and virtue was of particular significance during the sixteenth century as the legal profession expanded and

---

[132] Buc, *Third Universitie*, ff. 968, 971.   [133] *Ibid.*
[134] *Ibid.*, fo. 975.   [135] Fulbecke, *A Direction or Preparative*, fo. 9b.

common lawyers sought to assert their independence from, and precedence over, civil lawyers of the ecclesiastical courts. Title was crucial to the attainment of elevated status within the social hierarchy. The accusation of poverty was a devastating blow to potential advancement. Wealth and title were perceived also as crucial to the stability of the nation. In *The Governance of England*, for example, Fortescue remarked that the poverty of the king had been a principal cause of weakness in the House of Lancaster.

The hieroglyphic symbols of the legal profession developed from modest origins to their extravagant reinterpretation in the sixteenth century, demonstrating the influence of continental, Renaissance culture within an English environment. Hence the Inner Temple retained the horse, but the two riders were metamorphosed into wings, transforming their mount into the mythological flying horse, Pegasus. The original Knights Templar were evicted from the Temple at the instigation of Pope Clement I. He was probably persuaded to excommunicate them by King Philippe le Bell, who feared the power of the order, 'for they were very mightie'. Also he wanted to acquire their 'goodly possessions in Fraunce'. They were arraigned on charges of 'Heresie, of Idolatrie, of Sodomie, and of other horrible crimes'.[136] Whether these allegations had any factual basis, the Order was tainted by the charges, offering a further reason why members of the Inner Temple sought to alter the perception of their provenance. In *The Mirrour of Maiestie*, Pegasus is incorporated into the emblem of Lord Zouch. The winged horse stands on Mount Helicon, surrounded by swelling waters and overlooked by Apollo, seated on his throne (see cover illustration). An extract from the accompanying text reads:

> Divines (like Pegasus) divinely moove
> In Man, springs of profound, and precious love
> To heav'nly wisedom; who t'ech passing by,
> Poynts out the path-way to Eternitie.
> And whilst You doe your noble thoughts confine
> To what Divines preach, You become Divine.[137]

Accordingly, Pegasus does not merely inspire men to acquire divine wisdom; he actually enables them to become divine bodies. In *The Accedens of Armory*, Legh describes the birth of Pegasus, after Perseus had slain Medusa, and the subsequent flight of the winged horse to the heavens. This description leads to his account of an actual visit he made to the Inner Temple in 1561. Legh represents the Inner Temple as the home of divine, as well as earthly law: myth and reality integrate and are accommodated within the body of common law.[138]

---

[136] Buc, *Third Universitie*, fo. 971.
[137] *Mirrour of Maiestie*, p. 47.   [138] Legh, *The Accedens*, fo. 118b.

The evolution of Pegasus as the emblem of the Inner Temple demonstrates not only the pragmatism and invention of the legal profession, but also the tendency of common lawyers to interpret facts and events in a creative manner and without regard to external influences and sensibilities. It is a symbolic assertion of judicial independence, implying the determination of common lawyers to interpret law freely and without interference from the executive. There were earlier isolated incidents of judicial challenges to the royal prerogative. In 1234 one of the king's justices, William Raleigh, declared in the royal court that the outlawry of Hubert de Burgh was null, on the grounds that he had been neither indicted nor yet appealed, though he had escaped from prison and the king was treating him as a rebel.[139] By the early seventeenth century, the monarchies of continental Europe provided a model for English government, unhindered in scope by judicial constraint. In England, the threat was countered by a legal profession whose claim to represent the sovereignty of common law was asserted through the iconic symbols of its ancient provenance.[140] These symbols represented not only the legitimacy and sanctity of common law, but also the right of the legal profession to interpret both the origins of its institutional existence and the judgments of common law freely and without external interference.

The assertion of such a right and the concomitant attempt by the executive to restrict it finds parallels in the *Corpus Juris Civilis* of Justinian. In one sense this text represents an attempt to clarify a much more extensive body of legal texts, and thus to reduce the need for judicial interpretation and juristic commentary. Justinian was emphatic that where problems of interpretation occur, the judiciary should refer such cases to the apex of the empire, the emperor having the exclusive right to create and interpret laws.[141] This proclamation resembled the request of James I that, where important, innovative matters were concerned, the judiciary should consult the king and obtain his counsel before pronouncing from the courts, *ex cathedra*. Not only was it his stated belief that he was the author and interpreter of law; the king was equally emphatic that the function of the judiciary was to distribute and expound existing law, and not by adroit dissemblance to create new laws. Sir Richard Hutton reported a speech made in Star Chamber on 19 June 1616, in which James I protested that it had

---

[139] Pollock and Maitland, *History of English Law*, II, p. 581.
[140] On the suggestive power of imagery in Jacobean England and in particular the image of the king, see R. Ashton, *Reformation and Revolution, 1558–1660* (London: Paladin, 1985), p. 36.
[141] 'Si quid vero . . . ambiguum fuerit visum, hoc ad imperiale culmen per iudices referatur et ex auctoritate Augusta manifestetur, cui soli concessum est leges et condere et interpretari', *De confirmatione Digestorum*, quoted in I. Maclean, *Interpretation and Meaning in the Renaissance* (Cambridge University Press, 1992), p. 51.

never been his intention to alter the laws of England, because of their antiquity and their evident capacity to maintain order in the realm. But the king went on to remark that there was a case to be made for reforming the law and (as Justinian had before him) reducing the number of extant laws.[142] The standardisation and systematisation of law reporting during this period provided the means whereby the judiciary was able to develop the narrative logic of the common law. This logic was applied also to the heraldic symbols of the legal institution, which were graphic signs of the immutable link between the present and the pre-Christian past. They demonstrate the utility of aesthetics in asserting the right to independent judicial interpretation and in defying the oppressive extremes of the royal prerogative. Resistance to the prerogative would cost Coke his job as Chief Justice under James I: '"four P's have overthrown and put him down – that is, pride, prohibitions, praemunire, and prerogative"'.[143] But in 1628, through his eloquent proposal of the Petition of Right, Coke demonstrated in the House of Commons his continued adherence to the constitutional supremacy of common law and his implacable opposition to the inequitable exercise of the royal prerogative.

GENTILITY, FAMILY AND VIRTUES IN THE CITY-STATE

Advocates or Counsellors being Interpreters of the Law, their place is commendable, and themselves most necessary Instruments in a Commonwealth; wherefore, saith the Civill Law, their calling is honourable.[144]

The heraldic devices of the four Inns of Court represent and uphold the law of honour: in the classical, medieval and Renaissance worlds, honour and justice were synonymous. Ferne refers to the 'foure Cardinall vertues, to wit, Prudence, Justice, Fortitude, and Temperaunce, been the fountaynes, out of which al gentlenes, should and ought to streame'.[145] He offers an idiosyncratic interpretation of the four Platonic virtues: *andreia*, *sophia*, *dikaiosune* and *sophrosune*. The first two are frequently translated respectively as 'courage' and 'wisdom', rather than 'fortitude' and 'prudence'. The meanings of *dikaiosune* and *sophrosune* are more complex than the definitions of 'justice' and 'temperance' that Ferne offers. The former is spiritual rather than legal in intent (although it is often translated as 'justice'), referring to the particular function of each part of the soul. Of great interest however,

---

[142] *The Diary of Sir Richard Hutton, 1614–1639*, ed. W. R. Prest (London: Selden Society, 1991), p. 12.
[143] Quoted in Tanner, *Constitutional Documents*, p. 176.
[144] H. Peacham, *The Compleat Gentleman* (London, 1634), fo. 10.
[145] Ferne, *Blazon of Gentrie*, fo. 30.

in the context of the Inns of Court and *ius gentilitatis*, is the correct translation of the latter. *Sophrosune* does not imply merely temperance in the sense of restraint. In particular it is the aristocratic virtue of choosing not to abuse one's intrinsic power.[146] This is an important distinction to make, since it provides further evidence of an ethical code of manners which lay at the heart of the Ancient Constitution. 'Gentleness', in the sense that Ferne and his contemporaries implied, referred to the 'estate of Gentry', of which the bearing of arms was 'the signe, and outward badge'. He asserts that gentlemen are bound by the 'benefit and priviledges of that law, called *Ius Gentilitatis*'.[147]

Ferne linked this code of honour, which provides the framework for a hierarchic constitution, to the ancient world: 'this law was with Tully accounted as the most reverend and honorable, for the regard of the worthiness of the matter (to wit, Gentry) whereof it entreated'.[148] The primary function of this law was to allocate an appropriate role to the subject of law within a clearly delineated social stratum. As Macintyre observes, crucial to an understanding of roles in the heroic societies of Homeric poems are the related structures of kinship and household.[149] The basis of the constitution to which the four cardinal virtues apply is one of kinship: the bond that, in Aristotle's opinion, constitutes the *polis*. This form of friendship benefits the civic community as well as the household because it necessitates a recognition of and quest for the common good.[150] The recognition to which Macintyre refers is a shared factor in all communities; thus the moral imperative that informs the constitution takes the necessary step from the kinship group, on which the first social communities were based, to the city-state: the model for the ideal constitutions of Aristotle and Plato. Common to the four categories of human society defined by St Augustine was the recognition of kinship as the prerequisite for a lawful constitution, whether it existed in the lowest level of human society, *domus* (the household), or the highest, *mundus* (the universe). The individual in the Renaissance state was defined and identified according to the predetermined role allotted to him in the community that he inhabited. That community could be the family, the household, the city or the state; but the ultimate and primary allegiance of the individual was to the universe. According to Renaissance scholarship, the universe embodied a fundamental law of nature; it was a manifestation of divine order. The importance of virtue to such a society was that it demonstrated adherence to this cosmic law or, as Macintyre describes it, membership of the citizenry of

---

[146] See Macintyre, *After Virtue*, p. 128.   [147] Ferne, *Blazon of Gentrie*, fo. 86.
[148] *Ibid.*   [149] Macintyre, *After Virtue*, p. 115.
[150] *Ibid.*, p. 146. The influence of Thomist Aristotelianism on the political thought of Hooker is discussed in Lake, *Anglicans and Puritans?*, p. 225.

the universe.¹⁵¹ The familial obligation, based on kinship and civic friendship, defines the nature of the constitution with greater precision than any single text. Aristotle makes such a claim in the *Nicomachean Ethics*, stating that lawgivers make friendship a more important aim than justice. The virtue of justice can fulfil its classical function of rewarding desert and repairing the failure to reward desert only within an extant constitution; but the virtue of friendship, according to Aristotle, provides the essential conditions for the initial establishment of the constitution.

Foucault mentions the ancient attachment to a group, in which genealogy, tradition and status provide sustenance.¹⁵² He is here referring to the Nietzschean concept of *Herkunft*, which he equates with stock or descent. The constitution of the Renaissance state (and the Athenian city-state before it) sought to recreate the blood group of the household. The function of the law of honour within this constitution was to unite and enforce the three bonds to which Foucault refers above: tradition determines the importance of social status within the hierarchy, and the subject's particular social status is dependent on blood or genealogy. The laws of genealogy, or *ius gentilitatis*, were the artificial means whereby those virtues (which in Homeric societies guided kinships and households towards the acceptance of order) could be replicated in the extended kinship of the commonwealth. The knowledge of a common descent bound the group; in such a society, legitimacy was inherited from a distant original. In Roman law the father of the household was endowed with absolute power, as was the emperor in the public sphere.¹⁵³ The legitimacy of such absolutism was acknowledged by the civil law maxim, *quod principi placuit habet vigorem legis*. In the English legal system, paternal power did not vest in the king. Rather it existed in the artificial bonds of kinship that the institutional structures of common law sought to represent. Hence Buc's insistence that the king 'cannot make a gentleman' because although a monarch could create the various ranks of nobility, gentility was dependent upon proof of flawless ancestry.¹⁵⁴ Ferne also was insistent that a king could not create a 'gentleman of bloud' where only three previous generations of gentility were adduced: 'I am not ignorant how some have labored to shew, that if the coat-armor be given him by the King, that in such a case three discents (as aforesaid) shal make a Gentleman of bloud, whereunto I cannot subscribe.' Ferne insisted on the evidence of five previous generations, categorising them as *abavus, proavus, avus, pater* and *filius*. Paradoxically

---

¹⁵¹ Macintyre, *After Virtue*, p. 157.
¹⁵² M. Foucault, *Aesthetics, Method, and Epistemology*, trans. R. Hurley, 2 vols. (London: Penguin, 1998), II, p. 373.
¹⁵³ On the paternity of law and the *paterfamilias* in Roman law, see P. Goodrich (ed.), *Law and the Unconscious: A Legendre Reader* (Basingstoke: Macmillan, 1997), p. 9.
¹⁵⁴ Buc, *Third Universitie*, fo. 968.

the gentleman was the lowest in degree of the 'dignities of regalitie' cited by Ferne. His position in the hierarchy was beneath the six princely categories, 'Earl, Marquesse, Duke, Prince, King, and Emperor'. It was also the lowest of the six inferior positions of nobility, 'Gentleman, Esquier, Baneret, Knight, Baron or Lord, and Viscount'. The unique distinction of the gentleman was the mysterious significance of genealogy, rather than royal patronage, to his status within the hierarchy.[155]

A recurring theme in the historiography of the Elizabethan Inns of Court is that their members were of impeccable descent, bound together by a fraternity whose purpose was to practise and administer the law in a manner befitting their innate nobility. They owed their status not to the patronage of a beneficent monarch, but to their fathers and to the ancient customs of a patrimonial society. Fortescue, Ferne, Legh and Buc endowed the members of the Inns with an emblematic quality; human identity was discarded in favour of iconic representation. They were living symbols of ancient custom: the personification of the constitution. They embodied the classical virtues, defined by Aristotle as those qualities that permitted an individual to attain the state of *eudaimonia*, or blessedness (conversely the absence of these qualities prevented the attainment of this state of perfection).[156] For Aristotle, the city-state provided the ideal site where these virtues could be instanced (a sentiment shared by Stow in relation to sixteenth-century London), the social connection between virtue and the city-state being that a virtuous person was likely to be a good citizen. For Plato also, the virtuous man and the virtuous citizen were synonymous, although he distinguished between the actual city-state and the ideal constitution in which rational desire could be entirely satisfied. Despite Plato's distinction between the actual state and the ideal constitution, he believed that virtue was a political entity, because the virtuous citizen was comprehensible only as a *politikon zoon*.

The ancient world recognised the importance of storytelling as a means of both moral education and lawgiving. The use of didactic, allegorical narrative was important also in medieval and Renaissance societies. Categories of right and wrong, and the means of comprehending them, were created from such narratives, out of which a code of law emerged. The correlation between virtue and law was of paramount importance, because only those possessing the virtue of justice were fit to apply the law. In early modern England the challenge posed to the legal institution was to relate the classical virtues of courage, justice, temperance and wisdom to the Christian virtues of faith, hope and charity. At the Inns of Court an ancient rhetorical technique was adopted in order to demonstrate the synthesis of classical and Christian philosophy. The Inns incorporated dramatic representation

---

[155] Ferne, *Blazon of Gentrie*, ff. 87–8.   [156] Macintyre, *After Virtue*, p. 139.

into their public rituals in order to demonstrate the indivisible correlation between law and the virtues of the classical and Christian worlds. This technique had been popular in Athens, as a means of representing political and related philosophical concerns.[157]

Legh records such a ritual during his visit to the Inner Temple in 1561. After dinner a ceremony was enacted during which the knights of Pallas Athene were created from the assembled members. Legh delineates the official functions of this order of knights, allegorising the duties of the common lawyer within the ideal *polis*: '[a]n armed Mars, A campion politique, in fielde to fighte, or at home to defende, An ordered Justicer without respecte. Mercifull to the meke, Enemy to monstrouse Tirannye, Bountifull to the vertious, And clothed with secrecie, and counsell'.[158] The protagonists tacitly claimed descent from their Christian antecedents, the Knights Templar, and from classical forebears. The fact that the latter are fictional is irrelevant: belief in the existence of mythical ancestors was crucial to the classical and Christian worlds because both cultures defined their respective *polis* at least partly in terms of their perceived emergence from heroic societies.[159] The ceremony described by Legh provided a historical memory for the Inns of Court, the common law and the Ancient Constitution. His account records a jurisprudence that combines the xenophobic, Christian nationalism of the Knights Templar (and the Christian virtues of faith, hope and charity implicit in their ethos) with the cardinal virtues of courage, justice, temperance and wisdom. Legh relates the extraordinary synthesis of mythical, heroic societies. In so doing he acknowledges the importance of virtue, kinship, honour and tradition to the ideals of the Ancient Constitution:

> Wisdome the Guyde of armed strength,
> Upraise your knightly name
> By force of prowes hawte, to cliymbe
> The loftye tower of Fame:
> Advance your honours by your dedes,
> To lyve for evermore,
> As Pallas knightes, by Pallas helpe,
> Pallas serve ye therefore.[160]

[157] Ibid., pp. 129–30. [158] Legh, *The Accedens*, fo. 129b.
[159] Macintyre, *After Virtue*, p. 123. [160] Legh, *The Accedens*, fo. 130b.

3

Revels, feasting and role-playing: dreamland, drunkenness and the Utopian state

COMMUNITY, MAGISTRACY AND THE DEPICTION OF COMMONWEALTH

At night, before Supper, are Revells and Dancing; and so also after Supper, during the twelve days of Christmass. The antientest Master of the Revells, is after Dinner and Supper, to sing a Caroll, or Song; and command other Gentlemen then there present, to sing with him and the Company, and so it is very decently performed.[1]

The above passage from Dugdale's *Origines Juridiciales* suggests that the role of the Inns of Court was not confined to legal education in its strict technical sense. In *De Laudibus Legum Angliae*, Fortescue stated that students at the Inns were '[s]ons to Persons of Quality',[2] many of whom had no intention of practising law. Of the five admissions recorded by the Middle Temple in one month between 13 February and 14 March 1555, three were the sons of knights: 'Admissions. – <u>13 Feb.</u> Gilbert, son of John Talbott of Grafton, Worcestershire, knight . . . Carew, son and heir of Peter Courteney of Le Woode, Devon, knight . . . <u>14 March.</u> Richard, second son of Richard Molyneux, of Sefton, Lancashire, knight'.[3] Young men such as these would inherit and manage large estates, becoming the acknowledged guardians of a hierarchy that was governed by status, possession and exclusion. Fortescue records that 'Knights, Barons and the Greatest Nobility of the Kingdom, often Place their Children in those Inns of Court, not so much to make the Laws their Study, much less to live by the Profession (having large Patrimonies of their own) but to form their Manners and to preserve them from the Contagion of Vice'.[4]

---

[1] W. Dugdale, *Origines Juridiciales or Historical Memorials of the English Laws* (London: F. & T. Warren, 1666), fo. 155.
[2] J. Fortescue, *De Laudibus Legum Angliae*, ed. J. Selden (London: R. Gosling, 1737), p. 110.
[3] *A Calendar of the Middle Temple Records*, ed. C. H. Hopwood, 4 vols. (London: Butterworth, 1903), I, p. 105.
[4] Fortescue, *De Laudibus*, p. 112.

Guy has suggested that there is more to be discovered about the early modern Inns of Court, in particular concerning the prevalence there of the constitutional jurisprudence espoused by Christopher St German and the extent to which juristic thought reflected royal policy.[5] While acknowledging the importance of the readings and moots as signifiers of prevailing legal opinion, it should also be recognised that the annual Inns of Court revels provided evocative images of the ideal state and its constitutional mechanisms. Records suggest that the revels had been a major feature of institutional existence at the Inns since their foundation. During the reign of Elizabeth I these events attained levels of symbolism, spectacle and extravagance that have never been surpassed: '[t]he three grand days are All-hallow, Candlemass, and Ascension day; whereof All-hallow and Candlemass are the chief, for cost, solemnity, dancing, revelling and Musick.'[6] The creation of an artificial state for the duration of the revels, in which the functions of executive, legislature and judiciary were enacted by members of the Inns, enabled the legal profession to explore and develop the political concepts of constitutionalism and limited monarchy, and eventually to challenge the imperial theory of kingship.

In 1534 the Act of Supremacy had acknowledged that Henry VIII was 'the only supreme head on earth of the Church of England' and 'shall have and enjoy annexed and united to the imperial crown of this realm' all the necessary 'jurisdictions'.[7] The arrogation to the crown of unrestricted imperial power had the notable effect of blurring the distinction between *dominium regale* and *dominium politicum et regale*, as defined by Fortescue in *The Governance of England*. Fortescue advocated the use of administrative machinery to raise revenue for the re-endowment of the crown, but as Guy has noted, the success of such a régime ensured that *regale* would necessarily supercede *politicum*.[8] The pronouncement of Henry VIII that 'the Kings of England in time past have never had any superior but God alone' and that the king was 'under God but not the law' became an axiom of Tudor rule and threatened to diminish the practical significance of the common law maxim, *lex facit regem*. It is impossible to exaggerate the importance of Fortescue's theory of mixed monarchy to common lawyers of the sixteenth century, and in particular to Christopher St German. The constitutional theory of the sovereignty of king in Parliament, propounded in *Doctor and Student*, rendered church and

---

[5] J. Guy, 'Thomas Cromwell and the Intellectual Origins of the Henrician Revolution', in J. Guy (ed.), *The Tudor Monarchy* (London: Arnold, 1997), p. 230.

[6] Dugdale, *Origines Juridiciales*, fo. 161.

[7] On the *imperium* of Henry VIII, see J. Guy, 'Tudor Monarchy and its Critiques', in Guy, *Tudor Monarchy*, pp. 78–104.

[8] J. Fortescue, *The Governance of England*, ed. C. Plummer (Oxford: Clarendon, 1885), p. 109; J. Guy, *Tudor England* (Oxford University Press, 1990), p. 13.

state subject to the authority of the king but suggested that the king should govern both in a parliamentary way. St German asserted the harmonious coexistence of divine law, natural law and English common law. Crucial to the development of constitutional thought at the Inns of Court, *Doctor and Student* was a set text there. That a broader constituency than the Inns of Court was intended is suggested by its publication in English, rather than law-French or Latin.[9] In his introduction to the Second Dialogue, St German makes explicit his subversive intention that *Doctor and Student* should have as wide an audience as possible, far beyond the conventional educated readership:

> forasmuch as many can read English that understand no Latin, and some that cannot read English, by hearing it read, may learn divers things by it that they should not have learned if it were in Latin; therefore, for the profit of the Multitude, it is put into the English Tongue rather than into the Latin or French Tongue. For if it had been in French, few should have understood it but they that be learned in the Law, and they have least need of it.[10]

In the humanist–classical culture of the Henrician Inns of Court, where political theorists and jurists were influenced by Platonic and Aristotelian principles of civic republicanism, St German's constitutional theory was incompatible with the idea of imperial kingship.[11] Underpinning St German's theory of the king in Parliament is the notion that the legitimacy of any law enacted in the name of a sovereign body derives not from the king, but from the community. The supreme constitutional power resided not in the king alone but in a legislative assembly, representative of the entire commonwealth. The concept of the commonwealth was classical in origin, finding its earliest expression in the city-states of ancient Greece. Aristotle's principle that the ultimate purpose of the state was to enable men to live well, and that the ideal state might be realised only through the active political involvement of its citizens, was reinterpreted by humanist writers such as Sir Thomas Elyot in the context of an increasingly autocratic monarchy. Elyot's description of the ideal commonwealth, 'which is disposed by the order of equity and governed by the rule and moderation of reason',[12] has been interpreted as a critique of the imperial style of Henry VIII's government.[13]

---

[9] Guy, 'Tudor Monarchy', pp. 88, 104; Guy, 'Thomas Cromwell', p. 225.

[10] C. St German, *Two Dialogues in English, Between a Doctor of Divinity, and A Student in the Laws of England, of the Grounds of the said Laws, And of Conscience* (London: the Assigns of R. & E. Atkins, 1709), p. 119.

[11] On St German and the sovereignty of English common law, see J. Guy, 'Thomas More and Christopher St. German: The Battle of the Books', in *Reassessing the Henrician Age: Humanism, Politics and Reform 1500–1550* (Oxford: Blackwell, 1986), pp. 100–19; also J. Guy, *Christopher St. German On Chancery and Statute* (London: Selden Society, 1985).

[12] T. Elyot, *The Book Named the Governor* (London: Dent, 1962), p. 1.

[13] See Guy, 'Tudor Monarchy', p. 85.

As autonomous collegiate structures with independent quasi-civic status, the Inns of Court attempted to represent in microcosm the ideal humanist commonwealth, and invoked the ethical precepts of common law to shape the nature of their constitutions. The perception among lawyers that common law was natural law applied to the customs of an ancient nation[14] is represented clearly and unambiguously in the symbolic commonwealths depicted and enacted at the Inns during the revels. These were not optional entertainments, but a mandatory feature of formal legal education, at which attendance and participation by honourable members were compulsory. Their full title of 'Solemn Revells' reflects the seriousness with which the governing bodies regarded them. The Pension Book of Gray's Inn records that 'at a Pension held here in Michaelmas Term 21. H. 8. there was an Order made, that all the Fellows of this House, who should be present upon any Saturday at Supper betwixt the Feasts of All Saints, and the Purification of our Lady; or upon any other day, at Dinner, or Supper, when there are Revells, should not depart out of the Hall, until the said Revells were ended, upon the penalty of xiid'.[15]

The revels lasted for several weeks over the Christmas period, 'the first of these Feasts being at the beginning, and the other at the later end of Christmas'. As their form became more elaborate during the reigns of Elizabeth I and James I, so the duration of the revels extended, until in the 1630s a Parliament of the Inner Temple passed an Order 'that Christmas Commons should continue by the space of three weeks only, and no longer, according to the antient usage and custome of this House'.[16] These spectacular seasonal events permitted the Inns of Court to abandon temporarily their austere quotidian régime and devote themselves to the pursuit of extravagant feasting and elaborate entertainment. They were organised by members of the Inn elected to the seasonal offices of Master of the revels and Lord of Misrule: 'Parliament named and elected to undergo several offices for this time of solempnity, honour, and pleasance: Of which Officers, these are the most eminent; namely the Steward, Marshall, Constable-Marshall, Butler, and Master of the Game'.[17] For the duration of the revels, the patriarchs of the Inns ceded their governing authority to junior members, thus inverting the normal hierarchic structure. The effect of this temporary abdication was unexpected; order was not rejected, although the disruptive effect of the Lord of Misrule is instanced by the ensuing quarrels that erupted inside the Inn:

---

[14] See A. Cromartie, 'The Constitutionalist Revolution: The Transformation of Political Culture in Early Stuart England', *Past & Present*, 163 (1999), 82.
[15] Dugdale, *Origines Juridiciales*, fo. 285.   [16] *Ibid.*, ff. 205, 149.   [17] *Ibid.*, fo. 153.

About seaven of the Clock in the Morning, the Lord of Misrule is abroad, and if he lack any Officer or attendant, he repaireth to their Chambers, and compelleth them to attend in person upon him after Service in the Church, to Breakfast, with Brawn, Mustard, and Malmsey. After Breakfast ended, his Lordships power is in suspence, untill his personal presence at night, and then his power is most potent.[18]

Junior members created a fantastical but highly ordered community within the enclosed confines of the Inn. They presented archetypes from an ideal society, and so offered a glimpse of the Utopian state, one not subject to the uncertainties that existed beyond the walls of the Inn. In Nietzschean terms, the revels represented the coalescence of the Apollonian and the Dionysian;[19] the primitive force of Dionysus, personified by the Lord of Misrule, was tempered by the ordered dreamland or artifice of Apollo. This artificial, ordered world was created by the imposition of law, which restricted and regulated the excessive, disordered 'hostile demons of the non-Apollonian sphere'.[20]

The deployment of secular images of government occurred partly as a response to the destruction and denigration of iconography that implied the sovereignty of Rome. As the institutional authority of the Church was challenged and discarded by Henry VIII, so the absolute reference of sovereignty was predicated upon the image of the monarch. As Guy has suggested, in Tudor England the image of the king was the most important visible asset of the monarchy.[21] Literature and the arts replaced ecclesiastical iconography as the dominant means of expression for the art of government. Henry VIII was the first English monarch fully to appreciate the power of art to project the image of magistracy and the capacity of aesthetics to bind the private imagination of the subject to a public acceptance of his imperial authority.[22] But it was not until the reign of Elizabeth I that the theatre of government was developed as an art form, spectacularly by the monarch herself and discursively by the dramatists, poets and political theorists of the Elizabethan epoch.[23] Indeed, Sir Philip Sidney's *Arcadia* attempts the daunting task of setting down the whole art of government, asking of its readers, 'how can

---

[18] *Ibid.*, ff. 149, 156.
[19] F. Nietzsche, *The Birth of Tragedy*, trans. W. A. Haussmann (Edinburgh: J. N. Foulis, 1909), p. 21.
[20] *Ibid.*, p. 40.   [21] Guy, 'Tudor Monarchy', p. 78.
[22] On the political and religious symbolism of Holbein's portrait of Solomon receiving the Queen of Sheba, see *ibid.*, p. 84; and on the 'Rainbow' portrait of Elizabeth I in Hatfield House, *ibid.*, p. 81.
[23] On early modern government and the age of spectacle, see I. Ward, *Shakespeare and the Legal Imagination* (London: Butterworth, 1999), p. 200. On the theatre of Elizabethan government, see also S. Greenblatt, 'Invisible Bullets: Renaissance authority and subversion in *Henry IV* and *Henry V*', in J. Dollimore and A. Sinfield (eds.), *Political Shakespeare: New Essays in Cultural Materialism* (Manchester University Press, 1985), p. 44.

any laws (which are the bonds of all human society) be observed if the lawgivers and law rulers be not held in an untouched admiration?'[24] The dissemination of humanist literature and the concomitant influence of classical republicanism were instrumental in altering the aesthetic representation of magistracy and the commonwealth. This was particularly noticeable at the Inns of Court, where texts such as *Doctor and Student*, *The Book Named the Governor* and later, Richard Hooker's *Of the Laws of Ecclesiastical Polity* influenced not only the development of substantive law, but also its ethical context. One function of the revels was therefore to depict the form of this embryonic commonwealth, whose subjects (although still governed by a godly magistracy) were increasingly concerned with justice, fairness and their constitutional status. Above all, the origins of the Ancient Constitution, the source of political sovereignty and the legitimacy of the royal prerogative were recurring themes to be considered and represented through the unique imagery of the Elizabethan revels.

The form of the revels was unchanged throughout Elizabeth's reign: processions, feasts, music, masques and plays predominated. The correlation between magistracy and the constructed community was demonstrated by the presence and participation at these annual events of the queen, either in person or through her appointed representative. An analysis of two separate revels, those of Christmas 1561 at the Inner Temple and Christmas 1594 at Gray's Inn, provides evidence of the development of constitutional jurisprudence at the Inns of Court during the reign of Elizabeth and its expression through the medium of visual images. The revels suggested an increasing emphasis on the *pactum* or social contract as the basis for the tacit relationship between subject and ruler, and a rejection of the unlimited monarchy embodied by the *imperium* of Henry VIII. The particular depiction of commonwealth was modelled on the Ciceronian ideal of a society of men, endeavouring to attain the common good through the bond of a common law. The aesthetic of these stylised theatrical events is axiomatic of an institution that seeks to depict itself as the archetypal representation of order, fairness and repressive tolerance. A sovereign state, simultaneously real and imaginary, was created during the revels. Although this Utopia was an artificial state, it was one with real constitutional powers. It was a mythical creation, inhabited not by people, but by archetypes of order and their opposites: destructive, natural forces that law seeks to contain and repress in the interests of the common good, through the imposition of artificial structure. Crucial to a credible thesis that the revels presented a template for the ideal state is acceptance of the idea that early modern government was partly an aesthetic process, dependent to a considerable extent on the

---

[24] P. Sidney, *The Old Arcadia*, ed. K. Duncan-Jones (Oxford University Press, 1985), p. 349.

medieval perception of symbolism, not as an illustration of reality but as reality itself.[25]

THE INNER TEMPLE REVELS, CHRISTMAS 1561: AN ENGLISH UTOPIA

The revels held at the Inner Temple during Christmas 1561 were of conspicuous and extraordinary extravagance. Although the queen did not personally attend, the monarch was represented by her favourite: 'the Lord Robert Dudley (afterwards earl of Leicester) was the Chief person (his title Palaphilos) being Constable and Marshall'.[26] That Dudley was the formal representative of Elizabeth can be immediately inferred from his symbolic title: in classical literature, Palaphilos was the High-Constable of the goddess of war, Pallas Athene, and the defender of her temple. In 1561 Dudley played a peripheral, though influential role in Elizabethan politics. After the accession of Elizabeth he was named Master of the Horse, although it was not until October 1562 that he was admitted to the Privy Council (he was created earl of Leicester in 1564).[27] The connection between art and government is further emphasised by the fact that Pallas Athene also presided over the arts and literature. The enactment of myth reflects the artifice of political community: the staging of the body politic represents the subjugation of the individual to the greater interest of the commonwealth. The symbolic integration of monarch and common law, enacted by Dudley and the revellers, was perceived in terms of an imagined Ancient Constitution, affected by both feudal and classical–republican principles of government. The brief pantomime staged in Inner Temple hall after dinner on St Stephen's Day, 1561, provided a resonant image of limited monarchy:

Supper ended, the Constable-Marshall presenteth himself with Drums afore him, mounted upon a Scaffold, born by four men; and goeth three times round about the Harthe, crying out aloud, A Lord, A Lord, etc. Then he descendeth and goeth to dance etc. and after he calleth his Court, every one by name, one by one, in this manner. Sir Francis Flatterer of Fowleshurst, in the County of Buckingham. Sir Randle Rackabite, of Rascall Hall, in the County of Rake Hell. Sir Morgan Mumchance, of Much Monkery, in the County of Mad Mopery. Sir Bartholemew Baldbreech, of Buttocksbury, in the County of Brekeneck.[28]

---

[25] On the relationship between symbolism and reality, see O. von Simson, *The Gothic Cathedral: Origins of Gothic Architecture and the Medieval Concept of Order* (New Jersey: Princeton University Press, 1988). Concerning architecture at the Inns of Court and the medieval perception of symbolism as reality, see J. Allibore and D. Evans, *The Inns of Court*, ed. D. McCorquodale (London: Black Dog, 1996), p. 158.

[26] Dugdale, *Origines Juridiciales*, fo. 150.

[27] See E. Jenkins, *Elizabeth and Leicester* (London: Phoenix, 2002); S. Adams (ed.), *Leicester and the Court: Essays on Elizabethan Politics* (Manchester University Press, 2002); D. Wilson, *Sweet Robin. Robert Dudley: Earl of Leicester 1533–1588* (London: Allison & Busby, 1997).

[28] Dugdale, *Origines Juridiciales*, fo. 156.

The alliterative and allegorical titles of the participants suggest well-defined and circumscribed symbolic positions and roles. The overriding image conformed to the classical idea of natural order, in which social structure and hierarchy were central components of the cosmos.[29] The symbolic ruler summons his knights, who perform the Aristotelian function of 'friends', or counsellors to the prince. Drawn from the landed English gentry, as Elyot advised in *The Book Named the Governor*, they act as *amici principis* to limit the power of the sovereign. The formulaic scene depicted above has broad connotations of the royal court, in which some of the young revellers intended to prosper. The solemnity with which these revels were conducted and their strict adherence to an unchanging and unchangeable formula demonstrate the importance of ritual and its undeviating repetition within the common law tradition.

A notable feature of political culture in Tudor England was the use of literature as a medium of advice to the ruler, an observation made by the fictional Raphael Hythlodaeus in Thomas More's *Utopia*. Into this broad category can be placed Elyot's *The Book Named the Governor*, St German's *Salem and Bizance* and Thomas Starkey's *Dialogue between Reginald Pole and Thomas Lupset*, which considers civic humanism in the context of the Venetian system of limited monarchy. The actual role of the counsellor in Elizabethan government was limited. The Acts of Supremacy and Uniformity confirmed the imperial governorship of Elizabeth I and announced as fact the inherent supremacy of the monarch. The constitutional primacy of the Tudor monarchy was founded upon Thomist providential theology, which affirmed the divine provenance of civil magistracy, thereby rendering the authority of Parliament irrelevant. It is noteworthy that, despite Burghley's insistence that 'our part is to counsel', the primary function of the Elizabethan Privy Council was administrative and judicial, rather than advisory. Furthermore, the size of the Privy Council had shrunk from 227 members in the reign of Henry VII to 19 in the first year of Elizabeth's reign; by 1597 there were only 11 members.[30]

The theatrical depiction of community and shared government, to which the actions of the Constable-Marshall and his 'court' alluded, implies the existence of an earlier, mythical age of ancient and immutable custom. The form of ritual described by Dugdale contrasts starkly with the ascetic régime observed throughout the remainder of the year. The following account is for one day's food at the Inner Temple during the Christmas period: '3 loins of mutton, 3s. 3d.; 39 marrow-bones, 14s. 8d.; 19 mallards, 25s. 4d.; 5lbs. suet, 2s. 6d.; milk, 6d.; 1 bushel of onions, 2s.; eggs, 11d.; flour, 12d.;

---

[29] On the Elizabethan perception of community and cosmic order, see E. Tillyard, *The Elizabethan World Picture* (London: Penguin, 1963), pp. 7–8.
[30] Guy, *Tudor England*, pp. 310, 438.

18 shoulders of mutton, 24s.; 20 dozen larks, 18s. 4d.; 5lbs. butter (supper 3 lbs., sauce 2 lbs.), 4s.; spice, fruit, and sugar, 9s. 11d.; 1 peck of salt, 6d.'[31] The contrast with the quotidian diet normally enjoyed by members is notable, but the communal enjoyment of feasting has a biblical precedent. Christ was aware that both ascetics and hedonists would offend certain factions in society: '[f]or John the Baptist has come eating no bread and drinking no wine; and you say, 'He has a demon'. The Son of Man has come eating and drinking; and you say, 'Behold, a glutton and a drunkard, a friend of tax collectors and sinners!' Yet wisdom is justified by all her children' (Luke 7. 33–35).[32] The above inventory from the Inner Temple is the sign of an ordered, lawful commonwealth. In antithetical fashion, the alliterative vulgarity of 'Sir Bartholomew Baldbreech of Buttocksbury' affirms the primacy of genealogy and strict delineation of hierarchy in the ordered community of common lawyers. In *The Third Universitie*, Buc refers to the authority of the familial father (as opposed to the symbolic fatherhood of the monarch) as the original of societal status, asserting that 'no man can be made a Gentleman but by his father. And (bee it spoken with all reverant reservation of Duty) the King (who hath power to make Esquiers, Knightes, Baronets, Barons, Vicounts, Earles, Marquesses, and Dukes) cannot make a Gentleman'.[33]

Wigfall Green suggests that the younger members of the Inns enjoyed parodying the law and its rituals at these prescribed times in the academic year, as a welcome release from the rigours of legal education.[34] Licensed parody was a form of repressive tolerance on the part of the governing bodies of the Inns; it encouraged superficial rebellion against formal practices and institutions in a form that did not threaten the established or diurnal life of the law. Committed study of the law required application and discipline; according to Sir John Doderidge, 'it is the worke of many yeares, the attaining whereof will waste the verdour and vigour of youth'.[35] It was expedient that part of the year should be dedicated to the pursuit of pleasure among junior members of the Inns, but it cannot seriously be argued that the Elizabethan

---

[31] *Calendar of The Inner Temple Records*, ed. F. A. Inderwick, 5 vols. (London: H. Sotheran, 1896), II, p. 87. Despite the insularity of common law, foreign foodstuffs eventually infiltrated the Inns: the Inner Temple account for Christmas 1615 includes 'biscuits and carraways, 9d.; eggs for "Florantynes", 2s. 6d.; . . . "Oryngadoe", 12d.', *ibid.*, II, p. 93.

[32] On the hierarchy of dining rituals in Luke's gospel and for a depiction of Christ as travelling benefactor and banqueter, see W. Braun, *Feasting and Social Rhetoric in Luke 14* (Cambridge University Press, 1995).

[33] G. Buc, *The Third Universitie of England* (London: Society of Stationers, 1615), fo. 968.

[34] A. Wigfall Green, *The Inns of Court and Early English Drama* (New Haven: Yale University Press, 1931).

[35] J. Doderidge, *The English Lawyer: Describing A Method for the managing of the Lawes of this Land* (London: I. More, 1631), p. 29.

revels represented a rejection of order. Neither did they denote acceptance of unlimited, absolute government. Rather, they implied adherence to a traditional code of manners or honour as the basis of ideal governance. The concern with establishing the ancient provenance of common law was of crucial importance during the sixteenth century, as common lawyers sought to prove the existence of an antecedent legal system, prior to and independent of the royal prerogative. Unsurprisingly therefore, the practice of 'ancient' English custom at the Inns was considered to be of equal, if not greater, importance than knowledge of substantive law.

Fewer than one hundred years before the Christmas revels of 1561, Fortescue implied that the Inns of Court resembled the Academies and Gymnasia of the classical world, 'where they learn Singing, and all Kinds of Music, Dancing and such other Accomplishments and Diversions'.[36] Sir Henry Spelman allegedly joined Lincoln's Inn because membership of an Inn was generally considered 'as a useful Accomplishment of an English Gentleman'.[37] Implicit in the description offered by Fortescue is the claim that substantive educational exercises were less relevant to common law ideology than awareness of the traditions embodied in the unwritten constitution. These ancient traditions were visualised by common lawyers and depicted through the imagistic medium of the revels. Dugdale's *Origines Juridiciales*, which equates the history of English law with the institutional development of the legal profession at the Inns of Court, suggests that emphasis on formal, non-academic activities at the Inns of the sixteenth and early seventeenth centuries remained strong. The Inns were, above all, zealous observers of order and custom. Common law was characterised by jurists from Fortescue to Coke as ancient custom bestowed with judicial and divine authority: 'England has nevertheless been constantly governed by the same Customs, as it is at present: Which if they were not above all Exception Good, no Doubt but some or other of those Kings from a Principle of Justice, in Point of Reason, or mov'd by Inclination, would have made some Alteration or quite abolished them.'[38] As Bakhtin suggests, custom and familiarity confer on their subjects a certain level of freedom and a concomitant right to invert social norms.[39] This is of particular relevance to the revels, in which the inversion of conventional hierarchy augmented rather than diminished the importance of custom in the diurnal life of the legal community. In symbolic terms, the freedom and familiarity implied by custom were representative

---

[36] Fortescue, *De Laudibus*, p. 110.
[37] H. Spelman, *The English Works of Sir Henry Spelman, Kt.* (London: D. Browne, 1723), fo. a1.
[38] Fortescue, *De Laudibus*, p. 30.
[39] M. Bakhtin, *Rabelais and His World*, trans. H. Iswolsky (Bloomington: Indiana University Press, 1984), p. 200.

also of the equitable principles of common law and the inherent flexibility of a fair and just legal system.

In *The English Utopia*, Morton observes that common to the different fictional depictions of the ideal state are the conditions of self-sufficiency and exclusivity.[40] The Land of Cockaygne, for example, is temperate in climate, with fruits permanently in season and excellent soil, and is surrounded by sweet-tasting seawater. The inhabitants of this insular dreamland are unique, privileged and uncontaminated by contact with the chaotic world beyond their shores. This artificial environment was represented by the revels, in which exclusivity was undeniably a major effect. The walls surrounding the Inns, and the rules applied within, were indicative of an autonomous state – the realm of common law, in which the legal profession was the sovereign political body. The unique, fantastical character of the revels was unimpeachable and immune from external interference because an independent legal profession had determined and approved their form and content. Given that the revels were held to celebrate specific, Christian feast-days, the celebrations and rituals that attached to them were peculiarly pagan in nature. Dugdale relates the following account of the extraordinary events that followed the serving of the first course, during dinner at the Inner Temple on St Stephen's Day, 1561:

> Then cometh in the Master of the Game apparalled in green Velvet: and the Ranger of the Forest also, in a green suit of Satten; bearing in his hand a green Bow, and divers Arrows, with either of them a Hunting Horn about their Necks; blowing together three blasts of Venery, they pace round about the fire three times . . . This Ceremony also performed, a Huntsman cometh into the Hall, with a Fox and a Purse-net; with a Cat, both bound at the end of a staff; and with them nine or ten Couple of Hounds, with the blowing of Hunting-Hornes. And the Fox and Cat are by the Hounds set upon, and killed beneath the Fire.[41]

This extract illustrates the correlation between the Inns of Court, the royal court and the courts of justice: the role of Master of the Game was played by a future Lord Chancellor, Christopher Hatton.[42] The resemblance to pagan sacrifice is obvious: blood is spilt, a sacrifice is made and order is imposed by the Constable-Marshall, who ensures that the participants return to their 'appointed places'.[43]

The scene had a symbolic and didactic function, suggesting an ancient, golden age and (like the pantomime of the Constable-Marshall and his Lords) the idyll of 'Merry England': a land rich in forests and game, where archetypes of heroic, English nationhood exercised their ancient rights and

---

[40] A. L. Morton, *The English Utopia* (London: Lawrence & Wishart, 1952), p. 12. On the depiction of medieval Utopias, see H. Pleij, *Dreaming of Cockaigne: Medieval Fantasies of the Perfect Life*, trans. D. Webb (New York: Columbia University Press, 2001).
[41] Dugdale, *Origines Juridiciales*, ff. 155–6.   [42] *Ibid.*, fo. 150.   [43] *Ibid.*, fo. 156.

customs.⁴⁴ The fictional depiction of nationhood resembled the England described by Fortescue, a realm in which 'the Inhabitants are Rich in Gold, Silver, and in all the Necessaries and Conveniencies of Life'.⁴⁵ He attributed their felicitous condition to the inherent equity of the English legal system, suggesting that this unique quality of fairness was absent from the French legal system, which Fortescue characterised as arbitrary and unjust. The images of nationhood offered by Fortescue and the Inner Temple revellers were Utopian representations, but their rhetorical power lay in the iconic resonance of those images.⁴⁶ Ward makes the important observation that the Reformation had destabilised English provincial life by destroying the rituals determined by church festivals, thus posing a threat to local order and signalling for some a rejection of English mores.⁴⁷ The pastoral scene, enacted as described above at the Inner Temple, is a secular image intended to enhance the impression of an English nation, whose customs and laws were unique. Such a commonwealth was constructed around the principle of shared government, in which the trinity of civil magistrate, *amici principis* and active citizenry codetermine the form and content of the body politic.

Regular attendance by royalty and members of the royal court at these festive occasions necessitated considerable planning and expense by the Inns. From the ranks of junior members were elected stewards, marshals, and butlers: 'Elections for Christmas offices: Steward – Masters L. Arscott, Hunte, Hone and Welche. Marshal – William Thornhyll, Robert Mordaunte, John Butler, George Swyllyngton, Robert Balam, Edward Hasylwoode, John Vavasour, esquires. Butler – Nicholas Vaux, Edmund Mordaunte, senior, esquires'.⁴⁸ The members created a hierarchic society in which archetypes of service and order predominated. The duties incumbent on these offices were onerous; even during periods of celebration, role-playing was an essential part of the barrister's training, and was therefore accorded appropriate solemnity. The enactment of these seasonal offices was partly a didactic exercise, representing the natural hierarchy of the cosmic order. Failure to fulfil an allotted role rendered the offender liable to punishment by his Inn: '[i]f the Steward, or any of the said Officers named in Trinity Term, refuse or fail, he or they were fined every one, at the discretion of the Bench.'⁴⁹

The role of the 'Christmas' steward was of important practical significance, as he was responsible for paying the baker, brewer, chandler, and all the other

---

⁴⁴ See R. Hutton, *The Rise and Fall of Merry England* (Oxford University Press, 1994).
⁴⁵ Fortescue, *De Laudibus*, p. 83.
⁴⁶ On the image of law as an icon of an absent order, as well as a sign of degree and lineage, see P. Goodrich, *Oedipus Lex: Psychoanalysis, History, Law* (Los Angeles: University of California Press, 1995), pp. 108–14.
⁴⁷ Ward, *Legal Imagination*, p. 205.
⁴⁸ *Middle Temple Records*, I, p. 98.   ⁴⁹ Dugdale, *Origines Juridiciales*, fo. 153.

officers charged with serving the Inn during the Christmas period.[50] Election to this office demonstrated also the entrustment to him of the corporeal and spiritual welfare of fellow members. The role of the steward or householder has an important precedent in the events that preceded the original Eucharistic rite. Christ instructed his disciples to 'tell the householder, "The Teacher says to you, Where is the guest room, where I am to eat the passover with my disciples?" And he will show you a large upper room furnished; there make ready' (Luke 22. 8–12).[51] The acknowledged importance of the steward to the success of the Christmas festivities added an extra comic dimension to the performance of Shakespeare's *Twelfth Night* at the Middle Temple on Candlemas Day (2 February), 1602. Performed during the revels, forty years after the Inner Temple revels discussed above, the play demonstrates that the depiction of the English Utopia was a recurrent theme at the Inns of Court throughout the reign of Elizabeth.

Despite its Illyrian setting, the world of *Twelfth Night* is recognisably an agrarian English society, governed by a landed élite. The steward to the Countess Olivia, Malvolio, refuses to indulge the drunken excesses of the principal revellers, Sir Toby Belch and Sir Andrew Aguecheek. Malvolio's unpardonable fault (apart from opposing the spirit of disorder and misrule, which characterised the revels) is to reprimand his social superiors, and to believe that he could marry his mistress, Olivia. Paradoxically, although he appears to oppose all forms of disorder, Malvolio aspires to subvert the accepted norms of English society, according to which status was determined at birth. On the differences between ancient and modern law, Maine noted that in ancient law social position was fixed irreversibly at birth, whereas modern law allowed it to be created by convention. Under the ancient system, rules were derived from the station into which a person was born and from imperative commands addressed by the head of the household.[52] The marriage of a steward to a countess would, in classical terms, threaten the natural cosmic order.

The revellers at the Inns paid homage to the notion of an ideal order by their adherence to formulaic ritual and the portrayal of archetypal representatives of a feudal society. Shakespeare alludes to the revels and seasonal feasting throughout *Twelfth Night*, and in Sir Andrew Aguecheek he affectionately parodies the knight of the English shires whose formal education was traditionally concluded at the Inns of Court. Sir Andrew confesses that

---

[50] *Ibid.*, fo. 149.
[51] On the ritual of the Last Supper, its provenance and symbolism, see E. O. James, *Christian Myth and Ritual* (London: J. Murray, 1933).
[52] H. Maine, *Ancient Law* (London: Dent, 1917), p. 179.

'I delight in masques and revels sometimes altogether',[53] and despite his intellectual deficiencies is, by accident of birth, a member of the governing nobility. He represents a sense of English nationhood, founded upon the continuity of ancient custom and an acknowledgment of the central role played by a hereditary élite in the local governance of communities. Knights such as Sir Andrew often served simultaneously as royal courtiers, MPs and country justices.[54] Relevant to the depiction of government in Elizabethan England is not only the fact that Malvolio is 'a kind of puritan',[55] but that his downfall and humiliation is conceived and executed by the archetypes of immemorial English custom, Sir Andrew Aguecheek and Sir Toby Belch. It would be speculative to suggest that Malvolio's final line, 'I'll be revenged on the whole pack of you!'[56] presaged the momentous events of the 1640s, but the inclusion of this character suggests an awareness by Shakespeare of discontent in certain quarters with the prevailing system of governance.[57]

Richard Hooker's appointment in 1585 as master of Temple church (at which frequent discourse on the subject of predestination took place)[58] ensured that theological and political debate concerning puritanism were central to the institutional existence of the Inner Temple and the Middle Temple. Of great interest, concerning the possible influence of Hooker's thinking on the legal profession, was the elevated status of the master of Temple church within the hierarchy of both the Middle and the Inner Temple: '[h]is dyet he hath in either House at the upper end of the Benchers Table'.[59] Hooker's refutation of puritan criticism and the debate over his proposed religious and constitutional settlement became more widespread after the publication of Books I–V of *Of the Laws of Ecclesiastical Polity* between 1594 and 1597. The ceremonial and formulaic form of the Inns of Court revels was closely linked with Hooker's insistence on the crucial role of sacraments and ceremony within the Church. Once differentiated from popish idolatry,

---

[53] *Twelfth Night*, I. iii. 107–8. On *Twelfth Night* and Elizabethan society, see S. Greenblatt, *Shakespearean Negotiations: The Circulation of Social Energy in Renaissance England* (Berkeley: University of California Press, 1988); also G. Holderness (ed.), *Shakespeare: Out of Court* (London: Macmillan, 1990).

[54] Guy, *Tudor England*, p. 389.   [55] *Twelfth Night*, II. iii. 134.   [56] *Ibid.*, V. i. 375.

[57] While citing Clarendon's observation in *History of the Rebellion and Civil Wars* that 'I am not so sharp-sighted as those, who have discerned this rebellion contriving from (if not before) the death of Queen Elizabeth', Guy concedes that lack of intervention by Elizabeth in the 1590s and increased corruption at the royal court made the possibility of voluntary reform unlikely, Guy, *Tudor England*, p. 456.

[58] A. Cromartie, 'Theology and Politics in Richard Hooker's Thought', *History of Political Thought*, 21 (2000), 47.

[59] Dugdale, *Origines Juridiciales*, fo. 173. The Master is appointed 'by the King's Letters Patents, who hath administred the Sacraments, and performed other Divine service therein, without any Institution or Induction, as in other Churches, by the Bishop', *ibid.*

ceremonial forms could be reclaimed as symbols not only of a unique English church and state, but also of the unbroken relationship between these institutions and the Christian past. As Lake has argued, Hooker's reclamation of symbol and ritual from the Roman Church assisted in the rehabilitation of the image as a unique and important medium through which communication and instruction could be effected.[60]

The relative authority of text and sign was the basis of the theological dispute between Hooker and the Calvinist divine, Walter Travers, the latter complaining that Hooker predicated belief in God upon the perception of the senses rather than the written word.[61] The imagistic medium of the Inns of Court revels demonstrates the importance of ceremony and unwritten law to the claims of common law sovereignty. Legal ritual of purported antique origin implied that the institutional authority of common law was prior to, independent of, and took precedence over the textual authority of statutes and proclamations. The revels were notable for their deferential references both to ancient customs and the legitimacy that immemorial provenance conferred upon images of order:

> The Marshall at Dinner is to place at the highest Tables end . . . the most antient persons in the Company, present: The Dean of the Chapell next to him: then an Antient, or Bencher, beneath him. At the other end of the Table, the Sewer, Cupbearer, and Carver . . . When the first Table is set and served, the Steward's Table is next to be served. After him, the Masters table of the Revells: Then that of the Master of the Game. The high Constable-Marshall: Then the Lieutenant of the Tower: then the Utter-Baristers table; and lastly the Clerks table.[62]

Synonymous with age and seniority, or ancient standing, are legitimacy and authority. Common law derived authority from its venerable status; the Inns honoured that fact by showing appropriate respect to their own ancients, placing them at the 'highest' table. Similar respect for seniority was demonstrated after dinner, during the formal dancing: 'the Auncient, with his white staff, advanceth forward, and begins to lead the measures; followed, first by the Baristers, and then the Gentlemen under the Bar, all according to their several antiquities'.[63] As at moots and readings, and in the courts of justice, junior members of the Inn observed the repetition of ritual performed by the oldest and most learned members. In the above ceremony, the individual was subsumed into the corporate identity of common law through the stylised actions of the ancient who, physically and symbolically, demonstrated the measured steps that must be taken if wisdom was to be attained. Junior members imitated the actions of their elders, having shown deference by serving

---

[60] P. Lake, *Anglicans and Puritans? Presbyterianism and English Conformist Thought from Whitgift to Hooker* (London: Unwin Hyman, 1988), p. 165.
[61] Cromartie, 'Richard Hooker's Thought', 54.
[62] Dugdale, *Origines Juridiciales*, fo. 154.   [63] *Ibid.*, fo. 204.

them at dinner: 'Upon great Festival days the Gentlemen of the Inner Bar do serve up into the Hall, the first and second Course from the Dresser.'[64]

The revels were as significant to the spiritual life of common lawyers as the religious act of dining in hall, at which God and common law were symbolically unified and eaten. They were rhetorical devices, intended to depict the dreamland of perfect order. Regulations governing the form of conviviality imply a realm in which each minute action was controlled and ordered. There could be no clearer sign of community, hierarchy and order than the ancient, with his white staff, leading the dancing, followed in strict order of seniority by the utter-barristers and inner-barristers. At a doctrinal level, the revels demonstrated the adherence of the Inns of Court to the theology of Richard Hooker and its emphasis on the continued centrality of ritual to the post-Reformation English church. Symbol and ceremony were the demonstrable means through which the coextensive nature of state, church and commonwealth could be expressed.

EASTERN INFLUENCES ON THE ENGLISH UTOPIA

In the context of the Inner Temple, the hunting scene enacted at the revels of 1561 reinforced the fiction that common law was derived exclusively from ancient English custom.[65] The pastoral idyll and the ecstatic celebration of nature and the earth had their foundations in the Dionysian revels of ancient Greece, the influence of whose myths was gaining momentum in England during the sixteenth century. Mythical allusions are a salient feature of the description by Gerard Legh of his visit to the Inner Temple revels of 1561. Like Dionysus before him, Legh 'had traveiled through the Easte partes of thunknowen world'.[66] The traditions of Dionysus and (in Rome) of Bacchus were foreign to the English. They arrived from Europe and primarily through the church, the principal importer of the Latin tradition. The indigenous culture was Druidic and pagan, and contained its own rituals, which (like those of ancient Greece) paid homage to the earth and its produce.

The rites of ancient Greek sacrifice resembled the form of the feast attended by Legh. These included the wearing of ornate costume and processing to the sacrificial site, accompanied by music. The Inner Temple hall was the sacred precinct of common law in which the ritual was enacted; its walls replicated the circumference of the circle described by the participants in

---

[64] Ibid., fo. 158.
[65] On common law, custom and the English constitution, see J. G. A. Pocock, *The Ancient Constitution and the Feudal Law: A Study of English Historical Thought in the Seventeenth Century* (Cambridge University Press, 1987), a definitive analysis of early modern common law ideology and the 'immemorial' origins of the Ancient Constitution.
[66] G. Legh, *The Accedens of Armory* (London: R. Tottel, 1576), fo. 119a.

Greek sacrifice. At the Inner Temple feast of Christmas 1561, breadbaskets and water jugs were carried by servants; in ancient Greek ritual a basket of grain and a water jug were used to restate the act of consecration.[67] Legh's account demonstrates the enthusiasm with which the English legal institution was embracing the rediscovery and reinterpretation of ancient Greek mythology and ritual, and the facility with which these customs were assimilated into its indigenous, cultural practices. For example, when Legh writes of his encounter with Palaphilos in the grounds of the Inner Temple, his intention is to convince the reader that the mythical guardian of Pallas Athene's temple has been transported to England: '[a]nd emongest other, pleasauntlye washte over tholde forworen Temples, dedicate to Godes, as places meete for Pallas Muses, to inhabite and make there pastance. Where nowe is placed a souldier that doth defend the same, named Pallaphilos, the highe constable of the Goddesse her selfe, marshall of thinner Temple.'[68]

Legh's description of the Inner Temple reflects his sense of wonder at the images he encountered. An ordered structure was imposed on the convivial proceedings, and especially on the order of food; degeneration into lawlessness and Dionysian excess was proscribed. Legh describes 'tender meates, sweete fruites and dainty delicates, confectioned with curious Cookery: as it seemed wonder, a worlde to serve the provision'.[69] The notion of decadence suggested by the 'tender meates' and 'dainty delicates' belongs most clearly in this context to the monastic traditions, the excesses of which were offered by Protestant reformers as justification for the dissolution of the monasteries.[70] Analysis of the feast described by Legh reveals not a decadent institution but an ordered one that regularly, but not frequently (once a year), celebrates its majesty and timeless origin in a ritualised feast. Significantly, the feast occurred at Christmas, the celebration of the Word made flesh. It is the 'wonder' of the law (to which Legh alludes in the above passage) that was celebrated, and this quality manifested itself in the order of food: the meat was tender, the fruit was sweet and the 'delicates' dainty. Nature (in the form of the meat, fruit and other foodstuffs) was subjected to man's reason.

Concerning the act of eating, Bakhtin suggests that food represents the vanquished world and that its consumption symbolises the renewed vigour of the body and its victory over the world.[71] He further notes that one of the

---

[67] G. Hersey, *The Lost Meaning of Classical Architecture* (Cambridge, Mass.: MIT, 1988), p. 15. On Greek sacrificial rites, see W. Burket, *Homo necans: The Anthropology of Ancient Greek Sacrificial Ritual and Myth* (Berkeley: University of California Press, 1983).
[68] Legh, *The Accedens*, fo. 118b.   [69] *Ibid.*, fo. 123b.
[70] On the dissolution of the monasteries, see Guy, *Tudor England*, pp. 143–50.
[71] Bakhtin, *Rabelais*, p. 283.

most powerful images of man's encounter with the world is the mouth, and especially its capacity to open, bite and chew, by which means the world is symbolically tasted, introduced to the body and subjugated to the domination of mankind.[72] At the feast described by Legh, common law symbolically asserted its sovereignty and celebrated the Word made flesh – the law given corporeal substance. Order was ensured and enforced by the formal procession that accompanied the serving of food: '[a]t the first Course is served in a fair and large Bores-head, upon a Silver Platter, with Minstralsye. Two Gentlemen in Gownes are to attend at Supper, and to bear two fair Torches of Wax, next before the Musicians and Trumpetters, and stand above the Fire with the Musick, till the first Course be served in, through the Hall'.[73] Such reverence denoted the presence of deity: God was represented and substituted in the exquisite, ordered presentation of the feast. As Marin has noted of the prefix 're-', it introduces the idea of substitution, or the representation of an absent presence. Bakhtin alludes to this *re*-presentation with reference to the divine status accorded the sacrificial victim, and the procession that preceded it. The sacrificial ox processed to the accompaniment of musical instruments before its ritual slaughter, in accordance with the customs of the carnival. The ox was a symbol both of kingship and of the fecundity of the city, but it was simultaneously the sacrificial offering.[74] The ceremonial pomp that the minstrels, torchbearers, and trumpeters provided for the accompaniment of the first course was a prelude to the sacramental act of dining. In similar iconic fashion, the Middle Temple celebrated the Feast of All Saints: 'the Ancient, hath a white staff in his hand, the other a white Rod, with which they usher in the meat, following next after the Musick'.[75] The choice of words is noteworthy: the meat was 'ushered in' ceremoniously, marking the sacred moment when the Eucharist begins and the presence of God is invoked.

On holy days, which merited these feasts, attendance at church services and communal prayer was compulsory.[76] But the greater part of these days was devoted to eating, singing and dancing. In ancient Greece, Dionysus was worshipped with tumultuous processions in which the spirits of the earth and of fecundity appeared, their likenesses evoked by masks. The procession is a symbol of community or bonding, and was a notable feature of feasts at the Inns of Court. The status of each member in the immutable hierarchy of the Inn was reflected by his position in the procession. Like their Dionysian predecessors, participants in the revels wore symbolic costumes and masks.

[72] *Ibid.*, p. 281.   [73] Dugdale, *Origines Juridiciales*, fo. 155.
[74] L. Marin, *Portrait of the King*, trans. M. M. Houle (Basingstoke: Macmillan 1988), p. 5; Bakhtin, *Rabelais*, p. 202.
[75] Dugdale, *Origines Juridiciales*, fo. 204
[76] *Ibid.*, fo. 148; see also Wigfall Green, *The Inns of Court*, p. 10.

At the Inner Temple on St. Stephen's Day 1561, 'after the first Course served in, the Constable Marshall cometh into the Hall, arrayed with a fair, rich, compleat Harneys, white and bright, and gilt; with a Nest of Fethers of all Colours upon his Crest or Helm, and a gilt Pole-axe in his hand'.[77] The Constable Marshall was accompanied by halberdiers, drummers and trumpeters, befitting his elevated status. He was, according to Legh, 'an Herehaught' or king of arms, a symbol of flawless genealogy and a sign that the Inner Temple was an honourable place. The code of honour represented by martial iconography performed an important function in medieval law. For example, in the twelfth century a litigant could defend his right to land through the verdict of twelve knights of the grand assize, rather than by doing battle.[78]

The signal achievement of *The Accedens of Armory* was to integrate the medieval images of English nobility with those of Greek mythology in order to suggest the unique provenance and sovereignty of the early modern English legal system. Only Legh's status as a man of honour gave him access to the revels. He describes himself as a stranger, and legislation of the respective governing bodies prohibited the participation of strangers (and foreigners) in the rituals of the Inns, particularly during the Christmas period. Legislation was enacted at the Inner Temple to the effect '[t]hat no Stranger ... should be admitted to take any Repast, or be in commons in the time of Christmas, or to be present at any of the Christmas Parliaments.'[79] Insularity was at least partly a response to the insidious threat of rival, continental jurisdictions. Fortescue recognised the incipient danger and couched the polemical dialogue of *De Laudibus Legum Angliae* in appropriate nationalist terms. Common law was unique to England and taught only at the Inns of Court.[80] The abhorrence of strangers can therefore be seen to reflect not only the xenophobic instincts of common lawyers, but also the institutional fear of scrutiny, criticism and rejection. Rules prohibiting the admittance of aliens served to preserve and enhance the mystical aura of exclusivity and sanctity with which the Inns of Court actively sought to imbue the common law.

As Legh approached the Temple, he was surprised to hear 'the shott of double Canons in so great a number, and so terrible that it darkened the whole aire'.[81] On meeting the Constable Marshall, Legh is told that the

[77] Dugdale, *Origines Juridiciales*, fo. 155.
[78] P. Brand, *The Origins of the English Legal Profession* (Oxford University Press, 1992), p. 18.
[79] Dugdale, *Origines Juridiciales*, fo. 149.
[80] The rudiments of common law were studied at the Inns of Chancery: 'here they Study the Nature of Original and Judicial Writs, which are the very first Principles of the Law: After they have made some Progress here, and are more advanced in Years, they are admitted to the Inns of Court', Fortescue, *De Laudibus*, p. 110.
[81] Legh, *The Accedens*, fo. 119a.

purpose of the cannon-fire was to summon members of the Inner Temple to dinner. Of course, a bell would have performed this function as effectively, but it would not have suggested the autonomy of the Inner Temple and the associated sovereignty of common law. It is not only in a metaphorical sense that it is possible to describe the precincts of the Inns as representing the realm of law. Although the Temple was in London (Gray's Inn and Lincoln's Inn were in Middlesex), it has always been outside the jurisdiction of the City. As well as being a warning to members to prepare for dinner, the cannon-fire was an aural representation of the authority and independence of the common law.[82] Not only did the Inner Temple represent the symbolic realm of common law; it was literally a separate state, at the borders of which external jurisdictions ceased to apply.[83] The power of common law was demonstrated at dinner, where 'at every course, the Trompettes blewe the coragious blaste of deadlye warre, with noyse of dromme and fyffe'.[84] Marin has suggested that power is the ability to exert an action on something or someone, to have the force to do or act. In other words, power is to have a reserve of force that is not expended but that is in a state of being expendable. Its importance in the context of the above symbols is that representation puts force into signs.[85]

Legh's narrative describes an independent realm, whose model was the ideal city-states of ancient Greece, conceived by Plato in *The Republic*. There, the principle of governance was founded on the acknowledgment by all citizens of their respective duties and rights. Hence, Palaphilos is 'an honest Citizin' who prognosticates 'rather peace than peril'. Central to Legh's account is the implied existence of the freethinking, rational individual as an equable subject of law. Such an acknowledgment anticipates the Kantian principle that it is only as an autonomous moral being that man can be acknowledged as the purpose of creation.[86] Legh describes the Inner Temple as a 'province . . . auncient in trewe nobilitie. A place said he [Palaphilos] privileged by the most excellent princes, the highe governour of the Whole Iland, wherein are the store of Gentilmen of the whole Realme, that repair thither to learne to rule, and obeye by lawe, to yeelde there fleece to there prince and common weale'.[87] These prototypes of governance were

---

[82] In relation to the conversation between Narcissus and Echo in Ovid's *Metamorphoses*, Legendre suggests that images can be aural and that the idea that images are necessarily visual is essentially a modern one, *Law and the Unconscious: A Legendre Reader*, ed. P. Goodrich (Basingstoke: Macmillan, 1997), p. 216.

[83] D. Evans, 'The Inns of Court: Speculations on the Body of Law', *Arch-Text* 1 (1993), 17. On the metaphorical and physical boundaries of the Inns, see Allibore and Evans, *The Inns of Court*.

[84] Legh, *The Accedens*, fo. 123b.   [85] Marin, *Portrait of the King*, pp. 1–9.

[86] I. Kant, *The Critique of Judgment*, ed. J. Meredith (Oxford: Clarendon, 1991), pp. 110–12.

[87] Legh, *The Accedens*, fo. 119a.

personified by the various human representations of the common law ethos, whose participation in the events of the Inner Temple revels is recorded in *The Accedens of Armory*. In his narrative of events, Legh depicts himself as the ingenuous, impressionable figure of Everyman, a 'straunger' in the 'Iland' of the common law.[88] Palaphilos, the constable-marshall of the Inner Temple, is symbolic guardian of the legal institution, while the prince is the personification of human, natural and divine law. The narrative is related entirely in the first person singular. For example, '[t]he next day I thought for my pastime to walk to this temple, and enteringe in at the gates, I found the building nothing costly.'[89] But Legh's description of events is not only characterised by its subjectivity, it is notable also for the symbolic roles that he attaches to the protagonists of his narrative. In his evocative account these characters become prototypes of a social and legal order, incorporating elements of indigenous English culture, the Latin tradition and Neoplatonic humanism. In the legal system of which the Inner Temple (as described by Legh) is the microcosm, these three elements are coextensive and indivisible. Goodrich interprets *The Accedens of Armory* as an exposition of a figurative form of rhetoric at the Inn, through which the symbolic order of law can be understood and represented.[90] His analysis emphasises the importance of genealogy to the legal profession and the bonds of community that the revels nourished and enforced. In this context, *The Accedens of Armory* is at the forefront of an extensive literature that interprets the Inns of Court as embodiments of the ideal commonwealth. The ethical values of Neoplatonic humanism and the virtues of the ancient city-states cannot be extricated from the ecclesiastical polity inherent in their constitutions.

Dugdale's account of the same revels at the Inner Temple is concerned with reporting the order of quotidian existence, established during this period of prolonged celebration. So, for example, he notes that at one feast '[t]here were brought to the slaughter House twenty four great Beefes at 01l. 06s. 08d. the piece. From the Shambles one Carcass of an Oxe at 01. 04. 00. One hundred fat Muttons at 00. 02. 10. a piece. Fifty one great Veales at 00. 04. 08. a piece. Thirty four Porkes 00. 03. 03. a piece.'[91] Legh communicates a sense of the unique otherness of the Inner Temple and the events witnessed there. He implies that the world of the Inn is as mysterious and wonderful as the East, whence he has recently returned. Legh's literary style enhances the aura of mystery that surrounded the Inner Temple and its secret rites. It was an ideal state, the predilections, prejudices and arcane knowledge of whose subjects distanced and excluded it from the world beyond its walls.

[88] *Ibid.*, ff. 120a, 119a.   [89] *Ibid.*, fo. 120a.
[90] P. Goodrich, 'Eating Law: Commons, Common Land, Common Law', *The Journal of Legal History*, 12 (1991), 248.
[91] Dugdale, *Origines Juridiciales*, fo. 128.

The allusions to divine figures from Greek mythology and references to the ancient status of the Inner Temple suggest also that this strange world was inhabited by mythical heroes and archetypes of institutional probity. When Legh describes the order of dining, he is describing the order of a lawful world: '[t]hus the hall was served after moste auncient order of the Iland, in commendacion whereof I saye: I have also sene the service of greate princes, in solempne seasons and times of triumph, yet thorder hereof was not inferior to any.'[92] He makes the necessary imaginative leap from attending a feast at which only lawyers were present to being a visitor in the sovereign commonwealth of common law. The order of the 'Iland' to which he refers is the insular realm of the Inner Temple: an independent state, whose practices reflected the artificial reason and unchanging perfection of common law. He respects the customs and authority of the lawgivers without questioning their legitimacy or the source of their authority. He concurs with most Elizabethan commentators, who asserted that the origins of English law were traceable to no specific time, but had been handed down from God to His appointed representatives on earth. The foundation of common law had been variously attributed to Brutus, King Arthur, Romulus and Remus, Moses, the Druids and Lycurgus of Sparta.[93] Legh compounds the sense of mystery by arriving from the East, and as a stranger, like Dionysus before him. He refers not to Brutus or any other of the putative founders of English law listed above, but to heroic, divine archetypes drawn from classical mythology: Pallas Athene and her constable, Palaphilos.

Above all, Legh's account demonstrates that the aesthetics of English law were shaped during the early years of Elizabeth's reign by the classical and continental influences of the Renaissance. The associated implications of an active citizenry within a city-state are clear: the common-wealth, or *res publica*, existed for the good of the community, not for the private benefit of the ruler. This constitutional principle was expounded towards the end of Elizabeth's reign by Richard Hooker.[94] Although Hooker believed that monarchy was the best form of government, the correlation between Aristotelian republican ideals and common law ideology is expressed with

---

[92] Legh, *The Accedens*, fo. 123b.
[93] Coke refers variously to Brutus, King Arthur, Solon, and Romulus and Remus as founders of English law; see E. Coke, *The Reports*, 7 vols. (London: Rivington, 1777), Part II, p. B1a; Part IX, p. C2. Moses is cited in W. Lambard, *Archeion or Discourse upon the High Courts of Justice in England* (London: Seile, 1591); the Druids and Lycurgus of Sparta are mentioned in H. Spelman, *Of the Four Law Term: A Discourse* (London: Gillyflower, 1684). On the mythical hero as an archetype of nationhood, empire and religion, see S. Freud, 'Moses and Monotheism', in *The Origins of Religion*, trans. J. Strachey (London: Penguin, 1990), pp. 246–7.
[94] Cromartie notes that 'common-wealth' was an early modern translation of '*Res Publica*': Cromartie, 'Transformation of Political Culture', 100.

great clarity in *Of the Laws of Ecclesiastical Polity*. Hooker's view that kingship derived from the community rather than divine right finds its practical expression in Coke's belief that judges were authorised to restrict the exercise of the royal prerogative for the ultimate benefit of the English subject.

DIVINE RIGHT, PATRIARCHY AND COMMON LAW

The conduct of the revels at the Inns of Court during the last decade of Tudor rule reflects the confidence of the legal profession to challenge threats posed to its judicial supremacy by the arbitrary jurisdiction of the monarch. The divine right of kings was a thesis originally proposed by the Master of Trinity College, Cambridge, John Whitgift, prior to his elevation to the archbishopric of Canterbury in 1583. Its purpose was pragmatic: to attempt to justify the supreme governorship of the Church of England by a civil magistrate, in response to criticism from the Presbyterian leader, Thomas Cartwright. The Presbyterian principles of congregational autonomy, ministerial equality and the hierarchy of synods were ultimately incompatible with Tudor monarchic government. Central to Presbyterian polity were the distinction between governance of state and church and a rejection of the idea that monarchic authority was divinely ordained.[95] During the last two decades of Elizabeth's reign, use of the royal prerogative was increasingly justified on the basis that the queen was God's lieutenant and that therefore the authority of Parliament was unnecessary. The patriarchal model of government, which the divine right of kings appeared to sanction, was irreconcilable with the attachment of common lawyers to Bracton's dictum that the king was under God and the law, because the law makes the king.

In *The Governance of England*, Fortescue invoked biblical authority for the constitutional model of mixed monarchy. He articulated the concern, expressed by Hooker more than a hundred years later, that a society which recognised the crown as its supreme governor and lawmaker was not necessarily one best placed to interpret and act upon the will of God. He enunciated the intrinsic nationalism of common law, citing the Bible as authority for the establishment of an ideal legal system within the English state. He distinguished between two systems of government: *dominium regale* and *dominium politicum et regale*. Under the former system, the 'kynge mey rule his peple bi suche lawes as he makyth hym self'; under the latter, the 'kynge may not rule his peple bi other lawes than such as thai assenten unto'.[96] Broadly, this is the distinction that Fortescue made between civil law and

---

[95] See J. Guy, 'The Elizabethan Establishment and the Ecclesiastical Polity', in J. Guy (ed.), *The Reign of Elizabeth I: Court and Culture in the Last Decade* (Cambridge University Press, 1995), pp. 127–8; see also Lake, *Anglicans and Puritans?*, intro., pp. 1–2.
[96] Fortescue, *Governance of England*, p. 109.

common law, adjudging the former to be implicitly unjust. The fundamental injustice of civil law (with specific reference to the French legal system) is a principal theme of *De Laudibus Legum Angliae*. It is one to which Fortescue returned in *The Governance of England*, using the identical metaphor of an oppressed and hungry populace: '[t]hai drinken water, thai eyten apples, with brede right browne made of rye; thai eyten no flesshe but yf it be right seldom a little larde, or of the entrales and heydes of bestis slayn for the nobles and marchauntes of the lande'.[97]

The following three principles pertain to *dominium politicum et regale*, as envisaged by Fortescue. First, the judiciary is the sovereign arbiter of legal dispute and interpretation within the constitution; second, the primary function of the judiciary is to perform a sacerdotal role, acting as the divinely appointed link between the ultimate ruler, God Almighty, and his subjects on earth; and third, the crown performs a subordinate role within this judicial system. *The Governance of England* locates political sovereignty in the officers of the law: '[t]he childeryn of Israell, as saith Seynt Thomas, after that God hade chosen thaim *in populum peculiarem et regnum sacerdotale*, were ruled by hym undir Juges *regaliter et politice*.'[98] Fortescue mentions the gentiles, who had 'a man that reigned upon thaim *regaliter tantum*. With wich desire God was gretly offendyd, as wele for thair folie, as for thair unkyndnes; that sithyn thai had a kynge, wich was God, that reigned upon thaim politekily and roialy, and yet wold chaunge hym for a kynge, a verray man, that wolde reigne upon hem only roialy'. God was so angered by this ingratitude that he punished them 'bi thondres and other gasteful thynges from the hevene'.[99] Biblical imagery is invoked to condemn absolute monarchy. Fortescue continues his history of the English legal system by asserting that Brutus was the founder of the *dominium politicum et regale* in Britain. Brutus, the great-grandson of Aeneas, is reputed to have come to Britain from Troy, according to Geoffrey of Monmouth in *Historia Regum Britanniae*. The significance of Brutus to an analysis of the Ancient Constitution is that his provenance is Roman: the references made to his status as the founder of English law betray the classical and continental roots of common law ideology. Selden made the following important observation concerning Fortescue's claims for Brutus, emphasising the value of the latter as an iconic symbol of constitutional legitimacy rather than his mythical status as the definitive founder of English law:

---

[97] *Ibid.*, p. 114.
[98] *Ibid.*, p. 109. The independence that Fortescue attributes to the judiciary conflicts with the later opinion of Cowell, that judges 'have their authority by deputation, as Delegates to the King', J. Cowell, *The Interpreter; or Booke Containing the Signification of Words* (Cambridge: J. Legate, 1607), fo. Pp1.
[99] Fortescue, *Governance of England*, p. 110.

[s]ome have in like manner made enquiry concerning our British History, and stumbled at it. From hence we had Brutus, Dunvallo and Queen Martia: There are some both very Learned and very Judicious persons, who suspect, that that story is patched up out of Bards Songs and Poetick Fictions taken upon trust, like Talmudical Traditions, on purpose to raise the British name out of the Trojan ashes.[100]

Crucially, according to Fortescue, the populace 'ordenyd the same reaume to be ruled and justified by such lawes as thai all wolde assent unto; wich lawe therefore is called polliticum, and bi cause it is ministrid bi a kynge, it is called regale'.[101] The attraction to common lawyers of such a theory, in which law rather than an absolute monarch governs the populace, accounts for the enduring popularity of Fortescue among the legal profession during the sixteenth and seventeenth centuries. The analogy of the Israelites, the chosen race, being ruled not by a king but by divinely appointed judges; the suggestion that the legal institution (the king in Parliament, subject to the constraints of common law) rather than the person of the king, embodies the body politic; and the implication that the king is created by and is accountable to the law, were constitutional principles set down by Fortescue and re-presented more than a century later by Hooker.

It should of course be noted that Fortescue wrote *The Governance of England* and *De Laudibus Legum Angliae* a hundred years before the Inner Temple revels of 1561 discussed in this chapter. In particular, Fortescue's knowledge of government embraced neither the innovative centralisation that characterised the Tudor administrative machine nor the unprecedented level of sovereign power arrogated to the person of the monarch. Consequently it would be a mistake to extrapolate from the Elizabethan revels a literal depiction of the particular constitutional jurisprudence espoused by Fortescue. But it is reasonable to assert that Fortescue provided the textual foundations for the philosophical and juristic development of the early modern English legal profession, predicated upon the integration of insular national custom and Neoplatonic humanism. Implicit in such a model was the idea, developed by St German, that the natural order of the cosmos and the eternal law of God should be reflected in the equitable principles of English law. Fortescue and St German envisaged a system of governance in which the actions of the civil magistrate were accountable to the representative institutions of the law: the courts of justice and Parliament. The Elizabethan Inns of Court deployed the arcane insignia of institutional existence, of which the revels were archetypal, to provide a microcosm or template of the ideal state, in which the principles of mixed monarchy were graphically represented.

---

[100] J. Selden, *The Reverse or Back-Face of the English Janus*, trans. R. Westcot (London: T. Bassett & R. Chiswell, 1682), fo. 8.
[101] Fortescue, *Governance of England*, p. 112.

The influence of Hooker over the development of common law principles in accordance with the tenets of Judaeo-Christian teaching was of inestimable importance to the Elizabethan constitutional settlement. Hooker's unique contribution to the development of the early modern English state was to realign the guiding principle of the Henrician Act of Supremacy, which asserted the ancient right of the crown to control the liberties of its subjects within the framework of a sovereign, political and religious state. Hooker defined the immemorial polity that entitled the crown to exercise such power in terms of a triangular relationship between mankind, commonwealth and the Church of England, in which all sides were co-dependent.[102] The principal achievement of *Of the Laws of Ecclesiastical Polity* (and in particular, of Book VIII) is to suggest a mode of government in which church and state attain a level of parity that renders them indivisible. It is at least noteworthy that Books VI–VIII were published more than fifty years after the publication of Books I–V: Books VI and VIII in 1648, and Book VII in 1661. It is possible that Hooker was unable to find a willing publisher for his controversial opinions, in particular his reiteration of Bracton's assertion that the monarch was subject not only to the law of God, but to the law of the nation: '[t]he axioms of our regal government are these: "Lex facit regem".'[103] Still less could the theory of the divine right of kings be equated with Hooker's belief that the monarch governed 'with dependence upon that whole entire body, over the several parts whereof he hath dominion; so that it standeth for an axiom in this case, The king is "major singulis, universis minor".'[104]

Hooker's work had a profound effect on common lawyers such as Coke, who shared the fundamental belief that the common law, rather than the monarch, represented the ultimate order of the universe. Little suggests that Coke and Hooker shared the identical belief that the complete consistency and intrinsic harmony of the common law represented the unity and permanence of social life itself.[105] For Hooker, church and commonwealth co-existed as a single entity; their interests were mutual and identical. Within this religious commonwealth the rights of the Christian subject were sacrosanct. The prefix 'Christian' is important, since he or she accepts the law not as the coercive or restrictive threat of force, but rather as the liberating Word of God, enabling the subject to respond voluntarily and in accordance with the biblical injunction to 'love thy neighbour'. In such a society Christ

---

[102] On the triangular relationship described by Hooker, see D. Little, *Religion, Order, and Law: a Study in Pre-Revolutionary England* (Oxford: Blackwell, 1970), p. 153. On the Henrician Act of Supremacy as a restatement of ancient nationalist claims to political and religious sovereignty, see P. Goodrich, 'Poor Illiterate Reason: History, Nationalism and Common Law', *Social & Legal Studies*, 1 (1992), 12–13.

[103] R. Hooker, *Of the Laws of Ecclesiastical Polity*, ed. A. S. McGrade (Cambridge University Press, 1989), Book VIII, ch. II, XIII, p. 147.

[104] Ibid., Book VIII, ch. II, VII, p. 143.   [105] Little, *Religion, Order, and Law*, p. 175.

was the embodiment of law, representing its ultimate purpose – adherence and deference to the sovereign power of God Almighty.

Hooker's vision of a commonwealth governed by God and common law was similar to that envisaged by Fortescue in *The Governance of England*: 'every independent multitude, before any certain form of regiment established, hath, under God's supreme authority, full dominion over itself... God creating mankind did endue it naturally with full power to guide itself'.[106] He found no divine authority for a monarchic system of government, asserting that 'the Christian world should be ordered by Kingly regiment, the law of God doth not any where command'.[107] However, Hooker did not object to the institution of the monarchy as such. Rather he emphasised the primacy of the commonwealth of Christian subjects and the political sovereignty of common law, to which, of course, the king was subject: 'I mean not only the law of nature and of God, but very national or municipal law consonant thereunto. Happier that people whose law is their King in the greatest things, than that whose King is himself their law.'[108] Canon law taught that the church (and Christian society in general) was a *corpus mysticum*, the head of which was Christ. In post-Reformation England the influence of canon law on the development of the legal system was greatly diminished. Where conflict arose between the jurisdictions of ecclesiastical and common law, common lawyers asserted the authority of the latter. With reference to this dispute, in *Fuller's Case*, Coke declared that 'in any particular case, the determination of this belongs to the Judges of the common law'.[109] Hooker's image of the triangular relationship between the human subject, the Church of England and the commonwealth had a profound effect on the development of the early modern model of government. Paradoxically, it introduced the canon law doctrine of the *corpus mysticum* into a constitution shaped according to common law principles. The state was envisaged as a kind of 'mystical body',[110] an observation made by Coke in 1607: 'as we are all of one Nation, so let us be all of one Church, and Christ being onely our head, let us all desire as in one sheepfolde, to be the sanctified members of his glorious bodie'.[111]

Increasing use of the Court of High Commission in the last two decades of Elizabeth's reign, under the direction of Bishop Aylmer, threatened the autonomy of the common law courts and represented the insidious threat of rival jurisdictions. *Cawdrey's Case* (1591), concerning the deprivation of

---

[106] Hooker, *Of the Laws of Ecclesiastical Polity*, Book VIII, ch. II, V, p. 141.
[107] *Ibid.*, Book VIII, ch. II, VI, p. 142.
[108] *Ibid.*, Book VIII, ch. II, XII, p. 146.   [109] Coke, XII *Reports*, p. 42.
[110] On the *corpus mysticum* of the King, see E. Kantorowicz, *The King's Two Bodies: A Study in Medieval Political Theology* (New Jersey: Princeton University Press, 1957), p. 194.
[111] 'The Lord Coke His Speech and Charge', given at Norwich Assizes, 1607.

a minister's benefice by the commission, raised fundamental constitutional questions about the exercise of the 'imperial' prerogative by the queen and its authority to take precedence over common law. In particular, *ex officio mero* prosecutions in the Court of High Commission were clearly modelled on the procedures of Roman canon law. Richard Cosin, a civil lawyer and protégé of Whitgift, was responsible for the institutional assimilation of Roman canon law into *ex officio* investigations. His actions inevitably antagonised common lawyers, especially since canon law had limited jurisdiction following the Act of Supremacy of 1534. The inquisitorial nature of *ex officio* prosecutions, presided over by ecclesiastical judges, was antithetical to the principles of fairness and equity enshrined in common law ideology. But an appeal to Queen's Bench by the defendant in *Cawdrey's Case* failed, on the grounds that the queen's prerogative enabled her to empower the High Commission, because 'by the ancient laws of this realm this Kingdom of England is an absolute empire and monarchy'.[112] The Inns of Court revels of the latter part of Elizabeth's reign reflected growing concerns at the infringement of individual liberty by the state and the encroachment of the royal prerogative on the jurisdiction of the courts of common law.

'GESTA GRAYORUM': GRAY'S INN REVELS, 1594

Gesta Grayorum, or, the History of the Prince of Purpoole, Anno Domini, 1594 is an anonymous account of the Christmas revels held at Gray's Inn between 12 December 1594 and Twelfth-night (6 January) 1595.[113] It has been convincingly argued that the masque performed at these revels in the presence of the queen was written by Sir Francis Bacon. It confronted an audience largely made up of common lawyers with his proposals for the codification of the English legal system,[114] thus demonstrating the utility of the visual image to the art of Elizabethan government. That Bacon made a significant contribution to the revels is suggested by the following entry for 11 February 1595 in the Pension Book of Gray's Inn: 'On January 3rd the ambassador [of the Inner Temple] was again present, a Council was held, for which Spedding thinks Bacon wrote the speeches.'[115] Relevant to the particular depiction of a fictional realm suggested by these revels is that Bacon wrote his own Utopian work, *New Atlantis*. This work is, in most respects,

---

[112] See Guy, 'The Elizabethan Establishment', p. 132.
[113] The anonymous text was first published in 1688; for a discussion of its authenticity, see S. P. Kerr, 'Shakespeare and Gray's Inn', *Graya*, 32 (1950), 99–107.
[114] B. Shapiro, 'Codification of the Laws in Seventeenth Century England', *Wisconsin Law Review* (1974), 436.
[115] *The Pension Book of Gray's Inn*, ed. R. J. Fletcher, 2 vols. (London: Chiswick, 1901), I, p. 107, n. 1.

the antithesis of More's *Utopia*, which recognised the disparity between rich and poor, and expressed a genuine revulsion at the material excesses of the ruling class. Unlike More, Bacon viewed private property and the existence of class as the means of maintaining and ensuring happiness. His ideal family was strongly patriarchal, with no trace of the communism inherent in *Utopia*. More described education as a social and co-operative pursuit, for the potential increase in the happiness and enrichment of the populace. For Bacon, education was the exclusive domain of a body of specialists and was carried out in isolation from the masses: its object was not happiness but power.[116]

The events described in *Gesta Grayorum* record the creation of the fictional and symbolic realm of 'Purpoole', in which Bacon's masque was performed. The name derives from the Manor of Purpoole, where Gray's Inn first came into being and on whose site its hall was built. On his enthronement, the Prince was proclaimed 'Prince of Purpoole, Archduke of Stapulia and Bernardia, Duke of the High and Nether Holborn, Marquis of St Giles' and Tottenham, Count Palatine of Bloomsbury and Clerkenwell, Great Lord of the Cantons of Islington, etc. Knight of the most honourable Order of the Helmet, and Sovereign of the Same'.[117] The text emphasises the centrality of patriarchy to the writer's understanding of strong government. Of overriding importance to an analysis of the constitutional implications of the revels and the influence of the legal profession on the development of the English state was the unequivocal and violent rejection of the proposed model of government by the membership of Gray's Inn. *Gesta Grayorum* describes a fictional kingdom, peopled by archetypes of government: princes, privy councillors and ambassadors. The chief protagonist throughout this period was the Prince of Purpoole, in whom absolute power resided. The part was played by a member of Gray's Inn, chosen by his peers on 12 December 1594: '[w]hereupon, presently they made choice of one Mr. Henry Helmes, a Norfolk-Gentleman . . . and very active in Dancing and Revelling. Then was his Privy Council assigned him to advise of State-Matters and the Government of his Dominions . . . Also all Officers of State, of the law, and of the Household.'[118] The panoply of state was invoked in order to bestow legitimacy and order to these extravagant proceedings. The other Inns of Court were represented as sovereign states, and on 14 December it was requested that the Inner Temple send an ambassador to the court of the

---

[116] T. More, *Utopia*, trans. P. Turner (Harmondsworth: Penguin, 1965); F. Bacon, *New Atlantis: A Work Unfinished* (London: Macmillan, 1899). See L. Jardine & A. Stewart, *Hostage to Fortune: the Troubled Life of Francis Bacon, 1561–1626* (London: Phoenix, 1999).
[117] Anon., *Gesta Grayorum, or, the History of the Prince of Purpoole, Anno Domini, 1594* (London: W. Canning, 1688), fo. 9.
[118] *Ibid.*, fo. 2.

Prince of Purpoole. The Inner Temple accepted the invitation from Gray's Inn on 18 December, styling itself 'The State of Templaria' and despatching its ambassador, 'Frederick Templarius', to the Prince's court at Gray's Inn. In addition to the Prince of Purpoole, the members elected eighty officers of state, including a Speaker of the Parliament, a Lord Chief Justice of the Prince's Bench, a Chancellor of the Exchequer and a 'Master of the Wards and Idiots'.[119] The three functions of state – executive, legislature, and judiciary – were replicated. It is apparent that their intended role was that of subordinate adjunct to an imperial and absolute monarchy. Following the instatement of these offices, the Prince was duly enthroned in a coronation ceremony.

On 20 December, St Thomas's Eve, the Prince marched from his lodgings to the great hall of Gray's Inn and took his place on the throne, surrounded by his counsellors and lords: the majesty of kingship was enacted, and its power was instantly visible. Symbolic value attached to every nuance of dress and appellation. The Prince of Purpoole embodied principles of honour, tradition and flawless genealogy. He represented an unwritten, ancient law and his image was a visible object of attachment to which the subject of law was bound in obedience.[120] A trumpet sounded, 'and then entred the Prince's Champion, all in compleat Armour, on Horseback, and so cam riding round about the Fire'.[121] That the Prince was the personification of virtue and honour is emphasised by the armorial ornamentation of his shield, the symbolism of which was explained to the audience by the 'King at Arms':

> The most mighty Prince of Purpoole, etc. beareth his shield of the highest: Jupiter. In Point, a Sacred Imperial Diadem, safely guarded by the Helmet of the great Goddess Pallas, from the Violence of Darts, Bullets and Bolts of Saturn, Momus, and the Idiot ... For his Highness's Crest, the glorious Planet Sol, coursing through the twelve Signs of the Zodiack on a Celestial Globe ... supported by two anciently renowned and glorious Griffyns, which have been always in League with the honourable Pegasus.[122]

Prototypes were incorporated into the iconography, as a consequence of which the Prince's rhetorical significance was of greater importance than his physical presence. He was the 'most mighty' Prince, whose shield bore the 'highest' arms. It was the 'most heroical' order to which he belonged, and the 'glorious' planet Sol that adorned his crest. And they were two

---

[119] *Ibid.*, fo. 7.
[120] On the image and emotional attachment of the subject to law, see P. Goodrich, *Languages of Law: From Logics of Memory to Nomadic Masks* (London: Weidenfeld & Nicolson, 1990), p. 262.
[121] *Gesta Grayorum*, fo. 9.
[122] *Ibid.*, fo. 10. For a detailed exposition of the arcane symbolism of Elizabethan heraldic devices, see Legh, *The Accedens*; J. Ferne, *The Blazon of Gentrie* (London: Winder, 1586); and J. Bossewell, *Workes of Armorie* (London: R. Tottel, 1572).

'anciently renowned and glorious' griffins that supported the arms. It is noteworthy that in the heraldic order of government described above, the hieroglyphic symbols of two Inns of Court (the griffin of Gray's Inn and the flying horse of the Inner Temple) were subordinate to and supportive of the signs of imperial monarchy. The presence of the Prince fulfilled one of the main criteria of Aristotelian rhetoric, which was to produce a certain disposition in the audience.[123] He was an artificial creation, intended to persuade his subjects that the legitimacy of his *imperium* was irrefutable. In the words of Sir Philip Sidney, the Prince was '[a] speaking picture, with this end, To teach and delight'.[124] His reign was limited to the twelve days of Christmas (symbolised by the sun passing through the twelve signs of the Zodiac emblazoned on his crest), but the image of his noble personage is eternal.

The divine provenance of imperial monarchy was implied by the reference to Jupiter, the president of the council of Gods and source of legitimate authority. The 'Sacred Imperial Diadem' was an emblem of supreme authority, the use of which originated in the east. In symbolic terms, the east was the bringer of light: *ex oriente lux*.[125] The significance of the diadem is to imply that the light of providential monarchy has entered the world in order to eliminate chaos and provide enduring stability. The 'Bullets and Bolts of Saturn' mentioned above refer to the Roman Saturnalia, the days sacred to Saturn at the end of the year. They were characterised by festivals during which the social order was inverted: slaves gave orders to their masters, and the latter waited at table.[126] The imperial diadem was 'guarded by the Helmet of the great Goddess Pallas',[127] a popular contemporary allusion to the divine status of Elizabeth I. The immunity of the queen from all criticism can be inferred from the reference to *Momus*, the classical representation of blame or criticism, from whose 'Darts, Bullets and Bolts' the Prince was 'safely guarded'.[128]

Graphic devices of immense rhetorical power were employed to convince the subject of the legitimacy of imperial monarchy. The spirituality and corporeality of kingship was established through the use of sacred images. The

[123] *The Rhetoric of Aristotle*, trans. J. E. C. Welldon (London: Macmillan, 1886), p. 11.
[124] P. Sidney, *The Defense of Poesy* (Glasgow: R. Urie, 1752), p. 18.
[125] On the Eastern origins of heraldry, see A. C. Fox-Davies, *A Complete Guide to Heraldry* (London: Bracken, 1993), pp. 1–18.
[126] On the inversion of conventional social conduct, see D. Underdown, *Revel, Riot and Rebellion: Popular Politics and Culture in England, 1603–1660* (Oxford University Press, 1987); also, W. Carroll, *Fat King, Lean Beggar: Representations of Poverty in the Age of Shakespeare* (Ithaca: Cornell University Press, 1995).
[127] On the heraldic helmet and its indication of rank, see Fox-Davies, *Guide to Heraldry*, pp. 303–25.
[128] See L. B. Alberti, *Momus*, trans. S. Knight (Cambridge, Mass.: Harvard University Press, 2003).

Prince of Purpoole was a visual trope, *Imago Dei et Mundi*, a representation and earthly manifestation of the original father, God Almighty. The above symbols utilised mythology in order to express the reality of absolute rule. The Prince displayed magnanimity and benevolence by agreeing to pardon any offences hitherto committed in his realm. The order and harmony established by him were celebrated by formal dancing, 'until it pleased His Honour to take his way to his Lodging, with Sound of Trumpets, and his Attendants in order'.[129] The concern with order, which manifested itself that night in the formulaic deference to the Prince, demonstrates adherence to a code whose objective is the regulation of a patriarchal society. In its exaggerated depiction of an imaginary and Utopian realm, *Gesta Grayorum* represents a particular vision of England in which the private interests of the ruler are synonymous with the public benefits to the commonwealth. The symbolic importance of such a model of governance being presented in the hall of Gray's Inn cannot be overlooked.

The depiction of imperial monarchy was closely linked to the civilian maxim, *quod principi placuit habet vigorem legis* ('what pleases the prince has the force of law'). The actions of the Prince of Purpoole were those of an absolute ruler, whose benevolence did not disguise the fact that he lacked accountability: 'the Prince made a short Speech to his Subjects, wherein he gave them to understand, that although in Clemency he pardoned all Offences, to that present time; yet notwithstanding, his meaning thereby was not to give any the least occasion of Presumption in breaking his Laws'.[130] The suggestion that the crown represented a patriarchal system of government and that the monarch was therefore *pater patriae* has its origins in Roman law and in the absolute power exercised by the father within the familial unit.[131] Such a model was incompatible with the settlement proposed by Hooker in *Of the Laws of Ecclesiastical Polity*, the first five books of which were published between 1594 and 1597. Although, as Lake has suggested, the scope of Hooker's writing was academic rather than overtly political or polemical,[132] his appointment as master of Temple church placed him at the heart of institutional existence at the Temple. The influence of his political theology over the legal profession is evident from the central role played at all the Inns by sacramental ritual. The evolution of the Inns as religious commonwealths, in which the tenets of Aristotelian civic virtue provided constitutional guidelines, demonstrates the relevance to their governance of Hooker's belief that political authority resided in the whole of the common weal. Of particular significance to the imperial themes of *Gesta*

---

[129] *Gesta Grayorum*, fo. 20.   [130] *Ibid.*, fo. 19.
[131] See C. Downing, *A Discourse on the State Ecclesiasticall of this Kingdome in Relation to the Civill* (Oxford: Turner, 1634), fo. 64.
[132] Lake, *Anglicans and Puritans?*, p. 9.

Grayorum and their reception by common lawyers is the fact that Hooker's constitutional settlement was predicated on the model of limited monarchy rather than patriarchy, partly on the grounds that politic societies were too large to apply the familial analogy. The symbols of patriarchal government were violated and rejected on subsequent nights at Gray's Inn during the 1594 revels. The rebellion by common lawyers was an indication not only of the increasing corporate confidence of the legal profession, but also of its intention to influence the political development of the English state and, as Cromartie suggests, to concern itself with affairs which hitherto had been regarded as *arcana regni*.[133]

Licensed disorder, in which the conventional model of governance was threatened or inverted, was a familiar feature of the carnival and other seasonal festivities in the western tradition. In *The English Utopia*, Morton suggests that in medieval England, when the custom of crowning the Lord of Misrule in the Christmas period was founded, such conduct was revolutionary but harmless because this was an era when revolution itself was not objectively possible,[134] even though popular riots were frequent. Festivals of misrule preserved desires and aspirations that might otherwise have died away. The Tudor monarchy provided security and order, national as opposed to local organisation, and created the stability necessary for a flourishing market. The new merchant classes benefited, but the price paid was political absolutism. The erosion of feudalism, whilst emancipating the serfs, destroyed the basis of their security, the medieval village commune. According to Morton, Tudor England combined elements of hope and despair, of increasing wealth and increasing poverty. This observation is reiterated by Hill, who suggests that mounting poverty in late Elizabethan and Jacobean England led to the emergence of class divisions between previously undelineated groups.[135] It was a world turned upside down, and the revels of this period, although similar in form to those of an earlier age, reflected these concerns.

Central to the orchestration of events during the revels was the Lord of Misrule, who Dugdale reports was responsible for 'general scandal and obloquie', and of disturbing 'the peace and quiet of the House'.[136] The Lord of Misrule had licence to usurp all normal authority within the Inn. His role was subversive and, in the context of the ordered formality of the revels, both surprising and disturbing. It is not simply that his licence to disrupt

---

[133] Cromartie, 'The Constitutionalist Revolution', 106.
[134] Morton, *The English Utopia*, p. 23. On the rituals of carnival and the subversion of social norms, see Bakhtin, *Rabelais*; also, Underdown, *Revel, Riot and Rebellion*.
[135] C. Hill, *Intellectual Origins of the English Revolution Revisited* (Oxford: Clarendon, 1997), p. 285.
[136] Dugdale, *Origines Juridiciales*, fo. 149.

and parody the ordered proceedings of the Inn emphasised the importance of order and respect for custom during the remainder of the year. Staged misrule was circumscribed by the strictly limited duration of its licence, and the subsequent reassertion of order has led many commentators to characterise the rituals of misrule as an affirmation of community.[137] For example, on Twelfth Night at the Inns of Court the office of the Lord of Misrule expired, and the normal, established order was reinstated. On this night, the Marshal and the Steward came to the fire bearing torches, and their wands of office were ceremonially broken. The power exerted by the Lord of Misrule was restricted, regulated and eventually terminated by the institution that granted him his licence. He was a representation of the limited freedom of expression granted the individual by a supreme authority that regulated the conduct of its subjects in the interests of the commonwealth.

That his power was greatest at night suggests that the Lord of Misrule was a theatrical manifestation of dreams and darkness. Like Nietzsche's satyr, he symbolised 'the offspring of a longing after the Primitive and the Natural'. In *The Twilight of the Idols and the Antichrist*, Nietzsche characterised law (both temporal and spiritual) as the institutional repression of sensory pleasure. In relation to morality and the laws of the church, Nietzsche suggested that the most profound and superior desires of life were negated in the interests of a God who was the enemy of life, while in *Beyond Good and Evil*, he condemned English morality as self-interest masquerading as virtue.[138] Ward has noted the subversive connotations inherent in the various representations of misrule, and the associations with the Devil that such nocturnal power implied in early modern England.[139] This 'longing after the Primitive' is similar to the longing experienced by Puck, the spirit of misrule in Shakespeare's *A Midsummer Night's Dream*, written in 1596. The related themes of chaos, subversion of the immutable strata of society and the effects of this conduct on the commonwealth recur throughout Elizabethan and Jacobean

---

[137] See for example, Carroll, *Fat King, Lean Beggar*; K. Wrightson, *English Society, 1580–1680* (London: Routledge, 1982). The dramatic representation of misrule as an inversion of the bonds of community is discussed in I. Ward, 'A Kingdom for a Stage, Princes to Act: Shakespeare and the Art of Government', *Law and Critique*, 8 (1997), 191.

[138] Nietzsche, *Birth of Tragedy*, p. 63; F. Nietzsche, 'The Twilight of the Idols and the Antichrist', *The Works of Friedrich Nietzsche*, trans. T. Common, 11 vols. (London: Henry and Co., 1896), XI; F. Nietzsche, *Beyond Good and Evil*, trans. H. Zimmern (Edinburgh: Foulis, 1914). On psychoanalysis and law, see Goodrich, *Law and the Unconscious*, pp. 4–5. See also A. Pottage, 'Recreating Difference', *Law and Critique*, 5 (1994), 131–47; D. S. Caudill, 'Freud and Critical Legal Studies: Contours of a Radical Socio-Legal Psychoanalysis', *Indiana Law Journal*, 66 (1991), 651–97.

[139] Ward, *Legal Imagination*, p. 204. In relation to the social disharmony and inequitable law that initiate the action of Shakespeare's *A Midsummer Night's Dream*, see Ward, *Legal Imagination*, pp. 205–10. On the rituals of disorder, see also Hutton, *Merry England*, pp. 116–17, 187–99.

drama.[140] Puck personifies a tireless predisposition towards the disruption of accepted social norms. His conduct has a disruptive effect similar to that of the Lord of Misrule at the Inns of Court revels and is suggestive of dissatisfaction with existing societal arrangements. Puck is not merely the 'merry wanderer of the night'[141] (although, like the Lord of Misrule at the Inns of Court, his power is greatest at night), continuously playing puerile tricks on the mortals whom he encounters. He reminds the audience of fears and repressed desires, which emerge invariably in dreams and nightmares:

> ... Damned spirits all
> That in crossways and floods have burial
> Already to their wormy beds are gone.
> For fear lest day should look their shames upon.[142]

A Midsummer Night's Dream subtly criticises the inherent injustice of absolute, patriarchal government, represented in the play by the civil magistracy of Duke Theseus, a ruler who presides over a rigid and inequitable legal system, '[w]hich by no means we may extenuate'.[143] In this disjointed society, Puck is the catalyst through whose subversive actions the consciousness of the Athenian citizenry is animated. At the play's conclusion, a harmonious and inclusive commonwealth of artisans, gentry and aristocracy has replaced the exclusive model of absolute government enacted in the first scene. Throughout the play, allusions to Elizabeth I abound: she is the 'fair vestal throned by the west' and 'the imperial votaress ... In maiden meditation, fancy-free'.[144] Drama was an important medium of political discourse in Elizabethan England, a fact amply demonstrated when the supporters of Essex sponsored a performance of *Richard II* on the eve of the revolt in February 1601. Concerning *A Midsummer Night's Dream*, Montrose suggests that the edifying presence of the queen was a condition of the drama's imaginative suggestibility,[145] implying the mutual dependence of art and government in Elizabethan England. In the context of this congruency, considerable political significance attaches to the attendance by Elizabeth I of the masque presented at Gray's Inn in January 1595. Her visit followed a spontaneous rebellion in the realm of 'Purpoole' and a rejection of the fantastical, absolute government represented by the Prince. The conduct

---

[140] See R. Berry, *Shakespeare and Social Class* (New Jersey: Humanities, 1988); also G. Blakemore Evans (ed.), *Elizabethan–Jacobean Drama* (London: A. & C. Black, 1987).
[141] *A Midsummer Night's Dream*, II. i. 43.   [142] *Ibid.*, III. ii. 382–5.
[143] *Ibid.*, I. i. 120. On *A Midsummer Night's Dream*, see J. Kott, *Shakespeare: Our Contemporary* (London: Routledge, 1967); S. Greenblatt, *Renaissance Self-Fashioning: From More to Shakespeare* (University of Chicago Press, 1980); Greenblatt, *Shakespearean Negotiations*; and T. Hawkes, *Meaning by Shakespeare*, (London: Routledge, 1992).
[144] *A Midsummer Night's Dream*, II. Scene i. 158, 163–4.
[145] L. Montrose, ' "Shaping Fantasies": Figurations of Gender and Power in Elizabethan Culture', *Representations*, 1 (1983), 62.

Revels, feasting and role-playing 119

of the revellers on that night suggests discontent with the existing constitutional settlement, for implicit in their conduct was the revolutionary notion that governance according to the immutable precepts of ancient law was outmoded.

On Holy Innocents' Day, 28 December 1594, the ambassador of the Inner Temple was ushered into the Prince's presence, 'very solemnly, with Sound of Trumpets'.[146] The solemn presentation of credentials which usually precedes the acquaintance of monarch and ambassador was disrupted:

> When the Ambassador was placed . . . there arose such a disordered Tumult and Crowd upon the Stage, that there was no Opportunity to effect that which was intended: There came so great a number of worshipful Personages upon the Stage, that might not be displaced, and Gentlewomen, whose Sex did privilege them from Violence, that when the Prince and his Officers had in vain, a good while, expected and endeavoured a Reformation, at length there was no hope of Redress for that present. The Lord Ambassador and his Train thought that they were not so kindly entertained, as was before expected, and thereupon would not stay any longer at that time, but, in a sort, discontented and displeased. After their Departure the Throngs and Tumults did somewhat cease, although so much of them continued, as was able to disorder and confound any good Inventions whatsoever . . . So that Night was begun, and continued to the end, in nothing but Confusion and Errors, whereupon, it was ever afterwards called the Night of Errors.[147]

It is difficult to establish with absolute certainty whether the 'Lord Ambassador and his Train' were genuinely offended, or whether they were acting the roles of diplomatic officials who have received a rebuff from their host. It appears that a spontaneous breach of order occurred, and the persuasive power of rhetoric was tested to its limits. Its fragility was exposed, dependent as it is on an ordered reception by its audience. Collective rebellion by common lawyers visibly precipitated the rejection of ancient law.

Following the indignant exit of 'Frederick Templarius', a company of professional actors performed Shakespeare's *The Comedy of Errors* in the great hall. The choice of play is noteworthy: although at one level it operates successfully as a boisterous farce of mistaken identity (the plot is taken from Plautus's *Menaechmi*), Shakespeare incorporates into the frenetic action themes of considerable political relevance to an audience of the 1590s. In particular are the references throughout the drama to a powerful class of merchants, whose increasing personal wealth and capacity to affect the national economy were notable features of Tudor England.[148] The influence of a burgeoning middle class on government and the state is a related theme of the play, as the opening scene (in which the Duke of Ephesus condemns to

---

[146] *Gesta Grayorum*, fo. 21.   [147] *Ibid.*, fo. 22.
[148] On the theme of commerce in *The Comedy of Errors*, see D. Bruster, *Drama and the Market in the Age of Shakespeare* (Cambridge University Press, 1992).

death an innocent merchant, Egeon, according to the inequitable prescription of written law) demonstrates:

> Merchant of Syracusa, plead no more.
> I am not partial to infringe our laws:
> The enmity and discord which of late
> Sprung from the rancorous outrage of your duke
> To merchants, our well-dealing countrymen,
> Who, wanting gilders to redeem their lives,
> Have sealed his rigorous statutes with their bloods,
> Excludes all pity from our threat'ning looks.[149]

At the play's conclusion, order is restored after two hours of contrived chaos. Unity and tranquillity replace upheaval and social disorder, but only after the moral supremacy of unwritten law has been established and Egeon's life has been spared by the duke.

The life of Purpoole continued to imitate the farcical confusion of Ephesus in *The Comedy of Errors*. The night after its performance, an inquiry was set up to investigate 'a great Witchcraft used the Night before, whereby there were great Disorders and Misdemeanours, by Hurly-burlies, Crowds, Errors, Confusions, vain Representations and Shews, to the utter Discredit of our State and Policy'. The blame was levelled at 'a Sorcerer or Conjuror that was supposed to be the Cause of that confused Inconvenience'. The troupe of actors that performed *The Comedy of Errors* was also held to be accountable: 'a Company of base and common Fellows, to make up our Disorders with a Play of Errors and Confusions; and that that Night had gained us Discredit, and it self a Nickname of Errors. All which were against the Crown and Dignity of our Sovereign Lord, the Prince of Purpoole.'[150] The inquisitorial nature of the *ex officio* prosecutions that formed part of the inquiry clearly resembles the procedures of canon law and, in particular, the *ex officio mero* prosecutions in the Court of High Commission. Various 'court' officials were blamed for the lamentable events: a prisoner was arraigned at the bar, 'being brought thither by the Lieutenant of the Tower'.[151] The prisoner blamed 'all the Knavery and Juggling of the Attorney and Sollicitor, which had brought all the law-stuff on purpose to blind the Eyes of his Excellency'.[152] He alleged that everybody who attended the chaotic proceedings was deceived, because 'those things which they all saw and preceived sensibly to be in very deed done, and actually performed, were nothing else but vain Illusions, Fancies, Dreams and Enchantments'.[153] The tribunal's exaggerated emphasis on the inherent absurdity and injustice of a particular legal procedure drew attention to the abuse of executive power

---

[149] *The Comedy of Errors*, I. i. 3–10. [150] *Gesta Grayorum*, fo. 23.
[151] Ibid. [152] Ibid., fo. 24. [153] Ibid.

by unaccountable instruments of government such as the Court of High Commission.

In *The Defense of Poesy*, Sir Philip Sidney provides an illuminating explanation of the rhetorical function of comedy in Elizabethan art: '[c]omedy is an imitation of the common errors of our life, which he representeth in the most ridiculous and scornful sorts that may be; so as it is impossible that any beholder can be content to be such a one.'[154] It is noteworthy in the context of the 1594 revels that Sidney was a member of Gray's Inn and therefore accustomed to the comedic extravagance of its Christmas festivities. Although he died in 1586, Sidney's definition of comedy, when applied to the extraordinary events at Gray's Inn, suggests that the mock trial had a clear political intent. The chaotic proceedings of 28 December 1594 were excused on the grounds that they were 'Dreams and Enchantments'. If so, they were the aspirant dreams of common lawyers, enchanted by the imaginative possibilities of freedom, revealing a subversive tendency that for now confined its expression to the licensed misrule of the revels. It was not until the reign of Charles I that such dreams of freedom were expressed by common lawyers in Parliament, in terms of the fundamental liberty of the subject.

In a legal system whose freedoms were protected by custom, rather than codified in a written constitution, visual images of justice, fairness and liberty attained iconic significance. Despite the comedic confusion of the Night of Errors at Gray's Inn, there was an underlying seriousness to events in 'Purpoole' and a tacit acknowledgment of the rhetorical power of spectacle, theatre and symbols. The Elizabethan Inns of Court shared with Sir Philip Sidney the Platonic ideal that freedom was equated with self-realisation and the quest of the individual for perfection. This philosophy was irreconcilable with the absolute sovereignty of the royal prerogative, the claims of which obliged the individual to live in a state of servitude, dependent on the goodwill of the monarch. The incompatibility of individual liberty and arbitrary government was reflected in the themes of misrule and rebellion that came to dominate the Elizabethan revels. The model of government that emerged through these elaborate devices acknowledged an embryonic, constitutional relationship between civil magistrate and citizen, in which mutual rights and obligations were implied. The role of the legal profession in defining the nature of these rights and obligations was crucial: the importance of the Inns of Court revels in this process of definition is their significance as an initial response to modernity. Through an arcane system of signs they articulated an awareness of the existence of the rational individual and his relationship with the state, even though the precise nature of that relationship was yet to be defined. The construction by the legal profession of an imaginary

---

[154] Sidney, *Defense of Poesy*, p. 51.

constitution presaged the Kantian civil state, whose principles of freedom, equality and individual autonomy within the community were congruent with the rational notion of human rights. The ideal *polis* of the revels is discernible in Rawls's definition of the Kantian society as a community of individuals, creating their own morality, whose only constraint is their own rationality and autonomy.[155]

Change in the nature of English government had been extensive during the sixteenth century. The Tudor monarchy had overseen the development of a secure nation-state in which a recognisable middle class had emerged and prospered. These developments were accompanied by greater centralisation of government and an incipient absolutist monarchy. Morton makes the obvious but important point that the king, who under the feudalism of the Middle Ages was no more than the strongest landowner, became in the Tudor period the pivotal figure in the state.[156] Genuine subversive behaviour at the revels during the latter part of Elizabeth's reign suggests that discontent with excessive use of the royal prerogative was consolidated at the Inns of Court, providing an institutional framework for the development of an alternative constitutional settlement. The revels of this period reflected both the acknowledgement that fundamental change to the political structure of society was necessary, and anxiety as to the consequences of that change. The Utopian state represented by the revels had not been attained in England, despite the stability provided by the monarchy. The legal profession sought a new Utopia in which the sovereignty of common law was acknowledged by subject and ruler, but the means of realising this ideal state were not yet apparent. Fear of the chaos that might accompany fundamental alterations to social, legal and constitutional norms can be inferred from the repressive nature of the revels. At a symbolic level, they represented the obligation of common law to restrict and regulate individual freedom for the collective good of the commonwealth.

The arcane rules governing the conduct of the revels attempted to resolve the conflict between order and freedom, and between the compelling (and often conflicting) rights and duties of the individual citizen on the one hand and the governance of the state on the other. Their dreamlike, imaginary quality acted on the subconscious of participants and audience, enabling a subjective response to the suggested authority of the legal institution and an acknowledgement of its legitimacy. Legh's account of the Inner Temple revels of 1561 and the description in *Gesta Grayorum* of the 'Night of Errors' at Gray's Inn in 1594 evoke a similar illusory quality. They strongly

---

[155] J. Rawls, *A Theory of Justice* (Oxford University Press, 1971), pp. 140–9; *Kant: Political Writings*, ed. H. Reiss (Cambridge University Press, 1991), p. 74. See I. Ward, *Kantianism, Postmodernism and Critical Legal Thought* (Dordrecht: Kluwer, 1997), p. 93.

[156] Morton, *The English Utopia*, p. 49.

suggest the power of the image to capture the subject of law and generate submission to the authority of the legal institution.[157] These texts imply also the sovereignty of a confident professional body, asserting the legitimate authority of common law within an imagined body politic. In the context of the emergent legal profession and its institutional antipathy towards the royal prerogative, the Inns of Court revels can reasonably be interpreted as representations of the English Utopia, developed in accordance with the equitable principles of common law. The landscape of this realm was shaped by the aspirations of common lawyers, in particular by their collective desire to provide the necessary political, social and spiritual conditions for the creation of the ideal state.

[157] On Legendre and the capture of the subject of law by the image, see Goodrich (ed.), *Law and the Unconscious*, p. 218.

4

The theatre of law: dramatic symbols of crown, common law and the Ancient Constitution

THE ROLE OF THE MASQUE IN THE LEGAL COMMUNITY

it pleased his Maiestie to call for the Anticke-Maske of Song and Daunce which was againe presented; and then the Maskers uncovered their faces, and came up to the State, and kissed the King, and Queene, and Princes hand, with a great deale of grace and favour, and so were invited to the Banquet.[1]

The masquers described above were members of Gray's Inn, presented to James I following their performance of *The Masque of Flowers* at the Banqueting House in Whitehall on Twelfth Night, 1613. The description of events illustrates the ambiguous relationship between the Jacobean royal court and the legal profession. This was characterised on the one hand by patronage, advancement and a belief that the judiciary was a branch of executive office, and on the other, by a rigorous defence of judicial independence and a belief in the sovereignty of common law jurisdiction. This chapter is concerned with the representation of law in theatre and the utility of the visual and dramatic image in facilitating the comprehension of invisible concepts such as government, rationality and divine law. The masques examined here were not presented as educational devices for forensic rhetoricians, nor as a means of depicting a national idyll or Utopia. Instead they explore the mystical role of kingship: its benevolent predisposition and divine provenance, but also the limits to its earthly powers and the constitutional role of the judiciary in defining such restrictions.

Analysis of the printed versions of dramatic entertainments presented at the Inns of Court during the Elizabethan and Jacobean periods reveals their status as legal texts, embodying the content of the Ancient Constitution, as perceived and interpreted by common lawyers. The efficacy of this claim rests in the notion of the visibility of power, a phenomenon particularly associated

---

[1] I. G., W. D., and T. B., etc., *The Maske of Flowers. Presented by the Gentlemen of Graies-Inne, at the Court of Whitehall, in the Banquetting House, upon Twelfe night 1613* (London: R. Wilson, 1614), fo. C4.

with the early modern period. This was an era in which government was presented as a spectacular form of theatre, an art form with which Elizabeth I was entirely comfortable but that her successor, James, would never master.[2]

During the seasonal festivities described in chapter 3 it was customary for members of the Inns to present their own productions of dramatic entertainment, often in the form of the masque: a highly stylised, visually extravagant form of theatre, uniquely popular during the late sixteenth and early seventeenth centuries. These plays and masques were written either by members of the Inns or by eminent dramatists, commissioned for the occasion.[3] Actors were drawn exclusively from the membership of the Inn, and audiences consisted of fellow members, courtiers and, often, the monarch. I examine seven of the Inns of Court masques, spanning a period of fifty-eight years between 1561 and 1619. The dramatic entertainments examined in this chapter are instances of law presented as theatre. The staging of the drama of community and law, expressed through poetry, costume and scenery simultaneously exaggerates and exemplifies the social drama of law. Here the social enters law at the same time as law emerges into social, that is to say, into the non-reverential and imagistic domain of the public sphere. Common lawyers created roles for themselves, not only in the mythical world of the masques, but also in the formulation of the early modern constitution. The polemical content of all the masques considered in this chapter attests to the political ascendancy of common lawyers. Specifically, the masques assert the importance of an independent legal profession to the governance of the well-ordered state, and the elevated status of a divinely anointed judiciary as the supreme constitutional authority within the realm. Common law is depicted as the unassailable manifestation of natural order or divine judgment, rather than as a codified body of positive law. In this, it reveals its Judaeo-Christian, scriptural origins in the biblical principle that law was the earthly expression of divine rather than human will.[4]

---

[2] I. Ward, 'A Kingdom for a Stage, Princes to Act: Shakespeare and the Art of Government', *Law and Critique*, 8 (1997), 190, 191. See also C. Pye, *The Regal Phantasm: Shakespeare and the Politics of Spectacle* (London: Routledge, 1990); W. Iser, *Staging Politics: The Lasting Impact of Shakespeare's Histories* (New York: Columbia University Press, 1993).

[3] On the Inns of Court masques and dramas in general, and *Ferrex and Porrex* in particular, see F. S. Boas, 'Tragedy at the Inns of Court', in *An Introduction to Tudor Drama* (Oxford: Clarendon, 1933), pp. 29–41; L. B. Campbell, 'Dramatic Representations at the Inns of Court' in *Scenes and Machines on the English Stage during the Renaissance* (Cambridge University Press, 1923), pp. 83–98; S. P. Kerr, 'Shakespeare and Gray's Inn', *Graya*, 32 (1950), 99–107; E. Welsford, *The Court Masque: a Study in the Relationship between Poetry and the Revels* (Cambridge University Press, 1927).

[4] On the origins of the common law tradition in the Old Testament, see D. R. Kelley, *The Human Measure* (Cambridge, Mass.: Harvard University Press, 1990), p. 67.

MASQUE AND MONARCH: ICONS OF NATIONAL UNITY

Two issues of overriding constitutional importance at the start of Elizabeth's reign were the succession and the settlement. In hereditary terms, as granddaughter of Margaret Tudor and James IV of Scotland, Mary Stuart was the obvious heir presumptive, following the death of Mary I in November 1558. The main objection, of debatable legal foundation, was that she was queen of Scotland and therefore an alien at common law.[5] Also, the terms of Henry VIII's will favoured the descendants of his younger sister Mary and her husband the duke of Suffolk, rather than those of his elder sister Margaret. The question of the succession was directly linked to the nature of the future settlement. Mary I had restored England to the Roman Catholic faith, which in strict jurisprudential terms undermined the *imperium* established by Henry VIII and effectively subordinated English law to papal supremacy. As ecclesiastical law was administered by civil lawyers, the possible succession of another Catholic queen posed an obvious threat to the juridical hegemony of common lawyers.

On her accession Elizabeth I was regarded by the London authorities as a Protestant saviour. It is noteworthy that judicious use of the image was crucial in consolidating institutional opposition to rival claimants and jurisdictions. Guy cites a court masque, held on Twelfth Night 1559, in which cardinals, bishops and abbots were depicted by dancers as crows, asses and wolves.[6] During this period the principal contribution of the legal profession to the imagistic domain of the masques was to suggest for itself a central constitutional role as sagacious counsellor to the monarch. The Inns of Court masques were unanimous in their eulogistic depiction of the monarch as God's appointed representative on earth, but, in varying degrees, they suggested that such earthly power had its legal and natural limits. They provided a unique medium through which the idea of a modern constitution might be expressed and understood in pictorial and poetic terms. The texts reveal the nature of the constitution sought by common lawyers and the role envisaged for the monarch within the state. Classical imagery and ancient British myth were deployed as allegory, thereby avoiding the possible charge of explicit criticism of the regnant monarch.

The coexistence and mutual respect of the crown and common law were symbolised by the monarch's personal patronage of these events. Despite this, the subject matter of some of the masques emphasised an impending constitutional crisis, the origins of which could be traced to conflicting and irreconcilable ideologies, concerning the true and incontestable source of

---

[5] R. Ashton, *Reformation and Revolution, 1558–1660* (London: Paladin, 1985), p. 79.
[6] J. Guy, *Tudor England* (Oxford University Press, 1990), p. 258.

legal authority and constitutional supremacy. The form and content of government was depicted in a highly stylised and idiosyncratic manner, its crises and failings laid open to an influential audience, attuned to the overt symbolism and rhetorical power of the staged events.[7] Given the absence of any formal, statutory restriction over the exercise of prerogative powers, the Inns of Court played a significant role as institutional guardians of the common law. The content of the masques suggests that restraint would act in the interests of king, common law and country, and that the abuse of the royal prerogative would have dire consequences for the constitutional and civil stability of the nation. The physical presence of the monarch emphasised the startling and compelling polemic of these dramatic works.

Two common lawyers, Thomas Norton and Thomas Sackville, wrote *The Tragedie of Ferrex and Porrex* (also known as *The Tragedie of Gorboduc*). It was performed by members of the Inner Temple on 18 January 1561 in the presence of Elizabeth I.[8] The authors employed the deadly sin of pride as a metaphor for unlawful exercise of the royal prerogative. Gorboduc, the father of the eponymous princes, is the antithesis of good kingship. His deliberate subversion of ancient custom and the arrogation to his own person of unlawful prerogative powers initiated a descent into civil unrest and ultimately the destruction of the realm. Burgess has remarked that fear of civil disorder transcended intellectual distinctions concerning constitutional sovereignty and served as a pragmatic factor in uniting constitutional theorists of differing perspectives.[9] *Ferrex and Porrex* did not suggest that republican sentiments were prevalent at the Inns, although the Platonic ideal of *justitia* and the Aristotelian insistence on the congruency of natural and political order can readily be inferred from their constitutions. Rather, the text suggests an attempt to realign conventional providential jurisprudence of the king's two bodies (in which the transcendence of his 'divine' body provided the theological basis for the justification of absolute monarchy) within the framework of a sovereign common law. Under such a constitutional settlement, the judiciary was the ultimate determinant not of the legitimacy of the royal prerogative itself, but of individual acts taken under the name of the royal prerogative.

Ferrex and Porrex incorporated scenes of murder, rebellion and civil war, and vividly depicted the ensuing descent into chaos. More daringly, given the

---

[7] On the masque as a stylistic expression of art, government and the visibility of power, see Ward, 'A Kingdom for a Stage', 191, 195. For a classic, Whig interpretation of the impending constitutional crisis, see G. M. Trevelyan, *England Under the Stuarts* (London: Routledge, 2002).
[8] T. Norton and T. Sackville, *The Tragedie of Ferrex and Porrex* (London: J. Daye, 1570).
[9] G. Burgess, *Absolute Monarchy and the Stuart Constitution* (New Haven: Yale University Press, 1996), pp. 93–121.

presence of Queen Elizabeth, the play charted the inexorable slide towards civil war occasioned by confusion over the lawful succession and the absence of an heir to the throne. Gorboduc, king of Britain, divides his realm during his lifetime between his sons, Ferrex and Porrex. The ambitious younger son, Porrex, kills the elder. Their mother, Videna (who loves Ferrex more than Porrex), subsequently kills Porrex. The subjects rebel, killing Gorboduc and Videna. The nobility then violently suppress the rebellion, but continuing uncertainty over the succession leads to civil war, in the course of which many subjects were killed, 'and the land for a long time almost desolate and miserably wasted'.[10] Pride is perceived as the cause of chaos. Gorboduc had no constitutional right arbitrarily to divide the kingdom and appoint two new rulers, Ferrex and Porrex. The king has misused the royal prerogative and has failed to discharge properly his sacred duty to govern. The consequences for the crown, the constitution and the country are catastrophic. Gorboduc's hubris fatally impels him to reject and overturn the law of succession, a law vital to the maintenance of primogeniture, hierarchy and order. Early modern jurists were unanimous in their opposition to altering the ancient laws of the nation, perceiving in such precipitate action a genuine threat to civil order. Fulbecke, for example, asserted that 'lawes should not be altered without urgent occasion: for it is a fonde part to strive against the course and stream of lawes, and customs received'.[11] It is relevant to an understanding of the development of equity in English law that conscience was strongly linked by contemporary commentators to custom. St German, in his defence of equity, argued that '[t]hough a Custom in this Realm prevaileth not against a Statute as to the Law, yet it seemeth that it may prevail against the Statute in Conscience: for though Ignorance of a Statute excuseth not in the Law, nevertheless it may excuse in Conscience.'[12] Echoing these sentiments, in *Of custom, and not easily changing an accepted law*, Montaigne suggested that the laws of conscience were engendered by custom.[13] King Gorboduc is soundly advised that 'Custome (O King) shall bring delightfulnesse'.[14] His wanton disregard for the ancient customs of the realm instigates the ensuing catastrophe. As custom was considered by jurists to provide the foundations of common law legitimacy, then disregard for it indicated disdain for the common law itself. Infelicitous innovations were represented by common lawyers as potentially disruptive to the ordered administration of the state

[10] 'The argument of the Tragedie', in Norton and Sackville, *Ferrex and Porrex*, fo. A1.
[11] W. Fulbecke, *A Direction or Preparative to the Study of the Lawe* (London: T. Wight, 1600), fo. 5b.
[12] C. St German, *Two Dialogues in English, Between a Doctor of Divinity, and A Student in the Laws of England, of the Grounds of the said Laws, And of Conscience* (London: the Assigns of R. & E. Atkins, 1709), p. 95.
[13] M. Montaigne, 'Of custom, and not easily changing an accepted law', *The Complete Works of Montaigne*, trans. D. M. Frame (London: Hamish Hamilton, 1958), p. 83.
[14] Norton and Sackville, *Ferrex and Porrex*, fo. Bii.

Dramatic symbols of crown, common law and Ancient Constitution 129

or, in the words of Coke, as 'upstart and wild provisoes and limitations, such as the common law never knew'.[15]

In the court of King Gorboduc, the unheeded voices of wisdom and temperance were provided by learned counsellors, whose Graeco-Roman names (Arostus, Philander and Eubulus) indicate the influence of the ancient world over the practices of the Inns of Court. Their role in *Ferrex and Porrex* is similar to that exercised by the ancients, readers and benchers at the Inns. In the broadest sense, it is to educate young men; not only should they acquire technical expertise in the practice of common law but also, as Gorboduc intends for his sons:

> Maye so be taught and trained in noble artes,
> As what their fathers which have reigned before
> Have with great fame derived downe to them,
> With honour they may leave unto their seede.[16]

The reference to 'noble' arts is noteworthy, as it reflects the shift in emphasis from theology to rhetoric, which was a characteristic feature of education in the sixteenth century. In Selden's edition of *De Laudibus Legum Angliae*, he noted that students at the Inns of Court were referred to as '*Apprenticii Nobiliores*'.[17] Classical education (in which the works of Cicero dominated) was integrated with the medieval ideal of honour to train young men for the service of the nation-state, in accordance with the aims espoused by Elyot in *The Book Named the Governor*. Godfrey Goodman, for example, bishop of Gloucester during the reign of James I, articulated the belief of many that to be a lawyer was to be governor of one's country.[18]

The importance of humility in a ruler is emphasised throughout *Ferrex and Porrex*. Philander (a counsellor assigned by the king to his younger son, Porrex) reminds Porrex of the correlation between humility and law:

> See them obey, so shall you see them rule,
> Who so obeyeth not with humblenesse
> Will rule with outrage and with insolence.[19]

These lines serve as an injunction both to monarch and counsellor that the exercise of power should be characterised by humility, which is implicitly linked to the classical virtues of prudence and temperance. Elizabethan jurists were vehement that knowledge of law, self and universe could be acquired

---

[15] E. Coke, *The Reports*, 7 vols. (London: Rivington, 1777), Part IV, preface, p. vii.
[16] Norton and Sackville, *Ferrex and Porrex*, fo. Bi.
[17] J. Fortescue, *De Laudibus Legum Angliae*, ed. J. Selden (London: R. Gosling, 1737), p. 111, n. [c].
[18] W. R. Prest, *The Rise of the Barristers: a Social History of the English Bar, 1590–1640* (Oxford: Clarendon, 1991), p. 234. On the expectation of lawyers that they should be involved in government, see *ibid.*, p. 237.
[19] Norton and Sackville, *Ferrex and Porrex*, fo. Biiii.

only through the attainment of genuine humility. Fulbecke, for example, who contributed to the authorship of masques at Gray's Inn, emphasised the importance of humility in the student of the common law: '[l]et not the increase of his skil make his mind to increase, and swell.'[20] To question the validity, rectitude and customs of the legal institution was to question the omnipotence of God. Humility demanded the unquestioning acceptance of the sovereign authority of common law. In 1561, when the queen saw *The Tragedie of Ferrex and Porrex*, there was one public figure in particular whose hubris might constitute a threat to the throne. That year, Mary Stuart returned to Scotland from France, following the death of her husband, Francis II, in December 1560.[21] It was inevitable that so long as the successor to Elizabeth remained a matter of concern, hubris was perceived to be a fatal flaw.

Like many Elizabethan dramas, *Ferrex and Porrex* was preceded by a brief dumb show. In it, the main themes of the ensuing drama were condensed into a few minutes and acted in the form of a mime. The visual rhetoric was impressive and at least as important as the drama itself in demonstrating the burgeoning constitutional significance of the Elizabethan legal profession. The dumb show demonstrated the unity and fraternity inherent in the institutional existence of common lawyers at the Inns of Court, and the bonds of Aristotelian friendship to which the members adhered. Five men entered to dramatic musical accompaniment, covered in leaves. One of them had a bundle of sticks tied around his neck. The others tried to break the sticks, but were unable to do so until each of them took out one stick at a time from the bundle, and broke it: '[h]ereby was signified, that a state knit in unitie doth continue strong against all force. But being divided, is easely destroyed. As befell upon Duke Gorboduc dividing his land to his two sonnes which he before held in Monarchie.'[22] The bundle of sticks, or *fasces*, was the emblem of official authority in the ancient Roman republic. In the context of the Inns of Court and the particular depiction of government in *Ferrex and Porrex*, it is significant that *fasces* also symbolised the unity and strength of citizens within the city-state.[23]

Apart from raising issues concerning the constitution of the state, the dumb show also referred implicitly to the microcosm of that state, the Inns of Court. The corporate unity of the membership guaranteed their strength and represented shared spiritual and ethical values. Beneath the theatrical

---

[20] Fulbecke, *A Direction or Preparative*, fo. 11b.
[21] See S. Watkins, *Mary Queen of Scots* (London: Thames & Hudson, 2001). For an analysis of the numerous artistic depictions of Mary Stuart, from the Elizabethan to the Victorian age, see J. E. Lewis, *Mary Queen of Scots: Romance and Nation* (London: Routledge, 1998).
[22] Norton and Sackville, *Ferrex and Porrex*, 'The Order of the Domme shew', fo. A3.
[23] Benito Mussolini's Fascist Party of Italy was named for the *fasces*, which the members adopted in 1919 as their emblem; the word 'fascism' is derived from this use.

artifice was the serious concern that the royal prerogative should not be exercised to alter existing customs, 'without urgent occasion'.[24] The five members of the Inner Temple, clad in leaves, symbolised the correlation between natural law and common law. Elton argues that one effect of the Reformation was to assert the supreme jurisdiction of the king in Parliament, freeing the sovereign political power from the restrictions imposed by divine and natural laws.[25] While this assessment is undeniable in relation to the authority of foreign jurisdictions, it ignores the appeal made by common lawyers to the divine provenance of common law. In practical terms, the attempt by the legal profession to correlate common law with natural and divine law imposed an implicit duty on the judiciary (which Coke asserted on numerous occasions) to declare void those statutes which they considered irrational and offensive to God. The strength of the *fasces*, or bundle of sticks, was an apt symbol of the resolution demonstrated by common lawyers, confronted with the exigencies of absolute government. This resolution was to express itself overtly in the early seventeenth century in the common law courts, through the eloquent defiance of Coke, and by common lawyer MPs during the debates concerning the Petition of Right of 1628. At the start of Elizabeth's reign, when *Ferrex and Porrex* was presented, dissent and discontent within the legal profession were confined to symbolic acts of defiance. These included the presentation of the dumb show, above, in which the real presence of common law was encountered in an image: that of a united body of men, whose loyalty was primarily to the laws of God and the commonwealth.

On 28 February 1587, twenty-six years after the performance of *The Tragedie of Ferrex and Porrex*, Gray's Inn presented an entertainment entitled *Certaine Devises and shewes*, written by Thomas Hughes, with contributions from other members of the Inn, including William Fulbecke. It was performed in the presence of Elizabeth I, at her court in Greenwich. An introduction, written by Nicholas Trotte, preceded the main dramatic presentation. Three muses enter, escorting their captives: five students of the common law, all members of Gray's Inn. One of the muses presents the students to the queen, and greets her with appropriate deference:

> A Dame there is, whom men Astrea terme,
> Shee that pronounceth Oracles of Lawes,
> Who to prepare fit servants for her traine
> As by Commission takes up flowring wits.[26]

---

[24] Fulbecke, *A Direction or Preparative*, fo. 5b.
[25] G. R. Elton, *England Under the Tudors* (London: Routledge, 1991), p. 168.
[26] T. Hughes, *Certaine Devises and shewes presented to her Maiestie by the Gentlemen of Grayes-Inne at her Highnesse Court in Greenwich, the twenty eighth day of Februarie in the thirtieth yeare of her Maiesties most happy Raigne* (London: R. Robinson, 1587), introduction.

The obvious stylistic feature of this introduction is its allusion to classical mythology. The students emerge onstage into a mythical world of gods and goddesses. This is a recurring theme of the masques: members assume roles in a realm of ancient myth, in which archetypes of English kingship and custom are revered and deified. In *Violence and the Sacred*, Girard observes that one theory of primitive religion attributes the origins of ritual to myth, and that the discovery of some historical event, fact or belief is sought, to which can be attributed the particular ritual or practice. The real event of fundamental importance, whose revelation was sought in the masques, was the exposition of the origin of common law.[27] The themes and characters of the masques represent and emphasise the otherness of the common lawyer. He is depicted as a heroic figure of divine provenance, a theme to which I return later in this chapter.

Initially, my concern is with the portrayal of the crown, its status within this fictional representation, and its influence over the lives of the masque's protagonists and the legal system that they represent. In classical mythology, Astraea was the daughter of Zeus and Themis; she spread justice and virtue throughout the world in the Golden Age. When wickedness took over the world, Astraea returned to heaven, and became the constellation Virgo. Obviously, the inclusion of Astraea in the proceedings was a complimentary reference to the guest of honour, Elizabeth I, and was a familiar literary conceit. The introduction to *Certaine Devises and shewes* mythologised the queen, thus distancing her from the human process of lawmaking. The role of the monarch was represented as symbolic and iconic, and therefore of limited relevance to the creation and enforcement of legislation. If, as Marin suggests, the king acquires the symbolic status of monarch only through his representation in images,[28] then it is relevant to the perceived role of Elizabeth I that the image of the monarch presented in the masque was shaped not by the crown but by the legal profession. The choice of words in the introduction to the masque is distinctive: Astraea 'pronounceth Oracles of Lawes'. The writer communicates a sense in which the monarch acts as a mouthpiece for the law. She 'pronounces' (meaning, to articulate correctly) divine utterances concerning the law. But the laws themselves do not originate from her: their provenance is divine. The image of the monarch provides the visible link between common law and its divine creator. This interpretation of the monarch's iconic role requires that the image is understood in a classical or reformist sense as a real thing. Like the oracle to which the play's introduction refers, she is an agency or medium through which prophecy is transmitted and revealed.

[27] R. Girard, *Violence and the Sacred*, trans. P. Gregory (Baltimore: Johns Hopkins University Press, 1977), p. 89.
[28] L. Marin, *Portrait of the King*, trans. M. M. Houle (Basingstoke: Macmillan, 1988), p. 9.

The introduction reveals also a more pragmatic and parochial role, envisaged for the monarch by the author. It is that of patron of the common law, granting advancement to the royal court for the most accomplished rhetoricians of the Inn: the 'flowring wits' referred to above, who alone are 'fit servants for her traine'. These young men were removed from the harsh climate of legal practice and relocated to the rarefied environment of the royal court. The rhetorical skills acquired at the Inns (and the associated benefits of a humanist education) were represented as the foundation for their role as royal counsellors:

> The noble skils of language and of Arts,
> The wisedom, which discourse of stories teach,
> The ornaments which various knowledge yields.[29]

The visual climax of *The Maske of Flowers* was the transformation into flowers of those members of Gray's Inn who performed the masque in the presence of James I. As with *Certaine Devises and shewes*, the image of the stars and the heavens was incorporated into the action to embody the providential sanctity of kingship. The king was represented by the sun, whose miraculous power is such that it can turn men into plants, and reverse the process with equal facility. The interaction between heaven, earth and organic matter also suggests that reference was intended to the congruency of nature, God and the universality of natural law. A song was sung in praise of the transformation:

> Give place you ancient powers,
> That turned men to Flowers,
> For never Writers pen,
> Yet tolde of Flowers return'd to Men:
> But miracles of new event,
> Follow the great Sun of our firmament.[30]

Classical mythology provided the stylistic framework of the masque; in this case, Ovid's *Metamorphoses*, and the transformation of Narcissus into a flower, on gazing with self-love at his own reflection. At one level the above text clearly suggests elevation to the influential environment of the royal court. The king, 'the great Sun of our firmament', sitting before them in the audience, was the means through which the actors could achieve the transformation from common lawyers to royal favourites. The image of the king as the sun, the life-giving heavenly body, was a popular conceit. Shakespeare, for example, frequently incorporated the image in his history

---

[29] Hughes, *Certaine Devises*, intro.
[30] *The Maske of Flowers*, fo. C2. See also the myth of Echo and Narcissus in Ovid, *Metamorphoses*, trans. M. M. Innes (Penguin: Harmondsworth, 1973), pp. 83–7.

plays. *Richard III* opens with Gloucester informing the audience: 'Now is the winter of our discontent/ Made glorious summer by this sun of York.' The personal badge of Richard II was the sun emerging from a cloud, a recurring image throughout Shakespeare's *Richard II*.[31] But there is an additional political dimension to the symbolism of the sun and the flowers in *The Maske of Flowers*. The ambivalent sexuality of James I was reflected in the royal court by his preferment of handsome young men. As James VI of Scotland he had elevated Esmé Stuart to the dukedom of Lennox, and in 1611 James's passion for his fellow Scot, Robert Carr, was illustrated by his decision to create him Viscount Rochester. The remarkable rise of Buckingham (from knight in 1615 to viscount, earl, marquis and, finally, duke in 1623) and his extraordinary political hegemony exemplify the unique significance of the favourite in the government of Jacobean England.[32] As Ashton has noted, neither Leicester nor Burghley exerted as much personal influence over Elizabeth as did Carr (and later, Villiers) over James I.[33]

The text of *The Masque of Flowers* emphasised that the rule of the king was benevolent:

> The Sunne shines full upon your earth,
> Disclose out of your shady bowers,
> He will not blast your tender birth.[34]

The inference to be drawn was that the king would not abuse his prerogative powers. Whilst not a view shared by all common lawyers, it was expedient for aspiring favourites to impress on James I their confidence in his benevolence. Of course, individual members of the Inns benefited from royal patronage: the transformation of men into flowers, caused by the power of the sun, clearly alluded to this. But there is an obvious conflict between prospective elevation to the royal court and common law assertions of judicial independence and political sovereignty. The historical links between the courts of law and the royal court are well established: in one of its earliest guises, the court of law was the royal court. At a later date, when the king no longer presided in person, the provincial courts and assizes were simply the royal court sitting elsewhere, the king's person in the capacity of body politic rather than body natural.

---

[31] For further discussion of this symbol, see P. Reyher, 'Le symbole du soleil dans la tragédie de Richard II', *Revue de l'enseignement des langues vivantes*, 40 (1923), 254–60.

[32] On the 'favourite' in Elizabethan and Jacobean England, see J. H. Elliott and L. W. B. Brockliss (eds.), *The World of the Favourite* (New Haven: Yale University Press, 1999); and P. Hammer, *The Polarisation of Elizabethan Politics: The Political Career of Robert Devereux, 2nd Earl of Essex, 1585–97* (Cambridge University Press, 1999).

[33] Ashton, *Reformation and Revolution*, p. 197.   [34] *The Maske of Flowers*, fo. C2.

Despite the obvious utility of royal patronage, the relationship between the legal profession and the king was ambiguous. As the prerogative powers of the king extended into areas of common law jurisdiction, the Inns of Court affirmed their immunity from executive interference and common lawyers such as Coke vociferously asserted the political sovereignty of common law. The idea of a fundamental law, which guaranteed to its subjects certain rights and liberties, developed in the courts during this period and was expanded during the constitutional crisis of the late 1620s, culminating in the Petition of Right of 1628. In the reign of James I, the restraining power of the royal prerogative became a particular source of contention in relation to the granting of monopolies by royal charter. For example, concerning a monopoly of cloth-making, granted to the Merchant Taylors of London, 'it was adjudged, that the ordinance, although it had the countenance of a charter, was against the common law, because it was against the liberty of the subject ... every grant made in grievance or prejudice of the subjects is void'.[35] Coke attempted to address the absolutist tendencies of James I with reference to the individual liberties guaranteed by the Ancient Constitution. Until his dismissal as Lord Chief Justice in 1616, Coke played a central role in expanding the capacity of the judiciary to determine the legitimacy of executive actions exercised under the royal prerogative. He argued that there were defined limits to the executive authority of the crown. More than this, he depicted the monarch as a complex image of the nation and not as an active legislator. The king was, in Coke's phrase, 'an hieroglyphic of the laws',[36] rather than an omnipotent lawgiver whose providential powers entitled him to circumvent the informal constitutional constraints of common law jurisdiction.

In the wider social and political context, the monarch was the ubiquitous image of English nationalism. Although *Certaine Devises and shewes* depicted the queen not as a lawmaker but as a symbol of law, this image provided a single, highly visible sign of the spiritual unity, social community and political sovereignty that the common law sought to represent and uphold. Its appeal to nationalism and ethnicity made the common law unique among legal systems; it was specifically associated with a unified national and political identity. It was this sense of national identity that the masques addressed, in a manner which suggested that the English were God's chosen people. Thus, in a reference to the language of law, one masque mentions an idiom:

---

[35] *Davenant v. Harris*, discussed in 'the Case of Monopolies' (*Darcy v. Allen*), Coke, XI *Reports*, p. 86b.
[36] *Calvin's Case*, Coke, VII *Reports*, p. 11a.

> More bound to words then is the Poets love:
> And for these fine conceits she fitly chose,
> A tongue that Barbarisme it selfe doth use.[37]

The barbaric tongue that incurs the writer's censure was law-French, an idiom that had been in use since the Norman Conquest and which, paradoxically, was peculiar to the practice of English common law. The crucial significance of this fact was that the use of law-French ensured that common law created and retained a language of English nationalism.[38] The fact that a hybridised form of the French tongue formed an integral part of English legal practice undermined the assertion of common lawyers that the English legal system was rooted exclusively in England's ancient customs. Spelman, for example, expressed his amazement at Coke's refusal to address the historical and linguistic evidence of foreign influence, but this had no noticeable impact on those who argued for the fictional unity of the English nation.[39] Pragmatism necessitated that an instantly recognisable national identity should prevail over historical accuracy, providing a defence against the rival jurisdictions of civil and canon law. The threat to the English legal system was by no means imaginary: war against Spain was ongoing and the outcome less than certain. In 1586 the campaigns in the Netherlands had been unsuccessfully waged under the incompetent leadership of Leicester. On 7 February 1587, only two weeks before the performance at Greenwich of *Certaine Devises and shewes*, Mary Stuart was executed at Fotheringay Castle. Despite Elizabeth's ambivalent attitude towards her Catholic cousin and her sincere expressions of anger and sorrow at her sudden execution, the obvious effect of this conclusive act was to arouse French hostility.

Set in this context it is unsurprising that the Inns of Court valued so highly their exclusivity and their status as guardians of a unique ethnocentric legal system. Mistrust of strangers extended inevitably and particularly to foreigners, as the proscriptive legislation of the Inns demonstrated. The perceived threat of invasion by Spain and its Catholic allies in France served to distance still further English constitutional theory from its continental counterpart (as espoused in particular by Jean Bodin), which placed political sovereignty firmly and exclusively in the hands of the prince, acting as *rex solus*. Suspicion of foreign motives manifested itself as fervent nationalism and is apparent in the principal drama of *Certaine Devises and shewes*, entitled 'The misfortunes of Arthur'. In this interpretation of the ancient English myth, King Arthur leaves Britain for France, to do battle with Lucius Tiberius of Rome.

---

[37] Hughes, *Certaine Devises*, intro.
[38] J. H. Baker, 'The Three Languages of the Common Law', *McGill Law Journal*, 43 (1998), 7.
[39] H. Spelman, *Of the Four Law Terms: A Discourse*, 1614 (London: Gillyflower, 1684), pp. 99–101.

The outcome of the fighting is never in any doubt; nevertheless, a character informs the audience of Arthur's overwhelming victory, emphasising the fact that the battle was won in France:

> Brytaines erst paide tribute for their peace,
> But now rebell, and dare them at their doores:
> For what was Fraunce but theirs?[40]

The archetype of English nationalism, Arthur, has defeated Rome in a land subjected to Roman law. King Arthur was only one of several heroic icons of nationhood to whom Coke attributed the foundation of English law.[41] At one level therefore, the play operates as a metaphor for the nationalist certainties, inherent rectitude and divine authority of common law. This conceit would have been immediately apparent to performers and audience alike, conversant (and compliant) as they were with familiar legal perceptions concerning the origins of the English legal system.

The depiction of Arthur's wife, Queen Guinevere, as an intemperate, lustful adulteress demonstrates the contemporary relevance of 'The misfortunes of Arthur', by alluding to the perceived moral dereliction of the late Mary Stuart. While Arthur is in France, his illegitimate son, Mordred, seduces Guinevere (Mordred was the product of an incestuous relationship between Arthur and his twin sister, Anne). Following her seduction, Guinevere is consumed by lust for her stepson: 'Desire to joy him still, torments my mynde.'[42] She is dissuaded from repeating her crime by a lady-in-waiting, Fronia, who reminds her mistress of the laws of God and state which forbid such conduct: 'Eschew it farre: such love impugnes the lawes.'[43] Guinevere's function in the drama was to represent the antithesis of law: her excessive conduct, which transgresses the laws of God and man, threatens the ordered identity of the community. In the patriarchal society depicted in the play, she represents the feminine stranger, whose negative image affirms the jurisdiction of the commonwealth.[44] Its lawfulness is determined partly by the illicit image of outsiders, of their strangeness and unacceptable customs. Consequently the legitimacy of the legal community and of the state is asserted by presenting Guinevere as an idol, the empty mask of evil. Theatre is the chosen medium through which the idol, Guinevere, can be rejected and the legitimacy of law affirmed. Traditionally, iconoclasts interpreted the image as a harlot: Parker

---

[40] Hughes, *Certaine Devises*, fo. 12.
[41] On King Arthur and the immemorial origins of English law, see P. Goodrich, *Languages of Law: From Logics of Memory to Nomadic Masks* (London: Weidenfeld & Nicolson, 1990), p. 214.
[42] Hughes, *Certaine Devises*, fo. 5.   [43] *Ibid.*
[44] On the classical concepts of apology and antirrhetic, see P. Goodrich, *Oedipus Lex: Psychoanalysis, History, Law* (Los Angeles: University of California Press, 1995), pp. 41–67.

made this specific accusation in the *Scholasticall Discourse*.⁴⁵ But as *Certaine Devises and shewes* demonstrates, the Elizabethan legal institution distinguished between those images that offer nothing but the spurious visage, and those that draw the eye from the visible to the invisible. The former are examples of the antirrhetic, the antithetical form of the apology; the latter are icons, which legitimately direct the audience's gaze towards the will of God, and to an understanding of the correlation between common law and divine law.

THE JACOBEAN MASQUE: VIRTUE'S COURT AND THE IMAGINARY CONSTITUTION

The absolute power of law manifested itself, in legal form, as the royal prerogative. In 1607 John Cowell remarked that the prerogative gave the king power and privilege above other persons and above the course of common law. Cowell attempted to equate the prerogative powers of the English monarch with those absolute powers exercised by the prince under the civil code: 'our lawyers (*sub praerogitiva regis*) doe comprise also, all that absolute heighth of power that the Civilians call (*maiestatem, vel potestatem, vel ius imperii,*) subject only to god'.⁴⁶ As discussed in chapter 3, the theory of the divine right of kings was proposed initially by Whitgift in reply to Presbyterian claims that the institutions of church and state should be distinct and separate. Under James I, the mysterious power of the royal prerogative became inextricably entwined with the sacred theory of divine right. The providential claim by James I that kings were God's lieutenants on earth, called gods by God himself, provided the theological justification for the arrogation to him of absolute power, a model akin to the monarchies of continental Europe.⁴⁷ Accordingly, as the divine right of kings was derived through nature from God, it was not subject to legal constraint. It is in the context of (and as a response to) the potential such providential theory presented for unlimited monarchy that the Inns of Court masques of the Jacobean period should be interpreted. The principal stylistic development of Jacobean masques is the unprecedented visual extravagance of the settings. In thematic terms the most striking phenomenon is the allegorical depiction of common lawyers as divine bodies. In particular, the judiciary

---

⁴⁵ 'The image is an harlot', R. Parker, *A Scholasticall Discourse against Symbolizing with Antichrist in Ceremonies: Especially in the sign of the Crosse* (London, 1607), fo. 137.
⁴⁶ J. Cowell, *The Interpreter; or Booke Containing the Signification of Words* (Cambridge: J. Legate, 1607), fo. Ddd3.
⁴⁷ See James I, *Political Writings, King James VI and I*, ed. J. P. Sommerville (Cambridge University Press, 1994).

is represented as the supreme constitutional authority, administering justice independently and in accordance with the will of God.

The indivisibility of divine law, natural law and human reason was visualised by the members of Gray's Inn who devised and presented *The Maske of Flowers*, performed on the occasion of the marriage of the earl of Somerset to the daughter of the earl of Suffolk in 1613. Within a stylised representation of a city (with walls, battlements, a great gate, temples and houses) was an elaborate garden, depicting the harmonious fusion of nature's beneficence and man's reason: 'a Garden of a glorious and strange beauty, cast into foure quarters, with a crosse walke and allies, compassing each quarter. In the middle of the crosse walke, stoode a goodly Fountaine raised on foure columnes of Silver.' The elaborate fountain supported a statue of Neptune riding on a dolphin, and within the garden were pedestals, 'upon the toppes whereof were personages of golde, Lions of gold, and Unicornes of silver'. It is an ordered world of myth and symbolism, the realm of nobility (represented by the lion), ancient mystery (represented by the unicorn) and virtue (the 'personages of gold'). Cypress and juniper hedges bordered each quarter of the garden. In each of two quarters stood a pyramid, 'garnished with golde and silver, and glistering with transparent lights, resembling Carbuncles, Saphires, and Rubies'.[48] The pyramids represent human reason, the precious jewels encrusted therein the rewards for knowledge applied in harmony with the law of nature. At the end of the garden was an arbour covered by eglantine and honeysuckle, beyond which stood an orchard. In the arbour sat twelve 'Garden-Gods . . . apparrelled in long roabes of greene rich taffata, Cappes on their heads, and chaplets of Flowers. In the midst of them sate Primavera'.[49] The garden-gods (with Primavera at their head, representing continuance and rebirth) preside over a perfect natural world in which boundaries and paths are created by man's reason, for the greater benefit of the commonwealth. The correlation between God, nature and man (and the unwritten law that binds them) is evident in ancient Greek art, which abounds in sacred trees: sacrifices are made before them, and temples are built around and within them. The olive tree was both Athene's temple and her image, prior to the construction of architectural temples and sculptured images. Trees were often trimmed into the shape of columns: Vitruvius maintained that the first columns were trees, and, according to Pausanius, the first temple to Apollo at Delphi was a hut made of laurel trees.[50]

---

[48] *The Maske of Flowers*, fo. C. For observations on the design of masques, see P. Simpson and C. F. Bell, *Designs by Inigo Jones for Masques and Plays at Court* (Oxford University Press, 1924); see also J. Peacock, 'Inigo Jones's Stage Architecture and its Sources', *Art Bulletin*, 64 (1982), 195–216.

[49] *The Maske of Flowers*, fo. C2.

[50] G. Hersey, *The Lost Meaning of Classical Architecture* (Cambridge, Mass.: MIT, 1988), p. 11.

Similar themes emerge in *The Masque of Heroes*, written by Thomas Middleton and performed by members of the Inner Temple in 1619. The collateral, material benefit of harmonisation between man and nature was the creation of wealth, popularly understood to be the inevitable consequence of a virtuous life. In George Chapman's masque for the Middle Temple and Lincoln's Inn, presented in 1613, wealth was personified by Plutus, the god of earthly riches. Significantly, although Aristophanes depicted Plutus as blind, deformed and dull-witted, he was 'here by his love of Honor, made see, made sightly, made ingenious, made liberall'. Honour appeared in Chapman's masque as a heavenly goddess, and Riches as an earthly god. The importance of this relationship to Jacobean society was suggested by their status, 'Highest of all in the most eminent seate of the Tryumphall sat, side to side'. Law was personified in Chapman's masque as Eunomia, described as 'a Virgine Priest', consecrated to the goddess Honour.[51] The considerable wealth of successful lawyers was explained by Buc, in terms of virtue and godliness: 'chiefely by their due serving of God (who is the only and best rewarder of vertue, and honest industry) [they] get much wealth, and attayne to great places and dignities of offices in the law and in the commonwealth, and become rich, and famous lawyers'.[52] Wealth, and the associated power and influence it generated, was a vital factor in the creation of a distinct, professional class of lawyers. It enabled them to pursue careers in Parliament, and to bring their predilections to bear on the legislative process. This was of particular significance during the constitutional crisis of the late 1620s, when a disproportionate number of MPs were also common lawyers (Cromartie attributes this fact to the legal training provided for a class that Tudor government had burdened with administrative duties).[53]

During *The Masque of Heroes*, the character of Harmony ('with her sacred Quire') sang an encomium to virtue:

> Thy faire desires in Vertues Court are fil'de ...
> ... Thy Spring shall in all sweets abound,
> Thy Sommer shall be cleere and sound,
> Thy Autumne swell the Barne and Loft,
> With Corne and fruits, ripe, sweet and soft,
> And in thy Winter, when all goe,
> Thou shalt depart as white as Snow.[54]

---

[51] G. Chapman, *The Memorable Maske of the two Honorable Houses or Inns of Court; the Middle Temple, and Lyncolns Inne. As it was performd before the King* (London: G. Norton, 1613), ff. A8, A4, A8.

[52] G. Buc, *The Third Universitie of England* (London: Society of Stationers, 1615), fo. 975.

[53] A. Cromartie, 'The Constitutionalist Revolution: The Transformation of Political Culture in Early Stuart England', *Past & Present*, 163 (1999), 86.

[54] T. Middleton, *The Inner-Temple Masque or Masque of Heroes. Presented (as an Entertainment for many worthy Ladies:) By Gentlemen of the same Ancient and Noble House* (London: J. Browne, 1619), fo. C.

The natural order of the seasons and its relationship with man is an apt metaphor for man's acceptance of natural law. The implicit link between natural law and common law was suggested by the use of a felicitous image of the judiciary: 'Vertues Court' presides over an idealised, pastoral landscape. Virtue's Court was recognisably a representation of heaven, in which the God of Englishmen was the supreme judge. The allegorisation of virtue was a familiar rhetorical device during this period. Dugdale records the epitaphic details of John White, MP, Master of the Bench of the Middle Temple, who died in 1644 and was buried in the Inner Temple churchyard. His epitaph read: 'Here lieth a John, a burning shining light, His name, life, Actions, were all white.'[55] Middleton's masque concluded with the masquers, all students of the common law, sitting in heaven: 'Heroes Deified for their Vertues'. Finally, they descended from heaven, 'in their love to humane good', and walked upon the earth so that others might imitate their goodness.[56] The Christian interpretation of law as the Word made flesh is apparent in this image. It reflects the juristic thesis that the legal profession's role was sacerdotal rather than secular. *The Masque of Heroes* is significant in demonstrating the extraordinary capacity of a rhetorical device to exert a powerful influence over an audience. Its aural and visual images are coherent symbols of the common law's particular affinity with God and nature. In the encomium from *The Masque of Heroes*, the pulsating, repetitive nature of the four iambic feet in each line provides an exemplary poetic image of the inherent harmony and order of natural law.

Legh concluded his eulogy to the Inns of Court, *The Accedens of Armory*, with an image similar to that used by Middleton. He remarked, with reference to the Inner Temple that, '[h]erein I might compare your state (but that you are men) unto the heavenly Ierarches, for that you have the three thinges that Ierarches have, that is, Order, cunning, and working.'[57] Legh presents the archetype of the lawyer both as a human manifestation of divine order and as a member of the heavenly hierarchy. The masquers who descended from heaven in *The Masque of Heroes* were lawyer-poets. They maintained and asserted God's law, not by their knowledge of substantive law, but (in the words of Sir Philip Sidney, echoing the Ciceronian correlation between poets and the original lawgivers) because they were notable images of virtues, represented in a supposed state of nature. Although this ideal state has to be set out at a great distance from the social play of reason that is understood as law, the Inns of Court masques represented in graphic and exemplary form the coalescence of pre-Christian natural law and Thomist legal philosophy.

---

[55] Dugdale, *Origines Juridiciales*, fo. 179.   [56] *The Masque of Heroes*, fo. C2.
[57] G. Legh, *The Accedens of Armory* (London: R. Tottel, 1576), fo. 135b.

In Britain, the masque had its origins in the masks and mumming shows of seasonal feasts, in which the rites of pagan religions were observed, for example, giving thanks for the fertility of the earth, and appeasing the dead.[58] Certain visual aspects of the Inns of Court masques resembled these mumming shows, of which the dumb show preceding *The Tragedie of Ferrex and Porrex* was an obvious example. More often their sources were the epic works of Homer and Ovid, as in the case of the Inner Temple masque of 1615, *Circe and Ulysses*, in which a chapter from the *Odyssey* was staged; or *The Masque of Flowers*, whose inspiration was the tale of Echo and Narcissus in the *Metamorphoses*. At one level, these ancient narratives were concerned with the contemporary interpretation and pictorial representation of natural law in the pre-Christian world. Cicero provided a succinct definition of natural law, emphasising its eternal quality and its indissoluble association with reason:

> True law is, indeed, right reason, conformable to nature, pervading all things, constant, eternal; it incites to duty by commanding, and deters from crime by forbidding ... It is not lawful to alter this law, to derogate from it, or to repeal it ... nor will it be one law for Rome and another for Athens; one thing to-day and another to-morrow; but it is a law eternal and unchangeable for all people and in every age; and it becomes as it were, the one common god, master and governor of all. Reason is the author, publisher, and proposer of this law.[59]

For Christian scholars such as Anselm, the fundamental purpose of education was to realign these classical, ethical doctrines within the framework of Christian revelation. St Thomas Aquinas successfully integrated the two strands by asserting that human laws derived their legality from natural law, that segment of eternal law (or God-given rules governing all creation) which was discoverable through the process of reasoning, as invented by classical writers. To these he added the Christian element of divine law, revealed in Holy Scripture. Through the masques, the Inns of Court sought to represent the synthesis of classical and Christian doctrine in imagistic form. The incorporation of scenes and characters from a classical idyll demonstrated man's comprehension of God. These scenes represented a defence of faith and doctrine: faith in God Almighty, who sanctioned the doctrines of common law. Consequently, it should be understood that the images of English law referred to a Christian absolute or origin. The representations contained in the masques were not idols, or empty images without any legitimate cause. Their structural function was to establish the order and meaning of law,

---

[58] See W. Browne, *Circe and Ulysses, The Inner Temple Masque*, ed. G. Jones (London: Golden Cockerel, 1954), introduction, p. 41; also, A. Wigfall Green, *The Inns of Court and Early English Drama* (New Haven: Yale University Press, 1931), p. 15.

[59] Cicero, *The Republic*, trans. G. G. Hardingham (London: Bernard Quaritch, 1884), Book III, xxii, p. 257.

creating a relationship between the visible and the invisible, whereby incorporeal truth was manifested. Through the icons onstage, the audience was directed from the tangible to the intangible: to the creator of all that is natural. It is notable that images from classical (rather than Judaeo-Christian) mythology predominated. Such images enabled the legal institution to escape the opprobrium of Protestant, reformist iconoclasts, the object of whose opposition was the perceived idolatrous worship of images in the Roman Church. The masques presented at the Inns of Court did not condone such worship; rather they incorporated certain licit signs in order to direct the audience towards an understanding of the divine origins of common law.

In *The Masque of the Inner Temple and Gray's Inn*, by Francis Beaumont, presented before the king at the Banqueting House on 12 February 1612, the scenery consisted of a mountain

> wherein upon a levell after a great rise of the Hill, were placed two Pavilions ... In these Pavilions were placed fifteene Olympian Knights, upon seates a little imbowed neere the forme of a Croisant, and the Knights appeared first, as consecrated persons all in vailes, like to Coapes, of silver Tiffinie, gathered, and falling a large compasse about them, and over their heads high Miters with long pendants behind falling from them.[60]

The 'croisant' shape in which the lawyers were seated was probably an allusion to their forebears, the Knights Templar, and their virtuous struggle against the Saracen infidel, whose emblem was the crescent moon. The didactic function of this formalised scene was to depict the participating common lawyers as ministers of a legal system in which man was linked by nature (represented by the mountain) to God: 'upon the very top of the hill, being a higher levell then that of the Tents, was placed Jupiters Altar gilt ... and Jupiters Priests in white robes about it'. The priests had 'long white heads of haire. The high Priest a cap of white silke shagge close to his head.'[61] The symbolism was explicit: the law of God was articulated by His priests, the most revered of whom (symbolised by their position at the mountain's peak) were the most ancient. Jupiter was invoked, the supreme deity, one of whose functions was to oversee international relations through the mediation of his priests. The knights (all of whom were 'consecrated') were attired in copes and mitres. In the hierarchy of this imagistic state, the judiciary or 'Jupiter's Priests' were venerated for their antiquity and piety. They were depicted as the sovereign political power in the imaginary realm, 'upon the very top of the hill'. The above scene offers a pictorial microcosm of the

---

[60] F. Beaumont, *The Masque of the Inner Temple and Gray's Inn, Presented Before His Maiestie in the Banquetting House at White-hall on Saturday the twentieth day of Februarie, 1612* (London: G. Norton, 1612), fo. C3.
[61] *Ibid.*, fo. D.

nation-state, in which the judiciary was endowed with divine properties and irrefutable authority.

There was little dramatic narrative in the above masque, compared with the action of a drama such as *The Tragedie of Ferrex and Porrex*, which contained scenes depicting sibling rivalry, fratricide and civil war. By contrast, *The Masque of the Inner Temple and Gray's Inn* lacked any dramatic momentum. It offered nothing more than a representation of the intellectual and moral primacy of common law. The exclusive communities of the Inns interpreted law according to Cicero's advice concerning natural law, that it was unnecessary to look outside oneself for an expounder or interpreter of it.[62] As with the Christian faith itself, true knowledge of God's word was acquired through sacramental ritual. *The Masque of the Inner Temple and Gray's Inn* was peculiar for its extraordinary resemblance to religious ritual. Through the formal observance of specific rites, enacted by archetypal figures of immense symbolic significance, the subject was drawn by the image from the visible present to an understanding of a vast, incorporeal truth. It provided an image of common law at its most self-referential: it was unnecessary to look beyond the legal community for an exposition of law. The common lawyer was represented as oracle, archetype and icon. The political sovereignty of common law was intended to be inferred from the depiction of the judiciary as a representation of divinity. Elaborate scenery, extravagant costume and poetry combined to present a pictorial vision of the commonwealth as envisaged by the practitioners of common law. The masques outlined the structure and hierarchy of the state, in which social cohesion was to be attained by the synthesis of classical principles of natural law and the Christian revelation of divine law. The coalescence of these doctrines was revealed in the institutional practices of common law, the authority of which was represented in the masques as sacred and incontrovertible.

NATIONALISM, XENOPHOBIA AND COMMON LAW

The distinction between the maxims of common law and civil law (respectively *lex facit regem* and *quod principi placuit habet vigorem legis*) was partly a polemical one. Common lawyers castigated civilians for adherence to their axiom, while employing the same principle wherever the unwritten constitution required it. As Chief Justice, Coke regularly attempted to introduce innovations under the guise of immemorial practice, usually where he perceived the authority of common law jurisdiction to be threatened. Thorne

---

[62] On the elitism and insularity of Renaissance jurisprudence, see D. R. Kelley, 'Vera Philosophia: The Philosophical Significance of Renaissance Jurisprudence', *Journal of the History of Philosophy*, 14 (1976), 267–79.

suggests that wherever Coke provided a Latin maxim in order to demonstrate the continuation of an ancient legal custom, it was likely to herald a departure from existing law.[63] Hobbes made the identical observation of Coke, arguing that the insertion into his texts of Latin sentences was intended to convince the reader that these represented the law of the realm, even though they lacked either legal authority or intrinsic reason.[64] In an analysis of the practical differences between Elizabethan common law and the civil system employed by Britain's continental neighbours, Kelley notes the xenophobic zeal with which prominent Elizabethan lawyers defended their ancient birthright from external taint. He emphasises the misplaced nationalism that lay at the heart of English legal education during this period.[65] In the context of the Inns of Court masques, foreign legal systems were ridiculed with inexhaustible vigour whenever a suitable opportunity presented itself to the writers and performers. Underlying this apparent levity and obvious amusement at the strange and incomprehensible customs of foreigners was the serious theme of nationalism and, specifically, Englishness. Suspicion of Catholics in particular and foreigners in general was endemic to English society following the Bye Plot of 1603 and the Gunpowder Plot of 1605. The death in 1612 of Robert Cecil, first earl of Salisbury, marked the end of the Cecilian ascendancy. Francophile and pro-Spanish factions at court (the former led by the Scottish nobles, Lennox, Lord Hay and Lord Fenton, and the latter by the Howard family) increased the perception at the Inns of Court that rival, continental jurisdictions threatened the juridical dominance of common law.

The inherent suspicion of foreigners was highlighted to extraordinary effect in a comic interlude performed during *The Maske of Flowers*. Two characters, Silenus and Kawasha, debated the following issue, 'That Wine was more woorthy then Tobacco, and did more cheere and relieve the spirits of man.'[66] Silenus entered, riding 'an artificiall Asse, which sometimes being taken with straine of the Musicke, did bow down his eares'. Kawasha entered from the opposite side, 'borne upon two Indians shoulders attired like Floridans'. Silenus, proposing the motion, was presented in an affectionate manner, as a fat old man dressed in 'a crimson Sattin Doublet' that did not meet in the middle because of his huge paunch. He had 'a red swolne face, with a bunched nose, grey beard, bald head, pricke eares, and little hornes'.[67] He represented a particular image of common law, embodying qualities of compassion and humanity that were seen to distinguish the English legal

---

[63] S. E. Thorne, *Sir Edward Coke, 1552–1952* (London: Bernard Quaritch, 1957), p. 7.
[64] T. Hobbes, *A Dialogue between a Philosopher and a Student of the Common Laws of England*, ed. J. Cropsey (London: University of Chicago Press, 1971), p. 96.
[65] D. R. Kelley, 'History, English Law and the Renaissance', *Past & Present*, 65 (1974), 25–51.
[66] *The Maske of Flowers*, fo. A4.   [67] *Ibid.*, fo. B3.

system from its foreign counterparts. Although according to legend Silenus was very fat and rode an ass on which he could barely stay upright because he was so drunk, he was exceptionally wise. Silenus was a general term for an old satyr, but according to ancient mythology he was a demon, reputed to be the son of Pan and a nymph, and credited with bringing up the young Dionysus. When asked what was best for all men he replied, 'not to be born, not to be, to be nothing. The second best for you, however, is soon to die'.[68] These sentiments are familiar to readers of Sophocles' *Oedipus at Colonus*, in which the chorus, watching the horrific scene unfolding in Athens, cries out that the greatest boon was not to exist, but that once life had begun, it was best for it to end as soon as possible.[69]

An inference to be drawn from this bleak assertion is that life can be made bearable only by the imposition of structure and the acceptance of law, as represented by the Apollonian images depicted in the masques. Silenus retained only a vestigial trace of his Dionysian provenance, his 'pricke eares, and little hornes'. But this Silenus was not the primeval, fatalistic demon of legend. He has accepted the constraints of an ordered, lawful society, one that has harnessed nature's resources and uses them for the benefit of its subjects. Hence Silenus entered riding an ass and wearing a crimson, satin doublet. He was a symbol of man's unique ability to reason and impose his own, artificial structure on the pre-existing natural order. In the words of Thomas Carlyle, in his satirical treatise, *Sartor Resartus*, '[m]an is a Spirit, and bound by invisible bonds to All Men . . . he wears Clothes, which are the visible emblem of that fact. Has not your Red hanging-individual a horsehair wig, squirrel-skins, and a plush-gown, whereby all mortals know that he is a JUDGE?'[70] Silenus's ancient, venerable visage, his ample girth and his extravagant, red robe were suggestive of judicial office. Kawasha, opposing the motion that wine was 'more worthy' than tobacco, lacked the paternal, benevolent features that characterised Silenus. He was borne aloft on the shoulders of 'two Indians . . . attired like Floridans'. Silenus was mounted on a beast of burden, but Kawasha has subjugated his fellow humans, employing them inequitably. He is the personification of civil law, whose arbitrary code facilitated the abuse of monarchic power. As Fortescue observed, concerning the powers assumed by the ruler under civil law, 'a King of England does not bear such a Sway over his Subjects'.[71] Silenus and Kawasha represent the salient characteristics of two distinct and distinctive legal systems, of which they are recognisable caricatures.

[68] F. Nietzsche, *The Birth of Tragedy*, trans. W. A. Haussmann (Edinburgh: J. N. Foulis, 1909), p. 34.
[69] Sophocles, *The Three Theban Plays*, trans. R. Fagles (London: Penguin, 1984), lines 1261–2.
[70] T. Carlyle, *Sartor Resartus* (London: Chapman & Hall, 1885), p. 42.
[71] Fortescue, *De Laudibus*, p. 75.

The depiction of foreigners was mostly light-hearted and affectionate: Kawasha wore a chimney on his head, and held a native's bow and arrows in his hand.[72] The protagonists were preceded on to the stage by two sergeants, each bearing a symbol of his lawful authority, a mace. Kawasha's sergeant carried a mace in the shape of a giant tobacco pipe, illustrating the contempt shown towards foreign legal systems by the Inns of Court. One function of the debate between Silenus and Kawasha was to indicate that innocuous pleasures such as smoking and drinking had a significant part to play in an ordered society. They were a representation of communality and, less innocently, they were symbols of a masculine hegemony to which women had no access.[73] The debate also provided an opportunity for the custodians of common law to mock the strange customs of foreigners; in this case, the smoking of tobacco, only recently introduced into Britain, and despised by James I.[74] Xenophobia was only thinly disguised as good-humoured mockery, as the following extract demonstrates. The supporters of Silenus proposed to make Kawasha drunk: 'And when that he well drunke is, Returne him to his Munkeis, From whence he came.' His fellow countrymen were represented as monkeys. Kawasha replied that he would make Silenus fall down, and informed him that Kawasha and his followers would appear to him, 'All snuffing, puffing smoke and fire, Like fell Dragon'.[75] To be foreign was to be either an ape or a dragon; it was not to be human. The English followers of Silenus continued to taunt the foreigner, in predictable, puerile fashion: 'He is come from a farre Countrey, To make our Noses a chimney'.[76] The nationalist prejudices of the English legal profession guaranteed the appreciation of this joke at the expense of foreigners in general, and indigenous Americans in particular.

That there was a polemical aspect to these masques is indisputable, in particular, with reference to assertions of national unity and identity. Ancient mythological characters were incorporated into the action, and existing forms were thus rewritten and adapted to suit the circumstances of the institution.[77] Hence Silenus, a figure from ancient Greek mythology, was (in the context of *The Maske of Flowers*) emblematic of early-seventeenth-century English common law. That he is a mythical figure is important: he belonged

---

[72] *The Maske of Flowers*, fo. B3.
[73] On the theory of homosociality, see M. Borch-Jacobsen, *The Freudian Subject*, trans. C. Porter (Basingstoke: Macmillan, 1989), in which the concept is discussed in relation to the practices of professional institutions.
[74] On the expansion of the tobacco market after 1612, and the success of the Virginia Company in exploiting the indigenous American workforce, see Ashton, *Reformation and Revolution*, pp. 363–6.
[75] *The Maske of Flowers*, fo. B3.   [76] *Ibid.*, fo. B4.
[77] On the theoretical concept of tradition, see H.-G. Gadamer, *Truth and Method* (New York: Crossroad, 1988).

to an indefinite time in an imaginary, archetypal past. Consequently his function in the masque was iconic; he represented in imagistic form the ancient origins of common law. Silenus offered a complex image of common law: its wisdom and humanity, its inextricable links with nature and its classical provenance. But another archetypal figure, of equal iconic stature, was also a protagonist (albeit less active than Silenus) in *The Maske of Flowers*: King James I was a highly visible member of the audience. The real presence of common law and king was reinforced by the respective images presented to the audience, in the form of Silenus and James I. The simultaneous representation of common law and crown was a visible expression of the unity of the nation, seen here joined in common consent as an iconic whole.

HARLOTS, HAGS, AND WITCHES: THE DEPICTION OF WOMEN

In the patriarchal and patrimonial model of society that the masques presented as a template for the ideal commonwealth, women were peripheral and subservient, and lacked any legal status. The representation of the female form was entirely negative: the predominant image of woman was that of an irrational and occasionally inhuman creature, whose powers were destructive and did not derive from human or divine sources. They were perceived as a serious threat to the order of the commonwealth, and could reasonably be said to represent the antithesis of law and reason. In 'The misfortunes of Arthur' (1587), the most significant female character was an incestuous seductress; in *Circe and Ulysses, The Inner Temple Masque* (1615), the only females were sirens and sorceresses; and in the farce preceding *The Masque of Heroes* (1619), they were licentious temptresses and geriatric brothel-keepers. Their depiction indicates that the image is never innocent and that the form of the masque inherited the doctrinal concept of the image and the reformation of images: visual imagery could be perceived both as iconic and idolatrous. The representation of women in the masques demonstrated an institutional tendency towards misogyny in the early modern legal profession. This is unsurprising, given the exclusively male membership of the Inns of Court and the patriarchal government to which they were subjected. It was unlikely that the masquers would question the rectitude of the patrimonial system of inheritance upon which the law of property was founded, from which they stood to benefit personally as the principal beneficiaries of large estates. But the entirely negative portrayal of women marked a departure from the conventional use of images in the masques. Traditionally the image was employed as an iconic device, by means of which the viewer was directed from visible phenomena to an understanding of incorporeal concepts such as law, truth and reason. The positive depiction of masculine archetypes established the structure and order of law. But the image of women was idolatrous rather than iconic: through the depiction of transgression and excess, its function was to seduce and to concentrate vision on the emptiness of the image itself. Thus the masque provided a means of understanding law through its exceptions.

Fundamental to the structure of common law in Elizabethan and Jacobean England was the unchanging certainty that the status of women was subordinate to that of men. At a spiritual level, the legitimacy of this status was unchallengeable: the archetypal patriarch and original of all law, God the Father, spoke to mankind through the prophets, and subsequently through His son and his disciples, all of whom were men. The prototype of earthly written law, the *Corpus Iuris* of Justinian, is unequivocal in its depiction of women as inferior beings, lacking dignity, legal status and eligibility for public office, or *civilia officia*. All legal power resided with the male head of the family, to whom the woman was always subordinate.[78] In medieval England, the law relating to entails guaranteed the continuing dominance of a patriarchal society that refused to acknowledge the legal status of women, by ensuring that family estates passed to the eldest son by the convention of primogeniture. In early modern England the patriarchal model not only formed the basis of all legal relationships, it was also symbolic of the subordinate relationship of subject to sovereign in the early modern English state. James I referred to himself as *parens patriae*, the political father of the nation.[79] The post-Reformation, Protestant Church emphasised the subordination of wives to husbands; a relationship that Milton described as, 'He for God only, she for God in him'. But this does not explain the extraordinary depiction of women in the masques presented at the Inns of Court. Female characters appeared in all the masques to which I have referred in this chapter, but their overriding characteristic was not subordination. Men were portrayed as possessing heroic qualities, endowed with innate nobility and virtue, visibly of divine provenance. Alternative depictions of masculinity took the form of affectionate and benign representations of a benevolent patriarchy, such as Silenus in *The Maske of Flowers*. The portrayal of women, however, fell into three distinct and unsympathetic categories: lewd fornicators with rapacious sexual appetites, inhuman sorceresses and grotesque hags. The salient feature, common to all, is the violent antipathy with which their creators

---

[78] For an analysis of the legal status of women in Roman society, see Goodrich, *Oedipus Lex*, pp. 114–15.
[79] See L. Stone, *The Family, Sex and Marriage in England 1500–1800* (London: Penguin, 1979), p. 110; also S. Sheridan Walker, *Wife and Widow in Medieval England* (Ann Arbor: University of Michigan Press, 1993). The issue of women in English legal history is considered in W. P. MacNeil, 'Living On: Borderlines – Law/History', *Law and Critique*, 6 (1995), 167–91.

intended the audience to greet them. A true representation of the legal status of women in England during this period would necessarily involve images of subordination; instead, the audience is offered images of excess and transgression. Their interposition between and detraction from the divine and the human affirm their symbolic status as idols rather than icons. In behaviour and physical appearance they were represented as being either grotesque or specious; in either case they provided exemplary images of exceptions to law.

In the version of *Circe and Ulysses* presented at the Inner Temple in 1615, the opening scene was set on a cliff-top. On it were seated the two sirens, Hyginus and Servius, depicted as women only as far as their waists: their lower bodies were avian, resembling those of hens.[80] The introductory image was powerful and unequivocal: women were strange, outcast figures, and a perversion of nature. They were a monstrous hybrid whose resemblance to humanity was illusory, a grotesque and blasphemous parody of God's creation. The sirens were the enemies of natural law, personified by Ulysses, who traversed the oceans in search of knowledge and self-revelation. Ulysses and his worthy knights were the image of nature that the sirens and the cunning sorceress, Circe, sought to destroy. The depiction of Circe and the sirens was intended to be idolatrous: their specious surface offered a reading of law in inverted form. The traditional iconoclastic interpretation of the image as harlot was invoked to represent women as the self-proclaimed enemies of nature and reason. Opponents of the icon were damned because they transgressed the laws of nature and of reason, and in some cases, had the souls of dogs, pigs or savage beasts.[81] Circe exerted her magical, unnatural charms by changing men into wild animals with the minds of men. At her command, they became pigs, lions and dogs. The iconoclast thereby appeared to have thwarted natural law, and destroyed the icon. But the archetype and icon of human resourcefulness, Ulysses, employed natural reason to release his crew from Circe's spell.

Represented also in *Circe and Ulysses* was an image of the Inns of Court and their relationship with natural law. At the moment of Ulysses' triumph, the audience was suddenly presented with an image of nature and rational man in perfect harmony. As Ulysses approached his sleeping crew, two large gates opened, revealing a glade in the wood, in which was an avenue with brick walls on either side, over-canopied with trees.[82] The resemblance to the gardens of the Inner Temple is unmistakable and probably intentional. Extensive building work had been undertaken at the Inner Temple in the

---

[80] Browne, *Circe and Ulysses*, p. 7.
[81] The image is taken from Nicephorus, author of *Apologeticus Major* and the *Antirrhetici*, which were directed against the iconoclast, Constantine V; see Nicephorus. *Discours contre les iconoclasts*, ed. and trans. M.-J. Mondzain-Baudinet (Paris: Klincksieck, 1989).
[82] Browne, *Circe and Ulysses*, p. 29.

twenty-five years that preceded the masque of *Circe and Ulysses*.[83] The presence in their gardens of ornamental gates, avenues of trees, secluded glades and extensive brick walls is documented in the records of the Inns. This masque in particular demonstrates that the function of the antirrhetic is to attack the alien or other, in this case, the presence of the iconoclast (or that which is opposed to nature and reason) in the spiritual home of common law.

The pejorative depiction of women reached its nadir in the brief farce that preceded Middleton's *The Masque of Heroes*. It is indicative of cultural norms at the Jacobean Inns of Court that this masque was described on the title page of the original published edition as 'an Entertainment for many worthy Ladies'. The scatological tone of the entertainment was established in an exchange of insults between two characters, named 'Plumporridge' and 'Fasting day'. The former greeted the latter thus: 'I doe not love to meete thee fasting, thou art nothing but wind, thy Stomack's full of Farts, as if they had lost their way, and thou made with the wrong end upward, like a Dutch Mawe, that discharges still into'th Mouth!'[84] Following their meeting, the reading of a will was enacted, in which the doctrine of primogeniture was satirised and the inferior legal status of women emphasised with misogynous relish. Kersmas, the testator, leaves his younger sons, Gleeke and Primiviste, nothing but 'the full consuming of Nights and Dayes, and Wives and Children'. The female beneficiaries fare even worse: 'I give to my eldest Daughter, Tickle mee quickly, and to her sister my Ladies Hole, free leave to shift for themselves, either in Court, City, or Country'.[85] That the Inner Temple, in the presence of 'many worthy ladies', should present this lewd depiction of women and deride their diminished legal status was suggestive of the masculine hegemony of the Inns, and the extent to which it permeated institutional existence. The principal beneficiary of the will is of course the eldest son, whose name suggests a profound lack of intelligence: '[f]or the possession of all my Lands, Mannors, Mannor-houses, I leave them full and wholly to my eldest Sonne, Noddie.'[86] Women were not represented as subjects of law; they are the alien or other, whose legal status was inferior and whose physical access to the Inns of Court was restricted by legislation.

The perceived threat posed by females to the order of the legal community can be inferred from the following regulation at Gray's Inn: '[i]n 23 Eliz (30 Jan) there was an Order made, that no Laundresses, nor women called Victuallers, should thenceforth come into the Gentlemens Chambers of this

---

[83] Dugdale, *Origines Juridiciales*, fo. 146.   [84] Middleton, *Masque of Heroes*, fo. A3, B.
[85] *Ibid.*, fo. B. See J. Schroeder, 'Feminism Historicised: Medieval Misogynist Stereotypes in Contemporary Feminist Jurisprudence', *Iowa Law Review*, 75 (1990), 1135–217.
[86] Middleton, *Masque of Heroes*, fo. B.

Society, unless they were full fourty years of age: and not send their maid-servants of what age soever, into the said Gentlemens Chambers.'[87] The suggestion of sexual excess and transgression is implicit in the names of the two daughters in Middleton's brief play: 'Tickle mee quickly' and 'my Ladies Hole'. Their carnality threatened to undermine and confound the patriarchal structure of the common law and the ordered conviviality of its rituals. The mock will of Middleton's play emphasised the difference between the peculiar reverence which the senior members of the Inn, or ancients, were accorded and the contempt in which older women were held. This was graphically illustrated in the following bequest: 'I leave to their old Aunt, my Sow h'as Pigd, a Litter of Curtizans to breede up for Shrove-tide.'[88] The English legal institution represented the legitimacy of its patriarchal structure through images of flawless genealogy and ancient provenance: the 'titles of antiquity' to which Selden refers. The implicit antiquity of the aunt, 'my Sow h'as Pigd', attracted no such respect: her advanced age was a subject merely for derision and ribaldry. She was fit only to be a brothel-keeper, a transgressor of the laws of God, nature and man. Along with the other female representations of iconoclasm and irrationality considered in this chapter, the old aunt was a creation of fantasy, caricature and exaggeration.

The contemptuous treatment of women was not confined to fictional representations. For example, Stone refers to a will of 1599, in which one William Shaftoe bequeathed sixty sheep to his daughter Margery, before bestowing her in marriage to the son of a neighbouring landowner.[89] Selden recorded the barbaric and extraordinary treatment at English law of women merely suspected of murdering their husbands, while incidentally invoking the support of Sir Edward Coke for such a custom, on the basis of its antiquity.

When a Master of a Family, who is of higher birth and quality, dies, his Kindred meet together, that if the manner of his death were suspicious, they may by torture, as Servants were used, examine the Wife concerning the business, and if she be found guilty, they torment her miserably and burn her alive. To this story that most excellent Lawyer, and worthy Lord Chief Justice of the Common Pleas, Sir Edward Coke, refers the antiquity of that Law, which we at this day use of devoting to the flames those wicked Baggages, who stain their hands with the nefarious murder of their Husbands.[90]

Commenting on the exclusion of women from the right to succession to the French throne, Selden noted 'those Authors especially, who, propped up with the Salick Law (as they call it) write, that . . . The Government of women ('tis Bodin of Anjou sayes it) is contrary to the Laws of Nature, which hath

---

[87] Dugdale, *Origines Juridiciales*, fo. 286.   [88] Middleton, *Masque of Heroes*, fo. B.
[89] Stone, *The Family*, p. 135.
[90] J. Selden, *The Reverse or Back-Face of the English Janus*, trans. R. Westcot (London: T. Bassett & R. Chiswell, 1682), fo. 17.

bestowed upon men discretion, strength of body, courage and greatness of Spirit, with the power of Rule, and hath taken these things from women.'[91] The accreditation of these sentiments to Bodin serves to absolve Selden from the expression of a personal opinion on the fitness of women to govern. It is perhaps significant that, only a few years after the death of Elizabeth I (Selden records that some of the text was written at the Inner Temple on Christmas Day, 1610), he should be ambivalent on the subject of governance by women, preferring to quote Bodin on their inherent incapacity to rule than to commit personally to a particular evaluation of their fitness to govern.

In classical terms, the iconoclast was the physical manifestation of unreason or madness, whose chaotic language lacked any semblance of logic. The old aunt to whom the mock will in *The Masque of Heroes* refers was a familiar image of irrationality and iconoclasm: the ancient, senile woman.[92] The women of the masques were creatures of unnatural reason, a fact that manifested itself in their bestial characteristics, be they behavioural, physical or both. They were the antithesis of law, and the Inns of Court masques were unique in their graphic and plastic representations of such iconoclasts. Their representation suggests an inherent corporate fear in the legal profession of those reformers who rejected the iconic signs of institutional authority. Reason and anti-reason were vividly depicted and contrasted. The archetype of virtue, nobility and reason was represented in iconic form: common law and common lawyer were endowed with visible, divine attributes. They were the Word made flesh and their antithesis, the iconoclast, was represented as an idol: a monster or harlot, of bestial provenance, devoid of reason, nature or divinity. These powerful images demarcate in inverted form a law without desire, a law in which the woman was nothing.

The masques presented at the Inns of Court demonstrated the imagistic nature of the English constitution. The interpretation of law in the courts was partly determined by the prejudices and predilections of the judiciary, and in particular by the hostility of the legal profession to codification. The manifest reason, intrinsic excellence and immutability of English law were adduced by Coke and his fellow lawyers as evidence of the supreme constitutional authority of common law. Of those against the uncertainties of a legal system that acknowledged the primacy of the written word over the iconic signs of legitimacy, Coke was arguably the most articulate of the early modern period. On the inherent irrationality of civil law, he was unequivocal: '[u]pon the Text of the Civill Law, there be so many glosses and interpretations, and again upon those so many Commentaries, and all these written by Doctors of equall degree and authority, and therein so many diversities of opinions, as they do

---

[91] *Ibid.*, fo. 19.
[92] On the classical depiction of iconoclasts, see Goodrich, *Oedipus Lex*, pp. 52–4.

rather increase than resolve doubts.'⁹³ He argued that these interpretations and commentaries were merely the unauthorised opinions of highly educated individuals. In English law such commentaries, given in court by members of the judiciary, were *ex cathedra*, 'and therefore being collected together shall (as we conceive) produce certainty, the Mother and Nurse of repose and quietnesse, and are not like to the waves of the Sea.'⁹⁴ It is indicative of Coke's intellectual insularity that he failed to equate his own tendency, in *The Reports* and *The Institutes*, to represent opinion as law with the misguided presumptions of civil lawyers.

The antiquity of the English legal system was cited by Fortescue as irrefutable evidence of the superiority of common law to the civil code: 'Neither the laws of the Romans, which are cried up beyond all others for their antiquity, nor yet the laws of the Venetians, however famous in this respect, their island not being inhabited so early as Britain, neither was Rome at that time built. Nor in short, are the laws of any other Kingdom in the world so venerable for their antiquity.' ⁹⁵ It is unsurprising, bearing in mind the stylistic conformity of common law procedure to oral disputation and the exposition of narrative, that legitimacy should find a powerful mode of expression in the unique, visual and dramatic medium of the masque. Nor, given the importance of antiquity to claims of common law primacy, is it surprising that the myths of the ancient world should be reinvented and re-presented in an English setting. More surprising is that the elaborate, imagistic masques presented at the Inns should have attained such prominence in post-Reformation England. The iconoclastic Reformist movement sought to destroy the structural power of the figurative representation, associated as it was with the authority of the Roman Catholic Church.

The institutional expansion of the legal profession was accompanied by the enhancement of its spiritual and moral dimension, as commentators such as Fulbecke emphasised: 'where God is not, there is no truth, there is no light, there is no lawe.'⁹⁶ Where appropriate, the legal profession utilised iconography previously associated with the church, and adapted it to suit the temporal, as well as the spiritual imperatives of common law. The status of the Inns as autonomous, unincorporated institutions rendered them largely immune to the iconoclastic extremes of the Reformation.⁹⁷ Images continued

---

⁹³ E. Coke, *The Third Part of the Institutes of the Laws of England* (London: Flesher, 1644), preface.
⁹⁴ *Ibid.* ⁹⁵ Fortescue, *De Laudibus*, pp. 32–3.
⁹⁶ Fulbecke, *A Direction or Preparative*, fo. 10a.
⁹⁷ On the status of the Inns of Court as independent local authorities, see J. H. Baker, *The Inner Temple: A Brief Historical Description* (London: Inner Temple, 1991), p. 17; also J. Allibore and D. Evans, *The Inns of Court*, ed. D. McCorquodale (London: Black Dog, 1996), p. 153. On the autonomy of the Temple, see A. M. T. Eve (Baron Sisloe), *The Peculiarities of the Temple* (London: The Estates Gazette Ltd, 1972), pp. 92–3.

to play a vital and highly visible role in the institutional existence of common lawyers. The unique form of the masques enabled particular images of the state to be presented to a susceptible audience that included, on numerous occasions, the monarch. The threat of absolutism, and the development and consolidation of a powerful and independent legal profession alongside a flourishing and influential merchant class, inevitably created tension between the institutions of crown and common law.

The particular portrayal of the monarch demonstrates the prominent part played by common lawyers in defining the role of the crown in the early modern constitution. In so doing, the difference between medieval and modern interpretations of symbols is illustrated. Medieval kings embodied the invisible principles of godliness and were, by virtue of this embodiment, supreme judges, legislators and policy-makers. This was not a role envisaged by common lawyers for the 'great Sun' of Jacobean England. The acknowledged status of the monarch as emblematic head of state and church was an integral characteristic of the legal system. But the legal profession sought, through the presentation of its masques, to suggest that common law imposed definite limits on the exercise of the royal prerogative. The use of ancient images, drawn from classical and national mythology, suggested that common law predated the foundation of royal dynasties, thereby defeating the claim of James I to represent absolute sovereign authority. It also implied that the legitimacy of common law and the legal profession was divinely ordained and therefore immune to censure from the monarch. The monarch played an important, symbolic role in this constitution, but the limits to his power were defined and delineated by common law, as demonstrated in the unique, visual images of the Inns of Court masques. They convey graphic representations of a cohesive, rational society. The image was utilised variously as icon and idol, in accordance with the doctrinal concept of the sign and its reformation. For example, Ulysses was an archetypal image of the logic and rectitude of natural and divine law. His location in a contemporary stage setting that resembled the gardens of the Inner Temple provided a landscape in which classical and contemporary doctrines were accommodated and subsequently coalesced. Visible evidence was presented of the ancient provenance of common law and of its adaptation to contemporary social and political circumstances.

These entertainments were not simply examples of the cultural hegemony of the early modern Inns of Court, crucial though they were to the artistic development of the Inns and of the nation. The masques played an influential role in the development of a modern body of law and are legitimate subjects for legal, as well as literary and historical, analysis. They provided exceptional, visual representations of a constitution in which the power and restrictions pertaining to the organs of government were defined, and the central role of the legal profession as arbiters of constitutional probity was assured. They are imagistic portrayals of a rational community in which common law was co-extensive with God, nature and the universe. The claim of common lawyers to represent, interpret and uphold the Ancient Constitution was uniquely embodied in the pictorial and poetic imagery of the masques.

5

Reformation, regulation and the image: the English state and the subject of law

SUMPTUARY LAW AND THE CREATION OF THE NATION-STATE

I have myselfe met an ordinary tapster in his silke stockins, garters deepe fringed with gold lace, the rest of his apparel suteable, with cloake lined with velvet, who tooke it some scorne I should take the wall of him, as I went along the streete.[1]

The above passage from *The Gentleman's Exercise* by Henry Peacham, a former tutor in the household of the earl of Arundel, illustrates the sense of impending civil unrest represented by the abandonment of a visible order of signs, through which the societal status of individual subjects had been identifiable. In the period between the inception under Henry VIII of an imperial monarchy and the Restoration in 1660, reform of the image was a crucial factor in determining the political, social and cultural development of the English nation-state. The representational power of clothes and their capacity to embody institutional authority while simultaneously delineating societal status were of particular concern to Tudor legislators, as the autonomous nation-state gradually evolved from the medieval, feudal model of governance. Sumptuary laws, which related specifically to the regulation of clothes and the visible delineation of hierarchy, exemplify the concern of successive Tudor governments that the particular form of the English constitution should be both representational and enforceable. The repeal of sumptuary legislation during the reign of James I demonstrated the impossibility of enforcement rather than disillusionment with its desirability.

It is useful briefly to consider the reasons for the re-emergence during the 1530s of this form of legislation, whose origins are associated with the regulation of medieval society. The legitimacy of the medieval legal system had been founded on the lawful authority of immutable hierarchy, the image of which was the visible elucidation of rank, provided by costume. Before the

[1] H. Peacham, *The Gentleman's Exercise* (London: I.T., 1634), p. 134.

Act of Supremacy of 1534, sumptuary laws in England had two principal functions: to impose and enforce respect for feudal rule and to restrict the import of foreign goods. For example, in the reign of Edward IV an Act was passed which prohibited the import of 'velvet, damaske, satten... before that the Collectors of the subsidie of Tonnage and Pondage, and the Comptroller of the same, in the port where such marchandises is set upon land, hath surveyed and measured the same, and hath sealed every peece thereof in the one ende thereof'.[2] After the Henrician Reformation the rationale of sumptuary legislation subtly shifted to reflect an emergent constitution, embodying an Anglicised Protestantism based upon moderation, repression of excessive individualism and a belief in the divinity of common law and its institutions.

Sumptuary legislation enacted during the period of religious crisis surrounding the Henrician Act of Supremacy attempted to depict the monarch as the unique embodiment of divine law. The appearance or representation of divine sanction was a necessary expedient, as the Act of Supremacy merely declared that Henry was supreme head of the English Church. Such a declaration, although binding in law, did not indicate its acceptance by God. Only if the king could be successfully presented as *imago dei* could the legitimacy of the Act of Supremacy be asserted in theological rather than legal terms.[3] This was the underlying principle behind the legislation passed in 1533 to the effect that no person should 'use or weare in any maner their apparell, or upon their horse, mule, or other beast, any silke of the colour of purpure, ne any cloth of Gold of tissue, but onely the King' and specified close relatives.[4] Divine authority, legitimacy and justice were thus represented in the person of the king. In the context of sumptuary laws and the appropriation of the colour purple by the king, Legh's explanation of its hieroglyphic importance is helpful: '[i]t sheweth jurisdiction, a ruler of laws, and in justice, to be equal with a prince.' Ferne delineates the meaning of the 'five colours in Armes properly. Viz. Gewls, Azure, Sable, Vert, and Purpure [purple]'. He notes that the virtues associated with 'purpure' are temperance and prudence; the 'ages of man' with which the colour is linked is '[t]he age of gray heares, called *cana senectus*'; and the complexion which it denotes is 'Flegmatique with some choler'. Ferne applies a similar analysis to the colour gold. The planet associated with this colour is the sun; the virtues linked to it are faith and constancy; the relevant celestial sign is the lion; the 'ages of man' to which it pertains is 'Yong age of adolescentia. From 14 till 20 yeeres'; and

---

[2] W. Rastall, *Collection in English of the Statutes now in force* (London: Deputies of C. Barker, 1594), fo. 105.
[3] See J. J. Scarisbrick, *Henry VIII* (Harmondsworth: Penguin, 1971), p. 508.
[4] 24 Hen. 8. C. 13, Rastall, *Statutes*, fo. 14.

the complexion that it denotes is 'sanguine'.[5] The application of systematic analysis to the symbolism inherent in colour demonstrates the seriousness with which the project was regarded. Most important, with regard to the arrogation to the king of the colour purple is its historical association with imperial Rome. The comparison of Henry to a caesaropapist, managing the English Church like a late-Roman emperor, has been made by Guy.[6] It is significant to an analysis of Henrician sumptuary legislation that a statute was enacted in order to create this particular image of monarchy: a secular *imperium* with absolute spiritual supremacy.

One line of argument, to which Hunt subscribes, is that the intention of sumptuary legislation in the reign of Henry VIII was to preserve the emblems of class hierarchy.[7] Inferior subjects were forbidden to wear specific colours, types of cloth and precious metals. 24 Hen. 8 C.13 specified that nobody under the degree of earl may 'weare in any maner apparell of his body, or on his horse, mule, or other beast, or harneis of the same beast, any velvet of the colour of crimson, scarlet or blew'. No servant or yeoman 'shall weare any cloth in his hosen, above the price of ii.s. the yard'; and no man under the degree of a baron's son or a knight 'shall after the sayde feast, use or weare any Chein of Gold, bracelet, ouch, or other ornament of Gold'.[8] References to 'class' in the 1530s can create a misleading impression of the nature of the existing societal hierarchy. Although the commercial conditions necessary for the creation of a modern class structure were emerging, the structural composition of English society throughout Henry's reign was only beginning to change from a vertical to a horizontal model. The wholesale movement from status to contract had not yet taken place. The crucial point in relation to sumptuary law is that all forms of status, as Maine noted, are derived from the powers and privileges anciently residing in the family.[9] Whilst it is an indispensable condition of all sumptuary legislation that it should be concerned with the maintenance of an established order of governance, the particular hierarchy which early-sixteenth century, English sumptuary law sought to maintain can fairly be described as Aristotelian. It is concerned with the preservation of a natural order within the universe, based upon the honour and allegiance owed to the family and ultimately, to the father.

The image of the monarch was the representation of the absolute father. The arcane symbolism of colour which Legh and Ferne delineate in minute

---

[5] G. Legh, *The Accedens of Armory* (London: R. Tottel, 1576), fo. 10b; J. Ferne, *The Blazon of Gentrie* (London: Winder, 1586), ff. 163, 169–71.
[6] J. Guy, 'Thomas Cromwell and the intellectual origins of the Henrician Revolution', in J. Guy (ed.), *The Tudor Monarchy* (London: Arnold, 1997), p. 227.
[7] A. Hunt, *Governance of the Consuming Passions: A History of Sumptuary Law* (Basingstoke: Macmillan, 1996), p. 33.
[8] 24 Hen. 8 C. 13, Rastall, *Statutes*, fo. 14.
[9] H. Maine, *Ancient Law* (London: Dent, 1917), p. 100.

detail is fundamental to an interpretation of kingship as both the representation of divine law and the object of emotional attachment to which the subject is bound. The preamble to 24 Hen. 8 C.13 demonstrates that the purpose of sumptuary legislation was not to enforce 'class' distinction, but to uphold the natural order of the classical world in the context of the post-Reformation nation-state: '[f]or the better repressing of the inordinate excesse of Apparel by some moderation, and for a resonable order like to be observed, and performed in the wearing thereof'.[10] This constitutes an attempt by statutory means to manipulate the image for the purpose of representing a sovereign English state, not subject to papal jurisdiction. The state implied in the above legislation is the embodiment of the Ancient Constitution: it rejects foreign influences and its legality is founded upon the ethnocentric customs of a unique English race. Selden found similarities between the legally enforced hierarchy of Saxon England and that envisaged by the Henrician legislation, above. With reference to Saxon marriage customs, he observed that '[i]t was enacted by Laws, "That no rank in cases of Matrimony do pass the bounds of their own quality; but that a Noble-man marry a Noble-woman, a Free-man take a Free-woman, a Bond-man made Free be joyned to a Bond-woman of the same condition, and a Man-servant match with a Maid-servant".'[11] The Henrician sumptuary laws attempted to entrench these ancient customs in the context of a modernising nation-state, in which the iconic representation of the monarch as *imago dei* graphically demonstrates the indivisibility and legitimacy of spiritual and temporal authority.

THE ELIZABETHAN STATE, THE LEGAL INSTITUTION AND THEORIES OF THE IMAGE

... every man of this Society, should frame and reform himself for the manner of his Apparell.[12]

The relevance of this regulation (enacted by the governing body of Gray's Inn in 1574) to a study of sixteenth-century sumptuary law is twofold. First, use of the word 'frame' implies that it is the duty of the legal profession to apply a particular theory of the image to its institutional existence. Second, it contains an explicit command to effect reformation so that the image presented is acceptable to the governing body – the patriarchs of the legal profession and symbolic fathers of law. Regulation of the image at the Inns of Court

---

[10] Rastall, *Statutes*, fo. 14.
[11] J. Selden, *The Reverse or Back-Face of the English Janus*, trans. R. Westcot (London: T. Bassett & R. Chiswell, 1682), fo. 30.
[12] W. Dugdale, *Origines Juridiciales or Historical Memorials of the English Laws* (London: F. & T. Warren, 1666), fo. 282.

is traceable to the reign of Henry VIII. Dugdale notes similar legislation, passed by the Inner Temple Parliament in 1539, to the effect that 'Gentlemen of this company shall reform themselves in their cut or disguised Apparel, and not to have long beards.'[13] Immune from interference by the state, the legal community took upon itself the role of exemplifying the correct use of symbols and of elucidating the purpose of sumptuary law. The ecclesiastical polity inherent in such legislation is undeniable. A fundamental element of religious reformation was intrinsic to the sumptuary laws passed by the Elizabethan Inns of Court. Prest has observed that, from a religious perspective, the Elizabethan and Jacobean legal profession was not monolithic, and warns against generalising about a pervasive attitude. He notes the presence of recusants, anticlerical Erastians and secularists among the membership of the Inns.[14] His research suggests that a high proportion of those barristers whose religious affiliations were known tended towards Puritan doctrines,[15] although he concedes that 'puritanism' is an amorphous term that defies strict categorical analysis. Despite the difficulty of religious categorisation, an examination of sumptuary legislation enacted by the governing bodies of the Inns indicates that they sought to represent in visual terms the polity of the Protestant state, envisaged by the 1559 Acts of Uniformity and Supremacy. Following the Ridolfi plot of 1571 (the purpose of which was to facilitate an invasion of England by six thousand Spaniards, leading to the deposition of Elizabeth and the enthronement of Mary Stuart), anti-Catholic sentiment was inflamed. Despite Elizabeth's reluctance for the state to interfere in matters of individual conscience, events such as the Jesuit mission to England and the growing threat of Spanish invasion necessitated the introduction of coercive measures in order to enforce adherence to the Anglican state. The sumptuary legislation of the Inns of Court ensured that the legal profession embodied and reflected the spiritual, as well as the temporal, qualities of the Elizabethan settlement.

More than two hundred and fifty years after this legislation was passed at Gray's Inn, Thomas Carlyle published his fictional treatise on the philosophy of clothes, *Sartor Resartus*. A principal theme was the symbolic quality that attached to all clothes and the inherent, manipulative power of these symbols: 'all Symbols are properly Clothes; that all Forms whereby Spirit manifests itself to sense, whether outwardly or in the imagination, are Clothes; and thus not only the parchment Magna Charta, which a Tailor was nigh cutting into measures, but the Pomp and Authority of Law, the

---

[13] *Ibid.*, fo. 148.
[14] W. Prest, *The Rise of the Barristers: A Social History of the English Bar 1590–1640* (Oxford: Clarendon, 1991), pp. 209–10.
[15] *Ibid.*, p. 215; the religious affiliations of only 27.8 per cent of the membership were recorded by the Inns.

sacredness of Majesty, and all inferior Worships (Worthships) are properly a Vesture and Raiment'.[16] *Sartor Resartus* is an appropriate starting point for a consideration of a particular society in which order and adherence to the Aristotelian hierarchy were visibly and articulately expressed by the enforcement of sumptuary legislation. In the extract above Carlyle refers variously to Magna Carta, the majesty of kingship and the law itself as clothes or symbols. In other words (and of particular relevance to Magna Carta) the true significance of the text is that it is a sign, directing the viewer from the visible to the invisible; more precisely, it is an 'embodiment and revelation of the Infinite'.[17] Carlyle equates symbols of every kind with clothes, reducing man's existence itself to the status of an emblem: man's body acting as a 'visible Garment for that divine ME of his, cast hither, like a light-particle, down from Heaven'.[18] The expression of divinity (or what Carlyle terms 'the Divine Idea'[19]) through the medium of clothes is an important theme in Carlyle's interpretation of their symbolic status. If it is accepted that law manifests itself in images, an investigation into the particular form that these images take and especially into which images are acceptable and why they are, is of fundamental importance in establishing the nature of the constitution. Carlyle charts the decline in the social importance of clothes as a serious token of individual status. In this respect *Sartor Resartus* is a modernist work whose protagonist, Professor Tuefelsdrockh, urges the reader to see through the artifice of clothes to the essence of being.[20] Its principal significance to a study of English legal costume in the sixteenth century is the reformist tone of Professor Tuefelsdrockh, echoing the debate central to the European Reformation concerning the war of images.

In *De Laudibus Legum Angliae*, Fortescue traced the legitimacy of common law to the textual evidence of the Old Testament: 'Deuteronomy is the Book of Laws whereby the Kings of Israel were obliged to govern the People committed to their charge: Moses commands their Kings to read this Book, that they may learn to fear the Lord their God, and keep his Statutes which are written in the Law'.[21] He articulated the familiar belief that law was divinely ordained, but of greater interest to an analysis of the reformation of images is the emphasis he placed upon the text (as opposed to the image) as the embodiment of legitimate sovereignty. Of course, English law had no such comprehensive constitutional document for the guidance of the crown.

---

[16] T. Carlyle, *Sartor Resartus* (London: Chapman & Hall, 1885), p. 183. On the semiotics of clothes and sign systems as a form of discourse, see Hunt, *History of Sumptuary Law*, p. 58.
[17] Carlyle, *Sartor*, p. 149.
[18] *Ibid.*, p. 50.   [19] *Ibid.*, pp. 145, 151.
[20] On the importance of *Sartor Resartus* to jurisprudence, see N. E. H. Hull, 'The Romantic Realist: Art, Literature and the Enduring Legacy of Karl Llewellyn's "Jurisprudence"', *American Journal of Legal History*, 40 (1996), 115–145.
[21] J. Fortescue, *De Laudibus Legum Angliae*, ed. J. Selden (London: R. Gosling, 1737), p. 3.

The subject of English law was bound by the particular identity that the law presents. In contrast, the subject of civil law had his obligations to sovereign authority defined by a codified legal system. Traditionally, in English law the image played a more prominent role than the text as an object of attachment. As Legendre has noted, the image generates the capture and submission of the subject by the legal institution.[22] The injunction of the Judaeo-Christian deity that '[y]ou shall not make a carved image for yourself nor the likeness of anything in the heavens above' (Exodus 20.4), given to the people of Israel in the presence of Moses, has particular resonance in post-Reformation England. The text had not replaced the sign as the mark of attachment to law, but it was a fundamental tenet of the Reformation that the invisible presence of God should manifest itself through the proper signs. As Carlyle observed in *Sartor Resartus*, apparel has always been a matter of theological significance, embodying a religious principle and endowing 'the Divine Idea of the World with a sensible and practically active Body, so that it might dwell among them as a living and life-giving WORD'.[23] Sumptuary legislation at the Elizabethan Inns of Court facilitated the means by which this invisible order should be represented.

Sartor Resartus is of course fictional and broadly satirical, although the ideas expressed in it are no less convincing for the comic mode of expression. But it represents a view of truth from the first half of the nineteenth century, satirising the archaic rituals and ornamentation of an earlier unenlightened and unscientific era. A modern perspective on the societal importance of sartorial regulation is provided by *Governance of the Human Passions*, in which Hunt attributes the enactment of sumptuary legislation to a regulatory reflex in literate societies that excites the moral condemnation of luxury.[24] Hunt's interest in sumptuary law is primarily as a frame of reference for the exploration of Foucault's theory that modern power has two distinct forms: discipline acting on bodies and regulation acting on populations.[25] While agreeing with the assertion that sumptuary law was one instrument among many by which it was sought to establish a regulatory relationship between government and subject, Hunt's thesis that the objective of government is the materialisation of citizenship[26] is not elaborated in terms of the precise form that citizenship should take. His suggestion that sumptuary law is necessarily concerned with economic, moral and social regulation is, of course, valid.[27] To this I would add that in the case of the vast output of sumptuary legislation

---

[22] *Law and the Unconscious: A Legendre Reader*, ed. P. Goodrich (Basingstoke: Macmillan, 1997), p. 258.
[23] Carlyle, *Sartor*, p. 145.   [24] Hunt, *History of Sumptuary Law*, p. 77.
[25] *Ibid.*, p. 11.   [26] *Ibid.*, p. 7.
[27] *Ibid.* On socioeconomic developments in sixteenth- and early-seventeenth-century England, see R. Tawney, *Religion and the Rise of Capitalism* (London: Penguin, 1990).

in Elizabethan England the most important object of regulation was religion. The correlation between ecclesiastical polity, the governance of appearance and the war over images is crucial to the analysis of English sumptuary law during this period. Suppression of idolatry and the concomitant attempt to introduce a unique English ecclesiastical polity into the constitution are purposes expressed with particular clarity in the regulation of costume at the Inns of Court.

Writing of the regulations governing the apparel of members of the Middle Temple during the Elizabethan period, Dugdale made an observation that is crucial to an appreciation of the image and its inherent relationship with English law: 'for, even as his Apparell doth shew him to be, even so shall he be esteemed among them'.[28] Implicit in Dugdale's remark is the idea that legal costume is a central component of the common law's theatre of attachment. It is suggestive of a specific identity, which has the effect of binding the subject to law. Dugdale reiterated concerns, originally expressed in the ancient world, regarding the power of the visual image. For example, in *Dialogus de Oratoribus*, Tacitus wrote persuasively about the inadequacies of Roman legal costume, arguing that the gowns worn by lawyers in the courtroom restricted movement and were partly responsible for the denigration of the dignified image of the orator.[29] In relation to the aesthetics of English law, Fortescue expressed similar anxieties. Aware that authority could be represented only by the use of licit images and that legal costume was an eloquent and persuasive institutional device, Fortescue sought to enhance the image of the lawyer by means of sartorial embellishment: 'the Serjeant's Cape is always furred with White Lamb; which sort of Habit, when You [the Prince] come in Power, I could wish Your Highness would make a little more Ornamental, in Honour of the Laws, and also of Your Government'.[30]

The concerns of Tacitus and Fortescue were identical: the maintenance of order, the exclusion of chaos and the crucial role of the image in facilitating this end. The examples above illustrate Legendre's theory that the institutional use of the image is primarily concerned with assuring the prevalence of reason and the frustration of madness.[31] The distinction between icon and idol in a society in which law was predicated on the visibility of hierarchy, and represented partly by an order of clothes, was crucial. In post-Reformation England, the power of the image either to guide the subject

---

[28] Dugdale, *Origines Juridiciales*, fo. 197.
[29] C. Tacitus, *Dialogus de Oratoribus*, trans. W. Peterson (Cambridge, Mass.: Harvard University Press, 1970), p. 339. For the argument that Roman law and, more generally, the classics were the principal resource of early modern common law, see J. W. Tubbs, *The Common Law Mind: Medieval and Early Modern Conceptions* (Baltimore: Johns Hopkins University Press, 2000).
[30] Fortescue, *De Laudibus*, p. 120.   [31] *Law and the Unconscious*, p. 252.

towards truth and obedience to law, or to seduce vision into acceptance of a lie was necessarily a theme that concerned many writers. The perceived levity and carnality of femininity ensured the pre-eminence of the female form as the archetypal idol. In *A Quip for an Upstart Courtier* (1592), Robert Greene described women with 'faces like Angels, eies like stars, brestes like the golden front in the Hesperides, but from the middle downewards their shapes like serpents', recalling the hybridised sirens in the masque of *Circe and Ulysses*.[32] Greene incorporates the fantastical, comic device of a dialogue between two enormous pairs of breeches, one English, the other Italian, both conveniently anthropomorphised. With xenophobic fervour, 'Cloth-breeches' reminds 'Velvet-breeches' of the latter's foreign provenance: 'thou comest not alone but accompanied with multitude of abominable vices, hanging on thy bumbast nothing but infectious abuses, and vaine glory, selfelove, sodomie, and strange poisonings, wherewith thou hast infected this glorious Iland'.[33]

It is evident that clothes were interpreted both as icons of nationhood and as idols, or representations of falsehood. If it is accepted that clothing, more than any other symbol, establishes the inseparable bond between body and image, then the preoccupation of many sixteenth- and early-seventeenth-century writers with the appropriateness of feminine attire has an apparent discursive function that relates directly to Legendre's theory concerning the correlation between reason and the image. An example of this genre is an anonymous work, published in 1620, provocatively entitled *Hic Mulier: or, The Man Woman: Being a Medicine to Cure the Coltish Disease of the Staggers in the Masculine-Feminine of our Times. Exprest in a briefe Declamation. Non omnes possumus omnes. Mistris, will thou be trim'd or truss'd?* The writer expressed his horror at 'masculine' women, an image of transgression, falsehood and confusion. Such women were 'halfe fish, halfe flesh; halfe beast, halfe Monster: but all Odyous, all Divell, that have cast off the ornaments of your sexes, to put on the garments of Shame; that have laid by the bashfulnesse of your natures, to gather the impudence of Harlots'.[34]

Sumptuary legislation effected the manipulation of the image to facilitate a particular vision of order and reason. Hunt is specific in identifying the potential sources of disorder to which English sumptuary law was a response during the early modern period: urbanisation, the emergence of class as the pervasive form of social relations, and change in the structure of

---

[32] R. Greene, *A Quip for an Upstart Courtier* (London: I. Wolfe, 1592), fo. A4(i).
[33] *Ibid.*, fo. B2(i).
[34] Anon., *Hic Mulier: or, The Man Woman* (London: I.T., 1620), fo. A4. On the confusion of gender and the imposition of order through sumptuary legislation, see Hunt, *History of Sumptuary Laws*, p. 14. On the classical law of images see P. Legendre, *Le Désir politique de dieu: Étude sur les montages de l'état et du droit* (Paris: Fayard, 1989).

gender relations being principal among them.³⁵ But this does not account for the attempted resolution of religious crisis implicit in, for example, the legislation passed by Gray's Inn in 1574, demanding that members 'frame and reform' themselves in relation to their clothing. The linguistic construction of this regulation is noteworthy. The injunction is that the common lawyer should 'frame' himself. He must create an image of himself, or reconstitute himself as a semblance so that the subject, looking at the image, recognises the self as other. The framing of the image is a vital alienation device, by which means the relationship between the subject of law and the legal institution is articulated. The frame effectively separates the subject from the institution by initiating distance and perspective between them. The lawyer in the frame becomes the image in the mirror, which the subject identifies as both the representation and separation of self. As Legendre observes in relation to the myth of Narcissus, gazing lovingly at his reflection in the water, Narcissus engaged his image as though it were another person who happened to share the same body; thus establishing the indissoluble link between the image and the self.³⁶ Legendre makes the important observation in relation to Narcissus, that the love of self, declared by the protagonist, implies the existence of the other.³⁷ There is a point of recognition between the subject and the image; the recognition of the self as other enables the emotional bond of the subject to the legal institution.

Returning to the 'framing' and 'reform' of the honourable members of Gray's Inn, the legislation represents an attempt to depict an absolute or ultimate other: a social father, whom the subject can love in a similar manner to that in which a child loves its parents and recognises itself in them.³⁸ The moral and religious implications of 'reform', of particular relevance during the sixteenth century, suggest that the ultimate other to which the framed image refers is God the Father, the alleged source of all law. The fundamental objective of Elizabethan sumptuary laws at the Inns of Court was to represent, through a constitution of clothes and appearance, the perfect image of a Utopian society in which God the Father was manifested and embodied through the figure of the monarch (*imago dei*) and the institutional body of law. The image of the father was venerated above all others at the Inns of Court. Benchers occupied this symbolic role and a primary purpose of all legislation enacted by the Inns was to enhance their image as fathers of common law. The sacred importance of patriarchy is illustrated in the following regulation of the Inner Temple, which acknowledges the importance of ancient status and its primacy within the common law. If an honourable

---

³⁵ Hunt, *History of Sumptuary Laws*, p. 9.
³⁶ *Law and the Unconscious*, p. 211.   ³⁷ *Ibid.*, p. 223.
³⁸ On the importance of the paternal image to the symbolic system of law, see *ibid.*, p. 238. On psychoanalysis, religion and the image of the father, see S. Freud, 'Totem and Taboo', in S. Freud, *The Origins of Religion*, trans. J. Strachey (London: Penguin, 1990), p. 209.

member were 'called to the Bench, at that time being, or that thereafter should be a Knight, that notwithstanding such his dignity of Knighthood, he should take place at the Bench Table, according to his auncienty in the House, and no otherwise'.[39] In deference to this hierarchy, junior members of the Inn must 'yield due respect and observance to the Benchers and antients, their Governours'.[40] The legislation of the Inns promoted the image of the governor as an ancient, or father. Hence at the Inner Temple in 1557, during commons, only benchers (and knights) were permitted to wear beards beyond three weeks' growth. Transgressors were liable to a fine of '40s., and so double for every week, after monition, that he shall be so bearded in commons'.[41] At Lincoln's Inn, identical legislation was introduced, the intention of which was to define the licit image of the ancient or father. Such was the serious regard in which the image was held that, after the third offence, the transgressor was 'banished the House'.[42]

The beard is not only a masculine image, but also a symbol of wisdom, strength and authority. As Peacham observed in relation to the Greek God, Pan: '[h]is long beard noteth the ayre and fire, the two Masculine Elements, exercising their operation upon Nature being the Feminine'.[43] He represented '[a]ll, or the Universall, and indeed hee is nothing else but an Allegoricall fiction of the World'.[44] In similar allegorical fashion, an important function of sumptuary legislation at the Inns of Court was to depict the sovereignty of the absolute other and the position of the symbolic father at the apex of society. It should be noted that the fashion for wearing beards prevailed. The year after the above legislation was introduced at the Inns, 'all Orders before that time made, touching Beards, should be void and repealed';[45] an indication that the ancient customs of the Inns were responding to contemporary, external influences. This concession notwithstanding, the attempt to regulate the appearance of members demonstrated that the legal profession inherited from the church an awareness of the power of the image to play a crucial, manipulative role in the maintenance of order. The regulation of dress became an important means of expressing the propriety, authority and indivisibility of divine and common law.

CLASSICAL INFLUENCES AND THE ETHICS OF COMMON LAW

To paraphrase Foucault, ethics can be defined as freedom informed by reflection.[46] I have suggested that the early modern English constitution was

---

[39] Dugdale, *Origines Juridiciales*, fo. 148. [40] (Middle Temple), *ibid.*, fo. 192.
[41] *A Calendar of the Inner Temple Records*, ed. F. A. Inderwick, 5 vols. (London: H. Sotheran, 1896), I, p. 193.
[42] Dugdale, *Origines Juridiciales*, fo. 244. [43] Peacham, *Gentleman's Exercise*, pp. 120–1.
[44] *Ibid.*   [45] Dugdale, *Origines Juridiciales*, fo. 244.
[46] M. Foucault, *Ethics, Subjectivity and Truth: Essential Works of Foucault, 1954–1984*, ed. P. Rabinow (London: Penguin, 2000), p. 284.

modelled upon a system of ethics whose provenance lay in the synthesis of classical and Judaeo-Christian philosophies. The eclectic architecture of the Inns of Court was the public and monumental representation of a constitution that had never been codified but which was founded upon a notional insistence on *justitia* or righteousness. A similar analysis of legal costume provides a more personal and microscopic examination of the relationship between the citizen or subject of law and the governing body to which the subject owes allegiance. Of particular relevance to the definition of ethics provided by Foucault is the observation that the autonomous status of the Inns of Court enables them to be viewed as microcosms of the state, in which ethics, freedom and reflection are interactive and interdependent.

Possibly the most significant feature of an examination of costume, sumptuary legislation and the legal profession in the sixteenth century is the fact that members of the Inns of Court were entirely exempt from any proscriptive, statutory measures. Legislation on this point was specific. It did not extend 'to any Utterbarrester of any of the Innes of Court, for wearing in any of his apparel such silke (& furre) as is before limited for men that may dispend in landes, tenementes, rents, fees, or annuities for terme of life, rr. li. over al charges: nor to any other Student of the Innes of the Court'. The statute provided also that it 'shall not extend nor bee hurtfull or preiudiciall to any of the Kings most honorable Counsell, ne to Justices of the one Bench or the other ... Serieants at the Law ... they shall now at all times weare after the said feast, all such apparel in & upon their bodies, horses, mules, and other beasts ... as they have heretofore used to weare'.[47] Although this legislation did not represent an acknowledgment by the crown of the political sovereignty of common law, it was at least a tacit admission of the independence and autonomy of the legal profession. Of incalculable importance to common lawyers was the freedom such legislation provided for the Inns of Court to create and present an image of law which was entirely of their own formulation. The architecture of the Inns of Court was a representation of the ideal state, the means by which the communities envisaged in Plato's *Republic* and St Augustine's *City of God* were synthesised and manifested. The costume worn by individual members of the Inns was a representation of the ideal citizen within that state and of his relationship with other citizens. It was a representation also of his relationship with the state itself, and so was an important symbol of government.

Given the freedom specifically granted to them by statute in 1533, it is noteworthy that throughout the sixteenth century, and particularly during the reign of Elizabeth, the governing bodies of the Inns of Court regulated costume on an unprecedented scale. Control and manipulation of the image

---

[47] 24 Hen. 8. C. 13, Rastall, *Statutes*, fo. 15.

became the principal means whereby the ideal subject of law could be defined and recognised. During the reign of Edward VI the wearing of foreign clothes could, in a state trial, be evidence of treason. The earl of Surrey, renowned for his extravagant taste in dress, was depicted in a portrait by Scrots wearing highly ornate, Italian clothes. One of the charges at his trial in 1547 was that he wore foreign dress; he was found guilty of treason and executed.[48] The licit image of legal costume represented a social contract, in which the individual surrendered his absolute freedom to a sovereign power under a reciprocal agreement that guaranteed his status as a subject of the state, entitling him to the protection of a benevolent ruler. Such a model anticipates Rousseau by two centuries, but the initial formulation of the social contract is evident from the relations between subject and ruler that the legislation of the Inns of Court attempted to establish.[49]

A more precise definition of the particular system of power that the Inns of Court sought to represent is witnessed in legislation passed by the Middle Temple Parliament during the reigns of subsequent Tudor monarchs. Dugdale notes that '[i]n 4 & 5 Ph. & M. it was ordered, that none of this Society should thenceforth wear any great Bryches in their Hoses, made after the Dutch, Spanish, or Almon fashion; or Lawnde upon their Capps; or Cut doublets, upon pain of iiis. Iiiid. Forfaiture for the first default, and the second time to be expelled the House.'[50] It is significant that, during the reign of a Catholic queen married to a Spanish consort, the legal profession should have asserted its independence and nationalism in such an explicit manner. The threat of banishment pervaded the regulations of the Marian Inns in relation to sumptuary legislation and is relevant to the thesis that adherence to the Anglican settlement provided the religious foundation for all such laws. Salvation and damnation were implicit in the legislation passed by the Inner Temple in 1557, for example, forbidding foreign fashions such as 'double ruffs on their shirts, feathers or ribbons in their caps, upon pain to forfeit for the first default 3s. 4d., the second, expulsion without redemption'.[51]

The above legislation provides the clearest evidence of a corporate tendency towards xenophobic anti-Catholicism amongst common lawyers. Despite the protestation of Philip II that he did not intend to govern England, and the probable right to succession of Elizabeth if Mary died heirless, Spanish pretensions to power in the Netherlands and northern Italy aroused suspicion as to Philip's motives. Initial investigation therefore suggests that conflict, rather than consensus, provided the rationale for the sumptuary

---

[48] J. Ashelford, *A Visual History of Costume: The Sixteenth Century* (London: Batsford, 1983), pp. 56–7.
[49] See J.-J. Rousseau, *The Social Contract, and Discourses*, trans. G. D. H. Cole (London: Dent, 1973).
[50] Dugdale, *Origines Juridiciales*, fo. 191.   [51] *Inner Temple Records*, I, p. 192.

legislation of the Marian Inns of Court. Their constitutions appeared to represent a system of power that had rejected the juridical notion of sovereignty in favour of one that accorded to Foucault's theory that war was the eternal foundation of all national institutions of governance.[52] Law in such a model seeks to define the state in relation to its hostility towards and suspicion of neighbouring states. The Middle Temple legislation cited above delineates a code of sartorial regulation that attempts to represent the unique ethnicity of the Ancient Constitution, untainted by the invasion of foreign powers or the authority of rival jurisdictions. A predisposition towards strident nationalism was clearly manifested in these regulations, but further examination of the legislation relating to legal costume reveals that 'care of the self' was the other salient feature.

In ancient Greece, care of the self, or *epimeleia heautou*, was a civic obligation regulated by specific procedures. It was concerned with the governance of relationships at a domestic, familial level and with the constitutional relationship between ruler and subject. Foucault cites Xenophon, who related the concept of *epimeleia heautou* to the supervision of farming by the master of the household, and Dio of Prusa, who connected it to the benevolent actions of the sovereign in protecting his people and leading the city-state.[53] A. J. and R. W. Carlyle refer to the importance of the social contract between the king and the populace, as a fundamental tenet of governance in medieval society. They cite the medieval political theory of the *pactum*, in which each party was bound equally by a contract (defined by Manegold of Lautenbach in *Ab Gebehardum*),[54] as the intellectual antecedent of Hooker's religious commonwealth.[55] Of particular significance to the argument that the philosophical origins of the early modern English state can be traced to the constitutions of the classical world, is the suggestion of A. J. and R. W. Carlyle that the medieval social contract may be related to Platonic and Ciceronian political theories.[56]

The relevance of care of the self to the constitutions of the Greek city-states, the Inns of Court and the early modern English state is that a code of manners or ethics, regulating the relationships between individual members of a household, is considered the ideal model for a political system. In such a polity, a primary objective of government is the attainment of constitutional harmony between governor and subject. The end of feudalism was instanced by several events in sixteenth-century England. These included the expansion of a strong, centralised executive within a recognisable nation-state; the

---

[52] Foucault, *Ethics*, p. 61.   [53] *Ibid.*, p. 95.
[54] R. W. Carlyle and A. J. Carlyle, *A History of Mediaeval Political Theory in the West*, 6 vols. (Edinburgh: Blackwood, 1903–1936), III (1915), p. 168.
[55] *Ibid.*, VI (1936), p. 395.   [56] *Ibid.*, I (1903), p. 63.

standardisation and systematisation of common law and the legal profession; the emergence of a powerful merchant-class, dependent for its success on increased levels of trade with continental Europe and the Mediterranean countries; and the dissemination of knowledge brought about by innovative printing processes. A new system of social and political relations was evolving, and the unique freedom of the Inns of Court to regulate their own activities, unfettered by interference from the crown, enabled them to create and represent an image of the emergent constitution.

The sumptuary legislation of the Inns of Court attempted to replace the feudal model of government with one closely linked to the ancient Greek model. Inevitably, the interpretation of 'care of the self' in sixteenth-century England was different from its original interpretation in ancient Greece. Characteristic of the proscriptive regulations of the Inns was the requirement of repression and reformation, of atonement for past misdemeanours. The following extract from the regulations of the Middle Temple in 1584 provides evidence of the integration of neo-classical humanism and Protestant nationalism at the Inns of Court:

1. That no great Ruff should be worn.
2. Nor any white colour in Doublets, or Hosen.
3. Nor any facing of Velvet in Gownes, but by such as were of the Bench.
4. That no Gentleman should walk in the streetes, in their Cloaks, but in Gownes.
5. That no Hat, or long, or curled hayr be worn.
6. Nor any Gownes, but such as were of a sad colour.[57]

While the regulation of the image was a central feature of the European Reformation, the control of representations was also an important feature of ancient Greek philosophy. In *The Apology*, Plato presents Socrates berating his judges for their acquisition of wealth, reputation and honours at the expense of knowledge, truth and perfection of the self.[58] Epictetus emphasised the capacity of representations to affect reason and the necessity for their constant supervision. In relation to the effect of representations on human thought he used the analogy of the moneychanger (*arguronomos*) who examines, weighs and checks the nature of the coin and the effigy imprinted thereon.[59] As Foucault has observed, self-regulation in ancient Greece was linked to the belief that it was only through such self-possession (Seneca termed this *fieri suum*) that care of the self could be effected. The licit image was as important in ancient Athens as it was in post-Reformation

---

[57] Dugdale, *Origines Juridiciales*, fo. 191.
[58] 'Socrates' Defense (Apology)', in *The Collected Dialogues*, ed. E. Hamilton and H. Cairns (New Jersey: Princeton University Press, 1961), p. 16.
[59] Epictetus, *The Discourses and Manual*, trans. P. E. Matheson (Oxford University Press, 1916), p. 83.

England. The 'self-possessed' man in Greek society was the embodiment of the juridical and political model of sovereign government.[60] At a later date Christian asceticism placed a similar emphasis on self-renunciation as the means of self-knowledge and ultimately, of salvation. Gregory of Nyssa referred to the renunciation of the world and the detachment of oneself from the flesh as a means of recovering man's lost immortality. He cited the parable of the lost drachma (Luke 15.8–10), in support of his claim that one must search every corner of the human soul in order to find the true imprint of God, which has been tarnished by human corruption.[61]

It is evident therefore that the institutional control and repression of representations find their origins in ancient Greek society rather than in the war of images in sixteenth-century Europe.[62] Of course, the power (and concomitant danger) of the image to effect the attachment and obedience of the subject to law was a motivating factor for the Reformation movement and is of fundamental importance to any discussion of sumptuary legislation, the nation-state and the early modern constitution. The European Reformation became incidentally a means whereby the early modern state developed, unfettered eventually by interference from Rome. This development notwithstanding, the influence of the Renaissance (in particular the rediscovery, reinterpretation and publication of texts on ancient Greek philosophy and jurisprudence) on the form of governance within the emergent English constitution should not be underestimated. For example, Maclean suggests that the influence of Neoplatonic humanism was both disruptive of and aggressive towards existing jurisprudence. This he attributes to the fact that the Renaissance enabled hitherto unknown or poorly translated Greek passages from the *Digest* of Justinian to become widely available to a large audience.[63] Asceticism was considered to be an important means whereby care of the self (in ancient Greece) and self-knowledge (in the Christian world) were attained. In this context it is significant that the root of the Christian notion of self-knowledge was Platonic, it being a principal Socratic virtue. Techniques such as those outlined above, which acted upon individuals rather than institutions, established a personal basis to the creation of the constitutional relationship between subject and ruler in the post-medieval English state.

[60] Foucault, *Ethics*, p. 96.
[61] St Gregory of Nyssa, 'Treatise on Virginity', in *Saint Gregory of Nyssa: Ascetical Works*, trans. V. W. Callahan (Washington, D.C.: Catholic University of America Press, 1966), pp. 46–8.
[62] On the war of images and the Church, see S. Runciman, *Byzantine Style and Civilisation* (Harmondsworth: Penguin, 1987); also A. Grabar, *Christian Iconography* (New Jersey: Princeton University Press, 1968).
[63] I. Maclean, *Interpretation and Meaning in the Renaissance* (Cambridge University Press, 1992), p. 15.

In classical terms the insistence of the Middle Temple regulations, above, on 'sad' colours and the prohibition of white doublets and hose is significant. At Gray's Inn, it was ordered that 'none of this Society should wear any Gown, Doublet, Hose, or other outward Garment, of any light colour, upon penalty of expulsion', and at the Inner Temple in 1557 members were forbidden to wear 'in their doublets or hose any light colours' or 'white jerkins'.[64] A melancholic predisposition was, for the Stoics, a means of self-discovery. Foucault discusses the notion of *anakhoresis*, a form of retreat whose purpose is not self-indulgent, although the exercise is reflective and introspective, whereby the laws of behaviour are discovered and remembered.[65] In the *Dialogus de Oratoribus* of Tacitus, the melancholic retreat provides a means of self-discovery for Curatius Maternus, an advocate who seeks release from the specious rhetoric of forensic oratory. He asks the muses to restore his spiritual and emotional equilibrium by bearing him away from the noise and hazards of the forum. He wants to be transported to a tranquil, sacred place, far removed from the cares and anxieties of his quotidian existence.[66] The pastoral retreat that Maternus describes is a metaphor for reflective asceticism, the discipline of which it was believed led to an ethical awareness of self and the relationship between the individual and society. Discovery of the laws of behaviour informed the code of manners that was an acknowledged feature of the ancient city-state. Their discovery provided also the basis for the post-feudal English constitution, whose inherent fairness and justice was, according to commentators from Fortescue to Coke, unmatched by other legal systems. The seventeenth-century Anglican divine, Calybute Downing, suggested that the basis of the English constitution was nothing more than the organisation and assumption of good manners.[67]

Fortescue depicted the Inns of Court as a pastoral idyll of the kind that Curatius Maternus sought. They were sacred places where self-discovery and care of the self complemented and were coextensive with common law: '[t]he Place of Study is not in the Heart of the City it self, where the great Confluence and Multitude of the Inhabitants might disturb them in their Studies, but in a private Place, separate and distinct by it self, in the Suburbs, near to the Courts of Justice.'[68] Fortescue and Tacitus describe an idyll that is also a microcosm of the Stoic system, in which God is synonymous with the universal order of the cosmos. The order of nature creates the ethical imperative for obedience. Little argues that both Renaissance humanism and classical Stoicism recognised societal order as a manifestation of the

---

[64] Dugdale, *Origines Juridiciales*, at fo. 283; *Inner Temple Records*, I, p. 192.
[65] Foucault, *Ethics*, p. 238.   [66] Tacitus, *Dialogus de Oratoribus*, p. 265.
[67] C. Downing, *A Discourse of the State Ecclesiasticall of this Kingdome in Relation to the Civill* (Oxford: Turner, 1634), fo. 2.
[68] Fortescue, *De Laudibus*, p. 109.

recurring, inexorable *ordo naturae*, in the face of which no break or transformation was possible.⁶⁹ The incorporation of flamboyant, foreign styles and coloured fabrics into sartorial habit offended against the ordered principles of propriety, reason and authority, which informed the civic virtues of ancient Greece as much as they did the ethos of Renaissance humanism. The decision of the Inns of Court to standardise the dress of their members represented, in institutional terms, the movement towards the systematisation of common law in the sixteenth century. But at a symbolic level, the sumptuary laws of the Inns regulated the image so that the institution embodied by their members was perceived as the visible object of social authority: the exemplary legal community was the image of the ideal constitution.

Relevant to the argument that sixteenth-century sumptuary legislation at the Inns was a response to the Reformation is the lack of any restrictions on legal costume prior to this period. Baker draws attention to the fact that below the level of serjeant-at-law, there were no regulations concerning legal costume, the only distinguishing feature of medieval common lawyers being their long robes.⁷⁰ Although all barristers wore gowns in court, there was no standardised attire. Hence, as Mr Secondary Kempe, of the Court of King's Bench, recalled in 1602:

> In tymes past the counsellors wore gowns faced with satten, and some with yellowe cotton, and the benchers with jennet furre; now they are come to that pride and fantasticknes that every one must have a velvet face, and some soe tricked with lace that Justice Wray in his tyme spake to such an odd counseller in this manner: Quomodo intrasti, domine, non habens vestem nuptialem? Get you from the barre, or I will put you from the barr for your foolish pride.⁷¹

Implicit in the above condemnation of 'pride' and 'fantasticknes' is the classical principle that the repression of individual desire in the greater interest of the community is a prerequisite for social cohesion and the concomitant maintenance of order. For the purpose of subjective attachment to the legal institution, the reason and authority of law must be recognisable as a licit image of cosmic order. Consequently there evolved a plain, standard pattern of gown, dark in colour and generally recognised as appropriately modest. Baker refers to the full-length, monumental effigies of Robert Keilwey (d. 1580) and Edmund Plowden (d. 1584), benchers of the Inner and Middle Temple respectively (Keilway's effigy is at Exton, in Rutland; Plowden's is on the north side of Temple church). Each shows a plain gown with hanging or 'glove' sleeves. The only decoration seems to have been edgings to the

---

⁶⁹ D. Little, *Religion, Order, and Law: A Study in Pre-Revolutionary England* (Oxford: Blackwell, 1970), p. 37.
⁷⁰ J. H. Baker, 'History of the Gowns Worn at the English Bar', *Costume: The Journal of the Costume Society*, 9 (1975), 15.
⁷¹ J. Manningham, *The Diary of John Manningham of the Middle Temple* (London: Camden Society, 1858), p. 45.

elbow-slit and the bottom of the sleeve; perhaps these, and the facings, were of velvet. The garment would have been black or one of the dark colours approximating to black.[72] Ferne describes 'sable' [black] as one of the five colours recognised in heraldic arms, and therefore representative of the code of honour appropriate to a 'gentleman of blood'. Sable was associated with the planet Saturn (the god who presided over a golden age in Latium); it was linked with the virtues of 'prudence' and 'constancie', and denoted a 'melancholie' complexion.[73]

The sumptuary laws of the Inns represented an attempt to create a universal citizenship that acknowledged the primacy of reason in the body politic. Therefore the enhancement of reason was a strong, motivating factor for the regulation and repression of individual behaviour. Marcus Aurelius expressed similar thoughts in *Meditations* (Book IV), arguing that as reason distinguished humanity from other forms of life and was inherent to all law, then all citizens were active members of a universal body politic.[74] The fundamental importance of sumptuary legislation to the development of the English constitution was that it demonstrates the influence of Neoplatonic humanism on societal regulation and on the constitutional relationship between crown, common law and subject. Although their influence was marginal in comparison with the effect of statutes such as the Acts of Supremacy of 1534 and 1559, sumptuary laws were employed innovatively by the legal profession and the crown to depict the standardisation and efficiency of the early modern state and its organs of government.[75] Little argues that although Renaissance humanism facilitated significant intellectual developments, its effects were not experienced in the sphere of social progress.[76] But the sumptuary laws of Tudor England suggest that the social and political importance of Neoplatonic humanism was profound: it was instrumental in shaping a body politic in which an embryonic social contract was apparent.

The fictional, racial purity of English law was a popular polemical thesis proposed by the English legal profession as it sought to establish the political sovereignty of common law and its inviolability from the perceived threat of civil and canon law. Dugdale provided a genealogy of English law and lawgivers, suggesting that the constitutions of three distinct dynasties provided the basis of the common law. First, 'Dunwallo Molmutius (who apparently began his reign 440B.C.) was the first King that did constitute Laws in

---

[72] Baker, 'Gowns Worn at the English Bar', 16. [73] Ferne, *Blazon of Gentrie*, ff. 169–71.
[74] In C. N. Cochrane, *Christianity and Classical Culture* (New York: Oxford University Press, 1957), p. 166.
[75] On the incorporation of sumptuary legislation into the apparatus of early modern law, see P. Goodrich, 'Signs Taken for Wonders: Community, Identity and *A History of Sumptuary Law*', *Law and Social Inquiry*, 23 (1998), 707–28.
[76] Little, *Religion, Order, and Law*, p. 36.

Brittain, which were thereupon called the Molmucian Laws'. His successor, 'Mercia Queen of the Britans . . . made a Law, full of prudence and Justice, called the Mercian Law'. Second came the Saxon monarchs, Ethelbert, Ina, Alfred, Edward the martyr, Athelstan and Ethelred. And third, '[a]fter this, the Danes ruling here, here was a third Law of them constituted, which was called Denelega, id est, the Danes Law.' From these three bodies of law, Edward I (the English Justinian) selected 'the best and choicest, and reducing them into one body, called them the Common Law'.[77] Dugdale was in favour of the inherent racial purity of English law, as the following casuistic argument demonstrates: 'Sir Edward Coke expresseth it thus. – Because he [Henry I] abolished such Customes of Normandy, as his Father had added to our Common Laws he is said to have restored the antient Laws of England.'[78] Dugdale thereby rationalises the myth of the Ancient Constitution, offering an ethnocentric interpretation of the genealogy of common law, from which any foreign influences have been excised. Despite the attempts by Dugdale and other early modern jurists to justify the fiction of the immemorial nature of English law, it is apparent that the ethos of the sixteenth-century English constitution derived from the classical ideal of care of the self and the Christian principle of self-knowledge. The political influence of Renaissance humanism on the development of the post-medieval English state was pervasive, particularly with regard to acknowledgment of the rational individual and his role as a citizen of the state. Sumptuary legislation of the sixteenth century embodied and enforced a code of manners, tradition and honour, providing a visual image of the rational order inherent in the early modern English state.

ECCLESIASTICAL POLITY AND THE GOVERNANCE OF ENGLAND

Jurists of the sixteenth and early seventeenth centuries professed the belief that religion had a temporal, as well as an obvious spiritual, role to play in the governance of the nation. William Wilkes, for example, cited Justinian in defence of his thesis that religion was '[t]he safest defence of publicke state'. Wilkes quotes from several ancient philosophers, all of whom had observed the correlation between religion and the constitution of the citystate: '[a]mongst all things incident into the actions of men, there is none more excellent, then Religion saith Plato: In it, our cheefest good consisteth, saith Lactantius: It is the unmoveable foundation of Princely honour, saith Cyrill.'[79] It is certain that *ius commune* predates the common law as practised

---

[77] Dugdale, *Origines Juridiciales*, fo. 4.   [78] *Ibid.*, fo. 7.
[79] W. Wilkes, *Obedience or Ecclesiasticall Union* (London: G. Elde, for R. Jackson, 1605), p. 5.

by the early modern legal profession, its origins being ecclesiastical rather than secular. The phrase, *ius commune*, was well known to the canonists as a convenient means of distinguishing the general and ordinary law of the universal church from any rules peculiar to a particular, provincial church and from those papal *privilegia* that gave rise to much ecclesiastical litigation.[80] In the secular courts, common law was recognised as the general and ordinary law of the nation, and was distinguished from the acts of royal prerogative, which increased inordinately throughout the reign of James I.[81]

The potential and actual conflict between the executive and the legal profession in the late sixteenth and early seventeenth centuries accounts for the efforts of common lawyers to locate a legitimate source of sovereign constitutional authority that was prior to and independent from the authority of the crown. Coke's observation that an Act of Parliament in breach of the law of God was necessarily void[82] could only be valid if the constitutional primacy of ecclesiastical polity was accepted. The correlation between the constitutional supremacy of common law jurisdiction and divine authority prompted Coke publicly to compare the relationship between serjeant-at-law and client with that of spiritual confessor and penitent: 'Seeing therefore ye Clyent doth make you as his Confessour as great a Conscience as the religious Confessor whoe is bound at his odinacion by oathe not to reveale any thinge that is imparted unto him *sub stola Confessionis*.'[83] As Holdsworth observed in relation to the highly imaginative *The Mirror of Justices* (one of Coke's favourite sources of constitutional authority), it represented an attempt to construct 'an ideal system of law, out of the shifting legal panorama of his day, by going back to Biblical first principles'.[84] These principles were incontrovertible because they were sanctioned by the Almighty Father and were therefore of sovereign authority on earth. Consequently, if an irrefutable link between common law and the Word of God could be established, then common law could fairly be represented not only as the epitome of human reason but also as the supreme source of legal authority, to which the prerogative acts of the monarch were always subject. The attempt by Coke to predicate the foundations of common law upon holy writ was therefore as much an act of political expedience as one motivated by religious conviction.

---

[80] On *ius commune*, canonists and the common law, see F. Pollock and F. Maitland, *History of English Law*, 2 vols. (Cambridge University Press, 1898), I, p. 176.

[81] On the failure of successive monarchs to observe the legal limits of their sovereignty, and the conflicting ideologies of common lawyers and Tudor and Stuart monarchs, see Little, *Religion, Order, and Law*, p. 171.

[82] E. Coke, *The Third Part of the Institutes of the Laws of England* (London: Flesher, 1644), p. 181.

[83] B. M. Additional ms. 22591, fo. 94b, quoted in *Inner Temple Records*, II, appendix no. v, p. 349.

[84] W. S. Holdsworth, *Some Makers of English Law* (Cambridge University Press, 1938), p. 39.

In *De Laudibus Legum Angliae*, Fortescue drew attention to the difference between divine and human law. Employing the classical form of a dialogue between master and student (in this case, between Chancellor and Prince), he allowed the Prince to distinguish between theology and jurisprudence:

> I know, Good Chancellor, that the Book of Deuteronomy is a Part of the Holy Scriptures, that the Laws and Ceremonies contained therein are of Divine Institution and promulgated by Moses; upon which Account the Reading of them is Matter for a Pious and Devout Contemplation: But the Law, to the Study and Understanding whereof you now invite me, is merely Human, derived from Human Authority, and respects this World.[85]

Fortescue leaves his readers in no doubt that the youthful ignorance of the Prince prevents him from understanding that the laws of God and man are indivisible. He explains that the Book of Deuteronomy was the divinely ordained Book of Laws, according to which the kings of Israel were obliged to govern their subjects.[86] As many commentators have noted, in pre-revolutionary England the laws of God and man were for the most part indistinguishable and interchangeable.[87] Consequently, as the crown encroached upon the liberties of the subject during the latter years of Elizabethan rule and throughout the reign of James I, there was a strong political imperative for common lawyers to assert the indivisible correlation between divine law and common law, to which Fortescue referred above. In substantive terms, the effect of the arrogation to common law of biblical first principles was immediately apparent. The prerogative powers of the crown were curtailed by the courts, on the general grounds that such acts were offensive to God. At a symbolic level the suggestive and manipulative power of the image was the crucial and fundamental means whereby common law attained its pre-eminent role within the body politic.

The medieval concept of the *Character Angelicus*, hitherto associated exclusively with kingship, was invoked in the service of common law. As Kantorowicz has observed, the body politic of kingship appeared as a likeness of the seraphim because it represented, like the angels, that which was ageless and unalterable.[88] The quality of immutability has an obvious parallel with the unchanging and unchangeable character of common law. The symbols of the legal profession sought to represent its likeness to the celestial hierarchy and its tacit link with a Biblical past. Hence, the early modern

---

[85] Fortescue, *De Laudibus*, pp. 3–4.   [86] *Ibid.*, p. 3.
[87] See for example Little, *Religion, Order, and Law*, p. 133.
[88] E. Kantorowicz, *The King's Two Bodies: A Study in Medieval Political Theology* (New Jersey: Princeton University Press, 1957), p. 8. The literary source of the medieval *Character Angelicus* is the Old Testament: 'for my lord the King is like the angel of God to discern good and evil' (2 Samuel 14.17).

Inns of Court integrated and represented appropriate images of divine and temporal law. The legal profession presented itself as a secular priesthood, and the close association between lawyer and priest was exemplified by the lawyer's apparel, as regulated by the governing institutions of common law. Dugdale noted the biblical link between clerical and legal costume, implicitly confirming a fundamental tenet of the Reformation that the image must be an appropriate representation of the divine order.

> That peculiar and decent Vestments, have, from great antiquity, been used in religious services, we have the authority of God's sacred precept to Moses. 'Thou shalt make holy rayments for Aaron and his sons, that are to minister unto me, that they may be for glory and beauty.' And reason tells us, that in places of Civil judicature, it is not only proper, that the Magistrate should be distinguished from others, but all possible care used, that a venerable respect be had to his person and office.[89]

There was a specific intention on the part of the legal profession that legal costume should attain iconic significance. The invisible principles of divine law and their correlation with the English constitution were represented in the visual symbolism of legal costume. Waterhouse noted the association between sacerdotal and legal costume, and the divine provenance of both: '[r]obes were the best of garments, and those that signified excellency and State. And therefore as they were long from the collar to the foot, to import the extent of dignity over the whole person of the wearer, according to that pattern which I believe the Christian Church took for her long robe . . . one like the Son of man, cloathed with a garment down to the foot.'[90]

The particular order of knowledge that such costume embodies is elucidated in the following extracts from a speech of a Chief Justice of the Common Pleas during the reign of Henry VIII, concerning the costume of the Order of Serjeants-at-Law. The white coif, for example, 'betokeneth innocencye and clerenes, as well for understandinge as of conscience'. The colour of the coif is noteworthy in a religious context, since white is considered to signify godliness. In terms of the Reformation it is also the absence of colour or inscription. It is close to a blank space or vanishing sign, the most powerful because the most unobtrusive image. Coke attempted to explain the significance of the white coif at the installation of eleven serjeants-at-law in the Inner Temple hall in 1614. He emphasised the secular symbolism, rather than the religious connotations of the colour white, but his speech

---

[89] Dugdale, *Origines Juridiciales*, fo. 98.
[90] E. Waterhouse, *A Commentary On That Nervous Treatise De Laudibus Legum Angliae* (London, 1663), fo. 568. On robes as symbols of intellectual and social superiority, see J. H. Baker, *The Order of Serjeants at Law* (London: Selden Society, 1984), pp. 67–8.

is noteworthy for its elucidation of the meaning of a particular sign and its association with a mandatory code of ethics: '[h]is Coyfe is of whitt to shewe and represent unto him the integrity that he ought to retayne, And that as ye Coyfe being of whit Coullour is carryed by him upon the highest and most eminent parte of his Bodye, soe his Integritie ought to be Conspicuous and notorious.'[91]

Concerning the origins of the coif, Waterhouse observed that '[t]he Coyff called the Pileum in the Roman Stories, being a Priestly habit, and so by Saint Jerom owned under the name of Pileolum, as the fourth kinde of Sacerdotal habiliment.'[92] The tabard of the Serjeant 'betokenethe the weke bodye of the commonaltye, which without the cord and succour of lawys and justice shuld never be able to abide the strong, ferable, impetuouse blaste of wronge'; the hood and tabard were both 'single [unlined], in token that ye shall never doble the utterance of your knowledge with other consideration then of verite and justice . . . that is to saye, without all coloure or counterfet of coloure playnlye to saye that the wronge is wronge and that the right is right'. The symbolism of the parti-coloured tabard and hood is explained similarly, aligning Christian virtues with the fundamental principles of common law, in the body of the lawyer: '[t]he blew betokenethe fidelytie, the murrey stedfastnes and love.'[93] Coke had delineated the symbolism of the serjeants' robes in similar terms, differing slightly from the above description in suggesting that 'murrey' was the colour of 'prudentie', and adding that 'Parte Violett which takes noe Stayne, And for your Scarlett it is knowne to all men to be A judiciall Colour, Your Blacke betokeneth gravitie and patience'.[94]

The biblical parallel between God, law and the ministers of law was made explicit in a speech of Sir Edward Montague (Lord Chief Justice) to the newly appointed serjeants. The intended effect of his words was to evoke a visible image of the seraphim, or *Character Angelicus*, in the institutional body of serjeants-at-law. Hence, the coif was white because, 'as appereth Apocalip. 7, thos which shall assend to heaven shalbe clothed with white, signifiinge puritye of lif: which is verye necessarye in potentates and ministers of the lawe'. The gown was 'single' [unlined] because this 'doth presage that ye must be void of duplice, fraude, deceipte or coven. For the profete sayeth, in the persoune of God a deciptfull man shall not prosper here in erthe.' It was sewn up above the waist in order to 'betokenethe secretures. For, as Salamon

---

[91] B. M. Additional ms. 22591, fo. 93b, quoted in *Inner Temple Records*, II, appendix no. v, p. 348.
[92] Waterhouse, *Commentary On That Nervous Treatise*, fo. 568.
[93] B. L. ms. Harley 160, ff. 191-4v.
[94] B. M. Additional ms. 22591, fo. 94b, quoted in *Inner Temple Records*, II, appendix no. v, p. 349.

saiethe, procure as many frendes as thou canste, albehit make not one of a thousande thy counseler lest if thou make many they utter thy secretes to thy greate hurte and damage'.[95]

The above delineation of symbols demonstrates that legal costume can be subjected to a process of deconstruction and the individual components identified as signs of divine will, subsumed into the common law tradition. Costume forms part of *traditio* or *leges non scriptae*, the meaning of which it is the exclusive right of the legal profession to expound. An order of signs was designated, through which the subject of law could be made to understand the invisible truth of God's will, a mystery that the prosaic text alone could never reveal. The salient issues were those of ethical and moral sovereignty, the identification and recognition of the particular institutional body in which such sovereignty resides, and the willing attachment to that body by the subject of law. The importance of righteousness or *justitia* to the English constitution cannot be overstated: legitimacy depended on the licit signs of righteousness. Prior to the Reformation the church, acting as the appointed guardian of an invisible truth, was an institutional object of public veneration. Tainted by accusations of popery, idolatry and falsehood, its spiritual as well as its juridical authority had diminished.

For several centuries prior to the Reformation, Rome was aware of the threat posed by secular legal systems to the jurisdiction of ecclesiastical law. A version of *Collectio Dyonisiana*, entitled *Dyonisio-Hadriana*, was sent by Pope Hadrian to Charles the Great in 774, disseminating the principle that popes could declare, even if they could not make, law for the universal church, and thus were able to contract the sphere of secular jurisprudence.[96] But, following the Henrician Reformation, the juridical supremacy of the pope was replaced in England by the king in Parliament and the courts of common law. Conscious of the utility of religious iconography and its capacity to effect a binding relationship between institutional order and the individual subject, the legal profession strove to establish a religious commonwealth governed by judges, the legitimacy of whose ethical, moral and constitutional sovereignty was guaranteed by the Bible. In *The Birthpangs of Protestant England*, Collinson remarks that during this period in English history, the populace believed itself to be living within the Bible itself.[97] In accordance with the theological jurisprudence propounded by Hooker, ecclesiastical polity was central to the early modern constitution. Pursuing the analogy adopted by Collinson, above, in which the pages of the Bible

---

[95] B. L. ms. Harley 361, ff. 75–80.
[96] See Pollock and Maitland, *History of English Law*, I, p. 9.
[97] P. Collinson, *The Birthpangs of Protestant England: Religious and Cultural Change in the Sixteenth and Seventeenth Centuries* (London: Macmillan, 1988), pp. 7–10.

stand for a unique English commonwealth, the legal profession assumed the exclusive role of expounding the meaning of the biblical text. It illuminated the pages of the Bible with signs that were intended to capture the subject of law so that he willingly submitted to the authority of the legal institution. It also placed the legal profession (and in particular the judiciary) in an entrenched and sovereign position in the commonwealth. The Inns of Court played a decisive role in formulating the nature of these signs, devising a fictional genealogy whose origins lay in the books of the Old Testament that honoured judges as *elohim*, or gods, and in the New Testament injunctions to know thyself and to love thy neighbour. The self-regulating status of the Inns enabled them, without interference from external forces, to depict the original of law through an order of signs, designed to persuade the subject of the coextensive sovereignty of divine and common law.

The autonomy of the Inns of Court determined their power to convey images of an ideal form of law. Despite their statutory immunity, the Inns paid superficial deference to the movement for the reform of images, as the following extract from the Pension Book of Gray's Inn demonstrates.

In 6 Ed VI (8 Nov) in pursuance of the Act for Reformation there was an order made that the Pensioner and Steward of this House should make sale of certain Utensils then being in the said Chappell, for the behoof of the Society; viz: one Vestment with a cross of red velvet; a Holy Water Stock of Brass; two candlesticks; a little bell of brass; a vestment of silk, spect with gold, and a pair of organs.

That this was an act of political expedience rather than one of religious conviction is further demonstrated by the following entry in the same Pension Book during the first year of Mary's reign: 'the Romish Religion being restored, there was a new altar set up and ornaments for the same provided'.[98] The war of images, which these pragmatic actions exemplify, had a limited impact on the Inns of Court beyond affecting the form of worship in chapel. The sumptuary legislation of the Inns was effective in regulating the image of law in the presence of God, to imply humility and self-knowledge through self-renunciation. For this reason, the appearance of honourable members in chapel and hall was strictly regulated: '[h]is Habit is a Student's Gown, and in the term time a round Cap, which he wears both in the Hall, and in the Church. Boots and Spurrs, Swords and Cloakes are in those places forbidden; as also extraordinary long hair.'[99] Despite the alleged foundations of common law in the word of God, in relation to statutory regulation of the image the legal profession showed no more than cursory respect for the acts of God's anointed representative, the king.

---

[98] From Dugdale's extracts from the lost volume of the Pension Book, *The Pension Book of Gray's Inn*, ed. R. J. Fletcher, 2 vols. (London: Chiswick, 1901), I, appendix no. ii, p. 497.

[99] (Middle Temple), Dugdale, *Origines Juridiciales*, fo. 202.

ICONOCLASM AND THE RELIGIOUS IMAGE

During the reign of Edward VI legislation was enacted requiring the mass destruction of religious iconography: '[a]ny Images of Stone, Timber, Alabaster or Earth; Graven, Carved or Painted, taken out of any Church, etc. shall be Destroyed, etc. and not reserved to any Superstitious Use.'[100] Further evidence of the immunity of the Inns from the iconoclastic zeal of the Reformation was the survival of the grotesque, medieval Gothic heads that form the carved capitals around the aisle-wall arcade of Temple church. Among the diverse social range of characters (popularly believed to symbolise souls in heaven and hell) are depicted a serjeant-at-law, a peasant, a king, the devil and a toothless old woman.[101] In the decades following the enactment of the above statute, the great architectural expansion of the Inns of Court took place and religious iconography was incorporated into their ornamentation on an unprecedented scale.

Of conspicuous importance as a symbol of the autonomy of common law were the four windows of Lincoln's Inn chapel (two in the north elevation and two in the south elevation), installed in 1623 by Abraham and Bernard Van Linge, when the new chapel was completed. They attained national significance when they were cited during the trial of Archbishop Laud. Charged with 'traitorously endeavouring to alter and subvert God's True Religion by Law Established in this Realm, and instead thereof to set up Popish Superstition and Idolatry', Laud argued that the Edwardian legislation did not refer to 'Glass-Windows, nor the Images that are in them'. His accusers insisted that the Act 'requires the Destruction of all Images, as well in Glass-Windows, as elsewhere'.[102] Richard Butler assisted in painting the glass in Lincoln's Inn chapel and also repaired some of the windows of Lambeth Palace, thereby unwittingly providing evidence of Archbishop Laud's idolatry to his accusers. Laud, according to the common lawyer, pamphleteer and opponent of divine right episcopacy, William Prynne,

> caused these demolished superstitious Pictures in the Glasse windowes to be repaired, furbished, beautified and made more compleat and accurate with new painted Glasse, than ever before, setting them up againe in fresh lively colours, according to the very Patterne in the great Roman Missall, or Masse Booke ... so as no chapel in Rome could be more Idolatrous, Popish, superstitious in regard of such offensive Pictures, than his at Lambeth.[103]

---

[100] 3 & 4 Edw. 6. C. 10.
[101] See D. Lewer, *The Temple Church* (Andover: Pitkin, 1971), p. 7. On the English law of images, see also M. Aston, *England's Iconoclasts* (Oxford University Press, 1988).
[102] Anon., *The History of the Troubles and Tryal of William Laud, Arch-Bishop of Canterbury* (London: R. Chiswell, 1695), ff. 311, 312.
[103] W. Prynne, *Canterburies Doome; or the first part of a compleat history of the commitment, charge, tryall, condemnation, execution of William Laud, late Arch-bishop of Canterbury* (London, 1646), fo. 59

In 1637, for the second time in three years, Prynne was sentenced to have his ears 'cropped', along with Dr John Bastwicke and the radical anti-episcopalian, Henry Burton, following the publication of a seditious pamphlet. The fact that Prynne had been tried, convicted and sentenced in the past by the Courts of High Commission and Star Chamber probably contributed to the zeal with which Prynne attacked Laud. Ashton has noted the shared interest of Puritans and common lawyers in opposing the enhanced jurisdiction of the ecclesiastical courts during the reign of Charles I.[104] The spiritual courts, which were administered by civil lawyers, posed a serious threat not only to the unified jurisdiction of common law, but also to the livelihoods of common lawyers. That the power of these courts was increased under Laud's tutelage was interpreted by Puritan dissidents as evidence of the insidious ascendancy of Arminianism, whose emphasis on religious ritual and ceremony inevitably (if wrongly) led to accusations of popery.

The lawyer and MP Samuel Browne (a member of Lincoln's Inn) cited 3 & 4 Edw. 6. C. 10 in support of his allegation that Laud had installed idolatrous stained-glass windows in his private chapels at Lambeth and Croydon. Laud attempted to refute the allegation by referring specifically to the windows of the Lincoln's Inn chapel:

> I could not but wonder that Mr. Brown should be so earnest in this Point considering he is of Lincolns-Inn, where Mr. Pryn's Zeal hath not yet beaten down the Images of the Apostles in the fair Windows of that Chappel; which windows were also set up new long since that Statute of Edward 6. And 'tis well known, that I was once resolved to have returned this upon Mr. Brown in the House of Commons, but changed my Mind, lest thereby I might have set some furious Spirit on Work to destroy those harmless, goodly Windows; to the just dislike of that Worthy Society.[105]

But far from representing any incipient popish tendencies at Lincoln's Inn, the theme of the four windows in the chapel reflects the spiritual unity of the English constitution and the Biblical principles that the legal profession sought to embody and represent. One of the windows in the north elevation depicts four prophets: Zachariah, Amos, Ezechiel and Jeremiah. Above them are miniature portraits of medieval kings, holding sceptres. Jeremiah stands on a plinth decorated with a shield bearing the lion rampant, emblem of Lincoln's Inn. The other window in the north elevation depicts four apostles: Peter, Andrew, James and John the Evangelist. Peter and Andrew surmount angels supporting the arms of the earls of Southampton and Pembroke, each of which bears the motto of the Order of the Garter, *Honi soit qui mal y*

---

[104] R. Ashton, *Reformation and Revolution, 1558–1660* (London: Paladin, 1985), p. 281.
[105] Anon., *History of the Troubles and Tryal of William Laud*, fo. 312. The windows of Lincoln's Inn chapel are discussed in John A. Knowles, 'Stained Glass of Historic Interest in London', in *Journal of the British Society of Master Glass Painters*, 11 (1953–4), 141–2; also, M. Archer, 'Richard Butler, glass-painter', *The Burlington*, (May 1990), 311.

pense. Of the two windows in the south elevation, one depicts the saints Philip, Thomas, Bartholomew and Matthew. This window is of interest for its incorporation of classical imagery into an artefact of predominantly New Testament iconography. In the same window are represented the Christian virtues of faith, hope and charity alongside the classical virtues of fortitude, justice, prudence and temperance.

The remaining south window is of unique and conspicuous semiotic status,[106] containing the figures of four other apostles: St James the Less (holding a club and an open book), St Simon (holding a saw and a closed book), St Jude (holding a closed book) and St Matthias (holding an axe and a closed book). Each of them holds a book, evidence of the textual origins of common law in the Old Testament. In the background is a rare illustration of contemporary London, including Lincoln's Inn and its new chapel. St Simon and St Matthias are watching the diurnal activities depicted in the grounds of the Inn: a man in dark hat and cloak, walking his dog, greets another, more informally attired (they are reputed to represent, respectively, the Treasurer of Lincoln's Inn and Inigo Jones; see Fig. 4). A barrister walks through the grounds of the Inn, while in the background scenes purporting to represent the city of London are clearly visible. Above these is a depiction of heaven and the angels. The pre-eminent image is that of St Simon and St Matthias overseeing the quotidian life of the Inn, asserting in visual terms the eternal and indivisible correlation between divine and common law. There is an extraordinary iconic value to this window,[107] but its primary value to the aesthetics of law is that it marks the point of entry of the individual into the symbolic, thus enabling his institutional existence as the captive subject of law. In Lacan's definition of symbolic law, the implied presence of the father is crucial: his person has been consistently identified with the representation of law.[108] It is to the father that ultimate allegiance is owed, but the imagery in the south window in which St Simon and St Matthias are represented suggests a more complex relationship between the subject of law and the object of authority than was usually depicted in contemporary religious iconography.

Ecclesiastical art of the medieval and early modern periods invariably represented an absent God and the subjugation of the human individual in His

---

[106] On the capacity of the semiotics of law to comment on all aspects of legal regulation, see P. Goodrich, 'Language, Text and Sign in the History of Legal Doctrine', in D. Carzo and B. S. Jackson (eds.), *Semiotics, Law and Social Science* (Liverpool: Liverpool Law Review, 1985), p. 95.

[107] On the value of the icon and the attempt by the artist to manipulate the image in order to satisfy God, see J. Lacan, *The Four Fundamental Concepts of Psychoanalysis*, ed. R. Feldstein, B. Fink and M. Jaanus (New York: SUNY Press, 1995).

[108] J. Lacan, *Écrits*, trans. A. Sheridan (London: Tavistock, 1977), p. 67.

Fig. 4. The St Simon Light. Detail from the 'Van Linge' window in the south front of Lincoln's Inn Chapel.

symbolic presence. For example, the centre light of the east windows of Temple church, designed by Carl Edwards in the medieval style, depicts Christ sitting as the supreme judge.[109] Common to these depictions is the conventional, Judaeo-Christian representation of a deity who is at best dismissive and at worst condemnatory of the unity of human society. The seminal message of such iconography is that the true Christian is not, ultimately, of this world – a fundamental distinction between the ancient Greek and the Judaeo-Christian tradition. This observation was made by Hegel in relation to the book of Genesis and the insistence by God that Abraham leave his country, family and home for a land that the Almighty would show him. As Hegel noted, on his journey Abraham wandered with his herds over a vast expanse of land, making no attempt to cultivate or improve the soil, a

---

[109] Lewer, *Temple Church*, p. 8.

stranger to all men and an outsider in the world. For Abraham, God was the master of the earth and everything on it, providing sustenance for its inhabitants but remaining absent.[110] Hegel's objection to such a religion, or to the particular interpretation given to it by the church, was that it educated men to be celestial citizens who were unable or unwilling to engage with earthly, human emotions.[111]

The Lincoln's Inn window depicting St Simon and St Matthias demonstrates the intention of the Jacobean legal profession to redefine conventional Judaeo-Christian monotheism in which the ultimate figure of authority was supremely and conspicuously uninterested in the natural order of the *polis*. It depicts the Aristotelian bond between citizens that, in the classical world, formed the basis of an ethical and just society. The God of Judaeo-Christian tradition remains the ultimate and omniscient judge (and is represented here by St Simon and St Matthias), but there is a clear attempt to relate theology to society in a manner that would have been recognisable to the ancient Greeks. In other words, religion was predicated upon the belief that the deity is actively involved in the common life of citizens and the society that they inhabit. It is a philosophy closely linked to the Kantian principle that the existence of the rational individual is the pre-eminent justification for creation: without the immanent presence of man the act of creation lacks any ultimate purpose.[112] Early modern jurists articulated the belief that it was the duty of the legal institution to reinterpret Christian theology in the context of a just society, in which individual rights and obligations were emergent. Fulbecke argued that 'the chiefe end or last marke of ye law aswel as other sciences is God his glory. But ye next and immediate end, which is allotted to it, is to administer Justice to al, and in that sence it may be called the rule of Justice'.[113] In Hegelian terms, the divine, invisible spirit must manifest itself and be united with the visible societal relationships between individual citizens, in order that complete synthesis and perfect harmony may be attained.[114]

A phenomenological analysis of the window of St Simon and St Matthias leads to the inevitable conclusion that the early modern legal profession employed an aesthetic framework by reference to which the form and content of a unique English constitution could be expressed. Mythology, in the

---

[110] R. Plant, *Hegel: On Religion and Philosophy* (London: Orion, 1997), p. 13.
[111] *Ibid.*, pp. 13–14.
[112] See I. Kant, *The Critique of Judgment*, ed. J. Meredith (Oxford: Clarendon, 1991), p. 108. On the influence of Kant's *Critique of Judgment* on Hegel, see I. Ward, 'A Kantian (Re)turn: Aesthetics, Postmodernism and Law', *Law and Critique*, 6 (1995), 261.
[113] W. Fulbecke, *A Direction or Preparative to the Study of the Lawe* (London: T. Wight, 1600), fo. 1a.
[114] Plant, *Hegel*, p. 16.

form of the saints, was utilised to express a rational concept: the participation of the autonomous, free-thinking individual in the development of the body politic.[115] The particular form of the constitution depicted within this framework was affected by the influence of Neoplatonic humanism on the interpretation of Judaeo-Christian theology. Little has noted the influence of humanism and Stoicism on Calvin, and the latter's suggestion that a new social order was imminent.[116] The Inns of Court modified existing ecclesiastical iconography in order to present common law as the legitimate voice of theological (as well as jurisprudential) primacy. If the word of God had become barely distinguishable from the law of man, this was largely due to the reinterpretation of God's law by the English legal profession. Its role in integrating Judaeo-Christian tradition and classical, humanist philosophy ensured that the active involvement of God in the natural order of society was manifested not only in the spiritual unity and social community of the *polis*, but also in the political and ethical sovereignty of common law.

The power of the image lies in its capacity to generate an emotional response, in this case, the willing submission of the subject to the institutional authority of law. Without the image, the legitimacy, authority and sovereignty of unwritten law cannot be verified. Fundamental to the normative argument of this chapter is a rejection of the theory that the modern English constitution emerged solely from a post-Reformation, Protestant consensus that sought to impose a sovereign, national identity on the state and the church. Of course, in defence of their claim to independence from Rome, the Anglican reformers cited the existence of an ethnic church which predated the Roman Church. For example, Fulke expressed the opinion, familiar to Anglican polemicists, that 'the protestants are returned to the ancient faith which was in this land before Augustine came from Rome'.[117] In identical fashion, common lawyers referred to the ancient, English origins of common law and its foundation by mythical archetypes of nationhood. Despite these protestations, the classical and continental influences on common law and the constitution are clear and irrefutable. The political (as well as the cultural and intellectual) influence of the Renaissance over the formulation of a recognisable constitution has been consistently underestimated. During a period when the English state sought to assert its ethnicity, independence and political sovereignty, classical texts were rediscovered and

---

[115] On the importance of aesthetics and mythology to the expression of ideas, see G. W. F. Hegel, 'The Earliest System – Programme of German Idealism', in H. S. Harris, *Hegel's Development: Towards the Sunlight* (Oxford: Clarendon, 1972), p. 511.

[116] Little, *Religion, Order, and Law*, p. 37; see also M. Weber, *The Protestant Ethic and the Spirit of Capitalism*, trans. T. Parsons (London: Allen & Unwin, 1930).

[117] W. Fulke, *T. Stapleton and Martiall (Two Popish Heretics) Confuted and of their particular Heresies detected* (London: H. Middleton, 1580), fo. 14.

reinterpreted, and their contents disseminated among a readership wider than had ever previously existed. The principal beneficiaries of this intellectual effusion were the universities and the Inns of Court.

The perception of the Inns as legal innovators and creators of substantive law contributed to their emblematic status as communities or instances of order. The ideal of law that emanated from the Inns during the late sixteenth and early seventeenth centuries was represented in legislation concerning regulation of the image. Its formulation owes as much to the ethical ideals of Plato and the civic virtues expounded by Aristotle as it does to the Christian precepts of St Augustine and *The City of God*. The underlying theme of *The City of God* is the primacy of order and its crucial contribution to the maintenance of the body of law, a concern stated previously by Plato and subsequently by Hooker: '[t]he body's peace therefore is an orderly disposal of the parts thereof ... For order is a good disposition of discrepant parts, each in the fittest place.'[118] It was through the institutional existence of the Inns that the symbolic presence of law materialised. The signs of a legitimate order, the creation of which was the self-appointed responsibility of the legal profession, enabled the constitution to be embodied, understood and construed by the subjects of law. The Inns of Court shaped the development of the constitution through the creation of an order of signs, representing the ideal commonwealth. The semiotic system of representations formulated a language that articulates an unwritten law: a *lex terrae*, whose ethos guaranteed its subjects a fair, just, constitutional relationship with their ruler and their fellow citizens.[119]

---

[118] St Augustine, *The City of God*, trans. J. Healey (London: Dent, 1931), p. 249.
[119] On the continuous evolution of sign systems in human societies as a response to and a representation of changes in the social norms of communities, see R. Kevelson, *The Law as a System of Signs* (New York: Plenum, 1988), p. 4.

6

Common lawyers, fundamental law and the idolatrous mask of Charles I

'THE COMMON IDOLE, AND PREVAILING EVILL OF OUR DISSOLUTE, AND DEGENEROUS AGE'

If Monarchy the best of Governments degenerate into Tyranny, it becomes the worst of any.[1]

The identity of the composer of the above sentiments is surprising, given the popular association of his name with vehement opposition to the conduct of Charles I and his government. But his apparent (albeit qualified) support for monarchic government is also indicative of the difficulty to be found in categorising the different political groups in the period surrounding the English civil war. The quotation is from *Brief Animadversions on the Fourth Part of the Institutes of the Lawes of England*, by William Prynne, written after the restoration of the monarchy. That Prynne should be a supporter of the monarchy is extraordinary, given the appalling physical torture he suffered on two separate occasions following conviction in the king's courts. An addendum, inserted inside the front cover of the original edition of Prynne's *Histrio-Mastix: The Players Scourge, or, Actors Tragedie*, informs the reader that '[f]or this book Prynne was imprisoned eight years, fined 3000L. expelled the university of Oxford and Lincoln's Inn, degraded from his profession, stood twice in the pillory, lost both his ears, and had the book burned by the hangman.' His first clash with the royal authority of Charles I was in 1627 (while still a student at Lincoln's Inn) when, following the publication of his book, *The Perpetuitie of a Regenerate Man's Estate*, he was summoned to appear before the High Commission for Causes Ecclesiastical. He was accused of 'compiling, printing and publishing, or causing to be printed and published, a booke, without any lawfull lycense, warrant or auchtory; wherein ... there are divers passages tending to the great scandall

---

[1] W. Prynne, *Brief Animadversions on the Fourth Part of the Institutes of the Lawes of England* (London: T. Ratcliffe, 1669), fo. a2. The section heading is from W. Prynne, *Histrio-Mastix: The Players Scourge, or, Actors Tragedie* (London: M. Sparke, 1633), fo. 2.

of the Church of England'.² In 1637, four years after the appearance of Prynne's *Histrio-Mastix*, he suffered further mutilation to his ears following the publication of a pamphlet that was adjudged to be seditious, entitled *News from Ipswich*. In addition to this punishment, he was branded on the cheek with the letters 'SL', meaning 'Seditious Libeller'.

Prynne is invariably described as a Puritan,³ a word that at best denotes religious non-conformity, but lacks precise definition. As Russell has noted, if Puritanism has political connotations, then changes in the stated policy of ecclesiastical authorities could have the effect of creating Puritans:⁴ such was the outcome of Laud's devotion to Arminianism. Successive generations of historians have presented a caricature of Prynne as a maniacal extremist.⁵ Descriptions of his physical appearance tended to replicate the caricature of his clamorous opinions. Wren, for example, commented that Prynne had the countenance of a witch. Prynne took exception to the pejorative use of the word 'Puritan' in connection with his own religious conscience and mode of worship, preferring to regard himself as a sincere Protestant. In the diatribe against theatre, which constitutes most of Prynne's *Histrio-Mastix*, he complained that 'he that speaks against them [plays], or come not at them, is forthwith branded for a Scismaticall, or factious Puritan . . . they must be Puritans, and Precisions; not Protestants, who dislike them'.⁶ There is no evidence that Prynne was opposed to the proper ceremonial forms of the reformed Church, only that he resisted the idolatrous excesses that were associated with Roman Catholicism. Indeed, he argues in his idiosyncratic, zealous manner that the sacraments of the Church should be accorded appropriate respect. In his opinion, dancers 'offend against the Sacrament of the Altar, For on Easter-day they receive the Sacrament of the Altar, (And doe not our Bacchanalian Christmas-keepers, who spend that sacred time in revel-rout doe the like?) but immediately after they are like to Iudas the Traytor'. Further evidence that Prynne's non-conformist opinions were not of the most extreme type is provided by his belief that 'Musicke of it selfe is lawfull. Usefull, and commendable; no man, no Christian dares

---

² *Black Books of Lincoln's Inn*, ed. J. D. Walker, 5 vols. (London: Lincoln's Inn, 1897), II, p. 272.
³ See, for example, C. P. Hill, *Who's Who in Stuart Britain* (London: Shepheard-Walwyn, 1988), p. 93. More accurately, Ashton describes Prynne as a conservative Foxeian episcopalian: R. Ashton, *Reformation and Revolution, 1558–1660* (London: Paladin, 1985), p. 282.
⁴ C. Russell, *Parliaments and English Politics, 1621–1629* (Oxford University Press, 1979), p. 28.
⁵ Trevelyan, for example, refers to 'the Puritan with his short cloak and Prynne with his short ears', G. M. Trevelyan, *England Under the Stuarts* (London: Routledge, 2002), p. 172.
⁶ Prynne, *Histrio-Mastix*, fo. 3. On puritanism, pamphlets and the theatre in the early seventeenth century, see P. Lake (with M. Questier), *The Antichrist's Lewd Hat: Protestants, Papists and Players in Post-Reformation England* (New Haven: Yale University Press, 2002).

denie.' His acceptance of music is qualified only by his rejection of idolatry: 'that lascivious, amorous, effeminate, voluptuous Musicke . . . should be either expedient, or lawfull unto Christians, there is none so audacious as to iustifie it'.[7]

The antagonism towards plays, playwrights, playhouses, actors and audiences, vividly (if repetitively) conveyed by Prynne in *Histrio-Mastix*, is a thinly disguised metaphor for his disgust at the levity and inherent popery of the royal court. Suspicions of papal intrigue at the highest level of government centred on the queen, Henrietta Maria. Her public profession of the Roman Catholic religion and her particular interest in music, dancing and theatre reinforced prejudices against Catholicism and its insidious influence over the court of Charles I.[8] Prynne argued that plays 'advance the Divels scepter, service, Kingdome, by sowing, by cherishing the seedes of atheisme, heathenisme, prophanesse, incontinency, voluptuousnes, idlenes, yea, of all kind of wickednes both in their Actors and Spectators hearts'. But again, rebutting the stereotype of the joyless Puritan, he reluctantly conceded that plays were 'tollerable, if not lawfull', provided they were not obscene, profane or wanton; that they had no 'womans part' or 'Embracements', no heathen deities, no dressing in women's or 'sumptuous' attire; that they involved no unnecessary expense, were 'seldome Acted' and in Latin, 'for utterance, and learning sake alone'. In this tolerable category he placed 'academicall' plays, 'managed onely by Schollers in private Schooles, and Colledges at some certaine Seasons',[9] an apparent references to the use of drama as an educational device at the Inns of Court.

It is evident that Prynne would never have condoned the boisterous comedies associated with the dramatic entertainments presented during the revels, and it is possible that *Histrio-Mastix* was an allusion to the short play of the same name, written by John Marston and performed at the Middle Temple in 1599. Prynne would have disapproved entirely of the following sentiments, expressed by the character of Pride in Marston's play:

> Enlarge your mighty spirits, strive to excede,
> In buildings, ryot, garments gallantry.
> For take this note: *The world the show affects,*
> *Playne Vertue (vilie cladde) is counted Vice,*
> *And makes high blood indure base praeiudice.*[10]

---

[7] Prynne, *Histrio-Mastix*, ff. 257, 274.
[8] On the participation of Henrietta Maria in court masques and plays, see R. Malcolm Smuts, *Court Culture and the Origins of a Royalist Tradition in Early Stuart England* (Philadelphia: University of Pennsylvania Press, 1999), pp. 186, 250, 285; also, Q. Bone, *Henrietta Maria: Queen of the Cavaliers* (Urbana: University of Illinois Press, 1972), p. 83.
[9] Prynne, *Histrio-Mastix*, ff. **2b, 7–8.
[10] J. Marston, *Histrio-Mastix Or, The Player Whipt!* (London: T. Thorp, 1610), ff. D1b–D2a.

In a dedicatory epistle to the students of the four Inns of Court, Prynne expressed his disapproval of those members who 'learne as soone as they are admitted, to see Stage-playes, & take smoke at a Play-house, which they commonly make their Studie'. But in another dedicatory epistle, to the benchers of Lincoln's Inn, he distinguished that Inn from the others, which '(I know not by what (a) evill custome, and (b) worse example) admit of common Actors and Enterludes upon their two grand Festivals, to recreate themselves withall'. Citing numerous statutes (including 39 Eliz. C. 4 and 1 Jac. C. 7) and religious authorities that proscribed unlawful pastimes, he noted that Lincoln's Inn 'have prohibited by late publike Orders, all disorderly Bacchanalian Grand-Christmasses, more fit for Pagans than Christians; for the deboisest Roarers, than grave civill Students' and commented approvingly that the benchers 'have always from my first admission into your Society, and long before, excluded all Common Players with their lewd ungodly Enterludes, from all your solemne Festivals'.[11]

While that observation provides some indication of a possible nonconformist tendency in the corporate body of Lincoln's Inn (or of favouritism towards the Inn of which Prynne was a member),[12] and of the disinclination of the Council of Lincoln's Inn to imitate the seasonal rituals of the other Inns of Court, there is no documentary evidence to suggest that in religious terms, Prynne was anything other than a devout Protestant. During the constitutional crisis of the early seventeenth century religion was of fundamental importance, but it is misleading to suggest that Prynne's principled opposition to the government of Charles I was the consequence of religious extremism. The focus of Prynne's strident attack on the theatre was idolatry at the centre of court culture. But just as the question of symbolism is relevant in establishing that the inherent lewdness of the theatre was a metaphor for corruption at the royal court, it is important to emphasise that the archetypal exponent of symbols during this period was the king himself. At the trial of John Hampden in November 1637 for his refusal to pay ship-money, Sir Robert Berkeley stated categorically in judgment that the king *was* the law: 'I never read nor heard that *Lex* was *Rex*, but it is common and most true that *Rex* is *Lex*, for he is *Lex loquens*, a living, a speaking, an acting law.'[13] It was the characterisation of Charles I as a living mask, the embodiment of law, to which Prynne and many of his fellow common lawyers were opposed. In his relentless and painful quest for a satisfactory definition of law and legal rights, Prynne represented a class of lawyers, unprecedented in legal history,

---

[11] Prynne, *Histrio-Mastix*, ff. **3b, *1a, *2b.
[12] Prest suggests that during the period immediately preceding the civil war, Lincoln's Inn was more inclined towards Parliament than the other Inns: W. R. Prest, *The Inns of Court Under Elizabeth I and the Early Stuarts, 1590–1640* (London: Longman, 1972), pp. 236–7.
[13] S. R. Gardiner, *History of England*, 10 vols. (New York: AMS, 1965), VIII, p. 278.

whose political activities and public articulation of common law sovereignty contributed towards shaping the constitution along lines originally suggested by Fortescue and St German.

COMMON LAWYERS AND THE REJECTION OF FALSEHOOD: 'NO CONCORD WITH BELIAL'[14]

With total disregard for the likely personal consequences of his attack not only on the immorality of the royal court, but also on the abuse of the royal prerogative, Prynne declared that '[i]t is the prerogative royall of the King of heaven, to teach men virtue; and that not by Stage-playes, or lascivious Poems, but by his Word and Spirit onely.'[15] His emphasis on the authority of the word and the inherent falseness of the idolatrous image is important in establishing the primacy of the text as a source of supreme authority. But his appeal to the legitimacy of a heavenly prerogative recalls also the insistence of St German that if an earthly law was 'manifestly unreasonable', then 'he that would observe the Law, should break both the Law of God and the Law of Reason'. Furthermore, St German argued that 'against this Law [which he defined as the 'Law of Nature of Reasonable Creatures'], Prescription, Statute nor Custom may not prevail', being 'void and against Justice'.[16] Of course, it is not reasonable to infer from St German an injunction to disobey the rulings of a lawfully appointed civil magistrate, however unjust they may be. But St German's theories of the king in Parliament and the sovereignty of common law help to explain the belief in certain quarters of Henrician England that he posed a threat to the institutional authority of the church and the state. As Guy observes, the constitutional model suggested by St German established definite criteria for determining the legality of prerogative acts, and became an important point of reference for both practising lawyers and constitutional theorists of succeeding generations.[17] The imperial monarchy of Henry VIII, and the associated belief that the king was accountable to God but not the law, was antithetical to St German's humanist principles and has obvious parallels with the personal rule of Charles I. The moral dilemma posed by civil resistance to tyranny was raised by St Thomas Aquinas and was subsequently discussed by Luther in terms of a religious duty to oppose the acts of a quasi-divine tyrant. It is important in this context to note also

---

[14] Prynne, *Histrio-Mastix*, fo. 25. [15] *Ibid.*, fo. 102.
[16] C. St German, *Two Dialogues in English, Between a Doctor of Divinity, and A Student in the Laws of England, of the Grounds of the said Laws, And of Conscience* (London: the Assigns of R. & E. Atkins, 1709), pp. 53, 5.
[17] J. Guy, 'Tudor Monarchy and its critiques', in J. Guy (ed.), *The Tudor Monarchy* (London: Arnold, 1997), p. 88; see also A. Fox and J. Guy, *Reassessing the Henrician Age: Humanism, Politics and Reform, 1550–1550* (Oxford: Blackwell, 1986), p. 104.

Calvin's admonition that the subject should not obey the command of a civil magistrate whose actions were offensive to God.[18]

Common lawyers such as Prynne and Coke gained their knowledge and understanding of constitutional theory at the Inns of Court, where St German's *Doctor and Student* was a seminal text. While Prest is correct to emphasise that legal education at the Inns concentrated on the technical details of property law rather than on the broader constitutional implications of jurisprudence,[19] these issues were an important theme of *Doctor and Student*. Similarly, Fortescue's paean to the Inns of Court, *De Laudibus Legum Angliae*, and, to a greater extent, *The Governance of England*, present systematic, humanist theories of law in the specific context of the English legal system. Consequently, although the question of constitutional sovereignty did not arise in the course of formal legal exercises at the Inns, it was addressed obliquely by jurists, whose opinions were assimilated by common lawyers and reflected in the practical application of common law principles. For example, the assertion by St German that 'if any general Custom were directly against the Law of God, or if any Statute were made directly against it ... the Custom and Statute were void'[20] is indicative of the theological foundations of early modern jurisprudence. It was also the legal precedent for Coke's insistence in *Dr. Bonham's Case* that the common law would declare void those statutes which were repugnant, or which offended against right or reason.

A clear indication of the influence of St German on the particular constitutional theory espoused by early Stuart common lawyers is to be found in a pamphlet written by Prynne in 1636. At the time, he was imprisoned in the Tower of London for the crime of seditious libel, following the publication of *Histrio-Mastix* in 1633. In his *An Humble Remonstrance Against the Tax of Ship-money Lately Imposed*, Prynne employed the rhetorical device of a direct appeal to the king, in particular to his sense of justice and honour, in order to persuade him of the illegality of the tax levied in 1636. There is a neat irony enshrined in the fact that Prynne was already imprisoned for an offence of dubious illegality when he informed Charles I that 'this Tax of Shipmoney, is directly contrary to the fundamentall Lawes and Liberties of this Your Realme of England, which Your Majesty both in point of Iustice and Honour is obliged inviolably to preserve, according to the Oath made to God and Your Subjects at Your Coronation'.[21] Prynne founded the legitimacy of these fundamental laws and liberties in 'the ancient Law of

---

[18] Luther and Calvin are discussed in the context of moral law and conscience in I. Ward, *Shakespeare and the Legal Imagination* (London: Butterworth, 1999), pp. 175–80.
[19] Prest, *Inns of Court*, p. 221.   [20] St German, *Doctor and Student*, p. 18.
[21] W. Prynne, *An Humble Remonstrance Against the Tax of Ship-money Lately Imposed* (London: M. Sparke, 1643), fo. 1.

Edward the Confessor, and William the Conqueror (ratified by all our Kings by their very Coronation Oath'.[22] In other words, it was the ancient custom of the realm to which he appealed as the basis for the existence, recognition and lawful supremacy of fundamental liberties. His argument bore a striking resemblance to the suggestion of St German that 'our Sovereign Lord the King, at his Coronation, among other things, taketh a solemn Oath, that he shall cause all the Custom of his Realm faithfully to be observed'. St German went on to argue that this 'Custom' determined the legitimacy of the common law courts, and consequently the authority of the courts 'may not be altered' without the consent of Parliament.[23]

St German's theory provided the intellectual justification for common lawyers such as Prynne to reject the authority of the courts of Star Chamber and High Commission, and the judicial powers of the Privy Council and the episcopacy. While acknowledging the spiritual jurisdiction of the established church, St German was emphatic that its juridical competence was restricted to those matters 'that of right belong unto it'. He was unequivocal that the jurisdiction of neither the church nor the king could lawfully extend to interference with or alteration of the ancient customs of the realm. Because these customs were necessary for the maintenance of the commonwealth, they had attained the status of laws, 'inso-much that he that doth against them, doth against Justice: and those be the Customs that properly be called the Common Law'.[24] This assertion of common law sovereignty provided a theoretical foundation for the related concepts of fundamental law and liberty of the subject; but it should also be emphasised that neither St German nor Prynne (nor most of his fellow common lawyers) were opposed in principle to the lawful exercise of the royal prerogative. St German was emphatic that 'Law Eternal' was made known not only by natural reason and divine revelation, but also 'by the order of a Prince or any other secundary Governor that hath power to bind his Subjects to a Law'.[25] Prynne similarly acknowledged the legitimacy of prerogative rule in his assurance to Charles I '[t]hat the peoples Liberty strengthens the Kings Prerogative, and the Kings Prerogative is to defend the peoples liberty'. But St German and Prynne shared the belief that the king had accepted and approved as law the ancient customs of the realm, and that the coronation oath was a binding declaration of intent to protect and defend 'the just and ancient Liberties of our Subjects'.[26] For Prynne, the question of immeasurable importance was not the right of the king to exercise the royal prerogative, but the right of the courts of common law (including Parliament) to determine the lawfulness of such actions. In connection with the collection

---

[22] Ibid., fo. 2.   [23] St German, *Doctor and Student*, pp. 22, 23.
[24] Ibid., pp. 19, 21.   [25] Ibid., p. 3.   [26] Prynne, *An Humble Remonstrance*, fo. 2.

of ship-money (which had been levied from seaports without protest, but which in 1636 was collected on a national basis without the consent of Parliament), Prynne asserted the right of the subject (guaranteed by the Petition of Right) to freedom from imprisonment, unless 'by the Lawfull judgment of his Peers, and by the Law of the Land'. He complained that those subjects who had refused to pay ship-money had been imprisoned, and their goods seized and sold, without any legal judgment against them and before the legality of the tax was declared by Parliament.[27]

It is important to note that in his defence of common law sovereignty Prynne expressed no partisanship: he gave unqualified support to no particular faction, neither parliamentary nor royalist. Indeed, after the Restoration (and possibly for the pragmatic purpose of self-preservation) he expressed the strongest reservations about the legitimacy of the republic. Significant to an understanding of Prynne as a defender of common law ideology rather than as a Puritan pamphleteer, is the fact that he chose to address his thoughts on the body politic of the Interregnum to the students and professors of common law. Published in 1669, his observations on the *Fourth Part of the Institutes* of Sir Edward Coke paid valedictory homage to the archetype of constitutional freedoms. Prynne lamented that 'we have felt by sad experience during the late Lawlesse Anarchy and Tyranny, when the Law of the longest sword, not Land, was *Suprema Lex*'.[28] He begged common lawyers to endeavour to restore the purity, splendour and vigour of the law in the interests of king and kingdom, as well as subjects.

An incident that took place after the first civil war, in 1648, demonstrated clearly the dedication of Prynne to the principle that *lex terrae* was *suprema lex*, and his refusal to acquiesce in the unlawful exercise of coercive power, whatever the claimed source of authority. Inside the front cover of the first edition of *Histrio-Mastix* a letter was inserted some fifteen years after the book's publication, headed 'The Vindication of William Prynne Esquire' and dated 'January 10th 1648'. Prynne complained in the letter that a forged paper had been published in his name, defending stage plays and retracting the opinions expressed emphatically in *Histrio-Mastix*. He alleged that the perpetrators of this falsehood were 'some of the imprisoned Stage-Players or Agents of the Army'. Prynne stated that his judgment and opinion of plays and actors 'and their intollerble mischeivousness in any Christian state' was unaltered. But the interest of the *addendum* to this analysis is its embodiment of the nascent principle that an official body claiming the authority of the state for actions that infringed the liberty of the subject must not only act within the law, but must provide evidence of its lawful authority. According to Prynne, the House of Commons issued an order, demanding to know

[27] *Ibid*., fo. 3.   [28] Prynne, *Brief Animadversions*, fo. A.

whether the bogus pamphlet, in which the arguments of *Histrio-Mastix* were retracted, was written by Prynne. He replied, 'that when a sufficient authority was sent to Him, he would returne a speedy answer'. In response, Humphrey Edwards and John Fry were duly sent to Prynne's rooms at 'the Kings head in the Strand, & without shewing me any order, or commission; told me: that they were sent to me by the house of Commons' to establish the authorship of the pamphlet. The simple expedient would have been for Prynne to deny, in all honesty, that the forged paper was his; after all, it is certain that his religious sensibilities were greatly offended by the allegation that he now approved of idolatrous stage plays. But his adherence to the principle of the liberty of the subject, enshrined (he believed) in the Petition of Right, prevented him from issuing any such denial. Instead, when confronted by Edwards and Fry, he replied that 'I knew of no authority they had to demand the question of me; that I neither knew nor took them to be Members, their election being both void and illegal'. He freely agreed to answer any question, concerning any book he had written, 'when it should be demanded by a lawfull authority'. As the status of Edwards and Fry as MPs had been declared void by a committee of the House of Commons, Prynne refused to acknowledge their right to demand his acquiescence. He was forthright in his condemnation of the General Council of the Army, for 'many abuses in the New Elections . . . most of the elections of their adherents being very foule and void'.

Prynne's attack on the alleged illegality of actions taken by the army reflected concerns over its increased politicisation since the end of the first civil war. The seizure of Charles I by Cornet Joyce in June 1647 was the first of several momentous events that year, culminating in the Heads of the Proposals in August and the Putney Debates in November, signalling the unprecedented involvement of the army in the resolution of constitutional issues, often by coercive means.[29] But the principal interest of Prynne's characteristic, fearless opposition to coercion lies in his insistence on the provision of evidence of lawful authority. For Prynne, *suprema lex* was no more represented by individuals claiming to act on the authority of Parliament than it was in the specious claim, made by Sir John Finch during the trial of John Hampden in 1637, that 'no Acts of Parliament make any difference' to the unrestricted power of the king. The particular language used by Prynne to reject the authority of Edwards and Fry was redolent of the attacks he made on idolatry and falsehood, whether in the context of the unlawful prerogative

---

[29] On the fractious relationship between Parliament and the army in 1647–8, see Ashton, *Reformation and Revolution*, pp. 328–38; for *The Heads of the Proposals*, see S. R. Gardiner (ed.), *Constitutional Documents of the Puritan Revolution, 1625–1660* (Oxford University Press, 1906), pp. 316–26; for *The Agreement of the People*, proposed by the Levellers and considered by the Army Council during the Putney Debates, see *ibid.*, pp. 333–5.

actions of the king or the 'Heathenish Spectacles'[30] of stage plays. Citing the superior authority of Holy Scripture, he concluded his letter to the reader of *Histrio-Mastix* with the following quotation: 'ESAU 57.4 – "None calleth for justice; nor any pleadeth for truth: they trust in vanity and speak Lyes: they conceive mischief and bring forth iniquity".'

In all his work Prynne identified and condemned the arbitrary and unjust exercise of power, invariably offering himself as a sacrificial victim willing to suffer mutilation, imprisonment and ridicule so that attention might be drawn to the oppressive forces that threatened the ancient liberties of the English subject. He incorporated into his writing the image of the idolator and the language of the Old Testament prophet: the former represented the antithesis of law, while the latter was the earthly conduit for the true word of God. Although he cast himself in the role of prophet, one he played with utter conviction, he realised that it was only through the institutional resistance of an articulate and authoritative corporate entity that the liberty of English subjects would be assured. Consequently it was to common lawyers that Prynne appealed, not only for resistance to tyranny but for exposition of the law: '[t]hat speech of Christ himself to his Disciples in a spiritual, being likewise most true of the Courts of Law and Lawyers, in a temporal or politick sense; Ye are the salt of the earth (of our earthly Kingdom).'[31] The observation that common lawyers enacted a sacerdotal role was strongly linked with the theological jurisprudence of Fortescue, but here Prynne situated the legal profession in a specific political location: a nation-state at a moment of constitutional crisis, seeking guidance, exegesis and salvation.

THE PETITION OF RIGHT AND THE FOUNDATIONS OF MODERN LAW

Russell suggests that until the outbreak of the first civil war in 1642, Parliament failed to offer an alternative theory of government to that provided by the king, whatever the private beliefs held by individual members might have been.[32] He adds that the proposition of the divine right of kings was generally accepted and that as a concept it was uninformative about the extent of monarchic power.[33] It is true that the pre-civil war parliaments of the seventeenth century never imagined a constitution predicated on any system other than monarchy. It is reasonable notwithstanding to suggest that although there was an almost universal acceptance of the divine right of

---

[30] Prynne, *Histrio-Mastix*, fo. 25.   [31] Prynne, *Brief Animadversions*, fo. a2.
[32] C. Russell, *The Causes of the English Civil War* (Oxford: Clarendon, 1990), p. 135.
[33] *Ibid.*, p. 147. Russell's opinion is shared by Malcolm Smuts, who argues that the divine right of kings was a non-controversial concept and not a subject of debate until 1642, Smuts, *Court Culture*, p. 6.

kings, common lawyers in Parliament sought to limit its temporal powers. As Prest has noted, there was no uniform political outlook among common lawyers of this period, and the Bar included servants as well as critics of the crown. But it is fair to say that the political inclination of the Caroline royal court did not sit easily with the corporate spirit engendered by the Inns of Court.[34] It might even be argued that, during the parliamentary debates concerning the Petition of Right in 1628, common lawyer MPs proposed an alternative model of government. Their political system of choice would be predicated upon the sovereign power of common law to regulate the boundaries of rival jurisdictions and the right of Parliament to override the veto of the king when it presented itself as a court.

The position of common lawyers in Parliament enabled them to address the fundamental question of sovereignty within a political framework, an opportunity they grasped with tenacious confidence. The House of Commons had traditionally contained a substantial number of Inns of Court members. There was a continuous increase in the number of common lawyer MPs between the accession of Elizabeth I and the outbreak of civil war in 1642. Prest notes that the proportion of MPs who were either past or present residents of the Inns increased from a quarter in 1563 to approximately a third in 1584 and 1614, and more than half in 1640.[35] The increase in numbers of lawyer MPs was almost certainly connected to the institutional expansion of the Inns during this period. Cromartie suggests that whereas the Inns recorded admissions of perhaps a hundred members during the 1550s, this had increased to more than two hundred and fifty during the early seventeenth century, and that by 1625 there may have been as many as five hundred active barristers.[36] The presence in unprecedented numbers of a class of professional men, expert in rhetorical skills and familiar with the constitutional theories of Fortescue and St German, posed an obvious threat to the continued existence of unrestrained prerogative rule. In particular, the House of Commons provided a prominent platform from which common lawyers could question the legality of jurisdiction of the courts of Star Chamber and High Commission. The inclusion in the former of the entire body of privy councillors, and their power to summon, judge and punish any subject without reference to customary procedure, evidence or statutory

---

[34] W. R. Prest, *The Rise of the Barristers: A Social History of the English Bar, 1590–1640* (Oxford: Clarendon, 1991), p. 257.

[35] Prest, *Inns of Court*, p. 222. Cromartie estimates that at the opening of the Long Parliament in October 1640, approximately 60 per cent of the members were common lawyers, A. Cromartie, 'The Constitutionalist Revolution: The Transformation of Political Culture in Early Stuart England', *Past and Present*, 163 (1999), 86. See M. F. Keeler, *The Long Parliament, 1640–1641: A Biographical Study of its Members* (Philadelphia: University of Pennsylvania Press, 1954).

[36] Cromartie, 'The Constitutionalist Revolution', 85.

limitations offended every tenet of common law ideology. The power of the Court of High Commission to enforce the *ex officio* oath, whereby witnesses were compelled to incriminate themselves, was granted by the royal prerogative and resented not only by common lawyers but, as Trevelyan notes with an indignant flourish, 'by all Englishmen'.[37]

As chief justice under James I, Coke had doubted the legality of the Court of High Commission. As a member of parliament and unconstrained by judicial office, Coke unequivocally attacked the concept of an 'intrinsical' prerogative of the king, doubting its very existence in law. In drawing attention to its dubious legal status, he struck at the heart of the divine right theory of kingship: '[a]nd this intrinsical prerogative is entrusted him by God and then it is due *jure divino*, and then no law can take it away. Then it follows that for defense, etc., if his Majesty "shall find" cause to commit, he may. We are but where we were. We cannot yield to this.' Despite the valid claim that there was general acceptance of the principle of the divine right of kings (and there is evidence that, following the dismissal of Coke as chief justice, the judiciary became more consistent defenders of the royal prerogative), this is an explicit statement of intent to undermine the basis of its legality. In rejecting the resolution of the House of Lords for the retention of that sovereign power of the king 'wherewith your Majesty is trusted for the protection, safety, and happiness of your people', Coke distinguished between 'grace' and 'right'. Whereas the king governed by the grace of God, 'it is an act of right, not of grace, that we stand upon'. Accordingly, the rights of the subject, enshrined in Magna Carta, superseded the authority of the king 'graciously' to confirm the supreme authority of that statute.[38]

The analysis of the parliamentary debates concerning the Petition of Right in 1628 is here confined to the influence of a pervasive constitutional theory, associated with the humanist commonwealths of the Inns of Court, over the political events of the 1620s. In their references to ancient national customs, Fortescue and St German implied the existence of fundamental laws that were subsumed into the corpus of English law. But their theories were not specific and, although St German stated that it was reasonable 'in conscience' that a custom should prevail over a manifestly unreasonable statute, he made no reference to instances when such action might be appropriate or just. But Coke, most notably in *Dr. Bonham's Case*, was prepared to state in judgment that a statute that was either repugnant or devoid of reason was void. The synonymity of law and reason was the overriding theme of Coke's published work. Indeed, in *The First Part of the Institutes* he reiterated the

---

[37] Trevelyan, *England Under the Stuarts*, p. 161.
[38] *Proceedings in Parliament 1628*, ed. R. C. Johnson, M. F. Keeler, M. Jansson Cole and W. B. Bidwell, 6 vols. (New Haven: Yale University Press, 1977), III, (26 April) pp. 95, 100.

Ciceronian opinion that law was nothing else but reason. His familiar admonitions against the insidious threat of civilians and canonists represented a defence of the artificial reason of common law against the inherent irrationality and iconoclasm of alternative jurisdictions. For Coke, the civilian code represented uncertainty and incipient chaos and was therefore predisposed towards tyranny and falsehood.

The certainty of common law was symbolised by the existence of 'fundamental laws' (the use of the plural 'laws' by Coke is significant, implying the existence of a recognisable *corpus iuris* with greater conviction than the singular 'law'), superior in authority to statute. Consequently, monopolies 'are against the ancient and Fundamentall laws of the Realm'; therefore '[w]hatsoever offence is contrary to the ancient and Fundamentall laws of the Realm, is punishable by law';[39] and Magna Carta 'was for the most part declaratory of the principall grounds of the fundamentall Laws of England'.[40] But these quotations from *The Institutes* provide an interpretation rather than a definitive statement of the law, representing an attempt by Coke to systematise the principles of English law in accordance with the predilections of an English common lawyer. If judicial office had never effectively constrained Coke from attacking perceived abuses of the royal prerogative, the change of forum from King's Bench to House of Commons enabled him to express his opinions on ancient liberties and fundamental laws with unprecedented vigour. The extraction of the forced loan in 1626,[41] the arbitrary imprisonment for non-payment, the imposition of martial law and the enforced billeting of soldiers presented Coke and his common lawyer colleagues in Parliament with the opportunity to defend the credentials of constitutional government and enshrine those values in statute. The contribution of Coke to the parliamentary debates concerning the Petition of Right clearly demonstrated his belief that Parliament and common lawyers were not mutually exclusive; rather they were two sides of a legal system capable of addressing and remedying social and political iniquities.

Payment of the forced loan was mandatory for institutions as well as individuals. The benchers of the Inner Temple received a letter from the Council of State, dated 26 November 1626, whose tone was unequivocally coercive: 'likewise thought good (upon signification of Majesties pleasure as aforesaid) to direct our Letters to the severall Innes of Court . . . Hereof his Majestie and

---

[39] E. Coke, *The Third Part of the Institutes of the Laws of England* (London: Flesher, 1644), p. 181.
[40] E. Coke, *The Second Part of the Institutes of the Laws of England* (London: Flesher, 1642), preface.
[41] See R. P. Cust, *The Forced Loan and English Politics, 1626–1628* (Oxford: Clarendon, 1987).

this Board expects, a tymelie and reall Accounte from you.'[42] As *Darnell's Case* had shown in 1627, the King's Council threatened the existence not only of Parliament but of the courts as well. The council commissioned the forced loan, examined those who refused to pay and committed them to imprisonment. Detention without trial, habeas corpus and the principle that no subject should be committed without the cause being known were central issues in *Darnell's Case*. In the parliamentary debates of 1628 common lawyers asserted that the unwritten or fundamental law was superior to the arbitrary actions of the royal prerogative. In so doing they re-established in principle the constitutional supremacy of 'the safety of the people', enshrined in the Twelve Tables of Roman Law: 'Salus populi est suprema lex.'[43] A petition of right was by tradition a request for the remedy of demonstrated grievances. Its constitutional significance was as a judicial remedy, presented from Parliament as a court of law. Hence, on 6 May, Sir Nathaniel Rich suggested that 'the way of proceeding concerning our liberties shall be by petition in a parliamentary way'.[44] But the Petition of Right of 1628 attained significance far beyond that of a judicial remedy for grievances suffered. It is ironic, given his subsequent change of allegiance and the fatal consequences of his actions to him, that Sir Thomas Wentworth was a supporter of the petition, summarising its ultimate purpose in the simple sentence: 'I think it fit we declare what is *lex terrae*.'[45]

Before further analysis of the unique contribution of common lawyers to the formulation of the Petition of Right it is useful to recall the issues it sought to address and the remedies it provided for redressing abuses of prerogative power. Coke summarised the substantive contents of the petition in a speech to the House of Commons on 6 May. These included grievances on 'loans, commissions, instructions, imprisonment, confinement, with all the illegal raisings of money, billeting of soldiers, etc., and all other dependences'.[46] The legal principles raised by the Petition were as follows: (a) Magna Carta and the so-called 'six statutes' confirming its authority were binding lawful authorities; (b) according to statute, custom and law every subject had an irresistible claim to his goods and liberty of person; (c) subjects were guaranteed the liberties, privileges and rights of their ancestors; (d) cases within the common law, concerning liberty of the subject, should proceed according to the practices of that particular jurisdiction. The House of Lords attempted to introduce an amendment to the effect that the royal

---

[42] *Calendar of State Papers, Domestic, Charles I*, xl, no. 27, in *Calendar of the Inner Temple Records*, ed. F. A. Inderwick, 5 vols. (London: H. Sotheran, 1896), II, appendix vii, p. 352.
[43] On the insistence of the rebel propagandist Henry Parker that the royal prerogative was subservient to *salus populi*, see Cromartie, 'The Constitutionalist Revolution', 80–1.
[44] *Proceedings in Parliament 1628*, III, (6 May) p. 273.
[45] *Ibid.* (26 April) p. 99.   [46] *Ibid.* (6 May) p. 278.

prerogative was 'intrinsical' to the sovereignty of the king, entitling him to imprison for reasons of state and, within a reasonable time, express a cause. This clause was rejected entirely by the House of Commons.

Despite these statements of legal principle, the debate was essentially concerned with the fundamental question of establishing the boundaries of conflicting jurisdictions. In his reply to the House of Commons on 2 May 1628, Charles I was willing to state that he fully agreed to maintain the 'liberties of our persons and proprieties of our goods'. But his appeal to the mysterious, supernatural and sovereign authority of the royal prerogative rendered such acceptance all but worthless. Although he guaranteed that he would protect these liberties, his assurance was qualified by his insistence that 'he will have us to match ourselves with the best subjects by not encroaching upon that sovereignty and prerogative which God has put into his hands for our good'.[47] The king appealed directly to the sense of trust in his word and his honour. His secretary assured the House of Commons that if they accepted his royal word that he would at all times protect the liberty of the subject, then 'it shall be really performed'. It is indicative of the prevailing mood in the House that, following this declaration, it was reported that '[u]pon this there was a silence a good space.'[48] The common lawyers in the House, led by Coke, reminded members that the issue here was not one of trust or honour, but of accountability: on what 'cause' was the liberty of the subject deprived and upon whose authority? Coke assured the House that he readily accepted the word of the king, reminding members that the greatest bond of any subject was '*verbum regis*. This is an high point of honor.'[49] Although certain members suggested that the word of the king was synonymous with the exercise of power, and that therefore he should be trusted, the majority agreed with the opinion of Coryton, that '[w]e do not mistrust his Majesty; he is sworn to the law. But these breaches and violations enforce us to go by way of bill.'[50]

If there was a tendency among certain members to confuse the actions of the king as body natural with those as body politic, this was precisely because the king himself had blurred the distinction between the two phenomena. Sir Benjamin Rudyard, for example, feared that 'we are like to turn his favour into contempt and anger – not a childish anger, but the anger of a king, the roaring of a lion'.[51] The Speaker attempted to diffuse the personalisation of the dispute by suggesting to the king at the Banqueting House that the recent violations of laws and liberties had been the work of 'some of your Majesty's ministers',[52] a clear allusion to the invidious influence of Buckingham.[53]

[47] *Ibid*. (2 May) p. 213.   [48] *Ibid*. (1 May) p. 189.   [49] *Ibid*. (9 May) p. 338.
[50] *Ibid*. (2 May) p. 210.   [51] *Ibid*. (30 April) p. 179.   [52] *Ibid*. (5 May) p. 253.
[53] See R. Lockyer, *Buckingham: The Life and Political Career of George Villiers, First Duke of Buckingham, 1592–1628* (London: Longman, 1981).

John Selden stated the right of common law jurisdiction to arbitrate and give judgment in disputes concerning the arbitrary imprisonment of subjects: '[a]nd for convenient time, what is convenient time? Who shall judge of it but the judges?'[54] Questions such as these, posed by venerated common lawyers and expounding the supremacy of common law jurisdiction, expanded the debate from the futile ground of personality, trust and honour into the more profitable area of jurisprudence.

The question of whether the law was above the king, or the king above the law, was asked by Sir Dudley Digges on 26 April, the member concluding that 'Prerogative only has caused it.'[55] Even Coke was not opposed to the exercise of the royal prerogative, assuring the king from the floor of the House that 'we do not encroach on his prerogative'.[56] Three days later, he categorically stated in debate that 'He [Charles I] is God's lieutenant.' But the undoubted implication in all of his speeches is that Coke adhered to an Aristotelian interpretation of ideal governance: the power of the civil magistrate should be exercised for the public good of his subjects. The associated belief that the limitations of kingship were bounded by the jurisdiction of common law was antithetical to the royal notion of 'sovereign power', and, as Cromartie suggests, the incompatibility of these ideologies provided an intellectual foundation for rebellion.[57] The coexistence of two rival jurisdictions was implied by Alford on 20 May. In reply to the question 'What is "sovereign power"?', he answered that 'Bodin says it is that that is free from any condition. By this we shall acknowledge a regal as well as a legal power. Let us give that to the King that the law gives him and no more.'[58] The reference to Jean Bodin is an allusion to the political absolutism of continental monarchies, and Alford highlights the constitutional questions posed by the contemporaneity of two antithetical polities within the same realm. If the exercise of sovereign power by the king entitled him to govern according to his unchallengeable interpretation of the law, then, in the poetic phrase of Sir Nathaniel Rich, '[w]e have nothing thereby but shells and shadows.'[59]

It is unsurprising that while Coke accepted the legitimacy of the royal prerogative he should entirely reject the principle of the 'sovereign power' of the king, on the grounds that it 'is no parliament word in my opinion'.[60] In other words, if the constitutional principle (proposed by St German) of the king in

---

[54] *Proceedings in Parliament 1628*, III (26 April), p. 97. On Selden, see R. Tuck, 'The Ancient Law of Freedom: John Selden and the Civil War', in J. S. Morrill (ed.), *Reactions to the Civil War* (London: Macmillan, 1982), pp. 137–62.
[55] *Proceedings in Parliament 1628*, III (26 April), p. 102. Sir Dudley Digges became Master of the Rolls in 1630.
[56] *Ibid.* (3 May), p. 236.   [57] Cromartie, 'The Constitutionalist Revolution', 100.
[58] *Proceedings in Parliament 1628*, III (20 May), p. 494.
[59] *Ibid.* (6 May), p. 270.   [60] *Ibid.* (20 May), p. 495.

Parliament was valid then the undefined and unlimited 'sovereign power' to which the king laid claim has no basis in law. The only constitutional authority recognised by Coke as having absolute power was the body of existing laws that he claimed as the single legitimate source of rights and obligations. It was to Magna Carta that Coke repeatedly drew the attention of the House of Commons, as he did his readers in the preface to *The Second Part of the Institutes*. There he reassured his audience that his intention to expound the fundamental laws of England 'was no new declaration', but an exposition of the rights enshrined in the original Charter of 1215, and restated in the 'Confirm' Charter' of Edward I and the 'Great Charter' of Henry III. Coke emphasised the overriding concern of the latter statute with the liberty of the subject, citing its various titles as affirmation: 'Charta libertatum Regni'; 'Quia liberos facit'; 'Communis Libertas' and 'le Chartre des franchises'. According to Coke, since these charters were for the most part declarations of 'ancient Common laws of England', the king was bound and sworn to observe them, despite advice to the contrary from ministers whose motives were less concerned with good governance than with personal advancement. In a veiled reference to the level of influence exerted over Charles I by his advisers (especially, and obviously, Buckingham), Coke mentioned the 'evill Counsell' given to Edward II by Hubert de Burgo, who 'yet meaning to make this a step to his ambition (which ever rideth without reines) persuaded and humored the King that he might avoid the Charter'.[61]

In the parliamentary debates of 1628, Coke interpreted Magna Carta as a tangible representation of constitutional rights, attributing to it the architectural function of foundations on which the structure of English law was built. He warned the House that if the sovereign power claimed for the king was allowed to encroach upon the absolute authority of Magna Carta, such precipitate action would 'weaken the foundations of law, and then the building must needs fall'.[62] As I noted in connection with the physical expansion of the Inns of Court in the sixteenth century, the use by the legal institution of architectural metaphor enabled the boundaries of its jurisdiction to be physically represented. Within the walls of the Inns of Court, the ethos of the early modern legal profession evolved according to the principles of civic republicanism proposed by Aristotle, in which the best interests of the subject and the commonwealth were the ultimate objects of government. For common lawyers, whose loyalty to the humanist and republican ethos of the Inns was initiated as students and affirmed by their continued involvement in the institutional existence and governance of the Inns (in Coke's case, as a bencher of the Inner Temple), the House of Commons provided a public

---

[61] Coke, *Second Part of the Institutes*, preface.
[62] *Proceedings in Parliament 1628*, III (20 May), p. 495.

forum in which these ethical values could be articulated and from which they could be disseminated.

The substantive issue of fundamental importance to the Petition of Right, which common lawyers could immediately recognise, was the pre-existence of a *corpus iuris* that provided visible boundaries to the exercise of the royal prerogative. The association of this extant body of law with ancient national custom was repeatedly made by common lawyer MPs in the course of debate. In reply to the insinuation by the king that the attempt to restrain the royal prerogative was innovative and beyond the lawful power of Parliament, Edward Littleton made immediate reference to the immemorial antiquity of common law and the mystical authority of its ancient provenance. He protested that 'we are judged to produce new laws . . . We desire not to trench on the King's prerogative . . . We desire no new thing, but what is determined in the old.'[63] As with the architecture of the Inns of Court, allusion was made to an absolute original, located in an imaginary and mythical past, symbolised by the irrefutable sovereignty of Magna Carta.[64] One MP suggested that the authority of this statute prevailed over the jurisdiction of Parliament and the king: '[o]thers object it is not the language of parliaments to bind kings and the Council by express words. Answer: it is the language of *Magna Carta*.'[65]

On 7 June 1628 Charles I (dependent on Parliament for the supply of subsidy in the war against France) reluctantly accepted the terms of the Petition of Right, and it was enacted as a statute of the realm. Its constitutional importance rests on its principle, rather than its practical achievements. It imposed important restrictions on the power of the king to take certain actions, such as levying direct taxation, without common consent by act of Parliament. But in March 1629 Charles I dissolved Parliament and embarked upon eleven years of personal rule ended only by his need to raise money for the war against the Scots and the consequent summoning of the Short Parliament in April 1640. The constitutional significance of the Petition of Right was that it entrenched as principle the liberty of the subject, the existence of this right in law and the strict limitations on the state's ability to curtail it. The revels, masques and dramas enacted at the Elizabethan and Jacobean Inns of Court had been concerned to a greater or lesser extent with the capacity of the legal profession to present an ideal model of government that reflected their autonomous status as microscopic city-states, in which political

---

[63] Ibid. (3 May), p. 234.
[64] On Magna Carta and the relationship between custom, law and rights, see J. C. Holt, *Magna Carta* (Cambridge University Press, 1992), pp. 75–122.
[65] *Proceedings in Parliament 1628*, III (1 May), p. 187. This contribution was attributed in the original transcript of the debate to 'Mr. Sherwill'; the editors of *Proceedings in Parliament* suggest that this probably refers to Henry Sherfield.

arrangements were intended to promote the good of the commonwealth. In the various dramatic configurations, the rival jurisdictions of common law and civil law were presented as a debate between the conflicting maxims: *lex facit regem* and *quod principi placuit habet vigorem legis*. Since his accession to the throne in 1625, Charles I had aroused suspicions (fed largely by the unpopularity and perceived influence of his French, Catholic wife and his misguided faith in the judgment and ability of Buckingham) concerning his favoured model of government. His actions and insistence on the divine right to govern, constrained only by a promise to rule in accordance with the law, appeared to have more in common with the absolute monarchies of France and Spain than the models of mixed monarchy proposed by Fortescue and St German. With a higher proportion of common lawyers in the House of Commons than at any time in its history, it was inevitable that the humanist predilections of the Inns of Court should manifest themselves in parliamentary debate. This was especially so given the vociferous presence of the archetypal opponent of unlimited prerogative rule, Sir Edward Coke. At this time also the independence of the Inns of Court was threatened by the increasing interference of the monarch in their institutional activities, in particular, concerning religious worship and readings. As Charles I attempted to enforce conformity to his religious settlement and adherence to his personal rule at the Inns, it was no longer viable for the forum for constitutional debate to remain there. The parliamentary debates of 1628 represented a significant development in the influence of common lawyers over the polity of the English state. From contributing to a body of constitutional theory in the self-referential environment of the Inns of Court, as had been the case for the past hundred years, they were actually legislating for the constitution itself from the public arena of Parliament.

TYRANNY AND MANIPULATION OF THE IMAGE: THE PORTRAYAL OF PERSONAL RULE

A serious objection made by Prynne to the participation of students at the Inns of Court in seasonal plays and masques (notwithstanding that the plays met his criteria of acceptability on the grounds that their purpose and subject matter were 'academical') is the amount of time that was expended in preparing them for performance. He complained that months were sometimes wasted on writing a play, after which (he asked) 'how many houres, evenings, halfe-dayes, and sometimes weekes, are spent by all the Actors (especially in solemne academicall Enterludes) in copying, in conning, in practising their parts, before they are ripe for publike action?'[66] The closest

---

[66] Prynne, *Histrio-Mastix*, fo. 305.

parallel to this opinion, and to the injunction against common lawyers wasting their time in the writing and performance of plays, was to be found not in post-Reformation England, but in ancient Rome. In the *Dialogus de Oratoribus* of Tacitus, Aper rebukes Curiatus Maternus for neglecting his legal practice in favour of playwrighting. The latter argues that the scope of forensic oratory is too narrow, and that writing for the stage enables him to attain a higher form of eloquence than he is able to achieve in the forum. Aper rejects this argument, observing that lawyers are esteemed members of Roman society, venerated by citizens of every age and rank.[67]

The concern with maintaining the purity and integrity of law is an important theme of *De Oratoribus*, and one with which Prynne was apparently obsessed. I have noted his impassioned plea to common lawyers, after the restoration of the monarchy, to restore the splendour of the law, a lustrous quality that he equated with purity. Like Tacitus, Prynne emphasised the exalted status of lawyers. His claim that members of the Inns of Court were 'heires of heaven, coheires with Christ, yea, Kings and Priests unto God your Father'[68] is redolent also of the comparison made by Legh in *The Accedens of Armory*, that lawyers could reasonably be compared to the heavenly hierarchs because they 'followeth the conformitie, and likenes of god'.[69] In *Histrio-Mastix*, Prynne contrasted two antithetical images: the common lawyer as the true likeness of God and the actor as the personification of evil. Plays were the product of 'the very Devill himselfe; or at leastwise, Idolatrous, and Voluptuous Pagans'. Consequently, he considered actors to be inappropriate companions for lawyers, 'who were created for more noble objects, more sublime imployments than base infamous Enterludes'. He cited both classical and Christian authorities in defence of his abhorrence of stage plays: Tertullian and the Old Testament prophets were the most frequently quoted sources. St Augustine too was invoked, as an opponent of 'all diabolicall Enterludes, Vacillations, and Songs of the Gentiles'. Implicit in Prynne's thesis was the familiar polemical argument (deployed in the previous century by Bishop Aylmer) that God is an Englishman. The diatribe was directed as much against continental influences over the idyll of ancient Albion as it was against idolatry. Thus the initial purpose of stage plays was 'the superstitious worship . . . of Jupiter, Bacchus, Neptune, the Muses, Flora, Apollo, Diana, Venus, Victoria, or some such Devill-gods, or Goddesses, which the Idolatrous Pagans did adore'.

It should be emphasised that the objection to the performance of stage plays in general, and in particular by students of common law, was not on

---

[67] C. Tacitus, *Dialogus de Oratoribus*, trans. W. Peterson (Cambridge, Mass.: Harvard University Press, 1970), pp. 237, 251.
[68] Prynne, *Histrio-Mastix*, fo. **4.
[69] G. Legh, *The Accedens of Armory* (London: R. Tottel, 1576), fo. 135b.

purely religious grounds. For Prynne, as for most common lawyers of the early modern period, religion and politics were indivisible. His belief that the performance of plays was a waste of 'God's time', although expressed in an especially agitated manner, was predicated on the principle that '[t]he Common-Wealth is put to preiudice, by the generall corruption of mens mindes, and manners... which these Playes produce.' Although in relation to the ceremonial aspects of religious worship Prynne displayed a predilection for austerity not shared by Hooker, in political terms Prynne can be seen as his natural descendant. The fundamental tenet of both men's political philosophy was that Church and commonwealth were coextensive, and that within this theocratic framework the rights of the subject were protected by the sovereignty of common law. In such a polity, if certain practices were 'infamous, unseemly, unlawfull unto Christians',[70] then they were unlawful also to citizens of the commonwealth. In the context of Caroline court culture and the obvious influence on it of classical and continental art forms,[71] the attitudes expressed by Prynne were clearly subversive. As I have noted, Prynne did not object to the proper forms of sacramental church ritual. Just as Hooker had reclaimed the sacraments from Rome in order to re-present them in the image of an indigenous, ancient Anglican Church, so Prynne attempted to purge the Church and the commonwealth from the taint of idolatry and its associations with foreign jurisdictions. He was not opposed in principle to the Eucharistic rite, but was vehement 'that the Temple of God hath no agreement with Idoles: and that we cannot drinke the cup of the Lord, and the cup of Devils, nor be partakers of the Lords table, and of the table of Devils'.

The demonisation by Prynne of the ancient Greeks and their worship of false gods is a crucial factor in understanding the reaction of the government to his outspoken opinions and the numerous attempts to silence him. Prynne attributed responsibility for the popularity of theatre and its corrupt effects to 'the Athenians... in imitation of those drunken Husband-men, who Sacrificed, and made Playes to Bacchus, the God of their Vineyards'.[72] It was not only to the depiction of pagan and foreign rites in the theatre that Prynne objected: the contemporary fashion for adapting and portraying classical themes and myths in figurative art met with his severe disapprobation. He placed stage plays, games, dancing and feasting in the same unacceptable category as 'Meretricious Paintings'. The adjective was almost certainly

---

[70] Prynne, *Histrio-Mastix*, ff. 9, **4, 27, 28, 45, 831.
[71] On the patronage and collection of European art by Charles I, see Smuts, *Court Culture*, pp. 117–23.
[72] Prynne, *Histrio-Mastix*, ff. 25, 17.

intended to convey its original Latin meaning, of relating to a prostitute,[73] as well as suggesting the speciousness of the particular image.

It is probably not coincidental that *Histrio-Mastix* was published in the year following the appointment of Anthony Van Dyck as painter to the court of Charles I. Van Dyck had worked in Antwerp at the studio of Rubens *circa* 1620. There he had painted the subjects of classical myth with which Rubens was popularly associated: satyrs, the drunken Silenus and Arcadian shepherds.[74] Renowned already for his paintings of prominent Catholics in the royal courts of Europe and his incorporation of Biblical narrative into contemporary portraiture,[75] Van Dyck was responsible for a radical innovation in the depiction of the English monarchy. His royal portraits of the 1630s are notable, of course, for their heightened realism. They present idealised (and often sentimental) depictions of thoughtful individuals and differ in this important respect from the iconic portraits of Elizabeth I, which represented her in various guises as 'Gloriana', a virginal emblem of England.[76] Van Dyck's *Equestrian Portrait of Charles I* (*c.* 1638, Fig. 5) hung at Hampton Court palace during the lifetime of the king. Charles is depicted in Greenwich-made armour, wearing the lesser-George (an insignia of the Order of the Garter) and holding a commander's baton. The tablet hanging on the tree to his right reads 'Carolus Rex Magnae Britaniae'. The king sits astride a magnificent horse, whose left foreleg is raised as if poised for battle. The horse's head is disproportionately small, so as not to diminish the stature of the king. The background is an idyllic rural landscape, but the foreground reveals a rocky, arid terrain upon which the horse treads. The sky is grey, with only a few patches of blue, and behind the head of the king storm clouds are gathering. A groom, wearing a red damask tabard, stands behind the horse, presenting a plumed helmet to Charles. In the foreground, left of Charles, is a dead tree and a broken branch; only weeds are growing in the barren earth. The combination of pastoral and martial imagery is striking and clearly alludes

---

[73] From L., *meretrix*: prostitute; *merere*: to earn money.

[74] See for example, *Drunk Silenus supported by Satyrs* (National Gallery, London), details of which are attributed to Van Dyck, and produced in Rubens's studio, *c.* 1620. On Van Dyck, see R. Wendorf, *The Elements of Life: Biography and Portrait-Painting in Stuart and Georgian England* (Oxford: Clarendon, 2002), pp. 65–107.

[75] See for example, *The Balbi Children* (*c.* 1625, National Gallery, London), a depiction of members of an aristocratic Genoese family; *The Abbé Scaglia* (1634, National Gallery, London), the Abbot of Staffarda and Mandanici, diplomat in the House of Savoy and ambassador to Rome, Paris and London; *The Abbé Scaglia adoring the Virgin and Child* (National Gallery, London), in which the Virgin may be a representation of Christina of Savoy (wife of Duke Victor Amadeus I), and the child their son, Francis Hyacinth (born 1632).

[76] See for example, *A Procession by Queen Elizabeth*, by Robert Peake, which is compared to Van Dyck's *Charles I à la Chasse* in Smuts, *Court Culture*, p. 172.

Fig. 5. *Equestrian Portrait of Charles I* (*c.* 1638), Anthony Van Dyck. By permission of the National Gallery.

to a troubled land to which only an omnipotent ruler can bring relief. As Malcolm Smuts notes of Van Dyck's *Charles I à la Chasse* (Louvre, Paris), the style of these portraits is intrinsically continental.[77] The subtlety of their symbolism (to which all but the royal court were unaccustomed) and the unfettered power of the monarch to which they attested alienated the king still further from his subjects.

Despite the iconic power of the painted image, the masque provided a more public art form through which the absolute sovereignty of Charles I could be represented. The Neoplatonic traits of the Elizabethan and Jacobean masques, in which republican polities were sometimes depicted and the tyranny of absolute rule enacted and rejected, were abandoned in favour of extravagant and uncritical adulation of the king. The stylistic and thematic differences between the Caroline masques and those presented at the Elizabethan and Jacobean Inns of Court were exemplified by *The Triumph of Peace*, one of the most expensive masques ever staged. Presented by the four Inns in 1634, it was a spectacular affirmation of their collective loyalty to Charles I and Henrietta Maria and an unequivocal rejection of the opinions expressed by Prynne in *Histrio-Mastix*. Bulstrode Whitelocke, a member of the Middle Temple, kept a detailed account of preparations at the Inns of Court for *The Triumph of Peace*, noting that 'this action would manifest the difference of their opinion, from Mr. Prynne's new learning, and serve to confute his *Histro Mastix* against Interludes. This design took well with all the Inns of Court, especially the younger sort of them.'[78]

Although Prest acknowledges the important contribution made by common lawyers to the parliamentary debates of this period,[79] he has suggested that the Inns of the early seventeenth century played a peripheral role in politics, lacking both formal representation in Parliament and a corporate response to matters of public importance.[80] Although no MPs spoke on behalf of the Inns, there was a discernible group of members (led by Coke) whose arguments can be interpreted as representing the humanist, Neoplatonic polity of the Elizabethan and Jacobean Inns of Court. These libertarian sentiments were not replicated by the governing bodies of the Inns of Court during the reign of Charles I. The collaboration of the Inns on *The Triumph of Peace* suggests a public, corporate response to the tendentious

---

[77] Ibid., p. 177; see also T. N. Corns, *The Royal Image: Representations of Charles I* (Cambridge University Press, 1999). Similar idealised depictions by Van Dyck of members of the Stuart dynasty include *Lord George Stuart, Seigneur d'Aubigny* (c. 1638, National Portrait Gallery, London), in which the subject, a son of the third Duke of Lennox, is portrayed as an Arcadian shepherd; and *Lord John Stuart and his Brother, Lord Bernard Stuart* (c. 1638, National Gallery, London), in which the brothers of Lord George Stuart, theatrically costumed in sumptuous silks, pose languidly, with aristocratic disdain. The three sons of the duke were killed during the first civil war.
[78] B. Whitelocke, *Memorials of the English Affairs* (London: J. Tonson, 1732), fo. 19.
[79] Prest, *Rise of the Barristers*, p. 254.   [80] Prest, *Inns of Court*, p. 220.

issues of freedom of expression and worship raised by the publication of *Histrio-Mastix* and the subsequent punishment of its author. One of the most significant features of *The Triumph of Peace* is the crucial role played in its preparation and production by members of the Inns who happened also to be prominent royalists in positions of considerable political influence. The political temper of the masque was unequivocally suggested by Whitelocke, a member of the organising committee:

> the principal Members of the Societies of the four Inns of Court, amongst whom some were Servants of the King, had a design that the Inns of Court should present their Service to the King and Queen, and testify their affection to them, by the outward and splendid visible testimony of a Royal Masque of all the four Societies joining together, to be by them brought to the Court, as an expression of their Love, and Duty to their Majesties.[81]

Each Inn chose two of its senior members to be representatives on the organising committee. These included Whitelocke and Edward Hyde from the Middle Temple, Sir Edward Herbert and John Selden from the Inner Temple, Sir William Noy and Mr Gerling from Lincoln's Inn, and Sir John Finch from Gray's Inn (Whitelocke leaves blank the surname of the other representative, suggesting that Finch alone represented Gray's Inn).[82]

Whitelocke (who is characterised pejoratively by Ashton as a timeserver)[83] was a supporter of Parliament throughout the civil wars, attempted to mediate between the army and the king in December 1648, was appointed Commissioner of the Great Seal in the new Commonwealth and became an influential political figure during the Protectorate. As an MP, Edward Hyde (subsequently the first earl of Clarendon) became the effective leader of the royalist minority during the Long Parliament, joining Charles I in York when the king prepared for war in 1642, and proclaiming him the defender of the known laws of the land. Sir Edward Herbert was Recorder of Salisbury until 1635.[84] Selden had opposed the king in Parliament on several important constitutional issues, notably over the collection of tonnage and poundage and during the debates on the Petition of Right. Following the dissolution of Parliament in 1629, he was briefly imprisoned for his opposition to the king, but released swiftly following his apology and assurances as to his future conduct. Sir William Noy, an ardent critic of government in the 1620s, became a loyal supporter of the personal rule of Charles I and was appointed Attorney General in 1631. He was state prosecutor in several Star Chamber cases in the 1630s.[85] Sir John Finch was the pliant Speaker of the House of Commons at its dissolution in 1629. I have noted in connection with the trial of John

---

[81] Whitelocke, *Memorials*, fo. 19.   [82] *Ibid.*
[83] Ashton, *Reformation and Revolution*, p. 431.
[84] Prest, *Rise of the Barristers*, p. 251.   [85] *Ibid.*

Hampden that, as a judge in this case, Finch effectively declared the power of the king to control and command the liberty and property of his subjects to be unlimited. Following the imprisonment of Strafford in November 1640, Finch fled to Holland before he could be impeached by Parliament.

Whitelocke and Hyde attended meetings with the Lord Chamberlain and the Comptroller of the King's House (Sir Henry Vane), 'to advise with them, and to take order about the Scenes and other matters relating to the Masque'.[86] Whitelocke was also responsible for organising the music, for the composition of which he commissioned the musicians of the Queen's Chapel, 'Monsieur la Mare, Monsieur du Vall, Monsieur Robert, and Monsieur Mari, and of divers others of Foreign Nations, who were most eminent in their Art'.[87] The music indicates a Francophile predilection that would have been antithetical to the nationalist sentiments of the Elizabethan and Jacobean masques. The enormous procession that preceded the performance of *The Triumph of Peace* symbolised the unprecedented subservience of the Inns of Court, not only to the majesty of kingship but also (and in particular) to the putative *imperium* of Charles I.

The masquers were led from Holborn to the Banqueting House in Whitehall in four chariots, each drawn by six horses, 'after the fashion of the Roman Triumphant Chariots'.[88] Each chariot contained twelve men, dressed as gods and goddesses, embodying the idolatrous excess of which Prynne complained in *Histrio-Mastix*. Besides these 'proper and beautiful young Gentlemen', a hundred members of the Inns were mounted on 'the best Horses, and with the best Furniture that the King's Stable, and the Stables of all the Noblemen in Town would afford'. Whitelocke described the lavish procession as 'the most glorious and splendid shew that ever was beheld in England'.[89] The cost of the event was enormous: for the music alone the charge was £1,000. The liveries of the horsemen and pages cost £10,000 and the total bill was in excess of £21,000.[90] One aspect of the procession did engage directly with a controversial political issue: the granting by Royal Charter of monopolies and patents. Participants in the antimasque were dressed to represent 'projectors' of ridiculous inventions. One masquer rode 'upon a little Horse, with a great Bit in his Mouth, and upon the Man's Head was a Bit, with Headstall and Rains fastned'.[91] The nature of the monopoly sought by this projector was elucidated in the text of *The Triumph of Peace*:

---

[86] Whitelocke, *Memorials*, fo. 19.
[87] *Ibid*. On Caroline court music, see Smuts, *Court Culture*, pp. 124–5.
[88] Whitelocke, *Memorials*, fo. 19.   [89] *Ibid*., fo. 20.
[90] *Ibid*., ff. 21–2. Prest discusses Whitelocke's account of this masque in *Inns of Court*, pp. 230–1.
[91] Whitelocke, *Memorials*, fo. 20.

> He is to advance a rare and cunning bridle,
> Made hollow in the iron part, wherein
> A vapour subtly conveyed, shall so
> Cool and refresh a horse, he shall ne'er tire.[92]

Another masquer wore a bunch of carrots on his head and a capon on his fist. This fantastically costumed 'projector' was seeking 'a Patent of Monopoly, as the first Inventor of the Art to feed Capons fat with Carrots, and that none but himself might make use of that Invention, and have the Privilege for fourteen Years, according to the Statute'.[93]

In the reign of Charles I the granting of monopolies had become an important revenue-raising scheme: a type of indirect taxation, not necessarily linked to the uniqueness or ingenuity of the particular invention or product for which the monopoly was sought. The 1624 Statute of Monopolies had prohibited domestic monopolies (unless they were genuinely innovative), although excepted from the legislation were grants to corporate bodies. The exception provided an important and lucrative concession to chartered companies. The inclusion in *The Triumph of Peace* of the 'Antimasque of the Projectors' is probably connected with the granting of a monopoly in 1632 to the Westminster Soapmaking Company. This had been a contentious political issue, as the company received the financial backing of a Catholic syndicate and was the cause of public dissension between its principal supporters in government, Portland (Lord Treasurer), and Sir Francis Cottington (Chancellor of the Exchequer), and its implacable opponent, Archbishop Laud.[94] Whitelocke states that the Attorney General, Sir William Noy, had been one of the principal instigators of the antimasque, in which several other extraordinary projectors were presented. The unpopularity of monopolies can be inferred from the suggestion of Whitelocke that the antimasque 'pleased the Spectators the more, because by it an Information was covertly given to the King, of the unfitness and ridiculousness of these Projects against the Law'.[95]

This comical interlude is illuminating on several counts: in general terms it illustrates the continued relevance and utility of the image in the symbolic representation of law and its antithesis, chaos.[96] More specifically, it demonstrates that the legal advisers to the king (in this case his principal law officer, the Attorney General) did not always fulfil the function of 'lions under the throne', the notorious description applied to the judiciary by

---

[92] J. Shirley, *The Triumph of Peace*, ed. E. Gosse (London: Fisher Unwin, 1904), p. 452.
[93] Whitelocke, *Memorials*, fo. 20.
[94] See Ashton, *Reformation and Revolution*, pp. 248–9, 274–5.
[95] Whitelocke, *Memorials*, fo. 20.
[96] On the foundation of law and its links with the history and status of the image, see D. Freedberg, *The Power of Images* (Chicago University Press, 1990).

Bacon. They were occasionally prepared publicly to defend ancient customs against inequitable incursions by an unfettered executive. It is noteworthy that Whitelocke should have emphasised that monopolies were 'against the Law', when in the case of corporations they manifestly were not. Trevelyan is more accurate in his description of the grant of monopolies as inexpedient rather than illegal.[97] Whitelocke's remark tacitly refers the reader to the existence of a fundamental law against monopolies, according to which (in the words of Coke), 'therefore the use of a Monopoly is punishable by law'.[98] Coke had employed syllogistic logic to assert the illegality of monopolies: offences contrary to the fundamental laws are punishable by law; monopolies are contrary to the fundamental laws; therefore monopolies are punishable by law. The common lawyers who devised the 'Antimasque of the Projectors' utilised the suggestive power of the visual image for the same purpose.

This noteworthy diversion apart, the procession and the contents of the masque itself confirmed the impression that the corporate intention of the Inns of Court was to present themselves as pliant servants of an absolute monarch, complicit in the unilateral decision to govern without the consent of Parliament. The choice of James Shirley as writer of *The Triumph of Peace* demonstrated the strong influence of Queen Henrietta Maria and her Catholic coterie over the culture of the royal court. Shirley had attended St John's College, Oxford, as a student. There he had become known to Laud, who was president of the college at that time. He eventually obtained his degree from Cambridge and took orders in the Church of England before converting to Roman Catholicism. With deliberate irony, he had dedicated an earlier play, *The Bird in the Cage* (1633), to Prynne and, obviously intending to antagonise the writer of *Histrio-Mastix*, had included in that work a masque in which the parts were played by women.[99] It is interesting in the context of the controversy over the granting of monopolies that as a boy Shirley attended Merchant Taylors' School. When *The Triumph of Peace* was repeated at the request of the queen, following its original performance at the Banqueting House, the venue was Merchant Taylors' Hall. In 1602, *Davenant v. Harris* ('the Case of Monopolies'), concerning the grant of a monopoly to the Merchant Taylors, had decided that such grants were against the common law because they were incompatible with the liberty of the subject. The extraordinary extravagance of the masquers' costumes, including 'their Habits, Doublets, Trunkhose, and Caps of most rich cloth of Tissue, and wrought as thick with Silver Spangles as they could be placed,

---

[97] Trevelyan, *England Under the Stuarts*, p. 116.
[98] Coke, *Third Part of the Institutes*, p.181.
[99] Shirley, *Triumph of Peace*, introduction, pp. ix–xx.

large white Silk Stockings up to their Trunk-hose, and rich Sprigs in their Caps',[100] suggests the possible involvement of the Merchant Taylors and their vested interest in the granting of monopolies by royal charter.

There was a strong Italian influence, discernible in Inigo Jones's scenery for the masque: 'sumptuous palaces, lodges, porticos, and other noble pieces of architecture' and 'a spacious place' representing 'the piazza of Peace'.[101] The Elizabethan and Jacobean masques had invoked a timeless world of classical antiquity, implicitly linking the ancient English customs of common law to Platonic visions of the ideal commonwealth. In *The Triumph of Peace*, most of the images appeared vacuous by comparison, concerned only (as Whitelocke suggests) with the representation of 'earthly Pomp and Glory, if not Vanity'.[102] It is salutary to compare the inclusion of iconic characters such as Ulysses in *Circe and Ulysses* (1615) or the Olympian Knights in *The Masque of the Inner Temple and Gray's Inn* (1612) with the specious inanity of Opinion, Confidence, Fancy, Jollity, Laughter, Novelty and Admiration, all characters in *The Triumph of Peace*. The inclusion of a 'maquerelle' (an old French word for a bawd), two 'wenches' and 'two wanton Gamesters' was probably intended further to antagonise and alienate Prynne, who had argued against gamesters in *Histrio-Mastix* and praised the benchers of Lincoln's Inn for prohibiting the use of dice in hall at Christmas: 'a most pernicious, infamous game; condemned in all ages, all places'.[103] Although recognisable figures from classical mythology were incorporated into the action, their function was purely decorative, and their inclusion probably intended to satisfy the queen's enjoyment of dancing. Following a dance between four nymphs, three satyrs 'spy them and attempt their persons', but were driven away by a group of hunters who in turn danced with the nymphs. The emphasis on spurious pageant continued with the entrance of 'a Windmill, a fantastic Knight and his Squire armed. The fantastic adventurer with his lance makes many attempts upon the Windmill.' Although clearly a reference to *Don Quixote* by Miguel de Cervantes, the second part of which had been published in 1614, no allusion was drawn to the important themes of Cervantes' work, in particular, those concerning incompatible systems of morality and the distinction made by the writer between class and worth.

The finale of the masque paid sycophantic homage to Charles I and Henrietta Maria, and attempted to depict the function of law in the body politic. It is instructive to compare the portrayal of law in this masque with that of the Jacobean Inns of Court masques. The divine provenance of English law was strongly suggested by the emergence of Eunomia, the classical personification of law, from a 'cloud, of an orient colour, bearing a

---

[100] Whitelocke, *Memorials*, fo. 21.
[101] Shirley, *Triumph of Peace*, p. 446.
[102] Whitelocke, *Memorials*, fo. 21.
[103] Prynne, *Histrio-Mastix*, fo. *1b.

silver chariot curiously wrought'. Eunomia had been summoned by the principal character, Irene, or Peace, because 'I'm lost with them/ That know not how to order me'. The character of Diche, or Justice, also descended from a cloud, thus the presence of *ius* and *lex* were invoked in order to impose peace upon the commonwealth. It is significant that Eunomia and Diche bore the symbols of imperial office: the former wore a purple robe and the latter held a crown imperial in her hand, implying their subservience to the royal prerogative and the primacy of a jurisdiction alien to the ancient traditions of English law. The character of Eunomia featured also in *The Memorable Maske of the Middle Temple and Lincoln's Inn* (1613) by George Chapman. But her representation there as 'a Virgine Priest', consecrated to the goddess, Honour, emphasised a level of spiritual unity and social community, entirely lacking from the personification of law in *The Triumph of Peace*.

Having stated that they were 'Proud to wait upon that earth/ Whereon you move', the scene changed to a hillside, 'cut out like the degrees of a theatre', upon which stood all the members of the Inns of Court who participated in the masque. They then declared their unequivocal, willing subjugation to the personal rule of Charles I and his status as *parens patriae*:

> The children of your reign, not blood ...
> ... These have no form, no sun, no shade,
> But what your virtue doth create.[104]

GOVERNANCE OF THE INNS OF COURT AND POLITICAL INDEPENDENCE

This supine acceptance of their subordinate status was commensurate with the extent to which the king had compromised the autonomy of the Inns of Court since his accession to the throne in 1625. *The Triumph of Peace* was singularly successful in its public portrayal of the English legal profession as loyal servants of the crown. The cost of the masque was met partly by a compulsory tax, imposed upon members of the four Inns. Dugdale reports that benchers each paid £5, utter-barristers £2 10s and inner-barristers £2.[105] The *Pension Book* of Gray's Inn records that failure to pay the tax resulted in forfeiture of chambers and expulsion from commons. The cost of the masque was evidently greater than originally anticipated, as two substantial increases in the level of taxation were subsequently imposed.[106] The compliance with which these directives were met was facilitated by the presence on the bench of influential supporters of the government. For example, Sir John Finch

---

[104] Shirley, *Triumph of Peace*, pp. 454, 455, 457–8, 460–1.
[105] W. Dugdale, *Origines Juridiciales or Historical Memorials of the English Laws* (London: F. and T. Warren, 1666), fo. 150.
[106] *Pension Book of Gray's Inn*, ed. R. J. Fletcher, 2 vols. (London: Chiswick, 1901), I, pp. 318–19.

attended both meetings of the governing body of Gray's Inn at which the levy for the masque was increased. After its successful performance, the Lord Chamberlain wrote to the Inns informing them that the king was 'much taken with the noble entertainment which hath been brought unto him by the gentlemen of the Innes of Courte'.[107] Martial imagery, frequently employed to represent the imperial majesty of the king, was utilised by the crown to ascribe an unprecedented military role to the members of the Inns of Court. In a poem giving thanks to the Inns for the presentation of *The Triumph of Peace*, the masquers were described as

> The Flower of Gentrie, Hope of Chivalrie.
> Theis are the Sonnes of Charles his peacefull Raigne,
> Whom yet if warr's rude accents shall constraine
> To put on armes, will quickly understand
> The Lawes of Armes, as well as of the Land.[108]

A similar intention that the members of the Inns should act as an élite bodyguard to the king was expressed in a letter from Charles I to the benchers of Gray's Inn in 1628. He argued that, as the 'true religion' was threatened 'in all parts of Christendom', he required the benchers to encourage among the membership 'the exercise of archerie and armes ... and especially in horsemanshipp, a commendable and noble exercise and most necessarie in all occasions of warr'.[109]

In the years of his personal rule, Charles intervened on numerous occasions concerning various issues relating to the governance of the Inns. In 1630, members who failed to receive Holy Communion were, by order of the king, to be expelled from their Inn. In 1634, the king imposed religious conformity, instructing the Inns in a letter to conduct their religious services 'within the boundes of the doctrine and discipline of ye Church of England'.[110] There was a marked similarity between the educational exercises of the Inns and the lectures, sermons and exercises that differentiated Puritanism from Anglicanism.[111] I have noted the peculiar non-conformist tendency of Lincoln's Inn to which Prynne attests throughout *Histrio-Mastix*. It was probably at the instigation of the king that Council passed a resolution in January 1640, to the effect that 'some admonishment be given to them that resort to the sermon and usually neglect divine service'.[112] This edict

---

[107] *Black Books*, II, p. 315.
[108] *Ibid.*, p. 457 (from *Calendar of State Papers, Domestic, Charles I*, cclx, no. 15).
[109] *Pension Book*, I, p. xlviii (from *State Papers Domestic, Charles I*, cviii, no. 42).
[110] *Black Books*, II, p. 314.
[111] On the cultural differences between royalists and parliamentarians in the 1630s, see A. Fletcher, *The Outbreak of the English Civil War* (London: E. Arnold, 1981), p. 407; see also Smuts, *Court Culture*, pp. 5–6.
[112] *Black Books*, II, p. 354.

was clearly effective, as an inventory of May 1641 recorded the existence in chapel of communion cloths, surplices and hoods, tin and brass candlesticks, and 'one purple velvet cushion for the pulpit, with tassells of silke and gold'.[113] Evidence of a limited degree of religious independence is provided by Gray's Inn, where the Puritan preacher, Dr Richard Sibbes, remained in office until his death in 1635, despite his persecution by Laudians.[114] His survival in the post probably owed much to the influence of his powerful patron, the earl of Warwick. In 1631, the masters of the bench gave Warwick 'a convenient roome in the windowe at the east end of the chappell for theire better heareing the sermon in the chappell'.[115] After his death, Sibbes was succeeded by Hannibal Potter, a high-church Anglican and royalist. He was dismissed by the governing body in July 1641, but refused to leave office. It is significant that he was ordered to leave by the governing body in November 1641. This was the month in which the Grand Remonstrance was passed by the House of Commons, proposing (among a catalogue of grievances) that bishops be deprived of their votes in the House of Lords and that unnecessary religious ceremonies be removed.

Charles I was aware of the insidious influence exerted by the Inns of Court over the governance of the country and the political significance of the legal education acquired by their members. In a distant echo of Fortescue, he acknowledged in his letter of 1634 to the Inns that 'verie many of the gentrie spend some part of their time in one or other of the Innes of Court, and afterwards returning to live and governe as Justices of Peace or otherwise in their severall countries, there guide themselves according to such principles as in those places are infused into them'. To this end, the king interfered in the internal affairs of the Inns, attempting to enforce conformity and adherence to his personal rule. He issued orders for the form that readings should take during Lent, incidentally insisting that those who 'professe the Lawe, ought to be most forward and exemplarie in yielding conformitie thereunto'.[116] The governing bodies of the Inns were ordered to summon recalcitrant and dissident members to appear before the courts of High Commission and Star Chamber and, on conviction, were instructed to expel them from the membership. Prynne was one such member, expelled from Lincoln's Inn by order of Star Chamber following his conviction for seditious libel in 1634. The Inns also administered the oaths of supremacy and allegiance, whereby Irish and recusant members were required to swear their allegiance to the crown, under pain of expulsion.[117] The meeting of the governing body of

---

[113] *Ibid.*, p. 358.
[114] Prest notes that Sir John Finch made the expedient claim in the Long Parliament that he protected Sibbes from such persecution, *Rise of the Barristers*, p. 361.
[115] *Pension Book*, I, p. 300.   [116] *Black Books*, II, pp. 313–14, 308.
[117] *Ibid.*, pp. 272, 317, 360–2.

7 May 1630 records that the king had ordered a search of Gray's Inn to be conducted five times a year during term and once during each vacation, in order that 'ill subjects and dangerous persons' should be apprehended. To this effect, foreigners and 'discontinuers' were prohibited from admission to or accommodation in the Inn.[118]

Accounts exist of individual acts of rebellion against the personal rule of Charles I, after the dissolution of Parliament in March 1629. One such concerns a warrant for the arrest of Southcot Hewes, issued in August 1629 by the then Attorney General, Sir Robert Heath (treasurer of the Inner Temple and a member of its Parliament since the reign of James I). A messenger from Star Chamber was despatched to Lincoln's Inn in order to execute the warrant. When his purpose was discovered by members of the Inn, 'about thirty gentlemen sett him into the House violently, pumpt him, shaved him, and disgracefully used him, after they sawe his warrant, and otherwise carried themselves rudely and unworthily'.[119] The king ordered their prosecution in Star Chamber by the Attorney General, the Solicitor General and the Recorder of London. The suspects were ordered to attend a Council at Lincoln's Inn for the purposes of identification, but no witnesses were present to testify against them, despite being invited to attend.[120]

A Parliament of the Middle Temple, held in January 1631, recorded that students had complained 'of their liberties (as they termed it) being infringed', following the arbitrary dissolution of commons. Junior members had apparently drawn up their own constitution for the Inn. Consequently, a fracas ensued in hall, during which pots were thrown 'at random towards the Bench table, and struck divers Masters . . . the Masters complained to the Lord Chief Justice'. The main offenders were committed without trial to the King's Bench prison, and their alternative Parliament book was burned by order of the masters of the bench. They declared also that members claiming 'any power to govern otherwise than as subordinate to the orders of the Bench' would be immediately expelled. This case is noteworthy for its peculiar resonance with constitutional issues affecting the governance of England and its allusions to contemporary political themes, in particular those of freedom of expression, arbitrary trial and imprisonment, the burning of books, and the textualisation and standardisation of conceptual rights and obligations. The reaction of the masters of the bench to this incident, and their decision to involve the Lord Chief Justice, reflect the institutional links between the Inns and the juridical system. Clearly, the governing bodies of the Inns were sensitive to the perception of their authority by the government, and were anxious to dispel any impression that they might condone rebellious conduct within

---

[118] *Pension Book*, I, pp. 295–6.
[119] *Black Books*, II, p. 452, appendix, n. x.   [120] *Ibid.*, pp. 286, 290.

their sphere of jurisdiction. Consequently, in 1639 the Christmas revels were cancelled at the Middle Temple because 'the misgovernment of these times is become a public scandal, whereof the Judges and State take notice'.[121] The Council of State had expressed its displeasure at the excessive conduct of honourable members during the Christmas festivities, rebuking the governing bodies of the Inns. The Inner Temple was alone in offering a spirited defence of its ancient customs (which it equated with laws) and political autonomy. Its governing body informed the Council that 'our government and all our privileges are grounded only upon ancient custom, which we conceive to be a law ... We beseech your Lordships to have that honourable regard to the entire preservation of our ancient privelege as to give us leave to be the sole reformers of our own disorders.'[122] The response of the Council of State to this declaration of independence by the legal community is not recorded.

The civil war altered permanently the nature of legal education at the Inns of Court. At Lincoln's Inn, after 4 August 1642, there were three admissions only until June 1644, when admissions returned to the normal level of twenty to thirty per annum.[123] Gray's Inn recorded an average of forty-three admissions for the four years between 1642 and 1646, compared with its annual average of 102.7 admissions between the accession of Charles I and the outbreak of civil war. During the civil war, the *Pension Book* noted that there were no educational exercises, no calls to the Bar and very few members in residence. Readings at Gray's Inn were not resumed until 1661.[124] Throughout the sixteenth and early seventeenth centuries, complex ideas about the nature of the constitutional settlement and in particular about the contribution made to any such disposition by the legal profession had been expressed obliquely through the arcana of institutional existence at the Inns of Court. With the effective demise of an institutional forum for the dissemination of juristic theory, there was no corporate voice with which to express the nascent principles of constitutionalism. Instead, individual lawyers publicly articulated ideas concerning the constitutional primacy of common law, through the medium of the printed pamphlet. This particular mode of expression was ideally suited to the disputatious style of address to which lawyers were accustomed, the techniques of which were acquired through the educational exercises at the Inns of Court. The arguments presented in the pamphlets were succinct and usually interspersed with literary tropes, commonly associated with the presentation of legal argument.

---

[121] *A Calendar of the Middle Temple Records*, ed. C. H. Hopwood, 4 vols. (London: Butterworth, 1903), I, pp. 60–1, 70.
[122] *Calendar of State Papers, Domestic*, 1639–40, pp. 304–5, in *Inner Temple Records*, II, p. 369.
[123] *Black Books*, II, p. 362.   [124] *Pension Book*, I, introduction, pp. xliii–xliv.

In terms of the persuasive power of rhetoric, the poetics of law were probably more important during the civil war than they had been when Sir Philip Sidney memorably described poetry as a speaking picture, whose purpose was to teach and delight. And never more accurate was the injunction of Sir Thomas Wilson that the eloquence of the rhetorician had the potential power to win cities and entire countries. The rhetorical skills of the Elizabethan period had been handed down to a generation of common lawyers, who in the 1640s deployed them in print against the tyranny of absolute monarchy and in defence of the political sovereignty of common law.[125] Thus, in *A Miracle: An Honest Broker* (1642), the writer employed familiar arguments in favour of the principle of king in Parliament, originally proposed by Fortescue and St German. He adopted the same indignant tone and appeal to ancient custom that Coke skilfully deployed in the court of King's Bench and later in the House of Commons, when he asked 'by what *knowne Laws* hath his Majesty without the consent of Parliament levyed Arms: is it not against the *known Law* of Magna Charta, the Petition of Right, nay against his owne late *known Law* of Presse or Levy in this very Parliament?'[126]

As the argument develops, the stylistic influences of Elizabethan literature emerge, so that law is depicted imagistically, in a felicitous mixture of metaphors, as 'the fodder of all society, the Sanctuary, the flaming Sword of Right, brandisht against all violence & wrong'. The author develops the martial imagery in his assertion that law, without the means of execution, is 'Justices bare Scales without her Sword, a pistoll charged onely with powder, that can at most but threaten and make a empty noise'. The conceit of war is ingenious, as his argument concerns the illegality of Charles raising an army without the consent of Parliament and his related attempt to 'disarme and baffle' the law. Conversely, he argues that the lawful grounds on which Parliament levied forces were 'not whether a Bishop or no Bishop; no, nor whether Reformation or no Reformation; but whether Law or no Law: whether a Sword or an empty scaberd? Whether a living Law or but a dead letter? . . . and consequently, whether a Kingdome or no Kingdome?' The violent imagery concludes with the use of a familiar anatomical metaphor, in which laws are likened to the joints of the kingdom, 'which once cut asunder, must needs discontinue and unjoynt the whole frame to its certain ruine'.[127]

---

[125] On polemical pamphlets and literature, see T. N. Corns, *Uncloistered Virtue: English Political Literature, 1640–1660* (Oxford: Clarendon, 1992); see also T. N. Corns and D. Loewenstein (eds.), *The Emergence of Quaker Writing: Dissenting Literature in Seventeenth Century England* (London: Frank Cass, 1995).

[126] Anon., *A Miracle: An Honest Broker, or, Reasons urging a more liberall Loane towards the maintenance of Religion, Law, and the Kingdomes safety in them Both* (London, 1642), fo. 23.

[127] Ibid., ff. 36–7.

Aside from the specific issues addressed by the writer (concerning for example the liberty of the subject, the status of Parliament as a court of law, and the lawful boundaries to the exercise of the royal prerogative), the overarching effect of the pamphlet is to describe a disordered realm, whose chaotic condition is the fatal consequence of arbitrary and unjust governance. The resemblance to the themes of *Ferrex and Porrex* (presented at the Inner Temple in 1561) and the tragic mode in which that drama was expressed is notable. A particular literary style has been successfully adopted in order to convey the magnitude of civil and constitutional unrest. In the words of Sir Philip Sidney, '[t]ragedy, that openeth the greatest wounds, and sheweth forth the ulcers that are covered with tissue; that maketh kings fear to be tyrants, and tyrants to manifest their tyrannical humours.'[128]

After the rout of the royalist forces at Marston Moor in 1644, institutional existence at the Inns of Court gradually revived, but under straitened circumstances. Oliver St John, appointed Solicitor General, became treasurer of Lincoln's Inn when Council resumed in 1644, and presided over an unprecedented financial crisis, illustrated by this entry from the *Black Books*, dated 10 July 1644: '[u]ppon the peticion of Samuell Tayleure, Chiefe Butler, sheweinge that necessitie hath enforced him to pawne some of the House plate left in his custodie, for 20li., – It is thereupon ordered that the Steward shall redeeme the sayd plate, and sell the same.'[129] Commons could be provided only by charging members on each occasion that they ate a meal in hall. By 1645, many chambers at the Inns were empty, as their tenants had left London to fight in the civil war. Those members who had fought on the side of the king were, by order of Parliament, expelled from their Inns, and those suspected of being 'delinquents' had to prove their innocence before being granted readmittance. In October 1645, the Middle Temple noted a drastic diminution in the number of benchers, caused by the lack of readings during the past three years. By February 1646, the required standards for call to the Bar were lowered, due to the erratic attendance of members and students, so that 'whoever shall apply themselves to keep Commons, and perform exercises' would satisfy the bench as to their competence.

After the first civil war had ended in defeat for the royalist forces, the fortunes of the Inns appear to have improved. The Parliament Book of the Middle Temple records in its entry for 13 May 1647 that 'all passages are open to and fro all parts of the kingdom, and there is a competent number of Students and Barristers, Vacationers met in Commons, residing in the House'.[130] Consequently, a resolution was passed to the effect that mooting should recommence on 18 May. Despite the return to their customary

---

[128] P. Sidney, *The Defense of Poesy* (Glasgow: R. Urie, 1752), p. 52.
[129] *Black Books*, II, p. 365.   [130] *Middle Temple Records*, I, pp. 75, 76.

institutional régime, the governance of the Inns was subjected to external interference. Restrictions on the form of religious worship were enforced, as they had been during the personal rule of Charles I. Even before the defeat of the king in the first civil war, the dominance in Parliament of the Presbyterians was reflected at the Inns by the enforcement of the official state religion. At Gray's Inn in May 1645, it was ordered that 'Mr Reynolds is to attend at the next pencon to answere concerning the roll of the covenant'.[131] In August 1645 the Inns were declared a 'classical Presbytery' by parliamentary ordinance, and during the following year they were made a 'province' and ordered to put the ordinances for church government into execution.

Independence and autonomy were no more institutional features of the Inns of Court in the 1640s than they had been in the 1630s. The records of the Inns are conspicuously silent concerning the arrest, trial and execution of Charles I: at Gray's Inn, no governing body meeting was held between November 1648 and April 1649. Consequently no corporate attitude was expressed towards the abolition of the monarchy and the establishment of the republic. At the first Council of 1649 at Lincoln's Inn, on 6 February, no reference was made to the momentous events of the previous few months or their possible effect on the polity of the Inn and its future development. The *Black Books* record only that 'Mr Spence bee treated with by Mr Herne concerninge the furniture of the Preacher's chamber. Mr Hales, and the rest of those lately called to the Bench and not yet published, shall be published at the next moot.'[132] It was the clear intention of the governing bodies at the Inns that their role as patriarchs and guardians of the legal community should continue uninterrupted and unchanged. Their independence had been compromised by the enforcement of a state religion, first under Charles I and subsequently by order of a Parliament dominated by Presbyterians. During the reigns of Elizabeth I and James I, the Inns had developed as humanist commonwealths, their governance broadly modelled on the civic, ethical and political values of the ancient city-states. Common lawyers had dominated the parliaments of the 1620s and 1640s, and were prominent in the leadership of the new commonwealth. After the execution of the king on 30 January 1649 and the establishment of republic, an opportunity at last existed for the model of classical republicanism established at the Inns of Court over the course of the previous century, to be replicated in the governance of the English state.

---

[131] *Pension Book*, I, p. 353.   [132] *Black Books*, II, p. 380.

7

Interregnum: lex, ius *and de facto government*

THE PERCEPTION OF LAWYERS: 'THE NORMAN YOAKE ABOUT THE PEOPLES NECKS'[1]

Dick. The first thing we do, let's kill all the lawyers.
Cade. Nay, that I mean to do.[2]

Ever attuned to public sensibilities, in *The Second Part of King Henry VI* Shakespeare articulated the popular and obsessive resentment of lawyers that was as much a feature of Elizabethan life as it was during the Interregnum. Writing in 1600, Sir Thomas Wilson complained that no province, city, town or village in Britain was 'free from them, unlesse the Isle of Anglesey, which boast they never had lawyers nor foxes'.[3] During the last decade of the sixteenth century the legal profession enjoyed an unprecedented ascendancy; its influence over cultural, political and constitutional developments was profound. As Attorney General, Chief Justice and latterly a member of parliament, Sir Edward Coke played a crucial role in the reigns of Elizabeth, James and Charles as the defender of rights and freedoms, allegedly guaranteed by ancient statutes and the immutable customs of common law. He withstood attacks by professional rivals such as Sir Francis Bacon and defended the supreme jurisdiction of the courts of common law against the encroachment of prerogative rule by James I, for which he was eventually dismissed as Chief Justice. As a member of parliament during the reign of Charles I, Coke continued the principled fight for statutory recognition of individual liberty from the floor of the House of Commons. But fundamental issues of

---

[1] G. Winstanley, *Light Shining in Buckinghamshire*, 1648 (Thomason Tracts, E. 475 [11]), p. 9. See G. M. Shulman, *Radicalism and Reverence, the Political Thought of Gerrard Winstanley* (Berkeley: University of California Press, 1989).
[2] *The Second Part of King Henry VI*, IV. ii. 72–3. See C. Hobday, 'Clouted Shoon and Leather Aprons: Shakespeare and the Egalitarian Tradition', *Renaissance and Modern Studies*, 23 (1979), 63–78; T. Pettitt, '"Here Comes I, Jack Straw": English Folk Drama and Social Revolt', *Folklore*, 95 (1984), 3–20.
[3] T. Wilson, 'The State of England, Anno Dom. 1600', ed. F. J. Fisher, *The Camden Miscellany*, 16 (1936), 25.

constitutional importance such as those which Coke spent much of his career defending had no obvious relevance to the lives of most English subjects. For Jack Cade the clothier, Dick the butcher, Smith the weaver and the other artisan-rebels of *The Second Part of King Henry VI*, lawyers represented a privileged and avaricious class. The legal profession was visibly differentiated from working people by their long gowns, physically separated from the populace by the inaccessibility of the Inns of Court, and orally distinguished by the use of an arcane and incomprehensible language, law-French.[4]

After the execution of Charles I on 30 January 1649, the first action of the regicides was not to kill all the lawyers. In February 1649 the Rump Parliament established a committee 'to prepare an Act to restrain the preaching, and printing of any thing against the Proceedings of the House'.[5] Restrictions on freedom of speech and expression became important symbols of the oppressive nature of government under the Commonwealth and the Protectorate. They were unable notwithstanding to prevent the prolific publication of outlawed pamphlets, berating the republican government for perpetuating the tyranny of the sword, against which many of their authors had fought during the civil war.

The first Council of State, elected on 14 February 1649, consisted of thirty-eight members. In addition to senior army officers such as Fairfax and Harrington, it included eminent lawyers such as John Lisle, Henry Rolle, Oliver St John and Bulstrode Whitelocke. These men, and other lawyers who served the government of the republic, such as Roger Hill, Nicholas Lechmere, Lislebone Long, Edmund Prideaux and William Say were instinctively conservative (an observation made by Woolrych in relation to the committee nominated in 1651 for the preparation of a bill to set a terminal date for the sitting of the Rump Parliament[6]). Throughout the Interregnum, the inherent legal conservatism of these and other lawyers consistently thwarted attempts made by the various parliaments at reform of the law. They perceived in such precipitate action a real threat to the autonomy of the legal profession and (in broader terms) to the doctrines of realty and tenure which the law and the legal institution underpinned. Their conception of law, to the extent that it can be extrapolated from their actions in government, was necessarily concerned with the establishment and maintenance of order in a country that had been subjected to extraordinary levels of political and civil unrest. These men were not constitutional jurists in the mould of

---

[4] On the general mistrust of lawyers in early modern England and their unsympathetic representation, see C. W. Brooks, *Pettyfoggers and Vipers of the Commonwealth* (Cambridge University Press, 1986).
[5] B. Whitelocke, *Memorials of the English Affairs* (London: J. Tonson, 1732), fo. 377.
[6] A. Woolrych, *Commonwealth to Protectorate* (London: Phoenix, 2000), pp. 26–7.

St German or Fortescue, nor were they defenders of ancient liberties, whose irrefutable legality could be traced to a golden age of pre-Norman, common law tradition. The juristic ideals of Neoplatonic humanism, embodied by the Elizabethan Inns of Court, and the radical constitutionalism of Coke and the lawyer MPs who argued in favour of the Petition of Right were discarded in favour of the pragmatic imperatives of revolutionary government. In the opinion of the Council of State, order had to be imposed or anarchy would prevail. The theoretical distinctions between de iure and de facto government, which had concerned political theorists of the Renaissance such as Machiavelli, attained practical, political significance as the republican state sought to impose its authority on the British populace.

As Woolrych has noted, although more than two hundred MPs took their seats during the Rump Parliament between Pride's Purge in 1648 and its forcible dissolution in April 1653, only between sixty and seventy members attended the House of Commons regularly. Forty-four of these members were lawyers, their institutional resistance to innovation a fact that Woolrych attributes partly to the abysmal record of the Rump on reform of the law.[7] There was considerable resentment of lawyer MPs by non-lawyers in the House of Commons, a sentiment described memorably by Whitelocke as 'a great Peek against the Lawyers'. According to Whitelocke, on 4 November 1649 a sizeable body of non-lawyer members argued '[t]hat it was not fit for Lawyers who were Members of Parliament (if any Lawyers, ought to be of the Parliament) to plead or practise as Lawyers, during the time that they sat as Members of the Parliament'. Whitelocke draws an analogy with a parliament held during the sixth year of Henry IV's reign from which all lawyers were excluded: Walsingham disparagingly termed this 'the lack learning Parliament'. The popular perception of lawyers as 'gownmen' had alienated them from their fellow citizens. During the period of civil unrest and political upheaval surrounding the usurpation of the throne by Henry IV, these aggrieved subjects believed that lawyers 'had not undergone the Dangers and Hardships that Martial Men had done'. In defence of his profession, Whitelocke makes a comparison between the English Commonwealth and the republic of ancient Rome, in which soldiers were also gownmen, 'nor doth that Gown abate either a Man's Courage or his Wisdom, or render him less capable of using a Sword'.[8] William Leach of the Middle Temple referred to the attempt by certain members of the Rump to disqualify lawyers from membership of the House, as 'an Odium upon the Law and Lawyers'. He insisted that as good laws were 'grounded upon the quintessence of right

---

[7] *Ibid.*, pp. 5, 7. For a comprehensive analysis of the Rump and its dissolution, see B. Worden, *The Rump Parliament 1648–1653* (Cambridge University Press, 1972).
[8] Whitelocke, *Memorials*, fo. 430–1.

reason', there was a requirement that legislation should be deliberated upon by lawyers, 'being none other of any other profession have been heard of to attain to such learning and judgment'.[9]

Resentment at the acquisition of great wealth and their disproportionate political influence were undoubtedly significant causal factors in the negative attitude demonstrated towards lawyers by non-lawyer MPs. There was suspicion also of their role in the legislative process. As a lawyer, Commissioner of the Great Seal and an influential figure in government throughout the Interregnum, Whitelocke was in a position of considerable authority to observe of Parliament that 'those in Power have most reason to be displeased with this Profession, as a Bridle to their Power'.[10] Immediately before and throughout the trial of Charles I, prominent lawyers had displayed ambivalence towards the legality of proceedings and the right of Parliament to try the king. Maynard, Prideaux, Rolle, St John, Selden, Whitelocke and Wilde would not take part in the trial. William Steele, the Attorney General, excused himself on grounds of sickness and Algernon Sidney, on being appointed one of the judges, objected that the king could be tried by no court in the land and that this court did not have the jurisdiction to try any man.[11] Mindful of the obstructive attitude of lawyer MPs towards the executive in the Parliaments of the 1620s and early 1640s, it was inevitable that in 1649 Parliament should regard lawyers as a potential bridle to their power, particularly as at the time there was no effective separation of powers between the executive and the legislature.

The Council of State was elected on 14 February 1649 and given extensive military powers: commanding and settling the English and Irish militia, improving the navy, and allocating magazines and stores.[12] Following the abolition of the monarchy on 17 March 1649 and the House of Lords two days later, the Rump effectively committed executive authority to the Council of State. On 7 November 1652, as Cromwell's attitude towards the Rump hardened, he expressed his gravest misgivings about the 'Pride, and Ambition, and Self-seeking' of MPs: 'Nor can they be kept within the bounds of Justice, and Law or Reason, they themselves being the Supreme Power of the Nation, liable to no account to any.'[13] Throughout *Memorials of the English Affairs*, Whitelocke (mindful of the image he presents as a sagacious, equable lawyer and constitutionalist) depicts himself as a bridle to the power

---

[9] W. Leach, *A New Parliament or Representative for The perpetual Peace and quiet of this Nation* (London, 1651), fo. 2.
[10] Whitelocke, *Memorials*, fo. 432.
[11] *Sidney Papers, consisting of a Journal of the Earl of Leicester, and original letters by Algernon Sidney*, ed. R. W. Blencowe (London: J. Murray, 1825), p. 237. On Algernon Sidney, Harrington and Republican thought, see J. Scott, *Algernon Sidney and the English Republic, 1623–1677* (Cambridge University Press, 1988).
[12] Whitelocke, *Memorials*, fo. 381.   [13] *Ibid.*, fo. 549.

of Cromwell; counselling him and, with varying degrees of success, restraining his more impetuous instincts. As for example, on the same date, when Cromwell obliquely threatened to authorise the army to purge the Rump, Whitelocke reminded him that his commission came from Parliament and that '[w]e our selves have acknowledged them the Supreme Power.' Having counselled Cromwell against accepting the title of king, he consoled him by telling him that 'you have the full Kingly Power in you already, concerning the Militia, as you are General'. Whitelocke's advice to Cromwell to restore a limited monarchy, 'as will secure our Spiritual and Civil Liberties',[14] must be treated cautiously, as it might have been inserted at a later date as an indication of his loyalty to the restored monarchy. But his opposition, expressed in March 1653, to the ending of Parliament by force and his repugnance at its possible replacement by a military government appear to be genuine. His attitude indicates the constitutional adherence of the archetypal common lawyer to the rule of law, the abhorrence of martial law in a nation not at war and a vestigial attachment to the restraining principle of the king in Parliament.

Resentment and mistrust of the legal profession extended far beyond Parliament, and long after the Rump was dissolved on 20 April 1653. Lawyers were commonly considered to be parasites on the body politic of the nation. One pamphleteer objected that, since the execution of the king, Parliament had protected subjects 'from the oppositions and malice of foreign enemies (though not from the oppressions of some intestine inmates, I mean the Lawyers, and wicked men that oppressed by the Law).'[15] The same writer spoke for a large proportion of the populace when he proposed to Barebones Parliament that it abolish and repeal existing law. He objected to law reports and statutes 'that are either in a strange tongue or otherwise (which serve for no other end, but to enrich the Lawyers, and impoverish others)' and suggested that Parliament replace them with a brief code of laws. The new laws should be administered by godly men 'as never knew what those old laws meant . . . do his work, and your Lord when he cometh will blesse and reward you'.[16] To a writer such as this, the artificial reason to which William Leach referred, and which was implicitly the exclusive right of lawyers to expound, was a fallacy perpetuated by generations of lawyers. It served no other purpose than to enrich themselves and protect their profession from external interference. The matter of the 'strange tongue', law-French, is of particular importance following the execution of the king and the establishment of the republic, since its continued use symbolised for the majority of

---

[14] *Ibid.*, fo. 551.
[15] M. R., *Proposals to the Supreme Governours of the three Nations now assembled at Westminster* (London: R.C., 1653), p. 1.
[16] *Ibid.*, p. 11.

the populace willing subjection to the Norman yoke and, by extension, the bond between king and common lawyer.

The expression of discontent with the extant legal system, and the call for its replacement with a codified body of law – simplified, understandable to all and administered by untrained members of the local community – was sounded first by the radical democratic movements, the Diggers and the Levellers. In *Light Shining in Buckinghamshire*, the founder of the Diggers, Gerrard Winstanley, argued that '[t]he horsleech Lawyer cryes for a King, because else the supream power will come into the peoples Representatives lawfully elected, and so all Trials would be done in the country, in every Town etc. by the same Neighbourhood, and so the Law would no more be bought nor sold and then farewel caterpiller – Lawyer.'[17] He explains his unusual and memorable choice of metaphor, expanding it to elucidate fully the parasitic and destructive nature of the legal profession, 'which Lawyers are as profitable as magots in meat, and Caterpillers in Cabages, and Wolves amongst Lambs'.[18] The social and economic reforms proposed by Winstanley were revolutionary in intent. They sought to abolish the existing law of property, which governed the ownership of land in England. Instead, a written constitution would guarantee '[a] just portion for each man to live'. But his ingenious use of the literary image was as devastating as his proposed reforms, vividly portraying the monstrous nature of a tyrannical state, over which a corrupt magistrate governed.

Although *Light Shining in Buckinghamshire* was written in 1648, before the execution of the king, its political relevance is as a tract against absolute government, whether monarchic or republican. Of particular interest to the idea of law reform is Winstanley's insistence that the power of the law and lawyers derived from the illegal conquest and occupation of Britain by the Normans: 'William the Bastard sonne of Robert Duke of Normandy, with a mighty Army of his fellow-Tyrants and Theeves and Robbers enters Sussex, kils the inhabitants the Britains and their King . . . And all his tyrannical Lawes he caused to be in an Outlandish tongue.'[19] The image which Winstanley uses to depict the tyranny of absolute rule – the Beast – was not only familiar but provided the foundation of the political and theocratic philosophy of the Fifth Monarchists. Their core belief derived from the *Book of Daniel* in the Old Testament, and the association made between the four beasts of Daniel's vision and the four empires of the ancient world: Babylon, Persia, Greece and Rome. The execution of Charles I was the signal for the establishment of the Fifth Monarchy: the reign of King Jesus, ruling not in

---

[17] Winstanley, *Light Shining*, p. 5.   [18] *Ibid.*, p. 8.   [19] *Ibid.*, p. 7.

person but through his saints.[20] In the account of his vision, Daniel records that the fourth beast was different from the others. With its iron teeth and bronze claws it devoured and trampled everything in its path. This beast represented a kingly power, which was destined to be tried by a court, deprived of its sovereignty, destroyed and abolished, and its power ceded to the people of the saints (Daniel 7.15–28).

The unique hermeneutic contribution made by Winstanley to the interpretation of the bestial imagery of Daniel's vision concerns the horns on the head of the Beast. The largest of these 'had eyes and a mouth speaking proud words . . . As I still watched, that horn was waging war with the saints and overcoming them until the Ancient in Years came' (Daniel 7.20–21).[21] Winstanley is explicit in his claim that 'the Caterpillers Lawyers will prove the eyes' of the horn: instruments of the tyrannical government, 'and out of this rubbish stuffe are all our Creatures called Judges'.[22] It is noteworthy in connection with sumptuary legislation at the Inns of Court and the religious symbolism of legal costume, that Winstanley completely rejected the theory that the institutional iconography of the English legal profession represented the inherent divinity of common law. He drew the antithetical conclusion that legal robes and their accessories were idolatrous rather than iconic, demonstrating not the intrinsic truth and fairness of English law, but rather its inherent falsehood and tyranny. The corrupt legacy of its Norman provenance is exposed in the following attack on the vacuous ceremony of the legal institution:

> then their dread Tyrant, as he hath received power and dignity from the Dragon or Devil as aforesaid; doth shatter, breath out, and all-to-bedraggel them with it, with hairy skind Robes, resembling the subtle nasty Fox with his dirty tayl. And because the Lord Keeper, Privy Seal, and Treasurers long tails should not daggle in the dirt, they must have another Sycophant slave apeece to carry up for them with their hats off doing homage to their breech.[23]

John Warre made a similar observation in *The Corruption and Deficiency of the Lawes*, written in 1649: that corrupt laws are characterised by the obsequy, flattery and deference which subjects are obliged to show towards

---

[20] The Fifth Monarchists and the Rule of the Saints are discussed in A. Woolrych, *England Without a King, 1649–1660* (London: Methuen, 1983), pp. 16–26. For a more detailed account of millenarianism, see B. S. Capp, *The Fifth Monarchy Men: A Study in Seventeenth-Century English Millenarianism* (London: Faber & Faber, 1972).
[21] *The New English Bible* (London: Oxford University Press and Cambridge University Press, 1970), p. 1081.
[22] Winstanley, *Light Shining*, p. 8.
[23] *Ibid*. On Winstanley's belief that law is the 'declarative will of conquerors', see *The Works of Gerrard Winstanley*, ed. G. H. Sabine (Ithaca: Cornell University Press, 1941), p. 464.

the self-interest and worldliness of absolute rulers.[24] Warre was as forthright as Winstanley in levelling the accusation of corruption at common lawyers. He attributed their institutional ascendancy to two principal factors. First, and reiterating Winstanley's complaint, is the use of the Norman language in legal proceedings, making the law incomprehensible to and hidden from most English subjects. Warre makes the important observation that before the Norman conquest it was possible for a litigant to act as his own advocate without prejudicing his trial: the significance of this to the democratisation of English law was demonstrated by the trials for treason of John Lilburne in 1649 and 1653. Second, the centralisation of legal proceedings at Westminster, and the quarterly terms during which the courts sat, made it difficult if not impossible for the populace to attend cases and pursue litigation. Warre refers nostalgically to the pre-Norman, local system of justice, in which disputes between neighbours were resolved promptly and without recourse to lawyers. He suggests that when the courts and law terms were established at Westminster, but before the development of a distinct, secular legal profession, litigants from outside London would employ agents (usually articulate friends or neighbours), who would plead for them in court and lodge in London at inns. Warre claims that when the legal profession began its expansion and standardisation during the reign of Edward III, the hostels at which lawyers lived and learned retained the title of inns, but were elevated to the more honourable status of Inns of Court.[25]

Hill dedicates a chapter in *The World Turned Upside Down* to a discussion of Warre and his antipathy to common lawyers. In it he considers the radical and popular movement that proposed the abolition of an expert legal profession and the employment of tradesmen as ad hoc judges, arguing that the state and the legal institution existed in order to oppress the lower orders.[26] The principles of justice for which Warre eloquently argued had ramifications far beyond the narrow confines of the form of court proceedings. The expression of resentment at the monopoly exercised by the legal profession over the administration of justice, symbolised by its continued use of an archaic and exclusive foreign language, was a plea for all English subjects to have a louder voice in the government of the nation. In the evocative words of Trevelyan, it represented the 'plea of a lost birthright'.[27] The challenge thrown down by Warre, which in its broadest sense can be interpreted as a

---

[24] J. Warre, 'The Corruption and Deficiency of the Lawes of England Soberly Discovered: or Liberty Working up to Its Just Height', in D. Wootton (ed.), *Divine Right and Democracy: an Anthology of Political Writing in Stuart England* (London: Penguin, 1986), p. 151.
[25] *Ibid.*, pp. 160–1.
[26] 'John Warr and the Law', in C. Hill, *The World Turned Upside Down: Radical Ideas During the English Revolution* (London: Temple Smith, 1972), pp. 216–22.
[27] G. M. Trevelyan, *England Under the Stuarts* (London: Routledge, 2002 [1904]), p. 269.

demand for openness, accessibility and accountability of government, was eagerly accepted by the founder of the Levellers, John Lilburne. The ex-cloth dealer's apprentice, brewer, soldier and protégé of Cromwell had attended neither university nor the Inns of Court.[28] But this untrained lawyer of the populace was articulate, eloquent and thoroughly acquainted with the libertarian, constitutional arguments of Coke. He pointed the way towards a democratic state in which the people, rather than an absolute ruler or the elect of God, governed through their elected representatives. Like his *ex officio* mentor, Coke, Lilburne challenged contemporary, arbitrary legal practices with reference to the great constitutional charters. His first public insistence on the observance of legal forms took place in 1637, when, charged with sending scandalous books from Holland to England, he refused to take the High Commission oath. But it was his profound disappointment at the failure of the republican government to enact any of the constitutional proposals made by the army radicals in 1647 that provided the political background to his extraordinary, public demonstrations of dissent.

The origins of radical dissent in the army were traceable to the undertaking of Parliament in early 1647 to reduce the size of the army and pay them only part of their arrears. Soldiers organised themselves into a body opposed to Parliament, and expressed their grievances in documents such as *The Humble Petition of the Officers and Soldiers* (March 1647) and *The Book of Army Declarations* (September 1647). Unprecedented democratic aspirations were expressed in *The Heads of the Army Proposals* and *The Agreement of the People*, in particular with reference to regular elections to Parliament, the continuity of successive parliaments and liberty of worship. In the Putney Debates there had been open discussion concerning the extension of the franchise to all English subjects, regardless of their landed interests. At Putney a remark made by Commissary-General Ireton, in response to Colonel Rainsborough's suggestion that the poorest English subject had a right to consent to the government, highlighted the distinction between *lex* and *ius* that was to characterise much of the constitutional debate of 1649 and the 1650s. Ireton countered that if such a claim were recognised in law, it would entrench the primacy of natural right and negate the power of civil authority.[29] Lilburne sought to establish the absolute natural right to freedom of speech and conscience in a constitution that provided for a dissenting voice within the state, one that was not suppressed by the government. He perceived the actions of the Council of State to be as oppressive

---

[28] On the social backgrounds of Lilburne and the other leaders of the Levellers, see D. M. Wolfe, *Milton in the Puritan Revolution* (New York: T. Nelson, 1941), pp. 139–42; see also P. Gregg, *Free Born John: A Biography of John Lilburne* (London: Harrap, 1961).

[29] 'The Putney Debates: The Debate on the Franchise', in Wootton, *Divine Right and Democracy*, p. 286.

and unjust as those of the government that it had replaced. In a petition of 11 September 1648, Lilburne asked 'what was more incredible, than that a Parliament trusted by the people to deliver them from all kinds of oppression, and who made so liberal effusion of their bloud, and waste of their estates (upon pretense of doing thereof) should yet so soon as they were in power, oppress with the same kind of oppressions'?[30] For Lilburne, the Rump was the channel through which the decrees and determinations of the Council of State were conveyed to the populace.[31]

It is apparent that Lilburne had read several standard texts on constitutional jurisprudence, including St German's *Doctor and Student*. St German's theory of the primacy of eternal law and the law of reason can be equated with Lilburne's political philosophy. He was also influenced by the *Second Part of the Institutes* and in particular by Coke's interpretation of Magna Carta.[32] Coke provided Lilburne with his fundamental conception of statute law: that it must at all times be reasonable, or else it is liable to be declared void. Lilburne's appeal to conscience, custom and law was principled and unqualified. He spoke for natural law, divine in origin and imposing responsibility on rulers. Discussion of the democratic aspirations of Lilburne has tended to concentrate on comparisons with Cromwell. Gardiner, for example, regarded Cromwell rather than Lilburne as the archetypal Englishman. Other scholars have suggested that Lilburne rather than Cromwell was the articulate, guiding force for the democratic future of the English state.[33] Such comparisons tend to be glib and misleading, if only because Cromwell was concerned at a practical level wholly with the imperatives of government. After leaving the army, Lilburne devoted himself to dissent and asserting the illegality of arbitrary government power. As Woolrych has noted, the Levellers had no strategy for seizing power; indeed, they expressed great reservations about the use of force, being concerned principally with ideas and the reform of existing institutional forms.[34]

If a useful distinction between the two men can be made it is to refer us again to the difference between *lex* and *ius*. It is instructive to recall the definition provided by Hobbes in *A Dialogue between a Philosopher and a Student of the Common Laws of England*, in particular because he castigates

---

[30] J. Lilburne, *The Second Part of England's New-Chaines Discovered* (Thomason Tracts, E. 548 [16], 1649), p. 1.

[31] *Ibid.*, p. 12.

[32] See R. B. Seaberg, 'The Norman Conquest and the Common Law: The Levellers and the Argument from Continuity', *Historical Journal*, 24 (1981), 791–806.

[33] W. Haller and G. Davies (eds.), *The Leveller Tracts, 1647–1653* (New York: Columbia University Press, 1944), p. 2. For more recent discussion of the Levellers, see G. E. Aylmer, *The Levellers in the English Revolution* (London: Thames & Hudson, 1975); see also A. Sharp, *Political Ideas of the English Civil Wars, 1641–49* (London: Longman, 1983).

[34] Woolrych, *England Without a King*, p. 14.

Lilburne's source of constitutional jurisprudence, Coke, for failing to distinguish between them. The principal distinction made by Hobbes between *lex* and *ius* concerned the question of obligation: law obliges the subject to do, or to forbear to do something. Although he equates right with liberty, in Hobbes's restrictive interpretation it is a liberty only to do anything that the law does not forbid. The negative definition of right differentiates Hobbes's theory of law from the positive libertarianism of Coke, which asserted the legal status of fundamental rights.[35] Hobbes wrote *A Dialogue* in 1666 (it remained unpublished until 1681), with the memory of the momentous political upheaval of the Commonwealth and Protectorate years still fresh, and (for Hobbes) the certainty that powerful government was the only pragmatic alternative to anarchy. In it he confirmed the belief first expressed in his great work of constitutional and political theory, *Leviathan* (published in 1651), that right consists of the liberty to do or to omit to do whereas law determines the obedience of the subject because it creates a binding obligation upon him.[36]

The violence and political instability of the decade that preceded the publication of *Leviathan* undoubtedly contributed to Hobbes's pessimistic assessment of the natural condition of man as one in which all men were at war with each other. Accordingly, the life of man was 'solitary, poor, nasty, brutish, and short'.[37] It is probable also that the emergent themes of strong government and the failings of natural law were at least partly a response by Hobbes to the perceived threat to civil order posed by the Levellers. The prolific use of illegal pamphleteering had successfully disseminated their core philosophy that liberty of conscience and religious worship should be extended to liberty in the state.[38] Central to Hobbes's vision of political unity and order was the emergence in England of a Leviathan (the biblical monster of the deep, Job 3.8) who would impose order by strong leadership. Such leadership could vest in a republican governor as well as a monarch. In the state governed by Leviathan, the law was simply the will of the sovereign. He had the supreme power to make and repeal laws at will, freeing himself from subjection to particular laws by repealing them whenever such action was necessary or expedient.[39] The necessity for powerful government took precedence over

---

[35] T. Hobbes, *A Dialogue between a Philosopher and a Student of the Common Laws of England*, ed. J. Cropsey (London: University of Chicago Press, 1971), p. 73.
[36] T. Hobbes, *Leviathan*, ed. J. C. A. Gaskin (Oxford University Press, 1996), p. 86.
[37] *Ibid.*, p. 84.
[38] See D. Wootton, 'From Rebellion to Revolution: The Crisis of the Winter of 1642/3 and the Origins of Civil War Radicalism', *English Historical Review*, 105 (1990), 654–69.
[39] Hobbes, *Leviathan*, p. 176. On Hobbes, Harrington and the law, see G. Burgess, 'Repacifying the polity: the responses of Hobbes and Harrington to the "crisis of the common law"', in I. Gentles, J. Morrill and B. Worden (eds.), *Soldiers, Writers and Statesmen of the English Revolution* (Cambridge University Press, 1998), pp. 202–28.

the acknowledgement of individual conscience and its concomitant rights. The legal positivism espoused by Hobbes, according to which law was perceived as command rather than counsel and as the instrument of effective government power, was represented by a social contract in which the individual surrendered or renounced his natural state and acknowledged the authority of a sovereign power. Crucially, the sovereign was not contractually bound by such an arrangement, since the natural rights of the individual were surrendered unilaterally.[40] This coercive polity was incompatible with the equitable principles that Lilburne passionately defended, for which he was imprisoned intermittently during the 1640s and 50s.

Repeatedly throughout the Interregnum, the image of the sword was used by political theorists, politicians and dissident writers to represent a form of law that was far removed from the classical concept of *justitia*. Hobbes regarded as contrary to human nature the principles of justice, equity, modesty and mercy. He argued that the New Testament injunctions to love thy neighbour and to do unto others as we would be done unto ourselves were antithetical to natural passions such as pride and revenge. Accordingly, security could only be provided for all men if the fear of some external power lay behind such covenants. For Hobbes, law was indissolubly linked to the power of the sword.[41] Because it was not in the nature of man to act in a just and equitable manner, law must be imposed in order to enforce fairness. For Lilburne, if a particular law happened to impinge upon the fundamental liberty of the subject then equity and justice were outside the jurisdiction of positive law. As his associate William Walwyn had advised Lilburne in *Englands Lamentable Slaverie*, the liberty of men was guaranteed not by the law of England but by the law of nature.[42] In March 1647, while imprisoned in the Tower of London, Lilburne had written to Cromwell, insisting that the tyranny of Parliament as well as the tyranny of the monarch was resistible.[43] So it was predictable that under the Commonwealth he should regard the legal system as an instrument of the Norman yoke, oppressing the populace with the same vigour that it had under the Stuart kings.

Lilburne remained convinced that the only authority behind the republican government was the sword. Unlike Hobbes, who believed that power behind the law was the only means whereby the security of the state and of its subjects could be assured, Lilburne believed the exercise of such power to be illegal and tyrannical. It is curious that Hobbes should have used the image of a giant creature from the depths of the sea, as four years earlier Lilburne employed the same device in *Jonah's Cry*, composed while he was

---

[40] For a discussion of Hobbes and the origins of legal positivism, see I. Ward, *An Introduction to Critical Legal Theory* (London: Cavendish, 1998), pp. 79–86.
[41] Hobbes, *Leviathan*, p. 111.   [42] See Burgess, 'Repacifying the polity', p. 205.
[43] From *Jonah's Cry*, quoted in Haller and Davies, *Leveller Tracts*, p. 10.

imprisoned in the Tower in 1647. It is important to note that Lilburne felt the same moral imperative as Jonah to denounce injustice, fulfilling the divine injunction to '[g]o to the great city of Nineveh, go now and denounce it, for its wickedness stares me in the face' (Jonah 1.2). He cast himself in the role of the Old Testament prophet, who prayed for death and said to God 'I should be better dead than alive' (Jonah 4.8).[44] Lilburne showed a talent for self-dramatisation when he offered his life to his old friend, Cromwell, reminding him that he had once jokingly said that he would cut Lilburne's throat if he ever fell out with him.[45]

Although he was a devout man, Lilburne was not a religious zealot. It was precisely the quality of freethinking Protestant humanism, personified by Lilburne and his fellow Levellers, which posed a serious threat to the realisation of the rule of the saints. For example, the opinion of Richard Overton (imprisoned with Lilburne in the Tower) that '[t]he business is, not how great a sinner I am, but how faithfull and reall to the Common-wealth'[46] was not only a rejection of the theory of predestination, but also a tacit plea for a secular state, in which church and government were distinct and separate entities. Such a statement of intent was incompatible with the principle of government by godly men. As Cromwell was to observe of the Rump Parliament, 'they will destroy again, what the Lord hath done graciously for them and us; we all forget God, and God will forget us, and give us up to confusion'.[47] Lilburne had exclaimed, as he was whipped through the streets of London following conviction by the Court of High Commission, that 'I am cheerful and merry in the Lord.'[48] But he sought to separate the church and the state in the interests of liberty, as a letter to William Prynne, written in January 1644, demonstrated. Lilburne's extravagant use of the vernacular was a literary and oratorical device that he developed and exercised to great political effect in his subsequent tracts and public appearances. He suggested to Prynne that '[i]n your last Booke that you put out, you spend a great deale of paines in citing old rusty Authours, to prove that Kings, Councels, Synods and States have for so many hundred yeares medled with matters of Religion'; in so doing 'making the golden Lawes of Christ, to depend upon the leaden Lawes of man'.[49]

This letter is the first of many instances when Lilburne demonstrated an astute awareness of the political expediency of impending martyrdom, particularly if the martyr was a simple tradesman, unskilled in the labyrinthine complexities of the law, and if the court passing sentence was acting outside

---

[44] *New English Bible*, p. 1124–5.   [45] Haller and Davies, *Leveller Tracts*, p. 5.
[46] *Ibid.*, p. 22.   [47] Whitelocke, *Memorials*, fo. 549.
[48] Quoted in Wolfe, *Milton in the Puritan Revolution*, p. 141.
[49] J. Lilburne, *A Copie of a Letter Written by John Lilburne Lieut-Collonell. To Mr. William Prinne Esq*, 1644 (Thomason Tracts E. 24 [22]), p. 4.

its jurisdiction. He reminded Prynne of his own physical suffering at the hands of a tyrannical régime, '[y]ou have given away your ears & suffered as a busiebody in opposing the King and the Prelates', before willingly presenting Prynne with the opportunity to martyrise him: '[i]t may be instead of satisfying my desire, you'll run and complaine to the Parliament; and presse them upon their Covenant to take vengeance upon me, if you doe I weigh it not, for I blesse God I am fitted to doe, or suffer whatsoever the Parliament shall impose upon me.'[50] Lilburne shared with Prynne an extraordinary capacity for dramatising his suffering for the purpose of furthering his cause. Cromwell's fear of the disruptive power of the Levellers and their ready capacity to win public support can be inferred from his impassioned injunction to the Council of State in March 1649. On the occasion of Lilburne's appearance to answer charges following the publication of *The Second Part of Englands New-Chaines Discovered*, Cromwell insisted to the Council that it must break the Levellers or else be broken by them.

The popular image of Lilburne as a crowd-pleasing public performer derives to a great extent from his court appearances in 1649 and 1653, facing capital charges. Woolrych refers to his talent for playing to a large audience and to his apparent enjoyment at discomfiting the judges through his numerous procedural queries and consequent protraction of proceedings.[51] Opponents of Lilburne had noted his talent for publicising the cause of the Levellers with reference always to his personal condition, and mocked him for this perceived self-aggrandisement. In an anonymous letter written to Lilburne in September 1653 during his imprisonment at the Tower, the writer compared him to other rebellious populists. He predicted for Lilburne a similar fate to theirs: 'in our own histories you shall find that popular insurrections never raised their Ring-leaders above the gallows, as in Jack Straw, Cade and Wat Tyler'.[52] He favourably contrasts his own preference for anonymity to Lilburne's predilection for self-publicisation: '[f]or my name, I thought fit not to publish it, it being no part of my ambition to appear in print.'[53] He quotes from Lilburne's *The Upright Mans Vindication*, with the apparent intention of emphasising the crass appeal of Lilburne to a sentimental populace: 'with your party of *hobnails, clouted-shoes, private souldiers, leathern and wollen aprons*'.[54] But it was precisely this apparent sentimentality that ensured his popularity with a large portion of the populace who, like Lilburne, had not attended the universities or the Inns of Court. At his trial at

---

[50] *Ibid.*, p. 6.
[51] On the return of Lilburne to England in 1653 after his banishment in 1652, and his subsequent trial at the Old Bailey, see Woolrych, *Commonwealth to Protectorate*, pp. 250–9.
[52] Anon., *A Letter to Leiutenant Collonel John Lilburn now Prisoner in the Tower, Sept 8, 1653* (Thomason Tracts E. 712 [14]), p. 5.
[53] *Ibid.*, p. 8.   [54] *Ibid.*, p. 4.

the Guildhall in 1649, he deployed uncomplicated language with impeccable logic and clarity to defend the rights and liberties of English subjects. Prior to the creation of the English republic, the dissenting voice of constitutional reform had emerged invariably from the legal profession. This was either in its corporate capacity as the Inns of Court or through the oratorical, forensic and literary skills of individual members, of whom Coke was the archetype. It was a measure of the failure of the legal profession to offer sustained or effective resistance to the arbitrary actions of the republican government that the most potent voice of opposition should have come from Lilburne. His knowledge of law came exclusively from the selective reading of 'both old and new Laws, yea all of late that it was possible to buy or hear of'.[55]

The frontispiece of the published transcript of Lilburne's trial in 1649 is indicative of the nature of Lilburne's defence and its appeal to rights guaranteed as law by the Ancient Constitution. It portrays Lilburne, standing at the Bar, reading from a copy of Coke's *Institutes*. Above Lilburne's head are depicted the obverse and reverse sides of a coin. The obverse bears a profile of Lilburne's head, and around its perimeter is written: 'John Lilburne – Saved by the power of the Lord and the Integrity of his Jury who are juge of Law as wel as Fact, Oct. 26, 1649'. The reverse side carries the names of the jury, above which is the inscription, 'The names of the Iury. Of life and death'. Lilburne had questioned the authority of the judiciary with his provocative and inaccurate assertion that the jury was the judge of law as well as fact. He informed the bench that they were 'no more but Cifers', causing one of the judges to exclaim angrily, 'was there ever such a damnable blasphemous heresie as this is, to call the Judges of the Law Cifers?'[56]

Lilburne's favoured ploy as his own defence counsel was to question the legality of proceedings, both in court and at the time of arrest. He repeatedly stated that the administration of justice in the reign of Charles I had been exercised in a less arbitrary manner than it was under the republican régime. He constantly rejected the lawful authority of martial law when it was employed against civilian subjects. For example, at his arrest on 28 March 1649, when he was summoned to appear before the Council of State to answer charges relating to *The Second Part of Englands New-Chaines Discovered*, he complained that his house was surrounded by between a hundred and two hundred soldiers, consisting of both cavalry and infantry. He asked the arresting officer for evidence of his warrant, and was told that he had not brought it, whereupon Lilburne castigated the officer for failing to observe the rules of justice. In *The Picture of the Councel*

---

[55] Haller and Davies, *Leveller Tracts*, p. 196.
[56] *The Tryall Of Leiut. Colonell John Lilburne At the Guild-Hall of London (24 Oct 1649)* (London: T. Verax, 1649), p. 122.

of State, Lilburne records that following his objection, a platoon of foot soldiers rushed into the room. Lilburne asked their commanding officer to behave in a gentlemanly fashion and not to frighten his wife and children by the perpetration of 'incivilities'.[57] This episode from *The Picture of the Council of State* is instructive both in relation to Lilburne's literary and oratorical style and to the nature of the ideal constitution envisaged by him. With regard to the former, it is typical of Lilburne's disingenuous rhetorical style to demand exposition of authority for coercive actions taken in the name of the state, while simultaneously making a sentimental appeal to the humanity of a fellow subject. The de facto nature of military rule was repeatedly demonstrated during this period by the failure of individuals to withstand the force of arms, despite demanding by whose authority such force was empowered. A famous example was the seizure of the king by Cornet Joyce in June 1647. When asked by Charles what commission authorised him to take this action, Joyce pointed to his five hundred troopers, prompting Charles to reply that it was 'as well written as I have seen a commission in my life'.[58] A similar question was allegedly asked by William Prynne on the day of Pride's Purge, on 6 December 1648, when Colonel Pride and his soldiers debarred those MPs not considered favourable to the army's demands. Prynne received the same answer as Charles: his commission was the power of the sword. The Rump subsequently resolved that the House of Commons had the supreme power in the nation. Lilburne's signal contribution to the arguments over de facto and de iure government was to argue his case convincingly in legal tribunals, offering the evidence of the great constitutional charters such as Magna Carta and the Petition of Right in his attempt to elevate *ius* to the status of *lex*. But as this episode also demonstrated, he allied his knowledge of constitutional law to a depiction of himself as a simple man, subject to every human frailty and without the benefit of formal education. This was the crowd-pleasing, populist facet of his character that Cromwell recognised as a serious threat to the stability of government.

The Picture of the Council of State is not merely indicative of Lilburne's stylistic technique. It alludes also, albeit obliquely, to the ideal constitution proposed by the Levellers, in which a higher authority than the formal law of statutes and law reports was acknowledged. His reference to the protection of his wife and children, and to the possible 'incivilities' that might endanger them implies the existence of a moral or ethical code, to which all citizens should be subject, regardless of rank. The idea of *justitia*, or righteousness, as the governing factor in societal relations is one that

---

[57] Haller and Davies, *Leveller Tracts*, p.191.
[58] A notable account of the encounter between Charles I and Cornet Joyce is J. Holstun, *Ehud's Dagger: Class Struggle in the English Revolution* (London: Verso, 2000), pp. 3–8.

I have discussed, with particular reference to the Elizabethan legal profession. Lilburne constantly sought to establish the existence of a higher law, of divine provenance, to which the laws of earthly magistrates must defer. Although of strong religious convictions, he generally confined himself to the issue of secular relations between governor and governed, leaving metaphysical claims to freedom to associates such as William Walwyn, who rejected the Calvinist doctrine of predestination because it was incompatible with Christian liberty.[59] Walwyn's aim was the good of the commonwealth, not the communion of saints, and to this end 'more of the deeds of Christians, and fewer of the arguments would doe a greate deale more good to the establishment of those that stagger'.[60]

The existence of a higher authority than human law was suggested in *The Power of Love*, of which Walwyn was probably the author. In it he argues that 'I am not a preacher of the law, but of the gospell; nor are you under the law, but under grace.'[61] Indeed, in his trial at the Guildhall in 1649, Lilburne made use of the fact that he was not a lawyer, and therefore 'being no professed Lawyer, may through my own ignorance of the practick part of the Law . . . run my selfe with over-much hastinesse, in snares and dangers that I shall not easily get out of'.[62] He handled his defence skilfully, making extensive reference to 'the good old Lawes of England', reliance on which as a guarantee of his liberty was his 'Birth-right and Inheritance'. It was to the Ancient Constitution and its tenets of tradition, manners and honour that Lilburne appealed as the guarantor of his liberty, acclaiming Coke as 'that great Oracle of the Laws of England'.[63] With the single and honourable exception of Coke, he characterised the legal profession as the pliant instrument of tyranny. He accused William I of subduing 'that excellent Constitution, and instead thereof, introduced by His Will and Sword . . . the intolerable bondage of Westminster Hall, or Term Judges, and their Outlandish or Norman Law Practise in the French Tongue'.[64] Consequently, he unequivocally referred to his judges as 'no more than norman intruders'.[65]

The grounds for the charge of treason against Lilburne were that *The Second Part of Englands New-Chaines Discovered* vilified Parliament and the state, that it was intended to cause 'tumults, commotions and wars', and that it promoted division within the army. One of the judges, Lord Keeble,

---

[59] See J. Frank, *The Levellers. A History of the Writings of Three Seventeenth-century Social Democrats: John Lilburne, Richard Overton, William Walwyn* (Cambridge, Mass.: Harvard University Press, 1955).
[60] W. Walwyn, *Still and Soft Voyce*, quoted in Haller and Davies, *Leveller Tracts*, p. 22. There is an unabridged version of *Still and Soft Voyce* in Wolfe, *Milton in the Puritan Revolution*, pp. 365–74.
[61] W. Walwyn (attr.), *The Power of Love*, 1643 (Thomason Tracts E. 1206 [2]), p. 20.
[62] *Tryall of Lilburne*, 1649, p. 5.
[63] Ibid., pp. 3–4.   [64] Ibid., p. 20.   [65] Ibid., p. 122.

told Lilburne that 'if your intentions had taken effect, your plot was the greatest, that ever England saw, for it struck at no less then, the subversion of this Commonwealth'.[66] Despite the threat that the prosecuting authorities claimed Lilburne's writing posed to the state, the jury acquitted him, the foreman adding the equivocal comment: 'we are no Lawyers indeed my Lord'. On the one hand this remark was undoubtedly intended to reassure the bench that, contrary to Lilburne's claim, the jury were not judges of law as well as fact. Alternatively it can be taken to imply the existence of a higher authority than that exercised by the court, the supremacy of which no common lawyer could impugn. The popularity of the decision among the public bystanders in court was obvious: 'the whole multitude of People in the Hall, for joy of the Prisoners acquittal gave such a loud and unanimous shout, as is beleeved, was never heard in Yeeld-hall, which lasted for about halfe an hour without intermission: which made the Judges for fear, turn pale, and hang down their heads'.[67] It was a measure of the 'arbitrary waies' to which Lilburne was fundamentally and vociferously opposed that, despite his acquittal, Lilburne was escorted back to the Tower, from which he was released only by order of the Council of State, on 8 November 1649.

Lilburne had argued his case cogently, referring throughout to the ancient provenance of English law, and arguing that this genealogy implied constitutional superiority to the statutes of the 'norman intruders' and the decisions of their courts. He spoke with the authority of a lawyer in the language of ordinary people. Invoking the spirit of Coke, but discarding law-French and the Latin maxims to which the ex-Attorney General and Chief Justice was irresistibly drawn, he addressed the English nation in the English language on the subject of liberty. The Levellers failed to achieve their aim of constitutional and electoral reform, but even though the movement was destroyed, their ideas were not. Lilburne's impassioned plea for accountability and accessibility of government was, as Woolrych suggests, before its time.[68] That his libertarian objective failed was less important than that a lone voice spoke for freedom, dignity and the rule of law at a time when common lawyers and the legal institution were conspicuous by their silence.

THE DECLINE OF THE INNS AND THE FAILURE OF COMMON LAW

After the execution of the king in 1649, the records of the four Inns of Court suggest that the single most important reason for the unwillingness or inability of the legal profession to provide a corporate voice of dissent to the arbitrary actions of the government was the apparent diminution

---

[66] *Ibid.*, p. 148.   [67] *Ibid.*, p. 151.   [68] Woolrych, *England Without a King*, p. 14.

of independence and the growth in institutional ties between the Inns and prominent politicians. Inderwick argues that during the Interregnum, the majority of benchers at the Inner Temple were government officials of one sort or another.[69] At a Parliament of 9 February 1649, the governing body of the Middle Temple elected John Lisle, a Commissioner of the Great Seal (an office held also by Bulstrode Whitelocke, another member of the Middle Temple), to the bench of the Inn 'to Councell for the government of this House with the Masters in their Parliaments'.[70] The *Black Books* of Lincoln's Inn record that in May 1650 the Council of State imposed political conformity by ordering that a committee be set up by the Inn 'to make exact and effectuall search and scrutiny for the fyndinge out of all such persons . . . as have formerly bene sequestred, or bene adhereinge to the enemyes of the Parliament, or are otherwise justly to be suspected for the promoteing of any designe dangerous unto the Commonwealth'.[71] In February 1651, a new rite was created by the Inner Temple, whereby during commons all members present had to approach the bench table and there publicly 'take the engagement', swearing allegiance to the Commonwealth of England as it was then established, 'without a king or a house of lords'.[72]

The independence and autonomy of the four Inns were further compromised by the enforced payment of a tax specifically intended for funding the army. Until 1653, a fixed amount was payable by each Inn and tax was also levied on various commercial outlets rented to individual entrepreneurs by the Inns. For example, in January 1650 a shop belonging to the Middle Temple raised '[t]hirty-six shillings of Mercy Meigham, widow, for twelve months' tax for the Army of Lord Fairfax', and the treasurer's account for February 1652 records the payment of two pounds 'for payment of Parliament Army'.[73] In 1653 the commissioners for assessment for the army imposed a massive levy on the Inner and Middle Temple, of £100 per month, against which the two societies appealed on the grounds that they were 'like other Colledges and Societyes of learning'. Following the dissolution of Barebones Parliament in December 1653, the two temples petitioned the Lord Protector himself. A parliamentary committee of 1654 agreed with the argument made by the Inns that 'the study and profession of the lawes is as usefull to the publique and in the government of the Nacion as any of the artes or sciences studied or professed in the Universities'. The committee explicitly

---

[69] *Calendar of the Inner Temple Records*, ed. F. A. Inderwick, 5 vols. (London: H. Sotheran, 1896), II, introduction, p. cxi.
[70] *A Calendar of the Middle Temple Records*, ed. C. H. Hopwood, 4 vols. (London: Butterworth, 1903), I, p. 78.
[71] *The Black Books of Lincoln's Inn*, ed. J. D. Walker, 5 vols. (London: Lincoln's Inn, 1897), II, p. 386.
[72] *Inner Temple Records*, II, p. 297.   [73] *Middle Temple Records*, I, pp. 160, 163.

referred to the independence of the Inns, agreeing that they 'have their government intirely within themselves... a place distincte by itselfe and over and above and besides all London'.[74] Despite the acknowledgment by Parliament of the independence of the Inns of Court, overt criticism of government was not tolerated and was severely punished on the few, recorded occasions that it occurred. Three serjeants – Maynard, Twisden and Wadham Windham – were briefly imprisoned in 1655 for their conduct in *Cony's Case*. Twisden denounced Cromwell's use of arbitrary powers, denying the legality of his position as head of the Commonwealth. The three serjeants were incarcerated in the Tower, but were released soon after petitioning the Protector.[75]

Eminent lawyers in positions of political power openly interfered in the governance of the Inns. For example, Lord Chief Justice Rolle and Chief Baron Wilde gave express orders for the restoration of readings at the four Inns of Court, 'under a very great penalty on whomsoever shall fail therein'.[76] The readings and other educational exercises had fallen out of practice during the civil war years, as the Inns suffered a severe fall in admissions and existing members failed to attend commons. In February 1650, a Parliament of the Inner Temple, noting the importance of commons and exercises 'for the general good of this society and especially for the students', revived the custom 'under the usual penalties'.[77] In November 1652, the same Parliament attempted to enforce the orders of Rolle and Wilde by demanding that new benchers must deposit a sum of £50, returnable only if they completed a reading in hall 'or in default he may forbear to read'.[78] But the readings were never re-established as regular educational exercises, despite consistent attempts throughout the Interregnum to revive them. As late as November 1658, the *Black Books* record that 'Mr Recorder, Mr Prynn and Mr Williams, or any two of them, doe meete and treat with such as shalbee appoynted by the other Inns of Court, about reviveing of Readings.'[79] Prynne had been restored to the membership of Lincoln's Inn and his chamber in 1641, after his release from prison and by order of the House of Commons. He was elected bencher in 1648 and treasurer in 1657, and in November 1658 was 'discharged of all arrears due on the Preacher's Roll for such time as he was a prisoner'.[80]

The pragmatic truth, as Baker has noted in connection with the decline of learning exercises at the Inns during this period, was that the money exacted for not participating in the readings was of much greater importance

---

[74] *Inner Temple Records*, II, pp. 370–2, appendix XI. The Petition and the hearings of the subsequent parliamentary committee are in *A Calendar of State Papers Domestic* (1654), Commonwealth, lxvi, no. 5.
[75] *A Calendar of State Papers, Domestic* (1655), Commonwealth, xcvii, no. 48.
[76] *Inner Temple Records*, II, p. 289.   [77] *Ibid.*, p. 291.
[78] *Ibid.*, p. 304.   [79] *Black Books*, II, p. 422.   [80] *Ibid.*, p. 423.

to the maintenance of the Inns than the readings themselves. Baker goes on to note that where previously the readings had created a body of legal doctrine that prompted the decisions of the courts, the Inns of Court could no longer claim to be centres of legal authority. This role was now taken by the courts of justice, in which judges determined the meaning of law.[81] It was inevitable also that the increased textualisation of law and its ready accessibility in printed form should render obsolescent the continuation of oral exercises as the primary method by which knowledge of substantive law was acquired. The fines exacted from non-readers were crucial to the continued existence of the Inns. Admissions had declined drastically after 1641: the Middle Temple records indicate that, following the admission of fifty-eight members in 1640–1, admissions fell to a total of sixty-eight members for the period 1641–6, an annual average of fewer than fourteen new members. The decline in admissions continued after the civil war: thirty-eight in 1648–9, thirty-six in 1650–1 and only fifteen in 1651–2.[82]

Entries in the *Black Books* for the twelve months from November 1649 reveal the unprecedented financial hardship of Lincoln's Inn. Council of 19 November 1649 reported that 'Mr Doyly, a gentleman of the House, offers to lend £400 at 7 per cent. Accepted.'[83] A year later the situation had not improved, Council of 20 November 1650 noting that '[t]he servants of the Inn petition for some increase of wages. This cannot be granted, considering the present state of the revenue of the House.'[84] There was little if any reason to join one of the Inns of Court if learning exercises, commons and the associated rites were no longer practised there. The collegiate nature of the legal profession was imminently threatened if its communal activities ceased to operate. Throughout the sixteenth and early seventeenth centuries, the corporate structure of the Inns had facilitated the expansion of the legal profession and its recognition as an autonomous body of considerable political influence. Their only function otherwise was to provide board and lodgings to members. Consequently, compulsory commons was reinstated in April 1649: 'every one having a chamber or part of one to be in Commons one week in every Term'.[85] The punishment for continued non-attendance was forfeiture of chambers, although, demonstrating its reluctance to offend Parliament and its intention to gain favour there, Lincoln's Inn waived this rule for members who happened also to be MPs 'by reason of theire attendance uppon the publique service'.

---

[81] J. H. Baker, 'Why the History of English Law has not been Finished', *Cambridge Law Journal*, 59 (2000), 82. On the educational system at the early modern Inns of Court, see J. H. Baker, *The Third University of England: The Inns of Court and the Common Law Tradition* (London: Selden Society, 1990).
[82] *Middle Temple Records*, I, p. 167. [83] *Black Books*, II, p. 384.
[84] Ibid., p. 388. [85] *Middle Temple Records*, I, p. 78.

There was also a concerted attempt by the Inns to reinstate the traditional oral exercises undertaken by students, 'according to the auncient and laudable custome of this House and the example of other Inns of Court'.[86] Strict regulations were introduced by Gray's Inn, demanding that moots were to be 'performed' by inner-barristers 'without booke and every moote shall have its pleadings and it shalbe repeated without booke by him that bringeth in the case'.[87] The reintroduction of these ancient traditions appears to have had at least one noticeable effect on the collegiate fraternity of the Inns: between 1654 and 1657, at the petition of utter- and inner-barristers, the Parliament of the Middle Temple ordered that women and families must leave chambers in order that they could be inhabited exclusively by members of the Inn. This marked a genuine attempt to reinstate the masculine hegemony of the Elizabethan Inns, whose governing bodies had legislated for the creation of Neoplatonic academies of humanist learning, to which women were prevented access. Indeed, at the Middle Temple in 1654, the chambers of one Mr Jermin were seized 'for his entertaining strange women'.[88] Similar action was taken at Lincoln's Inn in 1657, when women were prohibited from lodging overnight within the Inn on the grounds of 'ancient Orders and customes' and because their presence offered 'too much opportunity to the gentlemen of the Society of using unfitting libertyes, without notice or controle'.[89] Such regulations reflected contemporary mores and the concomitant indivisible relationship between law and personal morality. They are indicative also of the continued male exclusivity at the Inns and of the depiction of women by the legal institution (in accordance with the doctrinal history of the sign) as vacuous images of falsehood and the antithesis of law.

The impact of the reimposition of traditional rites and practices on the number of admissions is difficult to assess. Membership of the Middle Temple increased from 1653 to 1658, but factors other than the internal government of the Inn might have been at least partly responsible. At the Middle Temple, from their lowest point of fifteen admissions in 1651–2, there was a slight increase to twenty-two in 1653–4. From the establishment of the Protectorate in 1653 until Oliver Cromwell's death in 1658 admissions increased drastically: between 1654 and 1658 the average number of annual admissions was just under sixty-two. These declined after Oliver's death and the accession of his son Richard to the title of Lord Protector. Forty-four members were admitted in 1658–9 and forty seven in 1659–60.[90]

---

[86] *Black Books*, II, pp. 386, 391.
[87] *The Pension Book of Gray's Inn*, ed. R. J. Fletcher, 2 vols. (London: Chiswick, 1901), I, p. 418.
[88] *Middle Temple Records*, I, pp. 85, 88, 91.   [89] *Black Books*, II, p. 418.
[90] *Middle Temple Records*, I, p. 167.

The single, most likely political factor to have favourably affected admissions at the Inns during the years of Oliver Cromwell's Protectorate was the triumph of conservatism over the forces of revolution. Hill ruefully observed that with the dissolution of Barebones Parliament, revolution had effectively ended; English propertied society had been saved by Cromwell.[91] Cromwell emphasised the primacy of property to his vision of English society in his speech on the first day of the new Parliament, 4 September 1654. His first reference was to 'the Danger of the levelling Principles ... The danger of that Spirit being not in the Nation, but in its preceding to a civil Transgression, when Men that come into such a Practice, as to tell us that Liberty and Property are not the badges of that Kingdom.'[92] The possible reasons for the failure of Barebones Parliament, and in particular the irreconcilable conflict between millenarians and constitutionalists, have been extensively explored by Woolrych in *Commonwealth to Protectorate*. His overriding theme is the effect of the tension between radical millenarianism and moderate constitutionalism on political groups and individuals, affecting the judgment and decisions of Cromwell himself as much as it did relations between the army and Parliament and within those institutions.[93] Hill refers to Cromwell's disillusionment after the failure of Barebones Parliament, and makes the important observation that he never again relinquished power to his parliaments.[94]

The significance to the Inns of Court of Cromwell's arrogation of power was that the influence of conservative lawyers in government (such as Whitelocke) was likely to mitigate the effect of demands for reform of the common law. Woolrych draws attention to the three distinct strands of law reformers in 1653. First, those who wished to retain the common law but make it more efficient; second, the radicals who wanted a simplified legal system administered by non-professional tribunals not subject to the 'Norman yoke'; and third, the millenarians who demanded the subjugation of earthly law to biblical edict.[95] The proposals on law reform, made by the Hale Commission in 1652, were not enacted by the Rump Parliament. Before its dissolution in December 1653, Barebones Parliament established several committees to consider the matter of law reform, one of which was intended 'to consider of the Laws, that hinder the Progress of the Gospel, and for repealing of them'. The possible consequences of this action posed an obvious threat to the autonomy of the legal profession, a threat that appeared to materialise on

---

[91] C. Hill, *God's Englishman: Oliver Cromwell and the English Revolution* (Harmondsworth: Penguin, 1972), p. 139.
[92] Whitelocke, *Memorials*, fo. 599.   [93] Woolrych, *Commonwealth to Protectorate*, p. 4.
[94] Hill, *God's Englishman*, p. 138. For a comprehensive analysis of political developments from 1653 to 1660, see B. Coward, *The Cromwellian Protectorate* (Manchester University Press, 2002).
[95] Woolrych, *Commonwealth to Protectorate*, p. 262.

3 November 1653, when a bill was 'committed for the taking away the High Court of Chancery'.[96] Only the dissolution of Parliament just over one month later prevented this revolutionary reform from becoming enacted in statute. The Court of Chancery remained a source of contention between reformers and common lawyers throughout the years of the Protectorate. Despite the endemic corruption and dilatory practices of the Court of Chancery, it was the only court in which the judiciary was able to exert its equitable influence in order to remedy injustice in the common law.

In historical terms, the jurisdiction of the Court of Chancery was independent from the king. The student of common law in Hobbes's *Dialogue* quotes Coke's explanation of the linguistic provenance of 'Chancellor': from *cancellando* – cancelling the letters patents of the king by striking through them like a lattice.[97] It is possible that the independent exercise of an authority to create rights and remedies in accordance with principles of justice was recognised by Cromwell as a threat to the unrestricted exercise of executive power, but it cannot seriously be argued that the Court of Chancery was not in need of reform. It was inefficient, and had been for many years prior to the Interregnum: Bacon and Coke had both admitted its inadequacies. It is noteworthy that when an ordinance concerning reform of the Court of Chancery was passed by the Lord Protector in 1655, common lawyers collectively opposed it, making a familiar appeal to the ancient authority of Magna Carta: '[t]he Commissioners and Master of the Rolls are by this Act of regulation made instrumental to deprive several Persons of their Freehold without Offence or legal Trial, which reflecting upon the Great Charter, and so many Acts of Parliament, they humbly desire they may have the Opinion of all the Judges of England in point of Law therein.' The judiciary rejected 'all the rest of the Articles, and Particulars of the new Ordinance touching the Chancery'. Whitelocke records that 'we proceeded in ordinary Business of the Court, according to the former Course'. The response of Cromwell to the collective disobedience of the judiciary reveals his reluctance to interfere with the traditional mechanisms of the legal institution when confronted with its unified opposition. Whitelocke reports that the Court of Chancery did not execute the new ordinance, 'which was inform'd to him, but he would not disturb us till the Term was over; and then he was quick with us for our Disobedience'.[98] Whitelocke and Widdrington were forced to resign as Commissioners of the Great Seal for their refusal to execute the ordinance, but the Court of Chancery continued to sit as normal.

---

[96] Whitelocke, *Memorials*, ff. 561, 568. On the attempt by the Barebones Parliament to abolish the Court of Chancery, see Woolrych, *Commonwealth to Protectorate*, pp. 295–8.
[97] Hobbes, *Dialogue between a Philosopher and a Student of the Common Laws*, p. 91.
[98] Whitelocke, *Memorials*, ff. 621, 624–6.

As Lord Protector Cromwell was reluctant to enforce change in the hereditary principles of English property law. Also, his apparent deference to the autonomy and independence of the legal profession, and the mitigating effect of conservative lawyers in positions of political influence contributed to the perception of landed families that their estates were no longer endangered by the reforming zeal of Levellers, millenarians or other radical groups. Following the disruption of the civil war, the stasis of the Rump and the ineptitude of Barebones Parliament, it appeared that stability and security had been restored under the Protectorate. Consequently the Inns of Court could once again be recognised as providing a useful and traditional foundation in management and local governance for the heirs to large estates. Cromwell's insistence to Parliament in September 1654 that 'there were some Things in the Government Fundamental, and could not be altered' was an affirmation of strong leadership. That a 'thing' of fundamental importance was the preservation of existing property rights provided reassurance to the gentry, and probably accounted for the drastic rise in annual admissions to the Inns of Court under the Protectorate of Oliver Cromwell.

The improved fortunes of the Inns of Court under the Protectorate were not reflected in their cultural and social activities, which had suffered immeasurably and irreversibly from prohibitions imposed by Parliament soon after the execution of the king. In November 1649 Parliament issued an order forbidding 'any publick Revelling or Gaming in any of the said Inns of Court or Chancery'.[99] In the same month, Council of Lincoln's Inn 'ordered that there should be no more Revills, Dancing nor Musique in the common Hall of this House, untill further Order taken'.[100] Similar austere injunctions applied to other aspects of collegiate existence at the Inns; at Lincoln's Inn students 'are not to expend above forty shillings in theire interteynements when they bring in theire Bar Moots, upon paine of being putt out of comons'.[101] The popular association (in particular among Presbyterian MPs) of the visual image with idolatry and the tyrannical excesses of the Caroline royal court militated against the traditional aesthetic of cultural activities at the Inns. The prohibition of revels (and the associated masques and dramas), dancing and music had as profound and deleterious an effect on the communality of the Inns as had the decline in readings and other oral learning exercises. The revels, and their frequent patronage by the monarch and the royal court, had facilitated a tacit relationship between the Inns of Court and the head of state whereby the legal profession had, by elliptical and allusory means, guided the direction of constitutional developments. Without such patronage, and the discreet means whereby political influence could be exerted over

---

[99] *Commons' Journal*, vi, fo. 327, in *Black Books*, II, p. 385.
[100] *Ibid.*, II, p. 385.   [101] *Ibid.*, II, p. 392.

a sovereign magistrate, the legal profession could no longer act effectively as a corporate restraint on the exercise of executive power.

The governance of the Elizabethan and Jacobean Inns was modelled on the ethical principles of freethinking, Neoplatonic humanism and was expressed to a great extent through the practice of sacramental rituals, of which the revels were arguably the dominant form. In chapter 3 I discussed the classical symbols that were incorporated into the action of the revels, and the eastern influences on the indigenous legal system. The use of ancient Greek mythology was a favourite device of the Elizabethan and Jacobean revels, intended to depict the indivisibility and coexistence of divine, natural and human law. The Aristotelian commonwealth, in which the individual was a *politikon zoon* or citizen of the state, actively involved in its governance, was re-enacted during the revels. Images of *justitia* combined with those of benevolent magistracy. The revels depicted a Utopian state that was republican, in the classical sense that political arrangements were directed to promote the good of the citizen body. While not anti-monarchical in subject matter, the masques and dramas performed at the Inns represented the king in accordance with Hooker's constitutional model, as *major singulis, universis minor*. Following the establishment of the English republic in 1649, these political sentiments were to prove unpopular both with royalist sympathisers and Puritan extremists.

The ideal of a mixed monarchy as proposed by Fortescue and St German was irreconcilable with the principle of rule by divine right. The archetypal apologist for the divine right of kings, following the execution of Charles I, was Robert Filmer. In *Observations upon Aristotle's Politiques*, Filmer dismissed the work of Plato, Aristotle and Cicero as the product of 'heathen authors, who were ignorant of the manner of the creation of the world'.[102] He traced the hereditary principle of monarchical government to 'the father of all flesh', Adam (an argument subsequently vilified by Locke in his *Two Treatises of Government*).[103] Filmer rebutted republican claims to government on the grounds that there was no biblical authority for the populace to govern itself or for it to choose its own governor. For him, the biblical commandment to honour thy father overrode the political and civic aspirations of the Aristotelian citizen.[104] Millenarians and other religious extremists also placed their trust in the primacy of biblical authority. In their case, they sought to introduce the rule of the elect by the innovative inauguration of a saintly order and the imposition of a religious commonwealth in which freedom of conscience and freedom of expression would not be tolerated.

[102] R. Filmer, 'Observations upon Aristotle's Politiques', in Wootton, *Divine Right and Democracy*, p. 110.
[103] On Locke's refutation of Filmer's theory, see Ward, *Critical Legal Theory*, p. 89.
[104] Filmer, 'Observations upon Aristotle's Politiques', p. 111.

According to the idiosyncratic interpretation of Daniel's vision by the Fifth Monarchists, the Greek and Roman empires (from which the myths enacted during the revels derived) were two of the four empires of which Daniel dreamt; their destruction was a necessary condition for the commencement of rule by the saints.

These models of government were incompatible with the humanist commonwealths of the Inns of Court and the utopian states represented in their revels. The enforcement by God's elect of a religious commonwealth, whose policies benefited only the saints themselves, was incommensurate with the principles of justice, ethics and individual liberty traditionally espoused by the Inns of Court. The quasi-civic governance of institutional existence at the Inns differed fundamentally from the oppressive acts of a powerful government such as that approved by Hobbes in *Leviathan*. Hobbes was emphatic that the teaching of classical texts at the universities (in particular those by Aristotle and Cicero) instilled in their students republican sentiments of the most violent kind. He raised the issue of the distinction between *lex* and *ius*, blaming the Athenians and the Romans for conferring on the word 'liberty' the status of civil rights and obligations. Specifically, he criticised the type of humanist education advocated by Elyot in *The Book Named the Governor*, in which classical writers provided the foundations for a range of subversive actions and opinions. In the opinion of Hobbes, the attribution to liberty of a spurious legal eminence was responsible for civil disorder and misplaced belief in the desirability of restricting the power of the sovereign.[105]

Attempts were made by the membership of the Inns to revive the revels before and during the Protectorate. The treasurer's accounts at the Middle Temple record that in February 1651, payment of 15s. 8d. was made for '[t]orches, staves, and candles for Revels in Michaelmas Term'. The same account for November 1652 notes payment of 10s. 0d. for '[r]evels, candles, Marshal's staff, white wands'. This was a rebuff to the order from Parliament, which explicitly forbade the practice of 'publick Revelling' at the Inns. No action was taken against the Middle Temple, and the accounts for February 1653 record payment of £20 to '[d]ancers and others, gratuity for instructing the gentlemen and for occasions of the House of that nature'. At the Inner Temple, between Easter 1654 and November 1655, the master of the revels was paid £6 on three separate occasions, by order of the bench.[106] During the first year of the Protectorate, the revels had been rehabilitated to the extent that the Middle Temple accounts note payment for '[m]usic in the Hall, six nights at 20s a night'.[107] Cromwell was well disposed towards

---

[105] Hobbes, *Leviathan*, p. 143.   [106] *Inner Temple Records*, II, p. 317.
[107] *Middle Temple Records*, I, pp. 162, 163, 164.

music, personally assisting the careers of musicians on several occasions.[108] His enthusiasm was such that in February 1657 a Committee for the Advancement of Music was appointed. The fortunes of musicians at the Inns revived during the Protectorate. William Saunders (one of the king's musicians after the Restoration) led a company of musicians at the Inner Temple in 1654. By 1656 '[u]pon the petition of the musicians for an augmentation of their allowance of 20s. a week, it is ordered they shall be allowed 4 nobles a night for their attendance.'[109]

The visual imagery that had been a central stylistic feature of the revels during the previous hundred years was firmly associated by their opponents either with pagan idolatry or the dissemination of libertarian, democratic dogma. It would anyway have been inexpedient for the Inns to present plays or masques after Parliament had passed ordinances against stage plays in 1642 and 1647, and in 1648 had banned actors from performing on stages.[110] There is evidence that some confusion existed as to the definition of a stage play, in particular, if music was a substantial component of the entertainment. A play with music, *The Countryman*, was performed in 1657 at the Inner Temple, and in 1658 at the Middle Temple (along with a work entitled *The Clown*, which received a second performance at the Middle Temple in 1659). It appears at least possible that *The Countryman* was acted by the regular musicians at the Inner Temple, thus conforming with the ordinance passed by Parliament against stage actors. The following entry exists in the records of the Inner Temple, which suggests that an inventive circumvention of the will of Parliament occurred: '[t]o the music for 5 November 1657, and their yearly fee, and acting "The Countrieman", 3li. 6s. 8d'.[111] The apparent revival of the theatrical traditions of the Inns was superficial and proved to be short-lived. With the death of Oliver Cromwell and the failure of the Protectorate under his son, Richard, Council of Lincoln's Inn legislated to the effect that '[i]n regard to the unsuitablenesse of mirth and jollitie to the condicion of this present time, it is thought fitt and ordered by the Masters of the Bench that for the future there shall be no musick in the Hall.'[112]

The use of allegorical drama or spectacle as a means whereby the regnant monarch could be influenced or criticised by the deployment of visual and verbal conceits developed throughout the reign of Elizabeth and attained

---

[108] See P. A. Scholes, *The Puritans and Music in England and New England. A Contribution to the Cultural History of Two Nations* (Oxford University Press, 1934); see also P. M. Young, *A History of British Music* (London: Ernest Benn, 1967).
[109] *Inner Temple Records*, II, pp. 313, 321.
[110] S. R. Gardiner, *History of the Great Civil War*, 4 vols. (London: Longmans, 1893), IV, p. 69.
[111] *Middle Temple Records*, I, p. 167; *Inner Temple Records*, II, p. 328.
[112] *Black Books*, II, p. 425.

unrivalled heights of complexity in the Jacobean Inns. Crucially, both Elizabeth I and James I had shown a level of respect for common lawyers and the legal profession to which Charles I never aspired. Elizabeth, more than any monarch before or since, reflected the visibility of power, commenting in 1586 that princes were 'set on stages in the sight and view of all the world'. James I, though less adept than his predecessor in the art of kingship, showed a serious interest in the cultural activities of the legal profession and its aesthetic representations of magistracy. Despite his differences with Coke over the legal limits to prerogative rule, James I was a regular guest at the Inns of Court. On these occasions many of the masques performed by members made a serious attempt to suggest ideal forms of governance, subject to the sovereignty of common law. As Russell fairly observes, it is inappropriate to attribute to James outright hostility to the English legal system when he depended on his Lord Chancellor (Egerton, later Lord Ellesmere) to explain the law to him.[113] But the idea of magistracy as an art form, and in particular a theatrical art form, suffered an irreversible decline under Charles I, as images of monarchy developed to represent the tyranny of absolute rule. The inherent sycophancy of *The Triumph of Peace* demonstrated the venality of the Inns of Court and their loss of genuine independence during the reign of Charles. After his death, doctrinal antipathy towards the visual image combined with the ascendancy of the written word to ensure that the text rather than the sign was the primary instrument of polemical discourse.

The disappearance of traditional ceremonial practices and cultural activities from the institutional life of the Inns was a crucial factor in the disintegration of a unified legal community. As might be expected during this period, the governing bodies of the Inns intervened in matters of religious worship, ensuring that preaching the word of God took precedence over sacramental rites. The *Black Books* report that in February 1654 'they will endeavour to have a minister to preach twice every Lord's Day in the terme'. In November 1656 the benchers of Lincoln's Inn 'are desired to inform John Thurlowe, Esq., Secretary of State to his Highness the Lord Protector, and one of the Masters of the Bench', explaining why the election of the preacher was postponed until the following term.[114] Deprived of the rituals that had defined the fraternal nature of legal community and its foundations in the ethical precepts of common law ideology, hall fulfilled only the utilitarian function of a dining room. Lacking the symbols of ancient fellowship that had signified and delineated the sacred precinct of common law, there was a commensurate increase in levels of disorder during commons. The *Pension*

---

[113] C. Russell, *The Causes of the English Civil War* (Oxford: Clarendon, 1990), p. 149.
[114] *Black Books*, II, pp. 402, 414–15.

Book of Gray's Inn records that in February 1655, '[t]he disorders in the hall being observed much more then in former times by throwing of bread, knocking and breaking of potts, refuseing to messe together'. Unruly conduct continued unabated, and in June 1658 the *Pension Book* again reports a collective refusal to obey the orders of the house relating to the ancient tradition of dining in messes of four members. The same entry notes disturbances to the service of food, the breaking of pots and the incompatibility of such conduct with 'civill societie, which ancient & good orders are not observed as in former times'.[115] The tone of these entries is valedictory: they lament the passing of a golden age and the subsequent descent into chaos, symbolised by the riotous behaviour described, and the consequent 'dishonour of the government' of the Inn.

The political sovereignty of common law was symbolised by its arcane rituals, representing divine origins and the sanctity of its practitioners. The appeal of such iconic rituals was emotional and imaginative, subjective rather than objective: binding the subject to obedience by reference to a symbolic father, God Almighty. In the absence of forensic evidence, appeals to the sovereignty of the Ancient Constitution depended on the acceptance by faith alone that its immemorial origins were genuine. The crisis for the Ancient Constitution during the period of the civil war and the Interregnum, as Burgess has noted, was in the development of rational (as opposed to emotional) arguments that assessed objectively the nature, success and suitability of real political structures.[116] In this respect the emotional power of the image could not compete with the rational supremacy of the word.

The parliamentary ordinances against stage plays and actors, and the disappearance of allegorical drama from the Inns of Court, did not succeed in eliminating dramatic works from public life. The dramatist and royalist, Sir William Davenant, compromised by straitened circumstances, offered his services to the Protectorate as a writer of propagandist drama, 'of which some use may be made'.[117] Davenant was closely associated with the Middle Temple. He wrote *The Triumph of the Prince D'Amour*, performed there for Charles I in 1635. He had shared lodgings with Edward Hyde (the future earl of Clarendon) at the Middle Temple in 1628, and remained on friendly terms with Bulstrode Whitelocke throughout his life. Whitelocke had been instrumental in his release from the Tower in 1652, and it was to Whitelocke that Davenant appealed in 1656 to license the performance of *The Siege of Rhodes* (which, like *The Countryman*, avoided the pejorative appellation of 'stage play' by its incorporation into the action of singing): '[w]hen I consider the nicety of the Times, I fear it may draw a Curtain between your

---

[115] *Pension Book*, I, pp. 414, 425.   [116] Burgess, 'Repacifying the polity', p. 204.
[117] A. Harbage, *Sir William Davenant, Poet Venturer, 1606–1668* (Philadelphia: University of Pennsylvania Press, 1935), p. 126.

Interregnum: lex, ius and de facto government 257

Lordship and our Opera, therefore I have presumed to send your Lordship, hot from the Press, what we mean to represent.'[118] The reliance of Davenant on friends in high office was clearly effective (the composer of the music for *The Siege of Rhodes*, Henry Lawes, was a friend and collaborator of Milton, who by now was a secretary to the Council of State), as the work was performed at Rutland House in September 1656.[119] Apart from the inclusion in it of probably the first woman to act professionally on the English stage (Mrs Coleman), the 'opera' was an undistinguished work. It demonstrated familiar xenophobic sentiments and antipathy towards non-Christian religions in lines of unremarkable verse, such as: 'Our Swords against proud Solyman we draw, His cursed Prophet, and his sensual Law.'[120]

Following the offer of his services as dramatic propagandist to the government of the Protectorate, Davenant's *The Cruelty of the Spaniards in Peru* was presented in July 1658 at the Cockpit in Drury Lane. Intending the piece to be a polemical attack against the Spaniards during the protracted naval and colonial war against Spain, he employed certain techniques that were familiar from the Jacobean masques at the Inns of Court, in which the foreigner, or other, is represented as the idolatrous mask of irrationality:

> What dark and distant Region bred
> For War that bearded Race,
> Whose ev'ry uncouth face
> We more than Death's cold visage dread?[121]

The Spanish soldiers indulge in cannibalistic practices, roasting members of the indigenous population on spits before eating them. Davenant describes them as 'beasts', a contemporary literary trope, suggesting the tyranny of absolute monarchy and its incompatibility with principles of justice and equitable governance. The work is episodic and, despite its theme, non-dramatic in style. The action was interrupted throughout by choruses, airs and dances. Its resemblance to the court masque was deliberate; in addition to the familiar stylistic devices, Davenant collaborated with renowned designers of scenery for these visual entertainments. The settings for *The Siege of Rhodes*, for example, were designed by John Webb, a protégé of Inigo Jones. Despite the artistic shortcomings of Davenant's work, which were manifest, the visual imagery of the masque form was anyway of less persuasive power during this period of increased textualisation than the rational argument of the printed word. In fairness to him, Davenant does make some appeal to

---

[118] Whitlelocke, *Memorials*, fo. 650.   [119] Harbage, *Sir William Davenant*, p. 245.
[120] W. Davenant, 'The Siege of Rhodes', *The Works of Sir William Davenant Kt.* (London: H. Herringman, 1673), fo. 3. For an assessment of Davenant's dramatic works and their relationship to contemporary political events, see J. L. Hotson, *The Commonwealth and Restoration Stage* (Cambridge, Mass.: Harvard University Press, 1928).
[121] Davenant, 'The Cruelty of the Spaniards in Peru', *Works*, fo. 109.

principles of justice and the coexistence of natural law and human law. With reference to the barbarity of the Spaniards in *The Cruelty of the Spaniards in Peru*, he poses the following question:

> If Man from sov'reign reason does derive
> Or'e Beasts a high prerogative,
> Why does he so himself behave,
> That Beasts appear to be
> More rational than he![122]

In works such as *The Tenure of Kings and Magistrates*, Milton had addressed similar issues of tyranny, governance and the sovereign reason of the citizenry. He had done so in an eloquent manner that Davenant could never match. But the demise of the theatrical image as a serious influence over constitutional and political developments was affected to a far greater extent by the textualisation of political philosophy. Works such as *Leviathan* appealed to reason, perceiving government as the means of effecting power, and law as the instrument of that power.

Of great relevance to the development of political theory during the Interregnum was the translation into English in 1640 of Machiavelli's *The Prince*, which subjugated the question of the legitimacy of a de facto ruler to the pragmatic necessity for strong government. Machiavelli cited Cesare Borgia, the efficient usurper and state reformer, who was accounted to be cruel but brought unity, order and obedience to the Romagna. The emphasis throughout *The Prince* on the art of warfare and the crucial importance to a ruler of its mastery has particular resonance when applied to Cromwell's military and political career. Machiavelli referred to Hiero of Syracuse, an ordinary citizen who became ruler of Syracuse. The Syracusans chose him as leader of their army, whereupon he disbanded the existing militia and created a new army. This action, combined with his destruction of former political alliances and the formation of new ones, provided the foundation for strong government.[123] The parallels with Cromwell's reorganisation of the army, giving him a firm base from which to launch his bid for executive power, are evident. Machiavelli rejected Aristotle's theory that the bonds of friendship formed the basis of stable civic existence. He argued that men would always break these bonds whenever it was advantageous for them to do so. Consequently, civil order could be imposed only by fear of punishment.[124] This theory was of course antithetical to the ideal commonwealth envisaged by the Levellers and the Diggers. In *The Power of Love*, for example, it was argued that men were governed not by human laws but by the embodiment of love, Jesus

---

[122] *Ibid.*, fo. 112.
[123] N. Machiavelli, *The Prince*, trans. G. Bull (London: Folio Society, 1970), p. 52.
[124] *Ibid.*, p. 91.

Christ. Winstanley also argued passionately for a commonwealth in which 'universal love unites not only mankind into an oneness, but unites all other creatures into a sweet harmony of willingness to preserve mankind'.[125]

Machiavelli's pragmatic theory of government was antithetical also to the humanist–classical traditions of the Inns of Court and the equitable principle of *justitia*, embodied in the iconography of common law. After the execution of the king, radical libertarian commentators cited Machiavelli as an archetype of unjust government. John Warre, for example, suggested that corrupt rulers act 'in a distinct way of opposition to the Rights and Freedomes of the People; all of which you may see in Machiavils Prince'. In the same pamphlet Warre argued that just government was 'seated in the People', using as authority for this claim the constitutional principle of Roman law: 'the Safety of the people is the supream Law'.[126] The appeal to ancient rights of the subject had obvious parallels with common law doctrine concerning the unassailability of the Ancient Constitution. Although Warre's constitutional theory was shared by the Levellers (in particular, his reference to the importance of elections in demonstrating the consent of the populace), his was not the dominant political theory of the 1650s. The two major Utopian works of that decade, *The Commonwealth of Oceana* by James Harrington and *A Holy Commonwealth* by Richard Baxter, both tended towards the Machiavellian idea of strong government.[127] Over the question of de iure and de facto government, Baxter argued pragmatically that where there was no legal magistrate, the wisest should govern on the basis of their natural aptitude rather than their right. He explicitly rejected the libertarian claim of the Levellers that the power of government derives originally from the people, asserting that the populace has no such power to create government.[128] Baxter fundamentally disagreed with Harrington over the particular form of government, criticising *Oceana* for its irreligious tone and for deriving its model of government from both heathen and popish exemplars.[129] Baxter was a fervent advocate of theocratic government by the saints, but he shared with Harrington the belief that the happiest commonwealth was one that most clearly attained the objectives of government.[130]

---

[125] G. Winstanley, 'A New-Yeers Gift for the Parliament and Armie', in Wootton, *Divine Right and Democracy*, p. 318.

[126] J. Warre, *The Priviledges of the People, or Principles of Common Right and Freedome asserted*, 1649 (Thomason Tracts E. 541 [12]), pp. 1, 8.

[127] On literary Utopias of the early modern period, see J. C. Davis, *Utopia and the Ideal Society: a study of English Utopian writing, 1516–1700* (Cambridge University Press, 1981).

[128] R. Baxter, *A Holy Commonwealth*, ed. W. Lamont (Cambridge University Press, 1994), p. 113.

[129] *Ibid.*, p. 135.

[130] *Ibid.*, p. 127. See N. H. Keeble and G. F. Nuttall (eds.), *Calendar of the Correspondence of Richard Baxter* (Oxford University Press, 1991).

As Pocock has noted, the republicanism of *Oceana* is Machiavellian rather than Platonic.[131] Harrington associates de iure government with the Aristotelian principle of the common interest of the people, memorably describing such a polity as the empire of laws, while de facto government represented the empire of men.[132] Like Cromwell, Harrington appreciated the central importance of land and its ownership to the stability of government, arguing that the system of 'agrarian' law was initiated by God Almighty, who divided the land of Canaan and distributed it between His people. That Cromwell, according to Hill, saved English landed society is explicable in terms of Harrington's prophecy that without agrarian law the duration of any form of government was necessarily limited.[133] *Oceana* is unusual among early modern Utopias in that it is set in England, but it is not the England of Coke, Hooker or Fortescue, in which the supreme magistrate was subject to the restraints of common law. As Burgess notes, Harrington's Machiavellian government of arms is incompatible with the Ancient Constitution and the government of laws.[134]

By 1654 the dissident opinions of the Levellers had been silenced and subsequent parliaments were dissolved for disagreeing with the policies of the Protectorate government. When MPs were barred from the House of Commons in September 1656 for their dissenting opinions, they published a Remonstrance, signed by Sir Arthur Hesilrige and ninety-seven others, stating that 'now he [Cromwell] hath assumed an absolute Arbitrary Sovereignty (as if he came down from the Throne of God) to create in himself, and his Confederates such Powers and Authorities, as must not be under the Cognizance of the Peoples Parliament'.[135] It is evident then that there was dissatisfaction with the arbitrary extremes of Cromwell's de facto government. As early as 1653, Whitelocke wrote that '[i]t was much wondered by some' that those summoned to become members of the Barebones Parliament should agree to 'take upon them the supreme Authority of this Nation; considering how little Authority Cromwell and his Officers had to give it, or these gentlemen to take it'.[136] In 1655, following Major Wildman's declaration of freedom 'against the Tyrant Oliver Cromwell', in which he called for the abolition of arbitrary powers and the recognition of the rights guaranteed by Magna Carta and the Petition of Right, Whitelocke noted that '[m]any who viewed this Declaration knew there was too much of Truth

---

[131] J. Harrington, *The Commonwealth of Oceana* and *A System of Politics*, ed. J. G. A. Pocock (Cambridge University Press, 1992), introduction, p. xv. On Harrington, see J. G. A. Pocock, *Politics, Language and Time: Essays on Political Thought and History* (London: Methuen, 1972); see also V. Sullivan, 'The Civic Humanist Portrait of Machiavelli's English Successors', *History of Political Thought*, 14 (1994), 73–96.
[132] Harrington, *Oceana*, pp. 8–9.   [133] *Ibid.*, p. 13.
[134] Burgess, 'Repacifying the polity', pp. 221–2.
[135] Whitelocke, *Memorials*, fo. 652.   [136] *Ibid.*, fo. 559.

Interregnum: lex, ius *and de facto government*   261

in it.' He stated that Cromwell suspected many of his former friends and advisers of plotting to restore the monarchy in order to guarantee 'a truly free Parliament'. Whitelocke admitted that Cromwell suspected him of such disloyalty, 'which was thought one main reason of his sending me out of the way to Swedland [as ambassador] and of his not taking me in to be of his Council'.[137]

Whitelocke's doubts concerning the legitimacy of Cromwell's rule reflect a career steeped in the freethinking, humanist traditions of the Inns of Court. For his generation of common lawyers, the legal positivism espoused by Hobbes, who declared categorically that the sovereign of a commonwealth was not subject to the constraints of civil law,[138] was irreconcilable with the appeals to conscience and custom made by St German. The coercive definition of *lex* and the negative interpretation of *ius* provided by Hobbes were incompatible with the suggestion of St German that 'in some cases it is necessary to leave the words of the Law, and to follow that Reason and Justice requireth'.[139] But the decline in the political and cultural influence of the Inns of Court deprived libertarians of a collective advocate for the Ancient Constitution and the natural rights and liberties of the subject, in defence of which previous generations of common lawyers had been outspoken champions.

Throughout the sixteenth and early seventeenth centuries, the legal community had created its own commonwealth at the four Inns of Court. In bricks and stone it built its city-states, attempting to reconstruct the civic republics of ancient Greece, guided by the idealism of Plato while acknowledging and honouring the Christian influence of St Augustine. *Justitia* was their guiding principle in the development of an unwritten constitution that recognised the fundamental liberties of the subject, and regulated conduct in the best interests of the commonwealth. In the Interregnum, the call by millenarians for enforcement of rule by the saints and for the saints was incompatible with humanist principles of intellectual freedom and broad religious tolerance. On the other hand, claims for the twin liberties of conscience and expression were irreconcilable also with the necessity for strong government. Their spokesmen were instinctively crushed by an increasingly intolerant government that perceived threats to its survival in every note of disagreement. In 1659, as the Restoration became imminent, the one great

---

[137] *Ibid.*, fo. 620. On the opposition of Wildman and other army officers to Cromwell's rule, see B. Taft, '*The Humble Petition of Several Colonels of the Army*: Causes, Character, and Results of Military Opposition to Cromwell's Protectorate', *The Huntington Library Quarterly*, 42 (1978), 15–41.
[138] Hobbes, *Leviathan*, p. 176.
[139] C. St German, *Two Dialogues in English, Between a Doctor of Divinity, and A Student in the Laws of England, of the Grounds of the said Laws, And of Conscience* (London: the Assigns of R. & E. Atkins, 1709), p. 53.

propagandist for the English Revolution, Milton, poignantly expressed his disappointment and disillusionment at the failure of the Commonwealth. If the example of the great architects of the common law had been followed, a genuine *Res Publica* might have succeeded. Instead, as Milton concedes, despite laying adequate foundations the edifice was ineptly constructed and never completed:

And what will they say of us, but scoffingly as of that foolish builder mentioned by our Saviour, who began to build a Tower, and was not able to finish it: where is this goodly tower of a Common-wealth which the English boasted they would build, to overshaddow kings and be another Rome in the west? The foundation indeed they laid gallantly, but fell into a worse confusion, not of tongues, but of factions, then those at the tower of Babel; and have left no memorial of their work behind them remaining'.[140]

---

[140] J. Milton, *The Readie & Easie Way To Establish a Free Commonwealth*, 1659 (Thomason Tracts E. 1016 [11]), p. 2. See *A Companion to Milton*, ed. T. N. Corns (Oxford: Blackwell, 2001); B. K. Lewalski, *The Life of John Milton: a Critical Biography* (Oxford: Blackwell, 2000).

CONCLUSION

The struggle between Liberty and Authority is the most conspicuous feature in the portions of history with which we are earliest familiar, particularly in that of Greece, Rome, and England.[1]

The discussion in *On Liberty* of the existence of individual rights, which protect the citizen from the actions of government, is a classic statement of liberal legalism. For Mill, right guarantees the sanctity of a private domain, to which the state has no access. But as Hobbes demonstrated in *Leviathan*, the proponents of legal positivism doubted not only the constitutional primacy of rights, but also the legal status of natural or fundamental right. Hobbes's definition of equity and justice as moral virtues rather than as rights enforceable in law emphasised their illusory nature.[2] While sharing Hobbes's scepticism concerning the existence of natural rights, ridiculing theories that propounded them as 'nonsense on stilts', Bentham perceptively noted that the capacity of common law to make use of the imaginary gave it its undeniable strength: the ability to encourage in the imagination of the subject a predisposition towards obedience.[3] Ward has observed in connection with the legal imagination that it is not only the precepts of natural law that are illusory and imaginary.[4] Sovereignty, the central conceptual tenet of legal positivism, implies the exercise of real political power, but the ability of a sovereign to impose legal order is similarly predicated on the encouragement of obedience in the political community. The exercise of sovereign power is subject therefore to the same attitudes and imagination that determine the acceptance or rejection of natural rights.

A central theme of this book is the representation of the conflicting imperatives of rights and sovereignty, embodied respectively by an expansionist,

---

[1] J. S. Mill, 'On Liberty', *On Liberty, Representative Government, The Subjection of Women* (Oxford University Press, 1963), p. 5.
[2] T. Hobbes, *Leviathan*, ed. J. C. A. Gaskin (Oxford University Press, 1996), p. 177.
[3] J. Bentham, *An Introduction to the Principles of Morals and Legislation* (London: Methuen, 1982), pp. 12–13.
[4] I. Ward, *Shakespeare and the Legal Imagination* (London: Butterworths, 1999), pp. 22–3.

politicised legal profession and a centralised, autocratic executive body. The creation by Henry VIII of the unitary sovereignty of church and state posed an institutional threat to the imaginary, libertarian safeguards of the Ancient Constitution. The arrogation to the king of spiritual supremacy was the inevitable precursor to the political theology of the divine right of kings: a monarch anointed by God and beyond the formal constraints of civil law. The legal profession was swift to recognise the threat posed by the absolutist tendencies of the Tudor monarchy to the historical and nationalist traditions of the common law.[5] As its institutional capacity expanded throughout the sixteenth century, the legal community gave visible shape and proportion to the illusory and fictive rights of the Ancient Constitution. It successfully exploited the imaginary quality of common law, constructing a political community that attempted to give form and shape to the invisible principles of justice. The governance of the Inns of Court during the sixteenth century replicated the terms of the social contract between magistrate and subject, in which the individual surrendered his natural rights in return for the benevolent government of a ruler who legislated in the best interests of the commonwealth.

The aesthetics of government that the early modern Inns of Court attempted, through their institutional *arcana*, to represent were located in an era of heightened political artifice, in which the medieval interpretation of symbolism as reality still prevailed. Each minute symbol of power was delineated to give form and substance to the idea of sovereignty. Thus at the coronation, according to Hooker, '[c]rowned we see they are, and enthronized, and anointed: the crown a sign of military, the throne, of sedentary and judiciall; the oil, of religion or sacred power.'[6] In a similar manner, the Elizabethan legal community at the Inns of Court attempted to elaborate and define its traditional symbols of institutional existence. The original of these was commons, at which the symbolic order of dining represented the oral tradition of common law and its inheritance from divine authority. The Word of God was eaten at a communal dinner and spoken in the various exercises undertaken in hall. The buildings and ornamentation of the legal community reflected the rational integration of classical and Christian philosophy: the coalescence of divine law, natural law and immemorial custom. The revels constructed a Utopian commonwealth, in which the ruler was counselled by learned advisers, or *amici principis*, whose function was to direct the polity of the idealised state in the best interests of the commonwealth.

---

[5] On the Tudors and the formulation of English absolutism, see G. Elton, 'Parliament', in C. Haigh (ed.), *The Reign of Elizabeth I* (Athens, Ga.: University of Georgia Press, 1987), pp. 79–100.

[6] R. Hooker, *Of the Laws of Ecclesiastical Polity*, ed. A. S. McGrade (Cambridge University Press, 1989), pp. 146–7.

The legal profession presented its own images of kingship in the various plays and masques performed at the Elizabethan and Jacobean Inns. Their explicit representation of limited monarchy, constrained by subjection to the common law, differed fundamentally from the images of providential monarchy presented by the royal court. Sumptuary legislation enacted by the Inns reflected the Protestant humanism of the early modern legal profession and its concern to create a standardised image of the common lawyer, emblematic of his sacerdotal role and the centrality of reason to the foundations of common law.

Although the successful reception of the images presented by the Inns during the early modern period depended on the subjective reaction of the individual, the singular development from medieval (and in particular ecclesiastical) iconography was the appeal made to reason rather than metaphysics. Opponents of the argument favouring the political sovereignty of a providential monarch were ultimately victorious. In an age in which the rational arguments of Plato, Aristotle and Cicero had been disseminated, assimilated and represented in the commonwealth of lawyers at the Inns of Court, claims to unlimited executive authority on the basis of divine providence were manifestly irrational. The regular attendance at the Inns of Court by Elizabeth I and James I signified a respect for the institutional practices of the common law and an astute awareness of the cultural and political influence of the legal profession. The presence of Elizabeth I at performances of polemical dramas such as *The Tragedie of Ferrex and Porrex* suggested the unprecedented confidence of the legal profession in addressing overtly the issues of sovereignty and misuse of the royal prerogative. The assertion by the legal profession of the supreme constitutional authority of the judiciary (represented in *The Masque of the Inner Temple and Gray's Inn*) led to the dismissal of Coke as Chief Justice in 1616, four years after the performance of this masque in the Banqueting House. In certain respects the legal profession of this period can be seen to anticipate Locke's idea of individual resistance to government, in particular by giving representation through the theatrical image to his conclusion that wherever law ends, tyranny begins.[7]

The organised opposition of common lawyers to the oppressive and arbitrary actions of the king was never more apparent than in the parliaments of the late 1620s. The lawyer MPs opposed to the king were arguing not only in favour of the liberty of the subject, and the right of the individual to freedom from forced loans and arbitrary trial and imprisonment: they were arguing publicly for the right to oppose the government without fear of reprisal. A significant development in the iconography of the

---

[7] J. Locke, *Two Treatises of Government* (London: Dent, 1989), pp. 190–219.

legal institution was marked in this period by the loss of independence by the Inns of Court. During the eleven years of personal rule by Charles I, it was perhaps inevitable that an embattled king should seek to reinforce the illusion of legitimacy and authority by gaining the support of the legal community. Consequently, he enacted numerous edicts which were concerned principally with religious conformity to the sacramental order of the Common Prayer Book, 'and in that manner administer the Sacrament of the Lord's Supper'. At all times, the king sought assurance 'that no one of those Houses will make use of any priveledge against government, civil or ecclesiasticall'.[8]

The enforcement of conformity with government policy was suggestive of a predisposition in the early Stuart kings to regard the legal profession as an ex officio ministry of the crown, and its senior members as lions under the throne. Hence in a proclamation concerning the form of readings at the Inns of Court during Lent, Charles I asserted that 'wee doubt not but all our subjectes, not ill affected to Government, will readilie and willinglie obey, and, most of all, those of yor Societies'.[9] Compliance was assured by the placement of prominent supporters of the government, such as Hyde, Noy and Finch, on the governing bodies of the Inns. With independence visibly compromised to such an extent, it was inevitable that the arcane rites of the legal community were no longer a viable means whereby dissent could be expressed. Furthermore, there was a growing perception in certain quarters that the visual image was indissolubly associated with the idolatry of a crypto-papist royal court. It was increasingly misappropriated by the Caroline court to represent an absolutist monarchy, whose favoured models were the autocratic régimes of continental Europe. Rational arguments in favour of a mixed monarchy, of the type envisaged by Fortescue and St German, were expressed by common lawyers in Parliament and, after its dissolution by Charles I, disseminated by means of printed pamphlets. The long association of the legal community with the political suggestibility of the visual image ended with the ascendancy of the printed word and the evolution of the House of Commons as a forum for debate, in which common lawyers predominated. The constitutional libertarianism expounded in Parliament by Coke had its intellectual foundations in the debate initiated by St German concerning the constitutional primacy of equity, conscience and reason. For the lawyer MPs of the 1620s the Aristotelian legal community,

---

[8] *The Black Books of Lincoln's Inn*, ed. J. D. Walker, 5 vols. (London: Lincoln's Inn, 1897), II, p. 314.
[9] *Ibid.*, p. 308. Identical letters were sent to the other Inns: see *The Pension Book of Gray's Inn*, ed. R. J. Fletcher, 2 vols. (London: Chiswick, 1901), I, pp. 313–14; *Calendar of the Inner Temple Records*, ed. F. A. Inderwick, 5 vols. (London: H. Sotheran, 1896), II, pp. 204–5.

as developed and regulated by the Elizabethan and Jacobean Inns of Court, served as a model for the government of English society.

The illusory nature of sovereignty was graphically illustrated by the trial and execution of Charles I. At his trial, the king presented an argument which suggested that sovereignty was absolute and unconditional: '[i]t is not for having Share in Government (Sirs) that is nothing pertaining to them, a Subject and a Sovereign are clean different Things.'[10] A few days later a scaffold was hastily erected outside the Banqueting House (whose ceiling had been painted in 1635 by Rubens, with images of divinely anointed kingship, at a cost to the Exchequer of £3,000).[11] The image of monarchical sovereignty was shattered, its illusory nature represented by the execution of a king. The maintenance of the precarious balance between sovereignty and rights was the single constitutional issue that determined the libertarian stance of many common lawyers throughout the late sixteenth and early seventeenth centuries. It was a balance that the Inns of Court had attempted to embody, by legislating for an ethical commonwealth in which reason was a central tenet of the body politic. In the English republic, the Rump claimed to derive its power from the populace and consequently assumed for itself supreme political authority. But, as Woolrych has noted, its depletion following Pride's Purge was so great that it could not seriously be regarded as representative of the people.[12] Its suppression of the Levellers and the protracted reluctance to call a general election demonstrated its innate anti-democratic tendency. The nominated assembly of 140 men from the regions of England, known as Barebones Parliament, represented an intention by Cromwell and the Council to create a parliament 'who should be as a Representative of the whole Nation' and a step towards an elected House of Commons.[13] Despite the religious zeal of some of its members, and their desire to introduce rule by the saints, the House acknowledged concern for the Commonwealth and its inability to achieve the necessary reforms for successful governance by resigning from Parliament after eight months and ceding power to Cromwell.

Cromwell's government was active in the suppression of dissent, but it has been persuasively argued by Woolrych and others that the government of the Protectorate was not a military tyranny. Cromwell consistently attempted to balance constitutional principles with the exigencies of strong government.[14] It was the perceived threat of anarchy rather than an aversion to

[10] B. Whitelocke, *Memorials of the English Affairs* (London: J. Tonson, 1732), fo. 375.
[11] R. Malcolm Smuts, *Court Culture and the Origins of a Royalist Tradition in Early Stuart England* (Philadelphia: University of Pennsylvania Press, 1999), p. 130.
[12] A. Woolrych, *Commonwealth to Protectorate* (London: Phoenix, 2000), p. 391.
[13] Whitelocke, *Memorials*, fo. 557.
[14] Woolrych, *Commonwealth to Protectorate*, pp. 391–8; see also, A. Woolrych, *England Without a King, 1649–1660* (London: Methuen, 1983), p. 31.

democracy that prompted Cromwell's fierce denouncement of the Levellers and the various sectarian, religious groups. A major difficulty in reconciling the government of the English Commonwealth during the Interregnum with the microcosmic commonwealths of the Inns of Court is that the republic did not emerge from a principled vision of the ideal republican state. It was brought about rather by the eventual awareness of the regicides that the only solution to the problems and dangers posed by a duplicitous and intractable monarch was to execute him. There was no precedent for government following the execution of a king and the abolition of the monarchy. Military dictatorship was the obvious de facto form of rule by which order could be imposed, but various changes to the form of governance during the Interregnum demonstrate reluctance to govern by force. Instead there is evidence of a tendency (sometimes thwarted by events or factions) to favour the constitutional government originally proposed by Fortescue in *The Governance of England*.

The Instrument of Government of 1653, by which Cromwell was formally recognised as Lord Protector, and the Humble Petition and Advice of 1657 provided a codified basis to the introduction of a *dominium politicum et regale*. The Instrument of Government took the unprecedented step of separating the powers of executive and legislature. It also imposed on the Lord Protector the obligation to govern with the advice of a council, consisting of twenty-one 'godly, able, and discreet Persons'.[15] The imposition of a council was intended to limit the sovereign power of the chief magistrate, and exactly replicates the advice offered by Sir Thomas Elyot in *The Book Named the Governor* that the prince should be surrounded by *amici principis*: Aristotelian 'friends' who counsel the sovereign. The constitutional principle of the king in Parliament, proposed by St German in *Doctor and Student*, was reflected in clause 6 of the Instrument, '[t]hat the Laws shall not be altered, suspended, abrogated or repealed, nor any new Law made, nor any Tax, Charge, or Imposition laid upon the People, but by common consent in Parliament.'[16] Clauses 7 and 8 guaranteed the existence of regular parliaments, to 'be summoned once in every third year', of at least five months' duration (unless Parliament itself consented to a shorter period).

The sovereignty of the common law in Parliament was further enhanced by the Humble Petition and Advice of 1657. Clause 6 provided that no laws were to be altered or repealed except by Act of Parliament, and clause 13 obliged the Protector to take an oath, swearing to govern according to the law. The constitutional supremacy of the common law maxim, *lex facit regem*, was thus given statutory authority. The significance to the legal institution of its flawless genealogy (the descent from perfect blood with which,

---

[15] Whitelocke, *Memorials*, fo. 571.   [16] *Ibid.*, fo. 571.

in *The Blazon of Gentrie*, Ferne associated the right to govern) was symbolised in the Humble Petition by the entrenchment of Cromwell's right to appoint his successor. Also, the creation of the 'other House of Parliament', similar to the abolished House of Lords, provided a visible structure for the common law traditions of ancient and distinguished provenance: there were sixty members, all of whom were nobles, knights or 'Gentlemen of ancient Families'.[17]

In an original draft of the Humble Petition, Parliament had offered Cromwell the title of king. He declined the offer, but at his inauguration as Lord Protector, the constitutional principle of mixed monarchy, by which government is conducted with the consent of Parliament, was enacted in emblematic form. It is of symbolic importance that Bulstrode Whitelocke, the common lawyer and constitutionalist, played an active part in the inauguration ceremony: '[a] Robe of Purple Velvet, lined with Ermin, which the Speaker assisted by me and others, put upon his Highness; then he deliver'd to him the Bible richly gilt and bossed; after that the Speaker girt the Sword about his Highness, and deliver'd into his hand the Scepter of massy Gold.'[18] Plots by royalists and Fifth Monarchists prompted the abandonment by Cromwell of parliamentary rule and the increased use of arbitrary powers. In February 1658, he dissolved Parliament, 'declaring several urgent and weighty Reasons, making it necessary for him, in order to the publick Peace and Safety'.[19] In April that year he wanted the plotters tried by special commissioners rather than a court of common law (Whitelocke refused to sit with the commissioners, 'it being against my Judgment'). These acts and others of an arbitrary, oppressive nature were motivated by the pragmatics of government during a period of political factionalism and national instability. But they do not diminish the relevance of common law ideology to the development of the constitution along lines originally proposed by Fortescue and St German. The Inns of Court had long since ceased to exert direct influence over the governance of the state, but the classical–humanist traditions of the legal community were pervasive. They can be detected in the various attempts during the Protectorate to formulate a balanced constitution, in which the imperatives of sovereignty were formally constrained by the authority of the common law in Parliament.

[17] *Ibid.*, fo. 665.   [18] *Ibid.*, fo. 662.   [19] *Ibid.*, fo. 673.

BIBLIOGRAPHY

Abbott, L. W., *Law Reporting in England, 1485–1585*, London: Athlone, 1973.
Ackroyd, P. *The Life of Thomas More*, London: Random House, 1998.
Adams, S. (ed.), *Leicester and the Court: Essays on Elizabethan Politics*, Manchester University Press, 2002.
Alberti, L. B., *Momus*, trans. S. Knight, Cambridge, Mass.: Harvard University Press, 2003.
Alciatus, A., *Emblemata*, Lugudini: M. Bonhomme, 1550.
Allibore, J. and Evans, D., *The Inns of Court*, ed. D. McCorquodale, London: Black Dog, 1996.
Anonymous, *Gesta Grayorum, or, the History of the Prince of Purpoole, Anno Domini, 1594*, London: W. Canning, 1688.
Anonymous, *Hic Mulier: or, The Man Woman: Being a Medicine to Cure the Coltish Disease of the Staggers in the Masculine-Feminine of our Times. Exprest in a briefe Declamation. Non omnes possumus omnes. Mistris, will thou be trim'd or truss'd?*, London: I.T., 1620.
Anonymous, *The History of the Troubles and Tryal of William Laud, Arch-Bishop of Canterbury*, London: R. Chiswell, 1695.
Anonymous, *A Letter to Leiutenant Collonel John Lilburne now Prisoner in the Tower, Sept 8, 1653*, Thomason Tracts E. 712[14].
Anonymous, *A Miracle: An Honest Broker, or, Reasons urging a more liberall Loane towards the maintenance of Religion, Law, and the Kingdomes safety in them Both*, London, 1642.
Anonymous, *The Tryall of Leiut. Colonell John Lilburne At the Guild-Hall of London (24 Oct 1649)*, London: T. Verax, 1649.
Aquinas, St Thomas, *Summa Theologica*, London: Burns, Oates & Washbourne, 1942.
Archer, M., 'Richard Butler, glass-painter', *The Burlington* (May 1990), 311–15.
Aristotle, *The Rhetoric of Aristotle*, trans. J. E. C. Welldon, London: Macmillan, 1886.
  Aristotle's Politics and Athenian Constitution, trans. J. Warrington, London: Dent, 1959.
Ashelford, J., *A Visual History of Costume: the Sixteenth Century*, London: Batsford, 1983.
Ashton, R., *Reformation and Revolution 1558–1660*, London: Paladin, 1985.
Aston, M., *England's Iconoclasts*, Oxford University Press, 1988.
Attridge, D. (ed.), *Acts of Literature*, New York: Routledge, 1992.
Augustine, St, *The City of God*, trans. J. Healey, London: Dent, 1931.

Aylmer, Bishop, *An Harborowe for Faithfull and Trewe Subjectes*, Strasborowe, 1559.
Aylmer, G. E., *The Levellers in the English Revolution*, London: Thames & Hudson, 1975.
Bacon, F., *New Atlantis. A Work Unfinished*, London: Macmillan, 1899.
Baker, J. H., 'History of the Gowns Worn at the English Bar', *Costume: The Journal of the Costume Society*, 9 (1975), 15–27.
  Manual of law-French, Amersham: Avebury, 1979.
  The Order of Serjeants at Law, London: Selden Society, 1984.
  The Third University of England: the Inns of Court and the Common Law Tradition, London: Selden Society, 1990.
  The Inner Temple: A Brief Historical Description, London: Inner Temple, 1991.
  'The Three Languages of the Common Law', *McGill Law Journal*, 43 (1998), 5–24.
  'Why the History of English Law Has Not Been Finished', *Cambridge Law Journal*, 59 (2000), 62–84.
Bakhtin, M., *Rabelais and His World*, trans. H. Iswolsky, Bloomington: Indiana University Press, 1984.
Barber, C., *Shakespeare's Festive Comedy: A Study of Dramatic Form and its Relation to Social Custom*, New Jersey: Princeton University Press, 1959.
Barker, E., *Essays in Civility: Eight Essays*, Cambridge University Press, 1948.
Baxter, R., *A Holy Commonwealth*, ed. W. Lamont, Cambridge University Press, 1994.
Beaumont, F., *The Masque of the Inner Temple and Gray's Inn, Presented Before His Maiestie in the Banquetting House at White-hall on Saturday the twentieth day of Februarie, 1612*, London: G. Norton, 1612.
Bentham, J., *An Introduction to the Principles of Morals and Legislation*, London: Methuen, 1982.
Berry, R., *Shakespeare and Social Class*, New Jersey: Humanities, 1988.
  Black Books of Lincoln's Inn, ed. J. D. Walker, 5 vols., London: Lincoln's Inn, 1897.
Blair, D. O. H. (ed.), *The Rule of our Most Holy Father Saint Benedict*, London: Burns & Oates, 1886.
Blakemore Evans, G. (ed.), *Elizabethan-Jacobean Drama*, London: A. & C. Black, 1987.
Bland, D. S., 'Rhetoric and the Law Student in Sixteenth Century England', *Studies in Philology*, 54 (1957), 498–508.
Blonsky, M. (ed.), *On Signs*, Baltimore: Johns Hopkins University Press, 1985.
Boas, F. S., *An Introduction to Tudor Drama*, Oxford: Clarendon, 1933.
Bone, Q., *Henrietta Maria: Queen of the Cavaliers*, Urbana: University of Illinois Press, 1972.
Borch-Jacobsen, M., *The Freudian Subject*, trans. C. Porter, Basingstoke: Macmillan, 1989.
Bossewell, J., *Workes of Armorie*, London: R. Tottel, 1572.
Brand, P., *The Origins of the English Legal Profession*, Oxford University Press, 1992.
Braun, W., *Feasting and Social Rhetoric in Luke 14*, Cambridge University Press, 1995.
Brooks, C. W., *Pettyfoggers and Vipers of the Commonwealth*, Cambridge University Press, 1986.

Brooks, P. and Gewirtz, P. (eds.), *Law's Stories*, New Haven: Yale University Press, 1996.
Browne, W., *Circe and Ulysses, The Inner Temple Masque, January 13, 1615*, ed. G. Jones, London: Golden Cockerel, 1954.
Bruster, D., *Drama and the Market in the Age of Shakespeare*, Cambridge University Press, 1992.
Buber, M., *Two Types of Faith*, London: Routledge & Kegan Paul, 1951.
Buc, G., *The Third Universitie of England*, London: Society of Stationers, 1615.
Burchell, G., Gordon, C. and Miller, P. (eds.), *The Foucault Effect: Studies in Governmental Rationality*, Hemel Hempstead: Harvester Wheatsheaf, 1991.
Burgess, G., *Absolute Monarchy and the Stuart Constitution*, New Haven: Yale University Press, 1996.
Burket, W., *Homo Necans: The Anthropology of Ancient Greek Sacrificial Ritual and Myth*, Berkeley: University of California Press, 1983.
Buxton, J., *Sir Philip Sidney and the English Renaissance*, London: Macmillan, 1987.
Camille, M., *Image on the Edge: The Margins of Medieval Art*, London: Reaktion, 1992.
Campbell, L. B., *Scenes and Machines on the English Stage during the Renaissance*, Cambridge University Press, 1923.
Capp, B. S., *The Fifth Monarchy Men: A Study in Seventeenth-Century English Millenarianism*, London: Faber & Faber, 1972.
Carlyle, R. W. and Carlyle, A. J., *A History of Mediaeval Political Theory in the West*, 6 vols., Edinburgh: Blackwood, 1903–36.
Carlyle, T., *Sartor Resartus*, London: Chapman & Hall, 1885.
Carroll, W., *Fat King, Lean Beggar: Representations of Poverty in the Age of Shakespeare*, Ithaca: Cornell University Press, 1995.
Carzo, D. and Jackson, B. S. (eds.), *Semiotics, Law and Social Science*, Liverpool Law Review, 1985.
Caudill, D. S., 'Freud and Critical Legal Studies: Contours of a Radical Socio-Legal Psychoanalysis', *Indiana Law Journal*, 66 (1991), 651–697.
Chapman, G., *The Memorable Maske of the two Honorable Houses or Inns of Court; the Middle Temple, and Lyncolns Inne. As it was performd before the King, at White-Hall on Shrove Munday at night, being the 15 of February 1613*, London: G. Norton, 1613.
Cicero, *The Republic*, trans. G. G. Hardingham, London: Bernard Quaritch, 1884.
  Brutus, trans. G. L. Hendrickson, London: William Heinemann, 1962.
Cochrane, C. N., *Christianity and Classical Culture*, New York: Oxford University Press, 1957.
Coke, E., *The Second Part of the Institutes of the Laws of England*, London: Flesher, 1642.
  The Third Part of the Institutes of the Laws of England, London: Flesher, 1644.
  The Reports, 7 vols., London: Rivington, 1777.
Collinson, P., *The Birthpangs of Protestant England: Religious and Cultural Change in the Sixteenth and Seventeenth Centuries*, London: Macmillan, 1988.
Corns, T. N., *Uncloistered Virtue: English Political Literature, 1640–1660*, Oxford: Clarendon, 1992.
  The Royal Image: Representations of Charles I, Cambridge University Press, 1999.
  (ed.), *A Companion to Milton*, Oxford: Blackwell, 2001.
Corns, T. N. and Loewenstein, D. (eds.), *The Emergence of Quaker Writing: Dissenting Literature in Seventeenth Century England*, London: Frank Cass, 1995.

Coward, B., *The Cromwellian Protectorate*, Manchester University Press, 2002.
Cowell, J., *The Interpreter; or Booke Containing the Signification of Words*, Cambridge: J. Legate, 1607.
  The Institutes of the Laws of England, Digested into the Method of the Civill or Imperiall Institutions, London: Roycroft, 1651.
Cox, L., *The Arte or Crafte of Rhetoryke*, London: R. Redman, 1529.
Cromartie, A., 'The Constitutionalist Revolution: The Transformation of Political Culture in Early Stuart England', *Past and Present*, 163 (1999), 76–120.
  'Theology and Politics in Richard Hooker's Thought', *History of Political Thought*, 21 (2000), 41–66.
Cust, R. P., *The Forced Loan and English Politics, 1626–1628*, Oxford: Clarendon, 1987.
Davenant, W., *The Works of Sir William Davenant Kt.*, London: H. Herringman, 1673.
Davies, J., *A Discourse of Law and Lawyers*, private circulation, 1876.
Davis, J. C., *Utopia and the Ideal Society: a study of English Utopian writing, 1516–1700*, Cambridge University Press, 1981.
Denning, A. T., *The Changing Law*, London: Stevens, 1953.
Doderidge, J., *The English Lawyer: Describing A Method for the managing of the Lawes of this Land*, London: I. More, 1631.
Dollimore, J. and Sinfield, A. (eds.), *Political Shakespeare: New Essays in Cultural Materialism*, Manchester University Press, 1985.
Douzinas, C., '*Whistler v. Ruskin*: Law's fear of images', *Art History*, 19 (1996), 353–69.
Douzinas, C. and Nead, L. (eds.), *Law and the Image: The Authority of Art and the Aesthetics of Law*, University of Chicago Press, 1999.
Downing, C., *A Discourse of the State Ecclesiasticall of this Kingdome in Relation to the Civill*, Oxford: Turner, 1634.
Dugdale, W., *Origines Juridiciales or Historical Memorials of the English Laws*, London: F. & T. Warren, 1666.
Dworkin, R., *Law's Empire*, London: Fontana, 1986.
Eden, K., *Hermeneutics and the Rhetorical Tradition*, New Haven: Yale University Press, 1997.
Eisenstein, E., *The Printing Press as an Agent of Change*, Cambridge University Press, 1980.
Elliott, G. R., 'Weirdness in *The Comedy of Errors*', *University of Toronto Quarterly*, 55 (1939), 95–106.
Elliott, J. H. and Brockliss, L. W. B. (eds.), *The World of the Favourite*, New Haven: Yale University Press, 1999.
Elton, G. R., *The Tudor Constitution, Documents and Commentary*, Cambridge University Press, 1960.
  England Under the Tudors, London: Routledge, 1991.
Elyot, T., *The Book Named the Governor*, London: Dent, 1962.
Epictetus, *The Discourses and Manual*, trans. P. E. Matheson, Oxford University Press, 1916.
Estienne, C., *De Dissectione partium corporis humani*, Paris, 1545.
Evans, D., 'The Inns of Court: Speculations on the Body of Law', *Arch-Text* 1 (1993), 5–24.
  'Theatre of Deferral: The Image of the Law and the Architecture of the Inns of Court', *Law and Critique*, 10 (1999), 1–25.

Eve, A. M. T. (Baron Sisloe), *The Peculiarities of the Temple*, London: The Estates Gazette Ltd, 1972.
Febvre, L. and Martin, H.-J., *The Coming of the Book*, London: New Left Books, 1976.
Ferne, J., *The Blazon of Gentrie*, London: Winder, 1586.
Finkelpearl, P. J., *John Marston of the Middle Temple: an Elizabethan dramatist in his social setting*, Cambridge, Mass.: Harvard University Press, 1969.
Fischer Taylor, K., *In the Theater of Criminal Justice*, New Jersey: Princeton University Press, 1993.
Fletcher, A., *The Outbreak of the English Civil War*, London: E. Arnold, 1981.
The Pension Book of Gray's Inn, ed. R. J. Fletcher, 2 vols., London: Chiswick, 1901.
Fortescue, J., *De Laudibus Legum Angliae*, ed. J. Selden, London: R. Gosling, 1737.
The Governance of England, ed. C. Plummer, Oxford: Clarendon, 1885.
Foucault, M., *The Use of Pleasure*, trans. R. Hurley, 2 vols., London: Penguin, 1987.
Discipline and Punish: the Birth of the Prison, trans. A. Sheridan, London: Penguin, 1991.
Aesthetics, Method, and Epistemology, trans. R. Hurley, 2 vols., London: Penguin, 1998.
Ethics, Subjectivity and Truth: Essential Works of Foucault, 1954–1984, ed. P. Rabinow, London: Penguin, 2000.
Fox, A. and Guy, J., *Reassessing the Henrician Age: Humanism, Politics and Reform 1500–1550*, Oxford: Blackwell, 1986.
Fox-Davies, A. C., *A Complete Guide to Heraldry*, London: Bracken, 1993.
Frank, J., *The Levellers. A History of the Writings of Three Seventeenth-century Social Democrats: John Lilburne, Richard Overton, William Walwyn*, Cambridge, Mass.: Harvard University Press, 1955.
Fraunce, A., *The Lawiers Logike, exemplifying the praecepts of logike by the practice of the common law*, London: How, 1588.
The Arcadian Rhetorike, Oxford: Blackwell, 1950.
Freedberg, D., *The Power of Images*, Chicago University Press, 1990.
Freud, S., *The Origins of Religion*, trans. J. Strachey, London: Penguin, 1990.
Fulbecke, W., *A Direction or Preparative to the Study of the Lawe Wherein is showed, what things ought to be observed and used of them that are addicted to the study of the Law*, London: T. Wight, 1600.
Fulke, W., *T. Stapleton and Martiall (Two Popish Heretics) Confuted and of their particular Heresies detected*, London: H. Middleton, 1580.
Furnivall, F. J. (ed.), *Early English Meals and Manners*, London: Bungay, 1868.
G., H., *The Mirrour of Maiestie: or, the Badges of Honour Conceitedly Emblazoned: with Emblems Annexed, Poetically Unfolded*, London: W. Jones, 1618.
G., I., D., W. and B., T., etc. [members of Gray's Inn], *The Maske of Flowers. Presented by the Gentlemen of Graies-Inne, at the Court of Whitehall, in the Banquetting House, upon Twelfe night 1613 . . . performed at the marriage of the right honourable the Earle of Somerset, and the Lady Francis daughter of the Earle of Suffolke, Lord Chamberlaine*, London: R. Wilson, 1614.
Gadamer, H.-G., *Truth and Method*, New York: Crossroad, 1988.
Gardiner, S. R., *History of the Great Civil War*, 4 vols., London: Longmans, 1893.
(ed.), *Constitutional Documents of the Puritan Revolution, 1625–1660*, Oxford University Press, 1906
History of England, 10 vols., New York: AMS, 1965.

Geminus, T., *Compendiosa totius anatomie delineatio*, London: J. Herfordie, 1545.
Gentles, I., Morrill, J. and Worden, B. (eds.), *Soldiers, Writers and Statesmen of the English Revolution*, Cambridge University Press, 1998.
Girard, R., *Violence and the Sacred*, trans. P. Gregory, Baltimore: Johns Hopkins University Press, 1977.
Goodrich, P., *Languages of Law: From Logics of Memory to Nomadic Masks*, London: Weidenfeld & Nicolson, 1990.
  'Eating Law: Commons, Common Land, Common Law', *The Journal of Legal History*, 12 (1991), 246–67.
  'Poor Illiterate Reason: History, Nationalism and Common Law', *Social and Legal Studies*, 1 (1992), 7–28.
  Oedipus Lex: Psychoanalysis, History, Law, Los Angeles: University of California Press, 1995.
  'Signs Taken for Wonders: Community, Identity, and A History of Sumptuary Law', *Law and Social Inquiry*, 23 (1998), 707–28.
Gould, T., *The Ancient Quarrel between Poetry and Philosophy*, New Jersey: Princeton University Press, 1990.
Grabar, A., *Christian Iconography*, New Jersey: Princeton University Press, 1968.
Graff, H. J., *The Legacies of Literacy*, Bloomington: Indiana University Press, 1987.
Green, M. A. E. (ed.), *Calendar of State Papers, Domestic, 1649–60*, 13 vols., London: Longman, 1875–6.
Greenblatt, S., *Renaissance Self-Fashioning: From More to Shakespeare*, University of Chicago Press, 1980.
  Shakespearean Negotiations: The Circulation of Social Energy in Renaissance England, Berkeley: University of California Press, 1988.
Greene, R., *A Quip for an Upstart Courtier*, London: I. Wolfe, 1592.
Gregg, P., *Free Born John: A Biography of John Lilburne*, London: Harrap, 1961.
Gregory of Nyssa, St, *Saint Gregory of Nyssa: Ascetical Works*, trans. V. W. Callahan, Washington, D.C.: Catholic University of America Press, 1966.
Grimal, P., *Dictionary of Classical Mythology*, ed. S. Kershaw, London: Penguin, 1991.
Gustafsson, H., '"As If": Behind Before The Law', *Law and Critique*, 7 (1996), 99–114.
Guy, J., *Christopher St. German On Chancery And Statute*, London: Selden Society, 1985.
  Reassessing the Henrician Age: Humanism, Politics and Reform 1500–1550, Oxford: Blackwell, 1986.
  Tudor England, Oxford University Press, 1990.
  (ed.), *The Reign of Elizabeth I: Court and Culture in the Last Decade*, Cambridge University Press, 1995.
  (ed.), *The Tudor Monarchy*, London: Arnold, 1997.
Hachamovitch, Y., 'The Ideal Object of Transmission: An essay on the faith which attaches to instruments (*de fide Instrumentorum*)', *Law and Critique*, 2 (1991), 85–101.
Haigh, C. (ed.), *The Reign of Elizabeth I*, Athens, Ga.: University of Georgia Press, 1987.
Haller, W. and Davies, G. (eds.), *The Leveller Tracts, 1647–1653*, New York: Columbia University Press, 1944.
Hammer, P., *The Polarisation of Elizabethan Politics: The Political Career of Robert Devereux, 2nd Earl of Essex, 1585–97*, Cambridge University Press, 1999.

Harbage, A., *Sir William Davenant, Poet Venturer, 1606–1668*, Philadelphia: University of Pennsylvania Press, 1935.
Harrington, J., *The Commonwealth of Oceana and A System of Politics*, ed. J. G. A. Pocock, Cambridge University Press, 1992.
Harris, H. S., *Hegel's Development Towards the Sunlight*, Oxford: Clarendon, 1972.
Hawkes, T., *Meaning by Shakespeare*, London: Routledge, 1992.
Hersey, G., *The Lost Meaning of Classical Architecture*, Cambridge, Mass.: MIT, 1988.
Hill, C., *Society and Puritanism in Pre-Revolutionary England*, London: Secker & Warburg, 1964.
  God's Englishman, Harmondsworth: Penguin, 1972.
  The World Turned Upside Down: Radical Ideas During the English Revolution, London: Temple Smith, 1972.
  Liberty Against the Law, London: Penguin, 1996.
  Intellectual Origins of the English Revolution Revisited, Oxford: Clarendon, 1997.
Hill, C. P., *Who's Who in Stuart Britain*, London: Shepheard-Walwyn, 1988.
Hobbes, T., *A Dialogue between a Philosopher and a Student of the Common Laws of England*, ed. J. Cropsey, London: University of Chicago Press, 1971.
  Leviathan, ed. J. C. A. Gaskin, Oxford University Press, 1996.
Hobday, C., 'Clouted shoon and leather aprons: Shakespeare and the egalitarian tradition', *Renaissance and Modern Studies*, 23 (1979), 63–78.
Holderness, G. (ed.), *Shakespeare: Out of Court*, London: Macmillan, 1990.
Holdsworth, W. S., *A History of English Law*, 17 vols., London: Methuen, 1924.
  Some Makers of English Law, Cambridge University Press, 1938.
Holstun, J., *Ehud's Dagger: Class Struggle in the English Revolution*, London: Verso, 2000.
Holt, J. C., *Magna Carta*, Cambridge University Press, 1992.
Homer, *The Odyssey*, trans. E. V. Rieu, Harmondsworth: Penguin, 1946.
  The Iliad, trans. E. V. Rieu, London: Methuen, 1953.
Hooker, R., *Of the Laws of Ecclesiastical Polity*, ed. A. S. McGrade, Cambridge University Press, 1989.
  Calendar of the Middle Temple Records, ed. C. H. Hopwood, 4 vols., London: Butterworth, 1903.
Horne, A., *The Mirrour of Justices: Written Originally in the Old French Long Before the Conquest*, trans. W. Hughes, New York: Augustus M. Kelley, 1968.
Hotson, J. L., *The Commonwealth and Restoration Stage*, Cambridge, Mass.: Harvard University Press, 1928.
  Shakespeare's Sonnets Dated, London: R. Hart-Davis, 1949.
Hughes, T., *Certaine Devises and shewes presented to her Maiestie by the Gentlemen of Grayes-Inne at her Highnesse Court in Greenwich, the twenty eighth day of Februarie in the thirtieth yeare of her Maiesties most happy Raigne*, London: R. Robinson, 1587.
Hull, N. E. H., 'The Romantic Realist: Art, Literature and the Enduring Legacy of Karl Llewellyn's "Jurisprudence"', *American Journal of Legal History*, 40 (1996), 115–45.
Hume, D., *A Treatise of Human Nature*, Oxford University Press, 1978.
Hunt, A., *Governance of the Consuming Passions: A History of Sumptuary Law*, Basingstoke: Macmillan, 1996.

Hutton, Sir R., *The Diary of Sir Richard Hutton, 1614–1639*, ed. W. R. Prest, London: Selden Society, 1991.
Hutton, R., *The Rise and Fall of Merry England*, Oxford University Press, 1994.
Calendar of The Inner Temple Records, ed. F. A. Inderwick, 5 vols., London: H. Sotheran, 1896.
Iser, W., *Staging Politics: The Lasting Impact of Shakespeare's Histories*, New York: Columbia University Press, 1993.
Jackson, B., *Law, Fact and Narrative Coherence*, Roby: Deborah Charles Press, 1988.
James, E. O., *Christian Myth and Ritual*, London: J. Murray, 1933.
James I, King of England, *Political Writings, King James VI and I*, ed. J. P. Sommerville, Cambridge University Press, 1994.
Jardine, L. and Stewart, A., *Hostage to Fortune: the Troubled Life of Francis Bacon, 1561–1626*, London: Phoenix, 1999.
Jenkins, E., *Elizabeth and Leicester*, London: Phoenix, 2002.
Proceedings in Parliament 1628, ed. R. C. Johnson, M. F. Keeler, M. Jansson Cole, and W. B. Bidwell, 6 vols., New Haven: Yale University Press, 1977–83.
Justinian, I., *The Digest of Justinian*, trans. C. H. Monro, 2 vols., Cambridge University Press, 1904.
Kafka, F., *Stories, 1904–1924*, trans. J. A. Underwood, London: Abacus, 1995.
Kant, I. *The Critique of Judgment*, ed. J. Meredith, Oxford: Clarendon, 1991.
Kant: Political Writings, ed. H. Reiss, Cambridge University Press, 1991.
Kantorowicz, E., *The King's Two Bodies: A Study in Medieval Political Theology*, New Jersey: Princeton University Press, 1957.
Selected Studies, New York: J. J. Augustin, 1965.
Calendar of the Correspondence of Richard Baxter, ed. N. H. Keeble and G. F. Nuttall, Oxford University Press, 1991.
Keeler, M. F., *The Long Parliament, 1640–1641: A Biographical Study of its Members*, Philadelphia: University of Pennsylvania Press, 1954.
Kelley, D. R., 'History, English Law and the Renaissance', *Past and Present*, 65 (1974), 25–51.
'Vera Philosophia: The Philosophical Significance of Renaissance Jurisprudence', *Journal of the History of Philosophy*, 14 (1976), 267–79.
The Human Measure, Cambridge, Mass.: Harvard University Press, 1990.
Kelly, J. M., *A Short History of Western Legal Theory*, Oxford: Clarendon, 1992.
Kernan, A., *Shakespeare, The King's Playwright: Theatre in the Stuart Court*, New Haven: Yale University Press, 1995.
Kerr, S. P., 'Shakespeare and Gray's Inn', *Graya*, 32 (1950), 99–107.
Kevelson, R., *The Law as a System of Signs*, New York: Plenum, 1988.
Klinck, D. R., '"This Other Eden": Lord Denning's Pastoral Vision', *Oxford Journal of Legal Studies* 14 (1994), 25–55.
Knowles, J. A., 'Stained Glass of Historic Interest in London', *The Journal of the British Society of Master Glass Painters*, 11 (1953), 135–47.
Kott, J., *Shakespeare: Our Contemporary*, London: Routledge, 1967.
Lacan, J., *Ecrits*, trans. A. Sheridan, London: Tavistock, 1977.
The Four Fundamental Concepts of Psychoanalysis, ed. R. Feldstein, B. Fink, M. Jaanus, New York: SUNY Press, 1995.
Lacey, R., *Robert, Earl of Essex: An Elizabethan Icarus*, London: Phoenix, 2001.
Lake, P., *Anglicans and Puritans? Presbyterianism and English Conformist Thought from Whitgift to Hooker*, London: Unwin Hyman, 1988.

Lake, P. (with Questier, M.), *The Antichrist's Lewd Hat: Protestants, Papists and Players in Post-Reformation England*, New Haven: Yale University Press, 2002.
Lambard, W., *Archeion or Discourse upon the High Courts of Justice in England*, London: Seile, 1591.
Leach, W., *A New Parliament or Representative for The perpetual Peace and quiet of this Nation*, London, 1651.
Legendre, P., *Le Désir politique de dieu: Étude sur les montages de l'état et du droit*, Paris: Fayard, 1989.
  Law and the Unconscious: A Legendre Reader, ed. P. Goodrich, Basingstoke: Macmillan, 1997.
Legh, G., *The Accedens of Armory*, London: R. Tottel, 1576.
Lewalski, B. K., *The Life of John Milton: a Critical Biography*, Oxford: Blackwell, 2000.
Lewer, D., *The Temple Church*, Andover: Pitkin, 1971.
Lewis, J. E., *Mary Queen of Scots: Romance and Nation*, London: Routledge, 1998.
Lieber, F., *Legal and Political Hermeneutics*, St. Louis: G. I. Jones, 1963.
Lilburne, J., *A Copie of a Letter Written by John Lilburne Lieut-Collonell. To Mr. William Prinne Esq*, 1644, Thomason Tracts E. 24[22].
  The Second Part of Englands New-Chaines Discovered, 1649, Thomason Tracts E. 548[16].
Lingis, A., *Excesses, Eros and Culture*, New York: SUNY Press, 1983.
Lissarague, F., *The Aesthetics of the Greek Banquet: Images of Wine and Ritual*, trans. A. Szegedy-Maszak, New Jersey: Princeton University Press, 1990.
Little, D., *Religion, Order, and Law: A Study in Pre-Revolutionary England*, Oxford: Blackwell, 1970.
Lockyer, R., *Buckingham: The Life and Political Career of George Villiers, First Duke of Buckingham, 1592–1628*, London: Longman, 1981.
Loftie, W. J., *The Inns of Court and Chancery*, Southampton: Ashford, 1985.
Locke, J., *Two Treatises of Government*, London: Dent, 1989.
MacEachern, C., *The Poetics of English Nationhood*, Cambridge University Press, 1996.
Machiavelli, N., *The Prince*, trans. G. Bull, London: Folio Society, 1970.
Macintyre, A., *After Virtue: a Study in Moral Theory*, London: Duckworth, 1981.
Maclean, I., *Interpretation and Meaning in the Renaissance*, Cambridge University Press, 1992.
MacNeil, W. P., 'Living On: Borderlines – Law/History', *Law and Critique*, 6 (1995), 167–91.
Maine, H., *Ancient Law*, London: Dent, 1917.
Maitland, F. W., *English Law and the Renaissance*, Cambridge University Press, 1901.
Major, J. M., *Sir Thomas Elyot and Renaissance Humanism*, Lincoln, Nebr.: University of Nebraska, 1964.
Malcolm Smuts, R., *Court Culture and the Origins of a Royalist Tradition in Early Stuart England*, Philadelphia: University of Pennsylvania Press, 1999.
Manderson, D., '*Statuta* v. Acts: Interpretation, Music, and Early English Legislation', *Yale Journal of Law & the Humanities*, 7 (1995), 317–66.
Manning, J., *The Emblem*, London: Reaktion, 2002.
Manningham, J., *The Diary of John Manningham of the Middle Temple*, London: Camden Society, 1858.

Marin, L., *Portrait of the King*, trans. M. M. Houle, Basingstoke: Macmillan, 1988.
Marston, J., *Histrio-Mastix Or, The Player whipt!*, London: T. Thorp, 1610.
Megarry, R., *Inns Ancient and Modern*, London: Selden Society, 1972.
Middleton, T., *The Inner-Temple Masque or Masque of Heroes. Presented (as an Entertainment for many worthy Ladies) By Gentlemen of the same Ancient and Noble House*, London: J. Browne, 1619.
Mill, J. S., *On Liberty, Representative Government, The Subjection of Women*, Oxford University Press, 1963.
Milton, J., *The Readie & Easie Way To Establish a Free Commonwealth*, 1659, Thomason Tracts E. 1016[11].
Mitchell, W. J. T., *On Narrative*, University of Chicago Press, 1980.
Montaigne, M., *The Complete Works of Montaigne*, trans. D. M. Frame, London: Hamish Hamilton, 1958.
Montrose, L., '"Shaping Fantasies": Figurations of Gender and Power in Elizabethan Culture', *Representations*, 1 (1983), 61–94.
More, T., *The Debellacyon of Salem and Bizance*, London: W. Rastell, 1533.
Tres Thomae, trans. P. E. Hallett, London: Burns, Oates & Washbourne, 1928.
Utopia, trans. P. Turner, Harmondsworth: Penguin, 1965.
The Yale Edition of the Complete Works of St. Thomas More, ed. L. A. Schuster, R. C. Marius, J. P. Lusardi, and R. J. Schoeck, 15 vols., New Haven: Yale University Press, 1973.
Morrill, J. S. (ed.), *Reactions to the Civil War*, London: Macmillan, 1982.
Morton, A. L., *The English Utopia*, London: Lawrence & Wishart, 1952.
Nairn, T., *The Enchanted Glass*, London: Radius, 1988.
The New English Bible, London: Oxford University Press and Cambridge University Press, 1970.
Nicephorus, *Discours contre les iconoclastes*, ed. and trans. M.-J. Mondzain-Baudinet, Paris: Klincksieck, 1989.
Nietzsche, F., *The Works of Friedrich Nietzsche*, trans. T. Common, 11 vols., London: Henry and Co., 1896.
The Birth of Tragedy, trans. W. A. Haussmann, Edinburgh: Foulis, 1909.
Beyond Good and Evil, trans. H. Zimmern, Edinburgh: Foulis, 1914.
The Genealogy of Morals, trans. W. Kaufmann and R. J. Hollingdale, New York: Random House, 1969.
Norton, T. and Sackville, T., *The Tragedie of Ferrex and Porrex shewed on stage before the Queenes Maiestie . . . the xviii day of Ianuarie 1561, by the gentlemen of the Inner Temple*, London: J. Daye, 1570.
Nussbaum, M., *Poetic Justice: the Literary Imagination and Public Life*, Boston, Mass.: Beacon, 1995.
Orr, D. Alan, *Treason and the State: Law, Politics and Ideology in the English Civil War*, Cambridge University Press, 2002.
Ovid, *Metamorphoses*, trans. M. M. Innes, Harmondsworth: Penguin, 1973.
Parker, R., *A Scholasticall Discourse against Symbolizing with Antichrist in Ceremonies: Especially in the sign of the Crosse*, London, 1607.
Peacham, H., *The Garden of Eloquence conteining the most excellent ornaments, exornations, flowers and forms of speech commonly called the figures of rhetorike*, London: H. Jackson, 1593.
The Compleat Gentleman, London, 1634.
The Gentleman's Exercise, London: I.T., 1634.

Peacock, J., 'Inigo Jones's Stage Architecture and its Sources', *Art Bulletin*, 64 (1982), 195–216.
Petherbridge, D., *The Quick and the Dead: Artists and Anatomy*, Manchester: Cornerhouse, 1997.
Pettitt, T., '"Here comes I, Jack Straw": English Folk Drama and Social Revolt', *Folklore*, 95 (1984), 3–20.
Phillips, W., *Studii Legalis Ratio or Directions for the Study of Law*, London: Kirkman, 1667.
Plant, R., *Hegel: On Religion and Philosophy*, London: Orion, 1997.
Plato, *Lysis, Symposium, Gorgias*, trans. W. R. M. Lamb, London: Heinemann, 1946.
   The Collected Dialogues, ed. E. Hamilton and H. Cairns, New Jersey: Princeton University Press, 1961.
   The Laws, trans. T. J. Saunders, Harmondsworth: Penguin, 1970.
   The Republic, trans. D. Lee, London: Penguin, 1987.
Pleij, H., *Dreaming of Cockaigne: Medieval Fantasies of the Perfect Life*, trans. D. Webb, New York: Columbia University Press, 2001.
Plowden, E., *Commentaries or Reports*, London: Brooke, 1816.
Plunket Barton, D., Benham, C. and Watt, F., *The Story of Our Inns of Court*, London: Foulis, 1924.
Pocock, J. G. A., *Politics, Language and Time: Essays on Political Thought and History*, London: Methuen, 1972.
   The Ancient Constitution and the Feudal Law: A Study of English Historical Thought in the Seventeenth Century, Cambridge University Press, 1987.
Pollock, F. and Maitland, F. W., *History of English Law*, 2 vols., Cambridge University Press, 1898.
Pottage, A., 'Recreating Difference', *Law and Critique*, 5 (1994), 131–147.
Prest, W. R., *The Inns of Court Under Elizabeth I and the Early Stuarts, 1590–1640*, London: Longman, 1972.
   The Rise of the Barristers: A Social History of the English Bar, 1590–1640, Oxford: Clarendon, 1991.
Prynne, W., *Histrio-Mastix: The Players Scourge or, Actors Tragedie*, London: M. Sparke, 1633.
   An Humble Remonstrance Against the Tax of Ship-money Lately Imposed, London: M. Sparke, 1643.
   Canterburies Doome; or the first part of a compleat history of the commitment, charge, tryall, condemnation, execution of William Laud, late Arch-bishop of Canterbury, London, 1646.
   Brief Animadversions on the Fourth Part of the Institutes of the Lawes of England, London: T. Ratcliffe, 1669.
Puttenham, G., *The Arte of English Poesie*, London: Field, 1589.
Pye, C., *The Regal Phantasm: Shakespeare and the Politics of Spectacle*, London: Routledge, 1990.
Quintilianus, M. F., *The Institutio Oratoria*, trans. H. E. Butler, New York: Loeb, 1920.
R., M., *Proposals to the Supreme Governours of the three Nations now assembled at Westminster*, London: R. C., 1653.
Rastall, W., *Collection in English of the Statutes now in force*, London: Deputies of C. Barker, 1594.
Rastell, J., *The Exposicions of the Terms of the Laws of England*, London: R. Totell, 1566.

Rawls, J., *A Theory of Justice*, Oxford University Press, 1971.
Ray, N., *Cambridge Architecture*, Cambridge University Press, 1994.
Read, P. P., *The Templars*, London: Phoenix, 2001.
Reyher, P., 'Le symbole du soleil dans la tragédie de Richard II', *Revue de l'enseignement des langues vivantes*, 40 (1923), 254–60.
Roper, W., *The Lyfe of Sir Thomas Moore, knighte*, Oxford University Press, 1935.
Rousseau, J.-J., *The Social Contract, and Discourses*, trans. G. D. H. Cole, London: Dent, 1973.
Roxburgh, R. F., 'Lawyers in the New Temple', *Law Quarterly Review*, 88 (1972), 414–30.
'Lincoln's Inns of the Fourteenth Century', *Law Quarterly Review*, 94 (1978), 363–82.
Runciman, S., *Byzantine Style and Civilisation*, Harmondsworth: Penguin, 1987.
Russell, C., *Parliaments and English Politics, 1621–1629*, Oxford University Press, 1979.
The Causes of the English Civil War, Oxford: Clarendon, 1990.
St German, C., *Two Dialogues in English, Between a Doctor of Divinity and a Student in the Laws of England, of the Grounds of the said Laws, and of Conscience*, London: the Assigns of R. & E. Atkins, 1709.
Scarisbrick, J. J., *Henry VIII*, Harmondsworth: Penguin, 1971.
Schoeck, R. J., 'Rhetoric and Law in Sixteenth Century England', *Studies in Philology*, 50 (1953), 110–27.
Scholes, P. A., *The Puritans and Music in England and New England. A contribution to the cultural history of two nations*, Oxford University Press, 1934.
Schroeder, J., 'Feminism Historicised: Medieval Misogynist Stereotypes in Contemporary Feminist Jurisprudence', *Iowa Law Review*, 75 (1990), 1135–217.
Scott, J., *Algernon Sidney and the English Republic, 1623–1677*, Cambridge University Press, 1988.
Seaberg, R. B., 'The Norman Conquest and the Common Law: the Levellers and the Argument from Continuity', *Historical Journal*, 24 (1981), 791–806.
Selden, J., *Titles of Honour*, London: W. Stansby, 1614.
The Reverse or Back-Face of the English Janus, trans. R. Westcot, London: T. Bassett & R. Chiswell, 1682.
Shakespeare, W., *A Midsummer Night's Dream*, ed. S. Wells, Harmondsworth: Penguin, 1967.
The Comedy of Errors, ed. S. Wells, Harmondsworth: Penguin, 1972.
Troilus and Cressida, ed. R. A. Foakes, London: Penguin, 1987.
Coriolanus, ed. G. R. Hibbard, London: Penguin, 1995.
Richard III, ed. E. A. J. Honigmann, London: Penguin, 1995.
Twelfth Night, ed. M. M. Mahood, London: Penguin, 1995.
The Second Part of King Henry the Sixth, ed. N. Sanders, London: Penguin, 1996.
Richard II, ed. S. Wells, London: Penguin, 1997.
Troilus and Cressida, ed. D. Bevington, Walton-on-Thames: T. Nelson, 1998.
Shapiro, B., 'Codification of the Laws in Seventeenth Century England', *Wisconsin Law Review*, (1974), 428–65.
Sharp, A., *Political Ideas of the English Civil Wars, 1641–49*, London: Longman, 1983.
Shirley, J., *The Triumph of Peace*, ed. E. Gosse, London: Fisher Unwin, 1904.
Shulman, G. M., *Radicalism and reverence, the political thought of Gerrard Winstanley*, Berkeley: University of California Press, 1989.

Sidney, A., *Sidney Papers, consisting of a Journal of the Earl of Leicester, and original letters by Algernon Sidney*, ed. R. W. Blencowe, London: J. Murray, 1825.
Sidney, P., *The Defense of Poesy*, Glasgow: R. Urie, 1752.
The Old Arcadia, ed. K. Duncan-Jones, Oxford University Press, 1985.
Simpson, P. and Bell, C. F., *Designs by Inigo Jones for Masques and Plays at Court*, Oxford University Press, 1924.
Simson, O. von, *The Gothic Cathedral: Origins of Gothic Architecture and the Medieval Concept of Order*, New Jersey: Princeton University Press, 1988.
Smith, T., *De Republica Anglorum*, Cambridge University Press, 1906.
Sommerville, J. P., *Royalists and Patriots: Politics and Ideology in England, 1603–1640*, Harlow: Pearson Education, 1999.
Sophocles, *The Three Theban Plays*, trans. R. Fagles, London: Penguin, 1984.
Spelman, H., *Of the Four Law Terms: A Discourse*, London: Gillyflower, 1684.
The English Works of Sir Henry Spelman, Kt., London: D. Browne, 1723.
Spencer, T., *Shakespeare and the Nature of Man*, New York: Macmillan, 1949.
Stewart, A., *Philip Sidney: a double life*, London: Pimlico, 2001.
Stone, L., *The Family, Sex and Marriage in England 1500–1800*, London: Penguin, 1979.
Stow, J., *The Survey of London*, London: N. Bourne, 1633.
Strachan, G., *Jesus The Master Builder*, Edinburgh: Floris, 1998.
Sullivan, V., 'The Civic Humanist Portrait of Machiavelli's English Successors', *History of Political Thought* 14 (1994), 73–96.
Summerson, J., *Architecture in Britain 1530–1830*, Harmondsworth: Penguin, 1953.
Tacitus, C., *Dialogus de Oratoribus*, trans. W. Peterson, Cambridge, Mass.: Harvard University Press, 1970.
Taft, B., 'The Humble Petition of Several Colonels of the Army: causes, character, and results of military opposition to Cromwell's protectorate', *The Huntington Library Quarterly*, 42 (1978), 15–41.
Tanner, J. R., *Constitutional Documents of the Reign of James I*, Cambridge University Press, 1930.
Tawney, R., *Religion and the Rise of Capitalism*, London: Penguin, 1990.
Thorne, S. E., *Sir Edward Coke, 1552–1952*, London: Bernard Quaritch, 1957.
Tillyard, E., *The Elizabethan World Picture*, Harmondsworth: Penguin, 1963.
Shakespeare's Problem Plays, London: Athlone, 1993.
Trevelyan, G. M., *England Under the Stuarts*, London: Routledge, 2002.
Trevor-Roper, H., *Archbishop Laud*, London: Phoenix, 2000.
Tubbs, J. W., *The Common Law Mind: Medieval and Early Modern Conceptions*, Baltimore: Johns Hopkins University Press, 2000.
Tuck, A., *Richard II and the English Nobility*, London: Edward Arnold, 1973.
Underdown, D., *Revel, Riot and Rebellion: Popular Politics and Culture in England 1603–1660*, Oxford University Press, 1987.
Verene, D. P., *The New Art of Autobiography: An Essay on the Life of Giambattista Vico Written by Himself*, Oxford: Clarendon, 1991.
Vesalius, A., *De humani corporis fabrica librorum epitome*, Basle, 1543.
Vickers, B. W., *In Defence of Rhetoric*, Oxford University Press, 1988.
Vico, G., *La Scienza nuova seconda*, trans. T. G. Bergin and M. H. Fisch, Ithaca: Cornell University Press, 1948.
Visser, M., *The Rituals of Dinner: the Origins, Evolution, Eccentricities, and Meaning of Table Manners*, Toronto: HarperCollins, 1991.

Walker, S. Sheridan, *Wife and Widow in Medieval England*, Ann Arbor: University of Michigan Press, 1993.
Walwyh, W. (attr.), *The Power of Love*, 1643, Thomason Tracts E. 1206[2].
Ward, I., 'A Kantian (Re)turn: Aesthetics, Postmodernism and Law', *Law and Critique* 6, (1995), 257–71.
  Law and Literature, Cambridge University Press, 1995.
  'A Kingdom for a Stage, Princes to Act: Shakespeare and the Art of Government', *Law and Critique* 8 (1997), 189–213.
  Kantianism, Postmodernism and Critical Legal Thought, Dordrecht: Kluwer, 1997.
  An Introduction to Critical Legal Theory, London: Cavendish, 1998.
  Shakespeare and the Legal Imagination, London: Butterworths, 1999.
  A State of Mind? The English Constitution and the Popular Imagination, Stroud: Sutton, 2000.
Warre, J., *The Priviledges of the People, or Principles of Common Right and Freedome asserted*, 1649, Thomason Tracts E. 541[12].
Warrington, R. and Douzinas, C., 'The Trials of Law and Literature', *Law and Critique* 6 (1995), 135–165.
Waterhouse, E., *A Commentary On That Nervous Treatise De Laudibus Legum Angliae*, London, 1663.
Watkins, S., *Mary Queen of Scots*, London: Thames & Hudson, 2001.
Weber, M., *The Protestant Ethic and the Spirit of Capitalism*, trans. T. Parsons, London: Allen & Unwin, 1930.
Welsford, E., *The Court Masque: a Study in the Relationship between Poetry and the Revels*, Cambridge University Press, 1927.
Wendorf, R., *The Elements of Life: Biography and Portrait-Painting in Stuart and Georgian England*, Oxford: Clarendon, 2002.
White, H., *The Content of the Form: Narrative Discourse and Historical Representation*, Baltimore: Johns Hopkins University Press, 1987.
White, J., *Heracles' Bow: Essays on the Rhetoric and Poetics of Law*, Madison: University of Wisconsin Press, 1985.
Whitelocke, B., *Memorials of the English Affairs*, London: J. Tonson, 1732.
Wigfall Green, A., *The Inns of Court and Early English Drama*, New Haven: Yale University Press, 1931.
Wilkes, W., *Obedience or Ecclesiasticall Union*, London: G. Elde, for R. Jackson, 1605.
Wilson, D., *Sweet Robin. Robert Dudley: Earl of Leicester 1533–1588*, London: Alison & Busby, 1997.
Wilson, T., *The Art of Rhetorique*, London: G. Robinson, 1585.
  'The State of England, Anno Dom. 1600', ed. F. J. Fisher, *The Camden Miscellany*, 16 (1936), 1–47.
Winstanley, G., *Light Shining in Buckinghamshire*, 1648, Thomason Tracts E. 475[11].
  The Works of Gerrard Winstanley, ed. G. H. Sabine, Ithaca: Cornell University Press, 1941.
Wolfe, D. M. *Milton in the Puritan Revolution*, New York: T. Nelson, 1941.
Wood, R. C., *The Sociology of the Meal*, Edinburgh University Press, 1995.
Woolrych, A., *England Without a King, 1649–1660*, London: Methuen, 1983.
  Commonwealth to Protectorate, London: Phoenix, 2000.

Wootton, D. (ed.), *Divine Right and Democracy: an Anthology of Political Writing in Stuart England*, London: Penguin, 1986.
 'From Rebellion to Revolution: The Crisis of the Winter of 1642/3 and the Origins of Civil War Radicalism', *English Historical Review*, 105 (1990), 654–69.
Worden, B., *The Rump Parliament 1648–1653*, Cambridge University Press, 1972.
Wrightson, K., *English Society, 1580–1680*, London: Routledge, 1982.
Young, P. M., *A History of British Music*, London: Ernest Benn, 1967.

INDEX

anatomy 54, 55–9
  Banister, John 55–6
  da Vinci, Leonardo 57
  Calvin's Case 57–8
Ancient Constitution 3, 8, 37, 44, 55, 61, 63, 90, 124, 135, 156, 160, 170, 176, 241, 243, 256, 259, 261, 264
Anselm, St 142
antiquity, classical 22, 47, 51, 86, 100, 129, 143, 252
  care of the self 170–1, 172, 176
  control of representations 171–2
  sacrifice 14, 99–100
  temples 61, 139
  theatre 33–4, 209, 210
Aquinas, St Thomas 142, 194
Aristotle 4, 35, 52, 73, 80, 81, 82, 159, 187, 189, 206, 252, 253
Arthur, King 105, 136–7
Augustine, St 45, 46, 80, 209, 261
  City of God, The 74, 168, 189
Aylmer, Bishop 21, 32, 69, 209

Bacon, Francis 111–12, 216–17, 227, 250
Baker, J. H. 23, 174, 246–7
Bakhtin, Mikhail 93, 100–1
Banqueting House 204, 215, 217, 265, 267
Baxter, Richard 259
Benedict, St 10–11, 14
Bentham, Jeremy 263
Bodin, Jean 152, 153, 205
Brutus, King 3, 30, 105, 107–8
Buc, George 44, 47–8, 75, 76, 92, 140
Buckingham, Duke of 134, 204, 206, 208
Burghley, Lord 91, 134

Carlyle, A. J. 170
Carlyle, R. W. 170

Carlyle, Thomas 146, 161–2, 163
Cecil, William, *see* Burghley, Lord
Cervantes, Miguel de 218
Charles I, King of England
  execution 226, 228, 267
  extraction of forced loan 202–3
  Henrietta Maria, queen 192, 213, 217, 218
  Joyce, Cornet 198, 242
  personal rule 7, 194, 207, 208, 219, 220, 221, 222, 266
  royal court 193, 194, 200, 210, 266
  ship-money 193, 195, 196–7
  see also Petition of Right; prerogative, royal
Cicero 129, 141, 142, 144, 170, 252, 253
  Brutus 23, 26
City of London, *see* Stow, John
Clarendon, Earl of 214, 256
Coke, Edward 8, 25, 37, 64, 110, 144–5, 153–4, 177, 179–80, 195, 227–8, 235, 236–7, 243, 244, 250
  conflict with James I 72–3, 135
  dismissal as Lord Chief Justice 72, 265
  Institutes, The 197, 201–2, 206, 217, 236, 241
  member of parliament 202, 203, 204, 205, 206
  Reports, The 13–14, 16, 18, 31, 41, 49, 129
Collinson, Patrick 181–2
Constitutionalism 85–6, 89, 155–6, 222, 223, 241, 249
Council of State 228, 229, 230, 235–6, 240, 241, 242, 244, 245
Cowell, John 40, 138
Cox, Leonard 22
Cromwell, Oliver 230–1, 236, 238, 239, 240, 242, 246, 248, 249, 250–1, 258, 260–1, 267–8, 269

Davenant, William 256–8
  Cruelty of the Spaniards in Peru, The 257, 258
  Siege of Rhodes, The 256–7
  Triumph of the Prince D'Amour, The 256
Davies, John 66
Derrida, Jacques 50
Devereux, Robert, *see* Essex, Earl of
Dionysus 88, 99, 101, 146
Doderidge, John 92
Downing, Calybute 173
Dudley, Robert, *see* Leicester, Earl of
Dugdale, William 11, 12, 13, 21, 32, 52, 93, 104, 141, 161, 164, 169, 175–6, 179, 219
Dworkin, Ronald 38–9

Edward I, King of England 12, 41, 176
Edward VI, King of England
  regulation of images 169, 182, 183
Edward III, King of England 55, 59, 234
Elizabeth I, Queen of England 88, 91, 130, 255
  Astraea 28, 131, 132
  Pallas Athene 83, 90, 100, 114
  religion 161
  succession of 126
  see also Inns of Court, revels
Elyot, Thomas 29, 34, 57, 86, 91, 129, 253, 268
emblems 67–71
  Mirrour of Maiestie, The 67–74
Epictetus 171
Essex, Earl of 31
Eucharist 14, 15–16, 17, 101, 210

Ferne, John 35–6, 58, 79–80, 81–2, 158–9, 175, 268–9
Fifth Monarchists, The 232–3, 253
Filmer, Robert 252
Finch, John 198, 214–15, 219
Fortescue, John 5, 9, 44, 194, 195, 199
  De Laudibus Legum Angliae 4, 19, 36, 46–7, 53–4, 67, 84, 93, 95, 154, 162, 164, 173, 178
  Governance of England, The 4, 77, 85, 106–8, 268
Foucault, Michel 81, 163, 167, 168, 170, 171, 173
Fraunce, Abraham 34, 35
Fulbecke, William 18, 31, 34, 47, 58, 128, 130, 131, 154, 187

Goodrich, Peter 104
governmentality 2, 7, 168, 264

Grand Remonstrance 221
Gray's Inn
  gates 51
  Gesta Grayorum 111–15, 119–21, 122
  griffin 74–5
  Sibbes, Richard 221
Greene, Robert 165
Gregory of Nyssa, St 172

Hampden, John 193, 198, 214
Harrington, James 8, 259–60
Heads of the Proposals 198, 235
Hegel, Georg Wilhelm Friedrich 186–7
Henry II, King of England 12
Henry VIII, King of England 55, 159, 264
  Act of Supremacy 85, 158
  imago dei 88, 115, 158, 166
  imperium 85, 89, 159, 194
  Reformation, Henrician 160, 163, 181
  heraldry 74, 77, 79, 113–14
  see also Gray's Inn, Inner Temple, Lincoln's Inn, Middle Temple
Hic Mulier: or, The Man Woman 165
High Commission, Court of 110–11, 120–1, 190–1, 196, 201, 221
Hobbes, Thomas 145, 238, 261
  Dialogue between a Philosopher and a Student of the Common Laws, A 236–7, 250
  Leviathan 8, 237–8, 253, 258, 263
honour, law of 45, 76, 79–80, 83
Hooker, Richard 4, 15, 33, 97–8, 170, 210
  Of the Laws of Ecclesiastical Polity 4, 67, 71–2, 105–6, 108–10, 115–16, 252, 264
Humble Petition and Advice 8, 268–9
Hume, David 29
Hunt, Alan 163–4, 165–6
Hyde, Edward, *see* Clarendon, Earl of

iconography, religious, *see* Lincoln's Inn, chapel
Inner Temple
  autonomy 103
  Christmas 1561 90–2, 94–5, 102
  Pegasus 76–8
  see also Legh, Gerard
Inns of Chancery 21
Inns of Court
  architecture 6, 44–5, 73, 168, 206, 264
  benchers 166–7
  bolts 32
  commons 9–10, 16–20, 60, 247, 264
  drama 7, 25–6, 82–3, 192, 193, 254
  gardens 60–2, 139
  hierarchy of membership 18–20, 60, 98–9

Index

imposition of order 19–20, 222–3, 255–6
independence 217, 219–20, 221–2, 223, 225–6, 244–6, 265–6
as microcosms of the Commonwealth 1, 2–3, 4, 30, 53, 87, 89–90, 189, 207–8, 268
moots 20–1, 248
readings 21, 23, 221, 223, 225, 246–7, 266
religion 17–18, 161, 220–1, 226, 255
revels 6, 84, 85, 87–8, 89–90, 92–4, 99, 121–3, 251–2, 253, 264
see also Gray's Inn; Inner Temple; Lincoln's Inn; Middle Temple
Instrument of Government 8, 268
Ireton, Henry 235

James I, King of England 148, 149, 255
author of laws 78, 79
favourites 133–4
proclamations 72
repeal of sumptuary legislation 157
tobacco 147
see also kings, divine right of; prerogative, royal
Jones, Inigo 185, 218, 257
Jupiter 113, 114, 143
Justinian, Emperor 78–9, 149, 172, 176
justitia 3, 46, 63, 64, 73, 168, 181, 238, 242, 259, 261

Kafka, Franz 50
Kant, Immanuel 103, 121–2, 187
Kantorowicz, Ernst 37, 178
kings, divine right of 5, 72, 106, 138, 199, 201, 264
Knights Templar 15, 47–8, 74, 76, 77, 143

Lacan, Jacques 185
Laud, Archbishop 13, 183–4, 191, 216
law, civil 106–7, 144, 146, 153–4, 163, 202
law, common
aesthetics 2
genealogy 36–7, 76, 81, 82, 244, 268–9
mistrust of lawyers 227–8, 229–30, 231–4, 238, 243
oral traditions 5, 40
origins 2, 3–4, 13, 63, 105
poetics 29, 37–42, 141
standardisation 39, 40–2
law, divine 1–2, 7, 47, 64, 71, 131, 142, 144, 160, 178, 179
law, ecclesiastical 1, 13, 110, 176–7, 181, 184

law-French 21–2, 86, 136, 228, 231–2, 234, 243, 244
law, natural 8, 87, 139, 141, 142, 144, 150, 155, 236, 263
Leach, William 229–30, 231
legal positivism 8, 261, 263
see also Hobbes, Thomas
Legendre, Pierre 163, 164, 165, 166
Legh, Gerard 36, 58, 66, 74–5, 77, 83, 99, 100–1, 102, 104–5, 122, 141, 158, 209
legislation, sumptuary 7, 27–8, 157–60, 161, 164, 165–6, 167, 168–70, 171, 172–3, 174–5, 176, 182, 233, 265
Leicester, Earl of 39, 90, 134, 136
see also Legh, Gerard
Levellers 8, 232, 236, 237, 240, 242, 244, 258–9
see also Lilburne, John; Overton, Richard; Walwyn, William
Lilburne, John 234–6, 238–44
Lincoln's Inn
Browne, Samuel 184
chapel 183, 184–8
finances 247
foundation 59, 75–6
lion rampant 75
non-conformity 193, 220–1
Locke, John 252, 265
Luther, Martin 194

Machiavelli, Niccolò 8, 229, 258–9
Magna Carta 64, 162, 201, 202, 203, 206, 207, 242, 250
Maine, Henry 61, 96, 159
Maitland, F. W. 11, 40
Marin, Louis 101, 103, 132
Mary I, Queen of England 126, 169–70, 182
Mary, Queen of Scots 126, 130, 136, 137, 161
masques 7, 124–5, 126–7, 138–9, 141–3, 144, 148–9, 154, 155–6, 254–5, 265
Certaine Devises and shewes 131–3, 136–8
Circe and Ulysses, The Inner Temple Masque 142, 148, 150–1, 165, 218
Masque of Flowers, The 124, 133–4, 139, 142, 145–8
Masque of Heroes, The 140–1, 148, 151–2, 153
Masque of the Inner Temple and Gray's Inn, The 143–4, 218, 265
Masque of the Middle Temple and Lincoln's Inn, The 140, 219
Tragedie of Ferrex and Porrex, The 127–31, 142, 144, 225, 265
Merchant Taylors Company, The 135, 217–18

Index

Middle Temple
  admissions 84, 247, 248
  butler 20
  gates 50–1, 52
  hall 43
  lamb and flag 16–17, 74
  Marston, John 26–8, 192
  steward 95–6
  Troilus and Cressida 26–35
  Twelfth Night 96–7
Mill, John Stuart 263
Milton, John 149, 257, 258, 261–2
Mirror of Justices, The 177
Misrule, Lord of 87–8, 116–18
monopolies 49, 135, 215–17
Montaigne, Michel de 40–1, 128
More, Thomas 16, 62
  Utopia 59–60, 69, 91, 111–12
Morton, A. L. 94, 116, 122
Moses 50, 105, 178, 179
music 33, 191–2, 215, 251, 253–4

Narcissus 133, 142, 166
nationalism 48–9, 63, 69, 136, 145, 170
Neoplatonism 44, 45, 55, 59, 63, 172, 175, 188, 229, 248, 252
Nietzsche, Friedrich 51, 88, 117
Noy, William 214, 216
Nussbaum, Martha 41

Orpheus 33
Overton, Richard 239

Parliament 140, 224, 229, 260–1
  Barebones 231, 245, 249–50, 267
  common lawyers in 199–200, 206–7, 208, 213, 226, 265
  dissolution by Charles I 7, 207
  law reform 249–51
  Rump, The 228, 229, 230, 231, 236, 239, 242, 249, 267
  see also Petition of Right; St German, Christopher
Paulet, Amias 51, 52, 53
Peacham, Henry 157, 167
Petition of Right 79, 198, 200, 201, 203–7, 242
Plato 24, 33, 59, 79, 82, 170, 172, 189, 252, 261
  Apology, The 171
  Laws, The 24
  Republic, The 3, 4, 5, 29, 45, 52, 58, 103, 168
Plowden, Edmund 38, 174

prerogative, royal 78, 79, 111, 121, 122, 123, 127, 131, 138, 155, 177, 194, 196, 201, 203–4, 207, 225, 265
Presbyterianism 106, 226
printing 5–6, 16, 22, 37, 41, 171, 247
Prynne, William 7, 183–4, 190–4, 195–9, 208, 209–11, 218, 221, 239–40, 242, 246
Puritanism, *see* Prynne, William
Putney Debates 198, 235

Renaissance, European 49, 52, 55, 58–9, 69, 77–9, 80–1, 105, 172, 173–4, 188–9
rhetoric 24–5, 29–30, 35, 52–3, 223–4
Rousseau, Jean-Jacques 61, 169
Rubens, Peter Paul 211, 267
Russell, Conrad 191, 199, 255

St German, Christopher 85–6, 108, 128, 194–6, 201, 205–6, 236, 261, 266
St John, Oliver 225, 228, 230
Selden, John 72, 129, 152–3, 160, 205, 214, 230
semiotics 3, 45
serjeants-at-Law 179–81
Shakespeare, William
  Comedy of Errors, The 119–20
  Midsummer Night's Dream, A 27, 117–18
  Richard II 61–2, 134
  Richard III 134
  Second Part of King Henry VI, The 227, 228
  see also Gray's Inn; Middle Temple
Shirley, James 217
  Triumph of Peace, The 7, 213–14, 215–20, 255
Sidney, Algernon 230
Sidney, Philip 31, 37, 39, 88, 114, 121, 141, 224, 225
Silenus 145–6, 147–8, 149, 211
Solon 3, 24
Spelman, Henry 93, 136
Stow, John 49–50, 58, 65, 66
Strafford, Earl of 203
Stuart, Mary, *see* Mary, Queen of Scots

Tacitus 164, 173, 209
Temple church 48, 55, 97, 174, 183, 186
theology 9, 49, 52, 91, 176, 178–81, 182, 187, 188
  see also Hooker, Richard

Van Dyck, Anthony 211–13
Vico, Giambattista 59
Villiers, George, *see* Buckingham, Duke of

Walwyn, William 238, 243
War, English Civil
  effect on Inns of Court 223, 225, 246
  publication of pamphlets during 7–8, 223–5
  politicisation of army 198, 235
Warre, John 233–4, 259
Waterhouse, Edward 34, 36, 179, 180
Wentworth, Thomas, *see* Strafford, Earl of
Whitelocke, Bulstrode 213, 214, 215, 216, 217, 218, 228, 229, 230–1, 245, 249, 250, 256–7, 260–1, 269

Whitgift, Archbishop 13, 106, 111, 138
Wilkes, William 176
Wilson, Thomas 22, 24–5, 32, 51, 224, 227
Winstanley, Gerrard 232, 259
Wolsey, Cardinal 51, 52
women 148–50, 151–2, 153, 248

xenophobia 44–5, 48, 62, 63, 66, 102, 145–7, 165, 169

Year Books 38

Titles in the series

The Common Peace: Participation and the Criminal Law in Seventeenth-Century England*
CYNTHIA B. HERRUP

Politics, Society and Civil War in Warwickshire, 1620–1660*
ANN HUGHES

London Crowds in the Reign of Charles II: Propaganda and Politics from the Restoration to the Exclusion Crisis*
TIM HARRIS

Criticism and Compliment: The Politics of Literature in the England of Charles I*
KEVIN SHARPE

Central Government and the Localities: Hampshire, 1649–1689*
ANDREW COLEBY

John Skelton and the Politics of the 1520s*
GREG WALKER

Algernon Sidney and the English Republic, 1623–1677
JONATHAN SCOTT

Thomas Starkey and the Commonweal: Humanist Politics and Religion in the Reign of Henry VIII*
THOMAS F. MAYER

The Blind Devotion of the People: Popular Religion and the English Reformation*
ROBERT WHITING

The Cavalier Parliament and the Reconstruction of the Old Regime, 1661–1667*
PAUL SEAWARD

The Blessed Revolution: England Politics and the Coming of War, 1621–1624
THOMAS COGSWELL

Charles I and the Road to Personal Rule
L. J. REEVE

George Lawson's 'Politica' and the English Revolution*
CONAL CONDREN

Puritans and Roundheads: The Harleys of Brampton Bryan and the Outbreak of the Civil War
JACQUELINE EALES

An Uncounselled King: Charles I and the Scottish Troubles, 1637–1641
PETER DONALD

Cheap Print and Popular Piety, 1550–1640*
TESSA WATT

The Pursuit of Stability: Social Relations in Elizabethan London
IAN W. ARCHER

Prosecution and Punishment: Petty Crime and the Law in London and Rural Middlesex, c. 1660–1725
ROBERT B. SHOEMAKER

Algernon Sidney and the Restoration Crisis, 1677–1683*
JONATHAN SCOTT

Exile and Kingdom: History and Apocalypse in the Puritan Migration to America*
AVIHU ZAKAI

The Pillars of Priestcraft Shaken: The Church of England and its Enemies, 1660–1730
J. A. I. CHAMPION

Steward, Lords and People: The Estate Steward and his World in Later Stuart England
D. R. HAINSWORTH

Civil War and Restoration in the Three Stuart Kingdoms: The Career of Randal MacDonnell, Marquis of Antrim, 1609–1683
JANE H. OHLMEYER

The Family of Love in English Society, 1550–1630
CHRISTOPHER W. MARSH

The Bishops' Wars: Charles I's Campaign against Scotland, 1638–1640*
MARK FISSEL

John Locke: Resistance, Religion and Responsibility
JOHN MARSHALL

Constitutional Royalism and the Search for Settlement, c. 1640–1649*
DAVID L. SMITH

Intelligence and Espionage in the Reign of Charles II, 1660–1685
ALAN MARSHALL

The Chief Governors: The Rise and Fall of Reform Government in Tudor Ireland, 1536–1588*
CIARAN BRADY

Politics and Opinion in Crisis, 1678–1681
MARK KNIGHTS

Catholic and Reformed: The Roman and Protestant Churches in English Protestant Thought, 1604–1640*
ANTHONY MILTON

Sir Matthew Hale, 1609–1676: Law, Religion and Natural Philosophy*
ALAN CROMARTIE

Henry Parker and the English Civil War: The Political Thought of the Public's 'Privado'
MICHAEL MENDLE

Protestantism and Patriotism: Ideologies and the Making of English Foreign Policy, 1650–1668*
STEVEN C. A. PINCUS

Gender in Mystical and Occult Thought: Behmenism and its Development in England
B. J. GIBBONS

William III and the Godly Revolution
TONY CLAYDON

Law-Making and Society in Late Elizabethan England: The Parliament of England, 1584–1601*
DAVID DEAN

The House of Lords in the Reign of Charles II*
ANDREW SWATLAND

Conversion, Politics and Religion in England, 1580–1625
MICHAEL C. QUESTIER

Politics, Religion and the British Revolutions: The Mind of Samuel Rutherford*
JOHN COFFEY

King James VI and I and the Reunion of Christendom*
W. B. PATTERSON

The English Reformation and the Laity: Gloucestershire, 1540–1580*
CAROLINE LITZENBERGER

Godly Clergy in Early England: The Caroline Puritan Movement, c. 1620–1643*
TOM WEBSTER

Prayer Book and People in Elizabethan and Early Stuart England*
JUDITH MALTBY

Sermons at Court, 1559–1629: Religion and Politics in Elizabethan and Jacobean Preaching
PETER E. MCCULLOUGH

Dismembering the Body Politic: Partisan Politics in England's Towns, 1650–1730
PAUL D. HALLIDAY

Women Waging Law in Elizabethan England
TIMOTHY STRETTON

The Early Elizabethan Polity: William Cecil and the British Succession Crisis, 1558–1569*
STEPHEN ALFORD

The Polarisation of Elizabethan Politics: The Political Career of Robert Devereux, 2nd Earl of Essex
PAUL J. HAMMER

The Politics of Social Conflict: The Peak Country, 1520–1770
ANDY WOOD

Crime and Mentalities in Early Modern England*
MALCOLM GASKILL

The Church in an Age of Danger: Parsons and Parishioners, 1660–1740
DONALD A. SPAETH

Reading History in Early Modern England
  D. R. WOOLF

The Politics of Court Scandal in Early Modern England: News Culture and the Overbury Affair, 1603–1660
  ALASTAIR BELLANY

The Politics of Religion in the Age of Mary, Queen of Scots: The Earl of Argyll and the Struggle for Britain and Ireland
  JANE E. A. DAWSON

Treason and the State: Law, Politics and Ideology in the English Civil War
  D. ALAN ORR

Pamphlets and Pamphleteering in Early Modern Britain
  JOAD RAYMOND

Preaching during the English Reformation
  SUSAN WABUDA

Patterns of Piety: Women, Gender and Religion in Late Medieval and Reformation England
  CHRISTINE PETERS

*Popular Politics and the English Reformation**
  ETHAN H. SHAGAN

Mercy and Authority in the Tudor State
  K. J. KESSELRING

Unquiet Lives: Marriage and Marriage Breakdown in England, 1660–1800
  JOANNE BAILEY

The Gospel and Henry VIII: Evangelicals in the Early English Reformation
  ALEC RYRIE

Images and Cultures of Law in Early Modern England: Justice and Political Power, 1558–1660
  PAUL RAFFIELD

*Also published as a paperback

For EU product safety concerns, contact us at Calle de José Abascal, 56–1°,
28003 Madrid, Spain or eugpsr@cambridge.org.